Theron S. E. Dixon

Francis Bacon, and his Shakespeare

Theron S. E. Dixon

Francis Bacon, and his Shakespeare

ISBN/EAN: 9783337063351

Printed in Europe, USA, Canada, Australia, Japan

Cover: Foto ©ninafisch / pixelio.de

More available books at **www.hansebooks.com**

FRANCIS BACON
AND HIS SHAKESPEARE

BY

THERON S. E. DIXON

Not to prove it, but perhaps to show it, — to make it manifest.

CHICAGO
The Sargent Publishing Company
1356 MONADNOCK BLOCK
1895

THE DIAL PRESS.

TO MY WIFE,

BERTHA L. DIXON,

THIS BOOK IS AFFECTIONATELY INSCRIBED;
FOR IT COULD NOT HAVE BEEN COMPLETED
EXCEPT FOR HER LOVING-KINDNESS AND HER
FAITHFUL CO-OPERATION.

T. S. E. D.

A too vivid realization of the fact, with all that it implies, is herein an obvious fault; one only to be forgiven when, in after years, this realization shall have become a part of the consciousness of the people.

CONTENTS.

"TO GET AT THE BEING OF A GREAT AUTHOR, TO COME INTO RELA-
TIONSHIP WITH HIS ABSOLUTE PERSONALITY, IS THE HIGHEST RESULT OF
THE STUDY OF HIS WORKS." — PROFESSOR HIRAM CORSON.

PROLOGUE.

The Tribunal of History is always open. Its session is one continuous term; and therefore, its judgments are ever subject to review. Nor is attendance at its bar limited to a privileged class : any one may at any time move a rehearing; and not even a "retainer" is required, as authority for his appearance. Nevertheless, and justly, there is no court in which it is so difficult to win a case. Old Father Time is almost always of the opposing counsel : and his wisdom, age, and experience have great weight in a tribunal where humanity sits in judgment upon itself; whose probity is the integrity of the race, and whose records are of the issues of its life. And, especially when its adjudication has been entered of record for three hundred years, it is not only apparently, but actually, the height of presumption, for one utterly unknown within its precincts to enter his appearance and deliberately ask for its reversal, —unless he succeeds. And as with the Sphinx and its riddles, whose solution was open to all, the penalty of his failure is in effect death, or at least banishment. Nevermore can he gain the ear of the court.

Dropping this pleasant fancy, for I would not have this book regarded as *fiction* (though were it false, it might perhaps be humorously termed a work of imagination; and if it be true, its truth is stranger than fiction), I would state, as the warrant for its appearance, that there are here presented data which have convinced me, beyond a reasonable doubt, that Francis Bacon wrote the Shakespearian Plays. It may be that my judgment is at fault, that I am the victim of illusion; but if so, as these data are here placed before the reader in just the light in which they appeal to my understanding, this fault must soon become glaringly apparent. But on the contrary, if I am right, and the data, in and of themselves, are really convincing, then I shall have good company.

Whatever be the event, I have already received an ample reward, in the acquirement of a better acquaintance with him of whom I write. This I would share with the reader: and I am confident that he will gain from the perusal of this book, if nothing else, at least additional knowledge of Francis Bacon,

> The greatest, the brightest, the least understood
> Of mankind.

FRANCIS BACON
AND HIS SHAKESPEARE.

—— · ——

CHAPTER I.

IT is a thrice-told tale of Gilbert Stuart, the painter, that having confided to a friend a secret in the mixture of colors, when this friend afterwards asked that it might be intrusted to another, Stuart refused: writing, " I know it, that is *1 ;* you know it, that makes *1 1 ;* tell your friend, and there are *1 1 1 ;* but that is one hundred and eleven."

This graphic portrayal of the cumulative effect of numbers upon the disclosure of a secret illustrates equally well the multiplied potency of evidence in the revelation of the truth, when it links together in a continuous sequence, instead of being merely an aggregation of disconnected facts. That which before had only a nominal value of three, is thereby, under the established laws of evidence, raised to an actual probative power of one hundred and eleven ; while the addition of another unit in the like relations increases its value to one thousand one hundred and eleven. If we continue this process indefinitely, Arithmetic at length becomes " dizzy " and we arrive at certainty, the end of mathematics. Always provided that it is possible for the human intellect, unaided, to arrive at certainty regarding anything ; — for only the Infinite One can comprehend all the relations, which in their whole constitute the Truth.

One after another, isolated parallelisms between the

plays and Bacon's acknowledged writings have been repeatedly pointed out, in ever-increasing numbers. But the general public still remains unconvinced of Bacon's authorship; evidently for some good reason, for it is but fair to presume the prevalence of sincerity and of a willingness to know and accept the reality, if only it be made clearly manifest.

The reason is to be found in that conservative instinct, dominant in the sound mind, which forbids the acceptance of a novel theory, if the facts presented in its support, interpreted in the light of experience, are fairly explainable in harmony with the old established beliefs.

This is altogether to be commended; for otherwise humanity, drifting from its moorings, without bearings or compass, would be perpetually tossed upon the waves of inconstant opinion, on a veritable *mare incognitum*.

Now, fairly stated, like parallelisms, though in much less numbers in each instance, have been found in the writings of many authors, ancient and modern, and where obviously, in many cases, they fall within the category of coincidences. Hence the attitude generally assumed towards these newly discovered parallelisms. While they are confessedly numerous, some of them very striking, nevertheless, this ready explanation, drawn from experience, is almost involuntarily applied to them; and in result, the conservative mind usually withholds its assent, regarding them merely as coincidences; interesting perhaps, and it may be inviting further investigation, but as wholly insufficient, in and of themselves, to establish the proposition advanced.

Coincidences, indeed, are in their essence simply developments of *chance;* capricious, intermittent, irregular, and desultory in their happenings. Such likewise are isolated parallelisms, and therefore the pertinent application of the theory of coincidences in their explanation.

But once eliminate these characteristics by the unfolding of a *continuous* parallelism, running through the whole of a material portion of one of the principal plays, involving a wide diversity of elements, and faithful both in detail and comprehensively, and obviously the theory of chance as an explanation would no longer be tenable, since it would cease to be applicable. We would then enter another domain, where law prevails, and where by continued application we must come at length to a definite and satisfactory conclusion; as surely as did Harvey, when he traced the blood through the veins and arteries till he arrived at the heart of the matter and the solution of the problem.

But is not the fulfilment of such a condition an impossibility with any author, comparing even his acknowledged writings, when upon different subjects? Truly, it would be so anomalous, so contrary to all recognized human experience, that to some minds, conservative ones too, if found in any production, it would be only explainable upon the hypothesis that it was thus written of purpose, with that design and intent — a difficult but not impossible undertaking. The reader, however, must be the judge as to whether this onerous condition be indeed here fulfiled.

We have selected for comparison Prospero's narrative to Miranda of their previous history, in *The Tempest*, Act I., Scene 2, it being admirably adapted for the purpose. It is from beginning to end deeply interesting, a revelation of humanity in its stern reality, uncovering the recesses of the heart, bringing into view its motives, its choices and their consequences, and enabling us to follow continuously its devious workings. It is of considerable length, extending over five pages in the " Handy Volume" edition: it is complete in itself, forming a well-rounded whole, and yet integral with the play, its very core, the central hub into which all the spokes converge.

The following brief quotations from Mr. Denton J. Snider's able commentary on *The Shakespearian Drama* sufficiently indicate the relative importance of the selection:

"*Tempest* stands very high in the list of Shakespeare's dramas; in some respects it is his supreme work. Its wonderful types, its perfect symmetrical structure, its bright poetic language, but, above all, its profound signification, must always make it a favorite among the thoughtful readers of the Poet."

"The play is often considered Shakespeare's last, and it may be regarded as a final summing up of his activity— or, indeed, that of any great poet."

"The Poet clearly enters the realm of conscious symbolism, in the present drama, and the reader must follow him or remain outside. . . . Hamlet is doubtless more fully delineated; still in Prospero the Poet is all his characters and himself too."

"The second scene of the First Act, which now follows, is the most important one in the play, for it gives the key to the action. . . . He lays down his magic mantle—that is, he assumes the individual relation to his daughter — and then begins to give an account of his life and conflicts as an individual."

This ostentatious laying aside of the magic garment, and with it his subtle power over the elements, is evidently part of the symbolism of the play: it invites our attention and possibly influences our choice.

The intrinsic importance of the proceeding would seem to justify the length of the selection, if indeed it be not a necessity of the situation; while doubters, at least, should be the first to commend and the last to complain. Whatever be the outcome, however, the reader's patience may perhaps be amply rewarded by the attainment, incidentally, of a better comprehension of Francis Bacon himself, and of his varied and wonderful powers; whose quality may be tasted even in the crumbs that have here fallen from his bountiful table. If the reader will kindly bear this in mind, the proverbial " dry crusts " of annotations may possibly be transformed, by his subtle alchemy, into both palatable and nutritious food.

The broader the lines traversed in the reader's mind, the more comprehensive the view that will open before him: and defects in details, incident to such a possibility, may perhaps be forgiven, in the greater satisfaction afforded by the enlarged prospect. Moreover, any structure is much more stable resting upon a base than upon a point : and certainly, in this case, the foundation will be the more solid, if the manifestation of the workings of one and the same unique mentality be made not only continuous, but continuously *abundant.*

(For convenient comparison, the quotations from Bacon's recognized writings are interposed between the lines of the play, the italies being in most cases our own.)

"Twelve years since, Miranda, twelve years since,"

The name *Miranda* is itself exquisitely significant, and according to ancient classic usage, symbolizes the quality therein expressed; thus delicately shadowing forth the essential character of the play.

" It may be that my reverence for the primitive time carries me too far, but the truth is that in some of these fables, as well in the very frame and texture of the story as in the propriety of the names by which the persons that figure in it are distinguished, I find a conformity and connection with the thing specified, so close and so evident, that one cannot help believing such a signification to have been designed and meditated from the first, and purposely shadowed out. . . . Then again there is a conformity and significance in the very names, which must be clear to everybody. Metis, Jupiter's wife, plainly means Counsel; Typhon, swelling; Pan, the universe; Nemesis, revenge; and the like."—*Preface to Wisdom of the Ancients.*

The Poet, indeed, later in the play (Act III., Sc. 1) gives beautiful expression to his conception of the significance of the name in one of its phases:

"Admired Miranda!
Indeed, the top of admiration."

If we turn to *De Augmentis*, Fourth Book, Chap. 1, it will afford us a glimpse not only of the height, but of the breadth and richness of the thought here expressed, and of its classic origin:

"But that other subject of the Prerogatives of Man seems to me to deserve a place among the *desiderata*. Pindar in praising Hiero says most elegantly (as is his wont) that he 'culled the tops of all the virtues.' And certainly I think it would contribute much to magnanimity and the honor of humanity, if a collection were made of what the schoolmen call the *ultimities*, and Pindar the *tops or summits* of human nature, especially from true history; shewing what is the ultimate and highest point which human nature has of itself attained in the several gifts of body and mind."

"So as there was nothing to be added to this great king's felicity, being at the top of all worldly bliss."— *History of Henry VII.**

"Thy father was the Duke of Milan and
A prince of power."

"Which words cost him his *Duchy* of Milan, and ut-

---

* "That thou, my brother, my competitor
In top of all design."—*Antony and Cleopatra, V., 1.*

"For princes being at the top of human desires, they have for the most part no particular ends whereto they aspire."—*Advancement of Learning, Second Book.*

terly ruined his affairs in Italy."— *Of the True Greatness of the Kingdom of Britain.*

"— and the like was done by that league (which Guiociardini saith was the security of Italy), made between Ferdinando *King* of Naples, Lorenzius Medicis, and Ludovicus Sforza, *potentates*, the one of Florence, the other of Milan."— *Of Empire.*

"But, my lords, I labor too much in a clear business. The king is so wise, and hath so good friends abroad, as now he knoweth *Duke* Perkin from his cradle. And because he is a great *prince*, if you have any good *poet* here, he can help him with notes to write his life; and to parallel him with Lambert Simnel, now the king's falconer."— *History of Henry VII.**

---

* It appears from the context that this Perkin was an impostor, feigning himself to be Richard, Duke of York, second son of Edward the Fourth, who in fact had been murdered by Richard III. Lambert Simnel was another impostor already exposed. The subtle play of wit in this reference to the poet's work will perhaps be better appreciated by reading the following from *As You Like It*, Act III., Scene 2:

"*Touchstone.* Truly, I would the gods had made thee poetical.

"*Audrey.* I do not know what *poetical* is; is it honest in deed and work? is it a true thing?

"*Touchstone.* No, truly; for the truest poetry is the most feigning; and lovers are given to poetry; and what they swear in poetry, may be said as lovers, they do feign.

"*Audrey.* Do you wish, then, that the gods had made me poetical?

"*Touchstone.* I do, truly; for thou swear'st to me thou art honest; now if thou wert a poet I might have some hope thou did'st feign."

"Yet this I must say, that it is a strange form of proof to put a number of cases where this writ hath been obeyed, which is directly against you; and then to *feign* to yourself what was the reason why it was obeyed, and to go on and imagine that if it had been and thus it would not have been obeyed. Sir, the story is good; but your *poetry* why it was done if the case had

"*Mir.* Sir, are you not my father?

Pros. Thy mother was a piece of virtue,"

This word *piece* has been somewhat perplexing to the critics. We learn from the admirable Henry Irving edition of the plays that the New Shakespeare Society, after

differed,—therein you do but please yourself; it will never move the Court at all."—*Case de Rege Inconsulto.*

But this play upon poetry was based upon a profound philosophy:

"Therefore, because the acts or events of true history have not that magnitude which satisfieth the mind of man, poetry *feigneth* acts and events greater and more heroical; because true history propoundeth the successes and issues of actions not so agreeable to the merits of virtue and vice; therefore poetry *feigns* them more just in retribution, and more according to revealed providence; because true history representeth actions and events more ordinary and less interchanged, therefore poetry endueth them with more rareness, and more unexpected and alternative variations. So it appeareth that poetry serveth and conferreth to magnanimity, morality, and to delectation."—*Advancement of Learning*, Second Book.

"With all that poets feign of bliss and joy."
　　　　　　　—*III., Henry VI., I., 2.*

"*Poet.* Sir, I have upon a high and pleasant hill
Feigned Fortune to be throned."—*Timon of Athens, I., 1.*

"Therefore the poet
Did feign that Orpheus drew trees, stones, and floods."
　　　　　　　—*Merchant of Venice, V., 1.*

"For herein the invention of one of the later poets [Ariosto in *Orlando Furioso*], by which he has enriched the ancient fiction, is not inelegant. He *feigns* that at the end of the thread or web of every man's life there hangs a little medal or collar, on which his name is stamped; and that Time waits upon the shears of Atropos, and as soon as the thread is cut, snatches the medals, carries them off, and presently throws them into the river Lethe; and about the river there are many birds flying up and down, who catch the medals, and after carrying them round and round in their beaks a little while, let them fall into discussion, endorsed Richard Grant White's interpretation, as meaning "woman." But possibly the word is used here in another and more special sense, distinctively peculiar, and arising out of a train of associations best indicated by the following brief quotations; which put the reader into line with Bacon's mode of thought, and also reveal his remarkable power of casting into the mould of material things such abstract qualities as virtue and justice:

"For I never saw but that business is like a child which is *framed* invisibly in the womb; and if it come forth too soon, it will be abortive."—*Letter to King James.**

the river; only there are a few swans, which if they get a medal with a name carry it off to a temple consecrated to immortality. Now this kind of swan is for the most part wanting in our age."—*De Augmentis,* Second Book.

("Why, then, let grievous, ghastly, gaping wounds
Untwine the sisters three! Come *Atropos,* I say!"
—*II., Henry IV., II., 4.*

"Why do you bend such solemn brows on me?
Think you I bear *the shears of destiny?*
Have I commandment on the pulse of life?"
—*King John, IV., 2.*

"Therefore, my lord, go travel for awhile,
Till that his rage and anger be forgot;
Or till the Destinies cut his thread of life."
—*Pericles, I., 2.*

"Was this easy?
May this be washed in Lethe, and forgotten?"
—*II., Henry IV., V., 2.*)

* "Frame the business after your own wisdom."
—*King Lear, I., 2.*

"'Tis wonder
That an invisible instinct should *frame* them
To royalty unlearned."—*Cymbeline, IV., 2.*

"When nature *framed this piece,* she meant thee a good turn."
—*Pericles, IV., 3.*

"[*Enter Coriolanus' wife, mother, and child.*]
My wife comes foremost; then the honor'd mould

" But to come to the present case ; the great *frame* of justice (my Lords) in this present action, hath a Vault and it hath a Stage ; a Vault wherein these works of darkness were contained ; and a Stage, with steps, by which they were brought to light."—*Charge against the Countess of Somerset.*

" Wherein first Mr. Lumsden plays his part, whose offence stands alone single, the offence of the other two being in consort ; and yet all three meeting in their end and center, which was to interrupt or deface this excellent *piece* of justice."—*Charge against Wentworth et al.*

" And for mercy and grace (without which there is no standing before justice) we see the King now hath reigned twelve years in his white robe, without any aspersion of the crimson dye of blood. There sits my lord Hobart, that served Attorney seven years. I served with him. We were so happy as there passed not through our hands any one arraignment for treason ; and but one for any capital offence ; which was that of the Lord Sanquhar ; the noblest piece of justice (one of them) that ever came forth in any King's times."— *Charge against St. John.*

" First therefore (my Lord) call to mind oft and consider duly how infinitely your Grace is bound to God, in this one point, which I find to be *a most rare piece,* and wherein, either of ancient or later times, there are few examples : That is, that you are so dearly beloved both of the King and Prince."— *Letter of Advice to Buckingham."*

And finally, and in a connection alike applicable to man or woman :

" I do esteem whatsoever I have, or may have in this world but as trash, in comparison of having the honor and happiness to be a near and well accepted kinsman to so rare and worthy a counsellor, governor, and patriot.

Wherein this trunk was fram'd, and in her hand
The grandchild to her blood."— *Coriolanus, V., 3.*

For having been a studious, if not curious observer, as well of antiquities of virtue as late pieces, I forbear to say to your Lordship what I find and conceive; but to any other I would think to make myself believed."—*New Year's Letter to the Earl of Salisbury.**

"and
She said thou wast my daughter;"

This subtle touch finds its counterpart in one of Bacon's *Apothegms :*

" There was a young man in Rome that was very like Augustus Cæsar : Augustus took knowledge of him, sent for the man and asked him, ' Was your mother never at Rome ?' He answered, ' No, Sir, but my father was.' "

As indelicacy appears in many of the plays, it is part of the *res gesta,* a factor in the problem : the reader is therefore referred to Bacon's *Apothegms,* and also to his *History of Henry VII.,* Spedding's *Works,* Vol. VI., page 215, or Bohn's ed. *Essays, &c.,* page 452, which will doubtless prove sufficient upon this point, and will illustrate his humor as well.

---

* " Thou art a piece of virtue,
And I doubt not but thy training hath been noble."
—*Pericles, IV., 6.*

" Their transformations
Were never for a piece of beauty rarer,
Nor in a way so chaste."—*A Winter's Tale, IV., 3.*

" And thou fresh piece
Of excellent witchcraft, who, of force, must know
The royal fool thou cop'st with."—*Id.*

" Yet to imagine
An Antony, were nature's piece 'gainst fancy,
Condemning shadows quite."—*Ant. and Cleo., V., 1.*

" All princely graces,
That mould up such a piece as this is,
With all the virtues that attend the good,
Shall still be doubled on her."—*Henry VIII., V., 5.*

"and thy father
Was Duke of Milan; and thou his only heir
And princess no worse issued."

Issued is a legal term, or rather the legal phrase or form of expressing the fact.*

" But to your Majesty, whom God hath already blessed with so much royal issue, worthy to continue and represent you forever, and whose youthful and fruitful bed doth yet promise many the like renovations, it is proper and agreeable to be conversant not only in the transitory parts of good government, but in those acts also which are in their nature permanent and perpetual."—*Advancement of Learning*, Second Book.

"*Mir.* O the heavens!"

"O the," *Promus of Formularies and Elegancies.*

" What foul play had we that we came from thence?
Or blessed was 't we did?
Pros.   Both, both, my girl:
By foul play, as thou say'st, were we heaved thence,
But blessedly holp hither."

The depth of the Poet's insight, and his exquisite portrayal of one of the subtler phases of human nature might here, as in the past, wholly escape us, but for the following acute observation :

" And he that is holpen, takes it for a *fortune* and

* " But if the eldest son leave any issue, though he die in the life of his father, then neither the second son nor the issue of the eldest shall inherit the father's lands, but the father there shall be accounted to die without heirs, and the land shall be escheat."—*The Use of the Law.*

" Of six preceeding ancestors, that gem
Conferr'd by testament to the sequent issue,
Hath it been ow'd and worn."—*All's Well, V., 3.*

thanks the times; and he that is hurt, for a *wrong*, and imputeth it to the author."—*Of Innovations.*

Moreover, Bacon's unaffected delight in *antithesis* will become manifest, both directly and incidentally, in subsequent citations.

> "*Mir.* O my heart bleeds
> To think o' the teen that I have turned you to." *

Taken in connection with other and more striking clauses, such as the following, one might well surmise that the Poet was master of the secret of the circulation of the blood :

> "Why does my blood thus muster to my heart,"
> —*Measure for Measure, II., 4.*

> "But there, where I have garner'd up my heart;
> Where either I must live, or bear no life;
> The fountain from the which my current runs,
> Or else dries up."—*Othello, IV., 2.*

> "Could I meet them
> But once a day, it would unclog my heart
> Of what lies heavy to 't."— *Coriolanus, IV., 2.*

> "As dear to me as are the ruddy drops
> That visit my sad heart."—*Julius Cæsar, II., 2.*

> "Or if that surly spirit, melancholy,
> Had baked thy blood, and made it heavy — thick,
> Which, else, runs tickling up and down the veins."
> — *King John, III., 3.*

> "Why, universal plodding prisons up
> The nimble spirits in the arteries :"
> — *Love's Labor Lost, IV., 3.†*

---

* Note the "turn" of the expression :

"—; which have turned your Majesty to inestimable prejudice."— *Letter to King James, on his Estate.*

† The above is an exemplification of a peculiar "spiritual" philosophy of man's constitution, which is given repeated and unmistakable development; in the exposition of an occult, but

Bacon also exhibits this same wonderful knowledge:

" Too continuous and copious an effusion of blood, such as sometimes takes place in hemorrhoids, sometimes in vomiting of blood from the opening or rupture of inner veins, and sometimes in wounds, causes speedy death ; *for the blood of the veins supplies the blood of the arteries,* which again supplies the *spirit*."—*History of Life and Death.*

" There are two great precursors of death, the one sent

thoroughly consistent physiology; and of which the following are further examples:

" Moreover, the course of life should if possible, be so ordered that it may have many and various restorations : and the *spirits* may not grow torpid by perpetual intercourse with the same things."—*History of Life and Death.*

" My spirits, as in a dream, are all bound up."—*Tempest, I., 2.*

"Nor I, my spirits are nimble." —*Id., II., 1.*

" Forth at your eyes your spirits wildly peep."—*Hamlet, III., 4.*

" But there is
No danger in what show of death it makes,
More than the locking up the spirits a time,
To be more fresh, reviving."—*Cymbeline, I., 5.*

" In his *Natural History,* Bacon observes regarding drunkenness:

" The cause is for that the spirits of the wine *oppress* the spirits animal, and occupate part of the place where they are; and so make them *weak to move.* . . . Besides they *rob* the spirits animal of their matter, whereby they are nourished ; for the spirits of the wine *prey* upon it as well as they: and so they make the spirits less *supple* and apt to move." Also: " Now the spirits are chiefly in the head and cells of the brain." And again, in his *History of Life and Death:* "We must be cautious about spices, wine, and strong drink, and use them very temperately, with intervals of abstinence; . . . For they supply to the spirits a heat not operative but predatory."

This hostility, or predatory action, is made the very essence of Cassio's memorable apostrophe in *Othello, II., 3:*

" O thou invisible spirit of wine, if thou hast no name to be

from the head, the other from the heart, namely, convulsions and extreme labor of the pulse; for that deadly hiccough is itself a kind of convulsion. But this laboring of the pulse has a remarkable quickness, *because* on the point of death the heart trembles so violently that contraction and dilitation are almost confounded. But together with this quickness there is a feebleness and lowness, and often

---

known by, let us call thee devil! . . . O that men should put an *enemy* in their mouths to *steal* away their brains!"

He further observes: "The power of opium to condense the spirits is remarkable; for perhaps three grains will in a short time so *coagulate* them that they cannot separate, but are quenched and rendered immovable. . . . Simple opiates, which are likewise called narcotics and stupefactives, are opium itself, which is the juice of the poppy, the plant and seed of the poppy, henbane, mandragora, hemlock, tobacco, and nightshade."

> "Not poppy, nor mandragora,
> Nor all the drowsy syrups of the world,
> Shall ever medicine to that sweet sleep
> Which thou ow'dst yesterday."—*Othello, III., 3.*

> " *Cleo.*   Ha, ha! —
> Give me to drink mandragora.
> *Char.* Why, madame?
> *Cleo.* That I might sleep out this great gap of time
> My Antony is away."—*Antony and Cleopatra, I., 5.*

> " O, I die, Horatio;
> The potent poison quite o'ercrows my spirits."
> —*Hamlet, V., 2.*

> " Upon my secure hour thy uncle stole,
> With *juice* of cursed hebenon in a vial,
> And, in the porches of mine ear did pour
> The leperous distilment; whose effect
> Holds such *enmity* with blood of man,
> That, swift as quicksilver, it *courses through*
> *The natural gates and alleys of the body;*
> And with a sudden vigor, it doth *posset*
> *And curd*, like eager dropping into milk,
> The thin and wholesome blood: so did it mine."
> —*Id., I., 5.*

a great intermission in the pulse, the motion of the heart failing, and being no longer able to recover itself stoutly and regularly."—*Id*.

And in metaphor:

"And while the life-blood of Spain went inward to the heart, the outward limbs and members trembled and could not resist."— *Speech on the Subsidy Bill*.

"— That the commerce between both nations be set open and free, so as the commodities and provisions of either may pass and flow to and fro without any stops or obstructions into the veins of the whole body, for the better sustentation and comfort of all parts ; . . . and that as well the internal and vital veins of blood be opened from interruption and obstruction in making pedigree and claiming by descent, as the external and elemental veins of passage and commerce."— *Report on Union of the Realms*.

"— and therefore might be truly attributed to a secret instinct and inspiring, which many times runneth not only in the hearts of princes, but in the pulse and veins of people, touching the happiness thereby to ensue in time to come."— *History of Henry VII*.

It is unnecessary to attribute this to Bacon's sagacity, for it is sufficiently explained by the fact that *Harvey* was his physician.*

---

* "He [Harvey] was twice censor of the college and in 1615 was appointed Lumelian lecturer. In the following year — the year of Shakespeare's death — he began his course of lectures, and first brought forward his views upon the movements of the heart and blood. Meantime his practice increased, and he had the lord chancellor Francis Bacon, and the earl of Arundel among his patients."— *Enc. Brit.*, HARVEY.

(It should be noted also that there is likewise the same philosophy of gravitation — prior to Newton's time:

"But the strong base and building of my love
Is as the very centre of the earth,
Drawing all things to it."—*Troil. and Cress., IV., 2.*

"Therefore we see that iron in particular sympathy moveth

"Which is from my remembrance!"

The point, or rather the occasion of this reference is made clear by the context immediately preceding the narrative, which, as if introduced for the purpose, unfolds

---

to the lodestone; but yet if it exceed a certain quantity, it forsaketh the affection to the lodestone, and like a good patriot, moveth to the earth, which is the region and country of massy bodies; so we may go forward, and see that water and massy bodies move to the centre of the earth."—*Advancement of Learning*, Second Book.

> "if you could hurt,
> Your swords are now too *massy* for your strengths,
> And will not be uplifted."— *Tempest*, III., 3.

> "But in the wind and tempest of her frown,
> Distinction, with a broad and powerful fan,
> Puffing at all, winnows the light away;
> And what hath *mass*, or matter, by itself
> Lies, rich in virtue, and unmingled."
> — *Troil. and Cress.*, I., 3.

> "That idea to which the human mind is prone, namely that hard bodies are the densest, is to be checked and corrected. . . . *Abundance and scarcity of matter* constitute the notions of dense and rare, rightly understood. . . . Dense and rare have a close connection with heavy and light."— *History of Dense and Rare*.

> "I love thee; I have spoke it:
> *How much the quantity, the weight as much,*
> As I do love my father."— *Cymbeline*, IV., 2.

> "And therefore, *as weight in all motions increaseth force*, so do I not marvel to see men gather the greatest strength of argument they can to make good their opinions."— *Debate on the King's Right of Imposition*.

> "And, *as the thing that's heavy in itself,*
> *Upon enforcement, flies with greatest speed,*
> So did our men, heavy in Hotspur's loss,
> Lend to this weight such lightness with their fear,
> That arrows fled not swifter towards their aim
> Than did our soldiers, aiming at their safety,
> Fly from the field."— *II. Henry IV.*, I., 1.)

the fundamental philosophy of memory: that things forgotten are recalled by or through their orderly association
with other things, whose *images* are impressed upon the
mind:

> "Canst thou remember
> A time before we came into this cell?
> I do not think thou canst; for then thou wast not
> Out three years old.
>
> *Mir.* Certainly, Sir, I can.
>
> *Pros.* By what? by any other house or person?
> Of anything the *image* tell me, that
> Hath kept with thy remembrance.
>
> *Mir.* 'T is far off;
> And rather like a dream than an assurance
> That my remembrance warrants. Had I not
> Four or five women once that tended me?
>
> *Pros.* Thou had'st, and more, Miranda. But how is it
> That this lives in thy mind? What see'st thou else
> In the dark backward abysm of time?
> If thou remember'st aught ere thou cam'st here,
> How thou cam'st here thou may'st.
>
> *Mir.* But that I do not."

Turning to *De Augmentis*, Fifth Book, we find the like
philosophy clearly taught:

" The Art of Memory is built upon two intentions; Prenotion and Emblem. By Prenotion I mean a kind of cutting off of infinity of search. For when a man desires to
recall anything into his memory, if he have no prenotion
or perception of that he seeks, he seeks and strives and
beats about hither and thither as if in infinite space. But
if he have some certain prenotion, this infinity is at once
cut off, and the memory ranges in a narrower compass;
like the hunting of a deer within an enclosure. And therefore order also manifestly assists the memory; for we have
a prenotion that what we are seeking must be something
which agrees with order. . . . Emblem, on the other hand,
reduces intellectual conceptions to sensible *images;* for
an object of sense always strikes the memory more forci-

bly and is more easily impressed upon it than an object
of the intellect; insomuch that even brutes have their
memory excited by sensible impressions; never by intellectual ones. And therefore you will more easily remember the *image* of a hunter pursuing a hare, of an apoth-
ecary arranging his boxes, of a pedant making a speech,
of a boy repeating verses from memory, of a player acting on the stage, than the mere notions of invention, disposition, elocution, memory, and action. Other things
there are (as I said just now) which relate to the help of
memory, but the art as it now is consists of the two above
stated."

> "Please you further.
> *Pros.* My brother and thy uncle, called Antonio,—
> I pray thee mark me* that a brother should
> Be so perfidious;—"

"There is no vice that doth so cover a man with shame
as to be found *false and perfidious*."—*Of Truth.*

> "he whom next thyself
> Of all the world I loved,"

The following from a letter to Essex, prior to his trea-
sonable insurrection, gives us, as in a chart, the bearings
of Bacon's course:

"I desire your Lordship also to think, that though
I confess I love some things much better than I love
your Lordship, — as the Queen's service, her quiet and
contentment, her honor, her favor, the good of my country, and the like, — yet I love few persons better than
yourself, both for gratitude's sake, and for your own virtues, which cannot hurt but by accident or abuse. Of
which my good affection I was ever ready and am ready
to yield testimony by any good offices, but with such res-

---

* "Or otherwise (mark what I say)"
    — *Charge to Grand Jury.*

ervations as yourself cannot but allow: for as I was ever sorry that your Lordship should fly with waxen wings, doubting Icarus' fortune, so for the growing up of your own feathers, specially ostrich's, or any other *save of a bird of prey*, no man shall be more glad. And this is the axletree whereupon I have turned and shall turn." *

"and to him put

The manage of my state;"

" For that which concerneth his crown and state, it is known . . . that for these last two years his Majesty

---

* " strong as the axletree
On which the heavens ride."—*Troil. and Cress.*, I., 3.

" So as the axletree, whereupon their greatness turneth, is soon cut in two by any that shall be stronger than they by sea." —*Considerations touching a War with Spain.*

Whence the origin of the figure?

" And assuredly as Aristotle endeavors to prove that in all motion there is some point quiescent; and as he very elegantly interprets the ancient fable of Atlas, who stood fixed and supported the heaven on his shoulders, to be meant of the poles or axletree of heaven, whereupon the conversion is accomplished; so do men earnestly desire to have within them an Atlas or axletree of the thoughts, by which the fluctuations and dizziness of the understanding may be to some extent controlled; fearing belike that their heaven should fall."—*De Augmentis*, Fifth Book, Chap. IV.

We begin to realize that Bacon was thoroughly saturated with " the wisdom of the ancients." He drank deep at the fountain of those waters, imbibing their subtle spirit, and seasoning his writings with their essence; sometimes so deftly that though we appreciate the richness, we are unable, in our ignorance, to distinguish the flavor.

We catch a glimpse also of his industry, for such an absolute mastery, as the educated world well knows, could only be acquired by years of close and patient study, and that too, we would almost add, in early youth, during the formative period.

hath been content to undergo the principal travel and manage of his affairs in his own person."—*Memorial for the King's Speech.*

"A fellow that thinks with his magistrality and goose-quill to give laws and manages to crowns and sceptres."—*Charge Against Talbot.**

---

* "Lorenzo, I commit into your hands
The husbandry and manage of my house."
— *Merchant of Venice, III., 4.*

"This might have been prevented and made whole,
With very easy arguments of love;
Which now the *manage* of two kingdoms must
With fearful bloody issue *arbitrate.*"
— *King John, I., 1.*

("And put thy fortune to the *arbitriment*
Of bloody strokes, and mortal-staring war."
— *Richard III., V., 3.*

The expression of a profound philosophy:

"It is the wars that are the tribunal seat, where the highest rights and possessions are decided."—*Bacon's Device.*

"Wars (I speak not of ambitious, predatory wars) are suits of appeal to the tribunal of God's justice, where there are no superiors on earth to determine the cause: and they are (as civil pleas are) plaints or defences." — *Considerations touching a War with Spain.*

"Strike up the drums; and let the tongue of war
Plead for our interest, and our being here."
— *King John, V., 2.*

"Will you show our title to the crown?
If not our swords shall *plead* it in the field."
— *III. Henry VI., II., 1.*

"In God's name, cheerly on, courageous friends,
To reap the harvest of perpetual peace,
By this one bloody *trial* of sharp war."
— *Richard III., V., 2.*

"So is the equal poise of this fell war,
Here on this molehill will I set me down,
To whom God will, there be the victory."
— *III. Henry VI., II., 5.*)

"as at that time
Through all the signiories it was the first,"

"This is now, by the providence of God, the fourth time that the line and Kings of England have had dominions and *signiories* united unto them as patrimonies, and by descent of blood."—*Case of the Post-Nati of Scotland.*

"And as for the Duke of Parma, he was reasonably well tempted to be true to that enterprise, by no less promise than to be made a fendatory or beneficiary king of England, under the *signiory* (in chief) of the Pope, and the protection of the King of Spain."—*Considerations touching a War with Spain.*

"And Prospero the prime duke,"

"I have been somebody by your Majesty's singular and undeserved favor: even the prime officer of your kingdom."—*Letter to King James.*

"Your grace being, as it were, the first born or prime man of the King's creatures, must in consequence owe the most to his children and generations: whereof I know your noble heart hath far greater sense than any man's words can infuse into you."—*Letter of Advice to Buckingham.**

"being so reputed
In dignity,"†

---

* "*King Henry.* Have I not made you
The prime man of the state?"
     —*Henry VIII., III., 2.*

† The following notes illustrate the intimacy of both thought and vocabulary:

"For as the works of wisdom surpass in dignity and power the works of strength."—*Wisdom of the Ancients.*

"I will take it for a good sign that you shall give honor to your dignity, and not your dignity to you."—*Letter to Villiers.*

"And though it must be confessed that the *ante-natus* and the *post-natus* are in the same degree in dignities; yet were they

> "and for the liberal arts,*
> Without a parallel:" †

If we adopt the theory of the critics that Prospero represents the Poet himself,‡ the resemblance is here so striking that we are almost led to venture the further conjecture that the whole play is likewise symbolical upon the broadest lines; the contest between Prospero and his brother typifying the conflict actually waged in the Poet's breast; engendered by the attractions of power on the one hand, and the love of learning on the other, and exemplified in the vicissitudes of his life. Leaving this, however, to the future, and to the exegesis of merciful critics, the following citations are perhaps pertinent

---

never so in abilities. For no man doubts, but the son of an Earl or Baron, born before his creation or call, shall inherit the dignity, as well as the son born after."—*Speech Against Motion for Union of Laws.*

* "In the course of your study and choice of books, you must first seek to have the grounds of learning, which are the liberal arts."—*Advice to Rutland,* on his Travels.

"Of all these arts those which belong to the eye and ear are esteemed the most liberal; for these two senses are the purest; and the sciences thereof are the most learned, as having mathematics like a handmaid in their train. . . . It has been well observed by some that military arts flourish at the birth and rise of States; liberal arts when States are settled and at their height; and voluptuary arts when they are turning to decline and ruin."—*De Augmentis,* Fourth Book, Chap. II.

† "For as Statuas and Pictures are dumb histories, so histories are speaking Pictures. Wherein, if my affection be not too great, or my reading too small, I am of this opinion, that if Plutarch were alive to write lives by parallels, it would trouble him for virtue and fortune both to find for her a parallel amongst women."—*Letter to the Lord Chancellor,* referring to the deceased Queen Elizabeth.

‡ "For in Prospero shall we not recognize the Artist himself."—*Lowell.*

3

> " to the present business
> Which now's upon us : "

" I now come to the Art of Empire or Civil Government, which includes Economics, as a state includes a family. On this subject, as I before said, I have imposed silence on myself, though perhaps I might not be entirely unqualified to handle such topics with some skill and profit, as being one who has had the benefit of long experience, and who, by your Majesty's most gracious favor, without any merit of his own, has risen through so many gradations of office and honor to *the highest dignity* in the realm and borne the same for four whole years; . . . and who also, *besides other arts,* has spent much time in the study of laws and histories."—*De Augmentis*, Eighth Book.

" Seeing now, most excellent King, that my little bark, such as it is, has sailed round the whole circumference of *the old and new world of sciences* (with what success and fortune it is for posterity to decide), what remains but that having at length finished my course I should pay my vows."—*De Augmentis*, Ninth Book, Chap. IX.

> "those being all my study,
> The government I cast upon my brother,[*]
> And to my state grew stranger,"[†]

" Not however that learning admires or esteems this architecture of fortune otherwise than as an inferior work. For no man's fortune can be an end worthy of the gift of being that has been given him by God; and often the

[*] " If I cast part of my burden, I shall be more strong and *delivre* to bear the rest."—*Note for Interview with the King.*

[†] " Surely I think no man could ever more truly say of himself with the Psalmist than I can, 'My soul hath been a stranger in her pilgrimage.' So I seem to have my conversation among the ancients more than among those with whom I live, and why should I not likewise converse rather with the absent than the present, and make my friendships by choice and election, rather than suffer them, as the manner is, to be settled by accident?"—*Letter to Casaubon.*

worthiest men abandon their fortunes willingly, that they may have leisure for higher pursuits."—*De Augmentis, Eighth Book, Chap. II.*

" My nature can take no evil ply ; but I will, by God's assistance, with this disgrace on my fortune, and yet with that comfort of the good opinion of so many honorable and worthy persons, retire myself, with a couple of men, to Cambridge, and there spend my life in my studies and contemplations without looking back."—*Letter to Essex,* in 1594.

" being transported
And rapt in secret studies."

" Amongst which (*if affection for learning transport me not*) there is not any more noble or more worthy than the further endowment of the world with sound and fruitful knowledge."—*De Augmentis,* Second Book, Dedication.

" Let those who distrust their own powers observe myself, one who have amongst my contemporaries been the most engaged in public business, who are not very strong in health (which causes a great loss of time), and am the first explorer of this course, following the guidance of none, *nor even communicating my thoughts to a single individual;* yet having once firmly entered in the right way, and submitting the powers of my mind to things, I have somewhat advanced (as I make bold to think) the matter I now treat of."—*Novum Organum,* Book I., 113.

We now pass, in transition, into the counter realm of statescraft and policy, governed by laws of its own, taught by experience. And here, as by a master hand, the very springs of action are laid bare before us, so that we may even discern the peculiar antithesis inherent in their movement; for as Bacon profoundly observes, in his Essay, *Of Empire,* " To speak now of the true temper of empire, it is a thing rare and hard to keep ; for both temper and distemper consist of contraries ; but it is one thing to mingle

contraries, another to interchange them,"— the meaning
of which will clearly appear as the theme is developed.

> "Thy *false* uncle —
> Dost thou attend me?
> *Mir.* Sir, most heedfully.
> *Pros.* Being once perfected* how to grant suits,
> How to deny them,"

" You are a new risen star, and the eyes of all men are
upon you : let not your own negligence make you fall like a
meteor. . . . And in respect of the suitors which shall attend you, there is nothing will bring you more honor and
more ease than to do them what right in justice you may,
and with as much speed as you may : for, believe me, Sir,
next to the obtaining of the suit, a speedy and gentle denial (when the case will not bear it) is the most acceptable
to suitors."—*Letter of Advice to Villiers.*

" But your Majesty is still in a straight, that either your
means or your mind must suffer. For *to grant all suits*
were to undo yourself, or your people. *To deny all suits*
were to see never a contented face."—*Letter to King
James.*

> "whom to advance," † and whom

---

* "It resteth that I express unto your majesty my great joy,
in your honoring and advancing this gentleman ; . . . Only
your Majesty's school (wherein he hath already so well profited,
as in this entrance upon the stage, being the time of greatest
danger, he hath not committed any manifest error), will add
perfection,— to your Majesty's comfort and the great contentment of your people."—*Letter to King James, regarding Villiers.*

† "And in places of moment, rather make able and honest
men yours, than advance those that are otherwise because they
are yours."— *Letter to Villiers.*

"The knot which is to be tied for his reputation must either

To trash for overtopping,—" [*]

"He (Henry VII.) kept a straight hand on his nobility, and chose rather to *advance* clergymen and lawyers, which were more obsequious to him, but had less interest in the people; which made for his absoluteness, but not for his safety. . . . He was not afraid of an able man, as Lewis the Eleventh was; but contrariwise, he was served by the ablest men that were to be found; without which his affairs could not have prospered as they did. . . . And as he chose well, so he held them up well; for it is a strange thing, that though he were a dark prince, and infinitely suspicious, and his times full of secret conspiracies and troubles, yet in twenty-four years' reign, he never *put down or discomposed* counsellor, or near servant, save only Stanley, the lord chamberlain. . . . He was a prince, sad, serious, and full of thoughts and secret observations, and full

be advancing or depressing of persons or putting by or forwarding of actions."—*Notes for Advice to Buckingham.*

"I should hope, that as your Majesty hath of late won hearts by depressing, you should in this lose no hearts by advancing: for I see your people can better skill of *concretum* than *abstractum*, and that the waves of their affections flow rather after persons than things."—*Letter to King James.*

[*] "There is use also of ambitious men in pulling down the greatness of any subject that *overtops;* as Tiberius used Marco in the pulling down of Sejanus. . . . As for the pulling of them down, if the affairs require it, and it may be done with safety suddenly, the only way is the interchange continually of favors and disgraces, whereby they may not know what to expect, and be, as it were, in a wood."—*Of Ambition.*

"And the like diligence was used in the age before by that league (wherewith Guicciardine beginneth his story, and maketh it, as it were, the calendar of the good days of Italy), which was contracted between Ferdinando, *King* of Naples, Lorenzo of Medici, *Potentate* of Florence and Ludovico Sfortza, *Duke* of Milan, designed chiefly against the growing power of the Venetians; but yet so, as the confederates had a perpetual eye one upon another, that none of them should *overtop*."—*Considerations Touching a War with Spain.*

of notes and memorials of his own hand, especially touching persons; as, *whom* to employ, *whom* to reward, *whom* to inquire of, *whom* to beware of, what were the dependencies, what were the factions, and the like."—*History of Henry VII.**

"new created
The creatures that were mine, I say, or changed them,
Or else new formed them;"

"And lastly, when all these means, or any of them, have *new framed or formed human will*, then doth custom and habit corroborate and confirm all the rest."—*Helps for the Intellectual Powers.*†

"having both the key
Of officer and office,"

"An instrument in tuning."—*Promus of Formularies and Elegancies.*

And in another sense: "This year also the King entered into a league with the Italian potentates for the de-

---

* "And for those she advanced to places of trust, she kept such a tight rein upon them, and so distributed her favors, that she held each of them under the greatest obligation and concern to please her, whilst she always remained mistress of herself."—*Memory of Elizabeth.*

† "Custom hath made it in him a property of easiness."
—*Hamlet, V., 1.*
"How use doth breed a habit in a man."
—*Two Gentlemen of Verona, V., 4.*
"That monster custom, who all sense doth eat —
Of habits evil — is angel yet in this, —
That to the use of actions fair and good
He likewise gives a frock or livery,
That aptly is put on. Refrain to-night:
And that shall lend a kind of easiness
To the next abstinence; the next more easy;
For use can almost change the stamp of nature."
—*Hamlet, III., 4.*

fense of Italy against France ; for King Charles had conquered the realm of Naples, and lost it again, in a kind of
felicity of a dream. He passed the whole length of Italy
without resistance ; so that it was true which Pope Alexander was wont to say, ' That the Frenchmen came into
Italy with chalk in their hands, to mark up their lodgings,
rather than with swords to fight.' * He likewise entered
and won, in effect, the whole kingdom of Naples itself,
without striking stroke. But presently thereupon he did
commit and multiply so many errors, as was too great a
task for the best fortune to overcome. He gave no contentment to the barons of Naples, of the faction of the
Angeovines ; but scattered his rewards according to the
mercenery appetites of some about him. . . . He fell too
soon at differences with Ludovico Sfortza, who was the man
that *carried the keys* which brought him in and shut him
out."—*History of Henry VII.*

> "set all hearts i' the state
> To what tune pleased his ear;"

" It is my desire that if any the King's business either of
honor or profit shall pass the house, it may be not only
with external prevailing but with satisfaction of the inward

---

* Later in the play [Act V., Scene 1], when all were amicably
reconciled, Gonzalo says:

> " Look down, you gods,
> And on this couple drop a blessed crown !
> For it is you that have *chalk'd* forth the way
> Which brought us hither."

Bacon repeats Pope Alexander's remark at least three times ;
in *De Augmentis*, Third Book, Chap. VI., continuing : " so I
like better that entry of truth which comes peaceably, as with
chalk to mark up those minds which are capable to lodge and
harbor such a guest, than that which forces its way with pug-
nacity and contention."

It is perhaps significant that the commentators upon the play,
for want of the key, have failed to comprehend the now clear

man. For in consent where tongue-strings not heart-
strings make the music, that harmony may end in discord.
. . . When Vespasian came out of Judea towards Italy
to receive the empire, as he passed by Alexandria he spake
with Apollonius, a man much admired, and asked him a
question of state: 'What was Nero's fall or overthrow?'
Apollonius answered again, 'Nero could tune the harp
well: but in government he always either wound up the
pins too high and strained the strings too far, or let them
down too low and slackened the strings too much.' Here
we see the difference between regular and able princes and
irregular and incapable, Nerva and Nero. The one tem-
pers and mingles the sovereignty with the liberty of the
subject wisely; and the other doth interchange it and vary
it unequally and absurdly."—*Speech on the King's Mes-
sages.*

"Until your Majesty have tuned your instrument you
will have no harmony. I, for my part, think it a thing inestimable for your Majesty's safety and service that you
once part with your parliament with love and reverence."

"That it doth well in church music when the greatest
part of the hymn is sung by one voice, and then the quire
at times falls in sweetly and solemnly, and that the same
harmony sorteth well in monarchy between the King and
his Parliament."—*Letters to King James.*

"This I apply to the King's business, which surely I
revolve most when I am least in action; . . . But still it
must be remembered, that the stringing of the harp, nor
the tuning of it, will not serve, except it be well played
on from time to time."—*Letter to Buckingham.*

"If a man so temper his actions, as in some one of them

_____

meaning of this *artificial* metaphor. (The same figure reap-
pears in unmistakable terms in *Henry VIII.*, I., 1:

"For, being not propp'd by ancestory, whose grace
Chalks successors their way;")

he doth content every faction or combination of people, the music will be the fuller."—*Of Honor and Reputation.**

" that now he was
The ivy which had hid my princely trunk," †
And suck'd my verdure out on't—"

" Nor is it without a mystery that the ivy was sacred to Bacchus, and this for two reasons : first, because ivy is an evergreen, or flourishes in the winter ; and secondly, because it winds and creeps about so many things, as trees, walls and buildings, and raises itself above them. . . . And for the second, the predominant passion of the mind

---

* We cannot withhold two other ornate but graceful variations of this musical theme :

"And when your Majesty could raise me no higher, it was your grace to illustrate me with beams of honor ; first making me Baron Verulam, and now Viscount St. Albans. So this is the eighth rise or reach, a diapason in music, even a good number and accord for a close."—*Letter to King James.*

" At length therefore having arrived at some pause and looking back into those things which I have passed through, this treatise of mine seems to me not unlike those sounds and preludes which musicians make while they are tuning their instruments, which produce indeed a harsh and unpleasing sound to the ear, but tend to make the music sweeter afterwards. And thus have I intended to employ myself in tuning the harp of the muses and reducing it to perfect harmony, that thereafter the strings may be touched by a better hand or a better quill."—*De Augmentis,* Eighth Book, Chap. III.

† " By all means it is to be procured that the trunk of Nebuchadnezzar's tree of monarchy be great enough to bear the branches and the boughs."—*Of the True Greatness of Kingdoms.*

" Your *princely* eye was wont to meet with any motion that was made on the relieving part."—*Letter to the King.*

" Were gracious in those princely eyes of thine."—*Titus And., I., 2.*

throws itself, like the ivy, round all human actions, entwines all our resolutions, and perpetually adheres to, and mixes itself among, or even overtops them."— *Wisdom of the Ancients.**

"Custom like an ivy which grows and clasps upon the tree of commerce."—*Notes of Speech on the King's Right of Imposition.*

"*But it was ordained that this winding ivy of a Plantagenet should kill the true tree itself.*"—*History of Henry VII.*

"Thou attend'st not.
Mir. O, good sir, I do."

In this truly "speaking picture," the arena of action has been opened to our view and the relative positions of the as yet uncontending forces fully disclosed. And now we are about to be taken, as it were, behind the scenes, and into the very "counsels," that we may witness the inception of the struggle, its genesis, and even the development of the causes producing it.

It is pregnant with instruction, which may be delivered to us, if we but follow Bacon's pertinent advice in the study of history:

"In the story of France, you have a large and pleasant field in the lives of their kings to observe their alliances and successions, their conquests and their wars, especially with us; their counsels, their treaties, and all rules and examples of experience and wisdom; which may be lights and remembrances to you hereafter to judge all occurrences at home and abroad."—*Letter of Advice to Rutland on his Travels.*

And he likewise condemns Epitomies, "where com-

---

* "So doth the woodbine the sweet honeysuckle
　　Gently entwist; the female ivy so
　　Enrings the barky fingers of the elm."
　　　　　　　—*Midsummer Night's Dream, IV., 1.*

monly in matter of art the positions are set down without their proofs, and in matter of story the things done without the counsels and circumstances, which indeed are a thousand times more in use than the examples themselves."—*Advice to Greville on His Studies.*

"*Pros.*   I pray thee, mark me,*
I thus neglecting worldly ends, all dedicated
To closeness."

"There be three degrees of this hiding and veiling of a man's self; the first, *closeness*, reservation, and secrecy; when a man leaveth himself without observation, or without hold to be taken, what he is."—*Of Simulation and Dissimulation.*

"It is not to be forgotten what Comineus observeth of his first master, Duke Charles the Hardy, namely, that he would communicate his secrets with none; and least of all, those secrets which troubled him most. Whereupon he goeth on and saith, that towards his latter time that closeness did impair and a little perish his undertakings. Surely Comineus might have made the same judgment also, if it had pleased him, of his second master, Lewis the Eleventh, whose closeness was indeed his tormentor."—*Of Friendship.*

"and the bettering of my mind
With that which, but by being so retired,
O'er-prized all popular rate,"

"Studies serve for delight, for ornament, and for ability. Their chief use for delight is in privateness and retiring."—*Of Studies.*

The critics have been in somewhat of a quandary as to the meaning of the text. The exquisite delicacy of its sig-

---

* "And to say truth, if one mark it well, this was in all memory the main piece of wisdom in strong and prudent counsels."
—*Considerations Touching a War with Spain*

nificance, its classical origin, and its pertinency are all however clearly unfolded in the following, from the *Advancement of Learning*, Book I.:

"As for retirement, it is a theme so common to extol a private life, not taxed with sensuality and sloth, for the liberty, the pleasure and the freedom from indignity it affords, that every one praises it well, such an agreement it has to the nature and apprehensions of mankind. This may be added, that learned men, forgotten in states and not living in the eyes of the world, are like the images of Cassius and Brutus at the funeral of Junia, which not being represented as many others were, Tacitus said of them that, '*They outshone the rest, because not seen.*'"

> "in my false brother
> Awaked an evil nature:"

"But let no man trust his victory over his nature too far; for nature will lie *buried* a great time, and yet *revive* upon the occasion or temptation."—*Of Nature in Men.* (See Angelo in *Measure for Measure.*)

"At this time the King's estate was very prosperous; secured by the amity of Scotland, strengthened by that of Spain, cherished by that of Burgundy, all domestic troubles quenched, and all noise of war, like a thunder afar off, going upon Italy. Wherefore nature, which many times is happily contained and refrained by some bands of fortune, began to take place in the King; carrying, as with a strong tide, his affections and thoughts into the gathering and heaping up of treasure." — *History of Henry VII.*

> "and my trust,
> Like a good parent,* did beget of him
> A falsehood,"

---

* This remarkable expression seems fully warranted by Bacon's close observation:

"Revolve in histories the memories of happy men, and you

" He (Cupid) is introduced without a parent, that is to say without a cause; for the cause is as the parent of the effect; and it is a familiar and almost continual figure of speech to denote cause and effect as parent and child."— *On Principles and Origins.**

" For *corruptio unius generatio alterius* holds as well in arguments as in nature. The destruction of an objection *begets* a proof."— *Case of the Post Nati of Scotland.*

" There is no pound profit which redoundeth to your Majesty in this course, but induceth and *begetteth* three pound damage upon your subjects, besides the discontentment."— *Speech to King James Touching Purveyors.*

" Another point was, that I always vehemently dissuaded him from seeking greatness by a military dependence, or by a popular dependence, as that which would *breed* in the Queen jealousy, in himself presumption, and in the state perturbation."— *Apology Concerning the Earl of Essex.*

" — glozing then, that because he had heard that by

---

shall not find any of rare felicity but either he died childless, or his line spent soon after his death, or else he was unfortunate in his children. Should a man have to be slain by his vassals, as the *posthumus* of Alexander the Great was? or to call them his imposthumes, as Augustus Cæsar called his? Peruse the catalogue: Cornelius Sylla, Julius Cæsar, Flavius Vespasianus, Severus, Constantinus the Great, and many more."— *Discourse in Praise of the Queen.*

* " Then let them anatomize Regan; see what *breeds* about her heart. Is there any *cause* in nature that makes these hard hearts?"— *King Lear, III., 6.*

(" To make an *anatomy* of it, and shew the lines and parts, which might serve to give a light, though not delight."— *Conference on the Question of Law.*)

" My brain I 'll prove the female to my soul;
My soul the father: and these two *beget*
A generation of *still-breeding* thoughts."
— *Richard II., V., 5.*

[See, please, *infra*, pages 60 and 80.]

strict exposition of law all treasons of rebellion did tend to the destruction of the King's person, it might *breed* a buzz in the rebels' heads, and so discourage them from coming in."—*Declaration against Essex.** (For the like argumentative "glozing," see *Troil. and Cress.*, II., 2.)

---

* "Now this follows,
(Which, as I take it, is a kind of *puppy*
To the old dam, treason) —Charles the Emperor,
Under pretence to see the queen his aunt,
(For, 'twas, indeed, his *color;* but he came
To whisper Wolsey,) here makes visitation:
His fears were, that the interview betwixt
England and France might, through their amity,
Breed him some prejudice."—*Henry VIII.*, I., 1.

[See *infra*, page 71.]

"*Ulyss.* I have a young conception in my brain,
Be you my time to bring it to some shape.
Nest. What is't?
Ulyss. This 'tis:—
Blunt wedges rive hard knots: the seeded pride
That hath to this maturity blown up
In rank Achilles, must or now be cropp'd
Or, shedding, *breed* a nursery of like evil,
To overbulk us all."— *Troil. and Cress.*, I., 3.

(Bacon was especially prolific in metaphors developed from nature's "nursery": "He entered into due consideration as well how to weed out the partakers of the former rebellion, as to kill the seeds of the like in time to come." "But that the true way is, to stop the seeds of sedition and rebellion in their beginnings." "But these blossoms of unripe marriages were but kindly wishes and the airs of loving entertainment." "And this was but a summer fruit, which they thought was almost ripe, and would be soon gathered."—*History of Henry VII.* "No mortal calamity is more moving and afflicting, than to see the flower of virtue *cropped* before its time."—*Wisdom of the Ancients.*

"A sweeter and a lovelier gentleman,
Framed in the prodigality of nature,
The spacious world cannot again afford:
And will she yet abase her eyes on me

> "in its contrary as great
> As my trust was;"

"—: always understood, that if you can reconcile all the words, and make no falsity, that is a case quite out of this rule, which hath place only where there is a direct *contrariety* or falsity not to be reconciled to this rule."— *Maxims of the Law*, Regula XXIV.

And, illustrating also his delight in playing with words:

"And yet they say that an use is but a nimble and light thing; and now, *contrariwise*, it seemeth to be weightier than anything else: for you cannot weigh it up to raise it, neither by deed nor deed enrolled, without the weight of a consideration."— *Reading on the Statute of Uses.**

> That *cropp'd* the golden prime of this sweet prince,"
> — *Richard III.*, I., 2.)

"Seldom but that pity *begets* you a good opinion, and that opinion a mere profit."— *Pericles*, IV., 3.

("For lies are sufficient to breed opinion, and opinion brings on substance."— *Of Vain Glory.*)

> "*Scroop.* Let him be punished, sovereign; lest example
> Breed, by his suffrance, more of such a kind.
> *K. Hen.* If little faults, proceeding on distemper,
> Shall not be wink'd at, how shall we stretch our eye
> When capital crimes, chew'd, swallow'd and digested,
> Appear before us?"—*Henry V.*, II., 3.

("Some books are to be tasted, others to be swallowed, and some few to be chewed and digested."—*Of Studies.*)

> "Know that this gold must coin a stratagem,
> Which cunningly effected, will beget
> A very excellent piece of villainy."
> — *Tit. Andron.*, II., 3.

* "—purse and brain both empty; the brain the heavier for being too light, the purse too light being drawn of heaviness; O! of this contradiction you shall now be quit."— *Cymbeline*, V., 4.

The following are a couple of like examples from a single *Letter to Queen Elizabeth:*

" As for profit, there appeareth a direct *contrariety* between that and all three courses."— *Gesta Grayorum.*

" Without it there can be no fortitude, for all other darings come of fury, and fury is a passion, and passions ever turn into their *contraries*, and therefore the most furious men, when their first blaze is spent, be commonly the most fearful."— *Advice to Rutland on his Travels.**

" I think I would *rest senseless* of that wherein others have *sense restless*, and that is of my particular estate and fortune. . . . Thirdly, your Majesty may by this redemption (for so may I truly call it) free me from the *contempt of the contemptible*, that measure a man by his estate."

And in the same vein:

" or to dissever so
Our great self and our credit, to esteem
A senseless help, when help past sense we deem."
                    — *All's Well, II., 1.*

" Above the sense of sense : so sensible
Seemeth their conference."— *L. L. L., V., 2.*

" I think you may use all the places of logic against his placing."— *Letter to Essex.*

" Open your mouth : this will shake your shaking, I can tell you, and that soundly."— *Tempest, II., 2.*

" For the greatness of the fault, I shall not insist upon it, it hath already been so soundly sounded."—*Speech on Telverton's Case.*

" To England will I steal, and there I'll steal."—*Henry V., V., 2.*

" Let me know of such roots, and I will root them out of the country."— *Speech to the Judges.*

" All this must be because you can pleasure men at pleasure."— *Letter to Sir Vincent Skinner.*

" And if what pleases him shall pleasure you."—*III., Henry VI., III., 2.*

" This concurrence of occurrents."—*Speech on Subsidy Bill.*

" O single-soled jest, solely singular for the singleness." — *Romeo and Juliet, II., 4.*

*" And all things change them to the contrary." — *Romeo and Juliet, IV., 5.*

" Excuseth memory :—Distracted by one day of astonishment, two of gladness : — Two *contrary* passions."—*Notes for Speech Touching Subsidy.*

These are but a few out of a multitude of examples, such was his *penchant* for antithesis.

> "which had indeed no limit,
> A confidence *sans* bound." *

Another peculiarity of Bacon was his frequent exaggeration of quantity or quality to the utmost limit of statement :

" Meaning that her goodness was *without limit*, where there was a true concurrence ; which I knew in her nature to be true."—*Apology Concerning the Earl of Essex.*

> "Sweet love, I see, changing his property,
> Turns to the sourest and most deadly hate."
> —*Richard II., III., 2.*

" But, my Lords, as it is a principle in nature, that the best things are in their corruption the worst, and the sweetest wine makes the sharpest vinegar; so it fell out with them that this excess (as I may term it) of friendship ended in mortal hatred."—*Charge Against the Earl of Somerset.*

* " I was three of my young years bred with an embassador in France."—*Letter to King James.* (See *Henry V., III.. 4.*)

In some instances, he even dropped into the peculiar French idiom :

" *Myself*, as I then took contentment in your approbation thereof, so I should esteem and acknowledge not only my contentment increased, but my labor advanced, if I might obtain your help in that nature which I desire."—*Letter to Dr. Playfair, Professor at Cambridge.*

In his old age and in distress, he thus appeals to Buckingham, formerly *Villiers*, to whom he had been of great service :

" *Myself* have ridden at anchor all your Grace's absence, and my cables are now quite worn. . . . My lord, do some good work upon me, that I may end my days in comfort, which nevertheless cannot be complete except you put me in some way to

4

" And his ambition was so exhorbitant and *unbounded*, as he became suitor to the King for the earldom of Chester, which ever being a kind of appendage to the principality of Wales, and using to go to the King's son, his suit did not only end in a denial, but in a distaste."—*History of Henry VII.*

His heart thus pours forth of its fulness, in expression of the tender affection between himself and Sir Toby Matthew:

"Whatsoever the event be (wherein I depend upon God, who ordaineth the effect, the instrument, all) yet your incessant thinking of me, without loss of a moment of time, or a hint of occasion, or a circumstance of endeavor, or a stroke of a pulse, in demonstration of love and affection to me doth infinitely tie me to you."—*Letter to Matthew.**

---

do your noble self service." And again: " For, as I writ before, my cables are worn out, my hope of tackling is by your Lordship's means."

This mournful note of the sea, whispering of the voyage of life, of loosening moorings and worn-out tackling, though in the sober measures of prose, as was befitting in correspondence, swells into a full diapason, in the tempest of poetic license:

"*K. John.* O cousin, thou art come to set mine eye:
The tackle of my heart is crack'd and burnt;
And all the shrouds, wherewith my life should sail
Are turned to one thread, one little hair;
My heart hath one poor string to stay it by,
Which holds but till thy news be uttered."
—*King John, V., 7.*

* " He is one of the noblest note, to whose kindness I am most infinitely tied."—*Cymbeline, I., 6.*

" A thousand oaths, an ocean of his tears,
And instances as infinite of love
Warrant me welcome to Proteus."
—*Two Gentlemen of Verona, II., 7.*

" Our duty is so rich, so infinite,
That we may do it still without accompt."
—*L. L. L., V., 2.*

Again; "But so it was, that not only the consent but the applause and joy was *infinite, and not to be expressed,* throughout the realm of England, upon this succession, whereof the consent, no doubt may be truly ascribed to the clearance of the right, but the general joy, alacrity and gratulation were the effects of different causes," etc. —*Fragment of the History of Great Britain.**

In the contrary sense, but the like pleonasm:

"But yet for all that, this liberty is not *infinite and without limits.*"—*Charge Against Whitelock.*

And to cap the climax: "I know I ought *doubly infinitely* to be her Majesty's."—*Letter framed for Essex.*†

"Neither mought I in reason presume to offer unto your Majesty dead lines, myself being excluded as I am; were it not upon this only argument or subject, namely to clear myself in point of duty. Duty, though my state lie buried in the sands, and my favors be cast upon the waters, and my honors be committed to the wind, yet standeth surely built upon the rock, and hath been, and ever shall be, unforced and unattempted."—*Letter written for Essex to the Queen.*

"*Wolsey.*   I am loyal, and will be,
Though all the world should crack their duty to you,
And throw it from their soul; though perils did
Abound, as thick as thought could make them, and
Appear in forms more horrid; yet my *duty,*
As *doth a rock* against the chiding flood,
Should the approach of this wild river break,
And stand unshaken yours."—*Henry VIII.,* III., 2.

* "I mean that her beauty is exquisite, but her favor infinite."—*Two Gentlemen of Verona,* II., 1.

"A satire against the softness of prosperity; with a discovery of the infinite flatteries that follow youth and prosperity." —*Timon of Athens,* V., 1.

"O, you shall be exposed, my lord, to dangers
As infinite as immanent."—*Troil. and Cress.,* IV., 1.

"In nature's infinite book of secrecy
A little I can read."—*Ant. and Cleo.,* I., 2.

† "Oh, were the sum of these that I should pay

But it was in his pleasantries that Bacon gave the freer rein to this propensity. The following from a Court Masque, in celebration of the Queen's day in November, 1595, entitled by Spedding (Bacon's *Works*, Vol. VIII., page 377) Bacon's *Device*, is well worthy of its space, as an example, to mention nothing else, of the extravagance in thought and language of which he was capable:

"Shall any man make his conceit as an anchor, mured up with compass of one beauty or person, that may have the liberty of all contemplation? Shall he exchange the sweet travelling through the universal variety for one wearisome and endless round or labyrinth? . . .

"If from a sanguine, delightful humor of love he turn to a melancholy, retired humor of contemplation, or a turbulent, boiling humor of the wars, what doth he but change tyrants? Contemplation is a dream, love a trance, and the humor of war is raving. These be shifts of humor, but no reclaiming to reason. . . .

"Nay, in his demonstration of love let him not go too far; for these silly lovers, when they profess such infinite affection and obligation, they tax themselves at so high a rate they are ever under arrest.* . . .

Countless and infinite, yet I would pay them."
—*Tit. Andron.*, V., 3.

"Beyond the infinite and boundless reach
Of mercy, if thou didst this deed of death
Art thou damn'd, Hubert."—*King John*, IV., 3.

—"he's a most notable coward, an infinite and endless liar."
—*All's Well*, III., 6.

"Valor and pride excell themselves in Hector.
The one almost as infinite as all,
The other blank as nothing."
—*Troil. and Cress.*, IV., 5.

* And in the like extravagance: "For these fellows of infinite tongue, that can rhyme themselves into ladies' favors, they do always reason themselves out again."—*Henry V.*, V., 2.
"Would now like him, now loathe him; then entertain him,

" But give ear now to the comparison of my master's condition, and acknowledge such a difference as is betwixt the melting hail-stone and the solid pearl. Indeed it seemeth to depend as the globe of the earth seemeth to hang in the air; but yet it is firm and stable in itself. It is like a cube or die form, which toss it or throw it any way, it ever lighteth upon a square. Is he denied the hopes of favors to come? He can resort to the remembrance of contentments passed: destiny cannot repeal that which is past. Doth he find the acknowledgment of his affection small? He may find the merit of his affection greater? Fortune cannot have power over that which is within.

" Nay, his falls are like the falls of Antaeus; they renew his strength. His clouds are like the clouds of harvest, which make the sun break forth with greater force; his wanes and changes are like the moon, whose globe is all light towards the sun when it is all dark towards the world; such is the excellency of her nature and of his estate.

---

then forswear him, now weep for him, then spit at him; that I drave my suitor from his mad humor of love, to a living humor of madness; which was to forswear the full stream of the world, and to live in a nook merely monastic."—*As You Like It, III.,* 2. And again:

" *Troilus.* In all Cupid's pageant there is presented no monster.

Cressida. Nor nothing monstrous neither?

Troilus. Nothing, but our undertakings: when we vow to weep seas, live in fire, eat rocks, tame tigers; thinking it harder for our mistress to devise imposition enough, than for us to undergo any difficulty imposed. This is the monstrosity in love, lady,—that the will is infinite, and the execution confined; that the desire is boundless, and the act a slave to limit.

Cressida. They say, all lovers swear more performance than they are able, and yet reserve an ability that they never perform; vowing more than the perfection of ten, and discharging less than the tenth part of one. They that have the voice of lions, and the act of hares, are they not monsters."—*Troil. and Cress., III., 2.*

" Attend, you beadsman of the Muses, you take pleasure in a wilderness of variety ; but it is but of *shadows*. You are as a man rich in pictures, medals, and crystals. Your mind is of the water, which taketh all forms and impressions, but is weak of substance. Will you compare shadows with bodies, picture with life, variety of many beauties with the peerless excellency of one? the element of water with the element of fire ? And such is the comparison between knowledge and love." *

---

* The reader has doubtless already discerned our broader purpose, which is to afford him an opportunity to become personally acquainted with Bacon's innate imaginative power. And to this end we add still another example:

Writing to Essex in 1596, he embodies his thought in this beautiful figure:

" Wherein I do not doubt but as the beams of your favor often dissolved the coldness of my fortunes, so in this argument, your Lordship will do the like with your pen."

Again, in writing to King James, he amplifies the same poetic imagery:

" And so expecting that that sun which when it went from us left us cold weather, and now that it is returned towards us brought with it a blessed harvest, will when it cometh to us disperse all mists and mistakings, I ever rest, etc."

The same expressive figure is utilized in the opening words of *Richard III.:*

> " Now is the winter of our discontent
> Made glorious summer by this son of York ;
> And all the clouds that lour'd upon our house
> In the deep bosom of the ocean buried."

This is indeed but a slight variation of the theme ; for it is but a hazy film that veils cold weather under the guise of winter, a blessed harvest in a glorious summer, and mists in lowering clouds. It is the same gorgeous transformation scene, utilizing poetically, in brilliant imagery, the subtle, inner, metaphorical meaning of the revivifying power of the returning sun.

CHAPTER I.— Continued.

> " He being thus lorded,
> Not only with what my revenue yielded,"

" Sure I am that the treasure that cometh from you to her Majesty is but as a vapor which riseth from the earth and gathereth into a cloud, and stayeth there not long, but upon the same earth it falleth again : and what if some drops of this do fall upon France or Flanders ? It is like a sweet odor of honor and reputation to our nation throughout the world."— *Speech on the Queen's Subsidy.*

" And first in general we acknowledge that this tree of Tenures was planted into the prerogative by the ancient common law of this land ; that it hath been fenced in and preserved by many statutes ; and that it *yieldeth* at this day to the King the fruit of a great *revenue.* But yet notwithstanding, if upon the stem of this tree may be raised a pillar of support to the Crown permanent and durable as the marble, by investing the Crown with a more ample, more certain, and more loving dowry than this of Tenures, we hope we propound no matter of disservice."—*Speech upon the Compounding of Tenures.**

> " But what my power might else exact,"

" And there is a great difference between a benevolence

---

* " And further, he that shall look into your revenues at the ports of the sea, your revenues in courts of justice, and for the stirring of your seals, the revenues upon your clergy, and the rest, will conclude that the law of England studied how to make a rich crown, and yet without levies upon your subjects."— *Of the True Greatness of the Kingdom of Britain.*

and an exaction called a benevolence; * which the Duke
of Buckingham speaks of in his oration to the city; and
defineth it to be not what the subject of his good-will
would give, but what the king of his good-will would take."
—*Charge Against St. John.*

"And this Solomon of England, for Solomon was too
heavy upon his people in exactions."—*History of Henry
VII.*

> "like one
> Who having unto truth, by telling of it,
> Made such a sinner of his memory,
> To credit his own lie,—he did believe
> He was indeed the duke;"

"Neither was Perkin, for his part, wanting to himself,
either in gracious or princely behavior, or in ready and
apposite answers, or in contenting and caressing those
that did apply themselves unto him, or in pretty scorn and
disdain to those that seemed to doubt him; but in all
things did notably acquit himself; insomuch as it was generally believed, as well amongst great persons as amongst
the vulgar, that he was indeed Duke Richard. Nay, himself, with long and continued counterfeiting, and with oft
telling a lie, was turned by habit almost into the thing he
seemed to be; and from a liar to a believer."— *History
of Henry VII.*†

---

* "And daily new exactions are devised —
  As blanks, benevolencies, and I wot not what;"
  —*King Richard II., II., 1.*

† In the interest of the earnest student of the plays, it should
be mentioned that Bacon found in the classics (Tacitus) the
germ out of which he developed this keen diagnosis of an abnormal or disordered state of the mental powers:

"And indeed let a man look into them, and he shall find
them the only triumphant lies that ever were confuted by circumstances of time and place, confuted by *contrariety* in themselves, confuted by the witness of *infinite* persons that live yet

" out of the substitution,*
And executing the outward face of royalty,†
With all prerogative : —"

The maintenance of the royal prerogative was Bacon's especial duty as Attorney-General for the Crown, and when Lord Keeper, he thus charged Sir John Denham, made Baron of the Exchequer :

" First, therefore, above all you ought to maintain the King's prerogative, and to set down with yourself that the King's prerogative and the law are not two things ; but the King's prerogative is law, and the principal part of the law ; the first born or *pars prima* of the law ; and therefore in conserving and maintaining that, you conserve and maintain the law."

And in humorous parlance, for in the words of Ben Jonson, Bacon's speech was nobly censorious, " when he could spare or pass a jest ":

---

and have had particular knowledge of the matters ; but yet avouched with such asseveration, as if either they were fallen into that strange disease of the mind which a wise writer describeth in these words, *fingunt simul creduntque ;*" etc., [They feign and at the same time believe it.]—*Observations on a Libel,* in 1592.

And, by the way, if the classics are capable of such fruitage, even in one mind in a generation, can we afford to omit them from the curriculum open to our youth?

* In his *Considerations Touching the Pacification and Edification of the Church*, Bacon condemns the holding of a benefice and executing its functions by a representative ; adding by way of exception, " and likewise for the case of necessity, as in the particular of infirmity of body and the like, no man will contradict but there may be some *substitution* for such a time."

† " The *outward face* of peace might flatter them into negligence, but their only real security was to be prepared for war."—*Speech on Motion and Supply.*

" And therefore whensoever it cometh to pass that one saith

"Then add to that some large allowance for waste (because the King shall not lose his prerogative to be deceived more than other men)."—*On Retrenchment in the Household.*

And again, poetically:

" His lordship further cited two precedents concerning other points of prerogative, which are likewise flowers of the crown."—*Report of Salisbury's Answer to the Merchants.*

" Your Majesty's prerogative and authority having risen some just degrees above the horizon more than heretofore, which hath dispersed vapors."— *On the Impolicy of the Alliance.*

The following is well worthy of place in illustration of Bacon's profound reverence for the " divine right of kings," a pronounced characteristic repeatedly manifested in the plays. Moreover, it lay at the foundation of the thorough respectability of the system then in vogue, of " suing " to the crown, as to the ordained source of earthly benefits, for the bestowal of privileges, favors, and advancements : all of which is to us as foreign as if it belonged to another world, and likewise as liable to be misjudged :

" The platforms are three : The first is that of a father, or chief of a family ; who governing over his wife by prerogative of sex, over his children by prerogative of age, and because he is author unto them of being, and over his servants by prerogative of virtue and providence (for he that is able of body, and improvident of mind, is *natura servus*) is the very model of a king. . . . And this is the first platform, which we see is merely natural.*

Ecce in deserto, another saith *Ecce in penetralis,* that is, when some men seek Christ in conventicles of heretics, and others in an *outward face* of a church, that voice had need continually to sound in men's ears, *nolite exire,*—' go not out.' "—*Of Unity in Religion.*

* " Yet no man will affirm, that the *obedience* of the child is

" The second is that of a shepherd and his flock, which, Xenophon saith, Cyrus had ever in his mouth. For shepherds are not owners of the sheep; but their office is to feed and govern; no more are kings proprietaries or owners of the people; for God is sole owner of people. 'The nations,' as the Scriptures saith, ' are his inheritance': but the office of kings is to govern, maintain and protect people. And it is not without a mystery, that the first king that was instituted by God, David (for Saul was but an untimely fruit), was translated from a shepherd, as you have it in Psalms lxxviii. This is the second platform; a work likewise of nature.

" The third platform is the government of God himself over the world, whereof lawful monarchies are a shadow. And therefore amongst the Heathen, and amongst the Christians, the word *sacred* hath been attributed unto kings, because of the conformity of a monarchy with a divine Majesty: never to a senate or people. . . . So, we see, there be precedents or platforms of monarchies, both in nature, and above nature; even from the monarch of heaven and earth to the king,* if you will, in a hive of

---

by law, though laws in some points do make it more positive: and even so it is of allegiance of subjects to hereditary monarchs, which is corroborated and confirmed by law, but is the work of *the law of nature.*"—*Case of the Post Nati of Scotland.*

* Curiously enough, the same intentional misnomer appears in the parallel passage in *Henry V., I., 2.*

> " *Bishop of Exeter.* For government, though high
> and low, and lower,
> Put into parts, doth keep in one consent;
> Congruing in a full and natural close,
> Like music.
>
> *Canterbury.* Therefore doth *heaven* divide
> The state of man in divers functions,
> Setting endeavor in continual motion;
> To which is fixed, as an aim or butt,
> *Obedience:* for so work the honey bees:
> Creatures, that, by *a rule of nature*, teach

bees. And therefore other states are the creatures of law: and this state only subsisteth by nature."—*Case of the Post Nati of Scotland.*

"Hence his ambition growing,"—

In his elegant exposition of the fable of Dionysius, Bacon gives a powerful delineation of the growth of all inordinate desire, from its first inception, through its development, to its final outbreak into overt, infamous action; the fidelity of which all must recognize:

"The fable seems to bear upon morals, and indeed there is nothing better to be found in moral philosophy. Under the person of Bacchus is described the nature of Desire, or passion and perturbation. For the *mother* of all desire, even the most noxious, is nothing else than the appetite and aspiration for apparent good; and the *conception* of it is always in some unlawful wish, rashly granted before it has been understood and weighed. But as the passion warms, its mother (that is the nature of good), not able to endure the heat of it, is destroyed and perishes in the

---

The act of order to a peopled kingdom.
They have a *king*, and officers of sorts:
Where some, like magistrates, correct at home;
Others, like merchants, venture trade abroad;
Others, like soldiers, armed in their stings,
Make boot upon the summer's velvet buds;
Which pillage they with merry march bring home
To the tent-royal of their emperor:
Who, busied in his majesties, surveys
The singing masons building roofs of gold;
The civil citizens kneading up the honey;
The poor mechanic porters crowding in
Their heavy burdens at his narrow gate;
The sad-eyed justice, with his surly hum,
Delivering o'er to executors pale
The lazy yawning drone. I this infer,—
That many things, having full reference
To one consent, may work contrariously."

flame. Itself, while still in embryo, remains in the human *soul* (which is its *father* and represented by Jupiter), especially in the lower part of the soul, as in the thigh; where it is both nourished and hidden; and where it causes such prickings, pains, and depressions in the mind, that its resolutions and actions labor and limp with it. And even after it has grown strong by indulgence and custom, and breaks forth into acts, it is nevertheless brought up for a time with Proserpina; that is to say, it seeks hiding-places, and keeps itself secret and as it were underground; until casting off all restraints of shame and fear, and growing bold, it either assumes the mask of some virtue or sets infamy itself at defiance. . . . Very elegantly too is Passion represented as the subjugator of provinces, and the undertaker of an endless course of conquest. For it never rests satisfied with what it has, but goes on and on with infinite, insatiable appetite, panting after new triumphs."—*Wisdom of the Ancients, XXIV.*

"And, as it fareth with smoke, that never loseth itself till it be at the highest, he did now before his end raise his style, entitling himself no more Richard, Duke of York, but Richard the Fourth, King of England."—*History of Henry VII.*

> "Dost thou hear?
> *Mir.* Your tale, sir, would cure deafness."

"*Auribus mederi difficillium.*" [To cure the ears most difficult.]—*Promus of Formularies and Elegancies.*

This mere association may be supplemented by the following equally poetic figures:

"unto your Majesty's sacred ears (open to the air of all virtues.)"—*Letter to King James.*

"wherein his Majesty's pen hath been so happy, as though the deaf adder will not hear, yet he is charmed that he doth not hiss."—*Speech in Reply to the Speaker's Oration.**

"Therefore your Lordship's discourses had need content my ears very well to make them entreat mine eyes to keep open."—*Advertisement Touching an Holy War.*†

"*Pros.* To have no screen ‡ between this part he
play'd
And him he play'd it for,"

"I think no man may more truly say with the Psalm, *Multum incola fuit anima mea,* than myself. For I do confess, since I was of any understanding, any mind hath in effect been absent from what I have done; and in absence are many errors which I do willingly acknowledge; and amongst the rest this great one that led the rest; that knowing myself by inward calling to be fitter to hold a book than *to play a part,* I have led my life in civil causes; for which I was not very fit by nature, and more unfit by the preoccupation of my mind. Therefore calling myself home, I have now for a time enjoyed myself; whereof likewise I desire to make the world partaker."—*Letter to Sir Thomas Bodley* (presenting a copy of his *Advance-*

---

* "For pleasure and revenge
 Have ears more deaf than adders to the voice
 Of any true decision."
    —*Troil. and Cress., II., 2.*

† And in the like vein:
   "If this be true,
 (As I have such a heart that both mine eyes
 Must not in haste abuse.)"—*Cymbeline I., 6.*

‡ "in short, to be a screen to your Majesty in things of this nature; such as was the Lord Burleigh for many years."—*Letter to King James.*

"for by that means, there be so many screens between him and envy."—*Of Envy.*

ment of Learning), written in 1605, sixteen years before his fall.

" Therefore I will reserve that till to-morrow, and hold myself to that which I called the *stage* or *theatre*, whereunto indeed it may be fitly compared: for that things were first contained within the invisible judgments of God, as within a *curtain*, and after came forth and were *acted* most worthily by the King, and right well by his Ministers."—*Charge Against the Countess of Somerset.*

And in pleasantry:

" And as for you, untrue Politique, . . while your life is nothing but a continual acting upon a stage; and that your mind must serve your humor, and yet your outward person must serve your end; so as you carry in one person two several servitudes to contrary masters."—*Device for Court Masque.*

"he needs will be
Absolute Milan."

" And that King Ferdinando, howsoever he did dismiss himself of the name of King of Castile, yet meant to hold the kingdom without account and in *absolute* command." —*History of Henry VII.*

" His Majesty's prerogative and his *absolute power* incident to his sovereignty is also *lex terrae,* and is invested and exercised by the law of the land, and is part thereof." —*Proceeding Against Whitelocke.*

" For it is plain that a kingdom and absolute dukedom, or any other sovereign estate, do differ *honore* and not *potestate.*"—*Case of the Post-Nati of Scotland.**

---

* " So the mistaking (whether voluntary or ignorant, but gross and idle I am sure) of the end and use of this writ hath *bred* a great buzz, and a kind of amazement, as if this were a work of *absolute* power, or a strain of the *prerogative,* or a checking or shocking of justice, or an *infinite* delay."—*Case de Reye Inconsulto.*

> "*Me*, poor man, my library
> Was dukedom large enough;"

See note to "*sans* bound," *ante* page 49.

Possibly the idea of a more satisfying enjoyment of power is implied, in a subtle way, in the use of the phrase, "dukedom large enough." The reader is referred to the lengthy passage in the *Advancement of Learning*, First Book, *Works*, Spedding's edition, Vol. III., page 316, or Bohn's edition, page 68, where in an eloquent plea to mankind in behalf of learning, Bacon characterizes it as a domain of real power, higher than that of any earthly dominion, and approaching "nearest to the similitude of the divine rule."

(Perhaps none will object if henceforth, for economy of space, in some minor matters, references merely be given, to be consulted at the reader's leisure.)

> "of temporal royalties
> He thinks me now incapable:"

Prospero's faults are here, as in life, working out their inevitable penalty; for as Bacon urged in his *Advice to Essex*, going into Ireland, "There is yet another kind of divination familiar in matters of state, being that which Demosthenes so often relieth upon in his time, when he saith, 'That which for the time past is worst of all, is for the time to come the best: which is, that *things go ill not by accident, but by errors*.'"

We may confidently believe that in the intent of the Poet, Prospero's persistent seclusion, his absorbing devotion to secret studies, his consequent neglect, and his excess of trust, were efficient causes contributing directly to his coming overthrow.

"Again, if you think you may intend comtemplations with security, your Excellency will be deceived; for such studies will make you retired and disused with your business, whence will follow a diminution of your authority."—*Gesta Grayorum*, Fourth Counsellor.

" And let men beware how they neglect and suffer matter of trouble to be prepared. For no man can forbid the spark, nor tell whence it may come. The difficulties in princes' business are many and great; but the greatest difficulty is often in their own mind."—*Of Empire.*

" 'There are seasons,' says Tacitus, ' wherein great virtues are the surest causes of ruin.' And upon men eminent for virtue and justice it comes suddenly, sometimes long foreseen."—*De Augmentis*, Eighth Book, Chap. II.

" confederates *
(So dry he was for sway) with the King of Naples,"

" But Richard, Duke of Gloucester, their unnatural uncle, first *thirsting* after the kingdom, through ambition, and afterwards *thirsting* for their blood, out of desire to secure himself, employed an instrument of his, confident to him, as he thought, to murder them both."

" For Pope Alexander, finding himself pent and locked up by a league and association of the principal states of Italy, that he could not make his way for the advancement of his own house, which he immoderately *thirsted* after, was desirous to trouble the waters of Italy, that he might fish the better."—*History of Henry VII.*

" To give him annual tribute, do him homage;†
Subject his coronet to his crown ‡ and bend
The dukedom, yet unbow'd, (alas poor Milan!)
To most ignoble stooping." §

---

* See *Works*, Vol. 7, page 171; Vol. 14, page 500.
† See *Works*, Vol. 6, pp. 63, 65; Vol. 7, pp. 334, 482.
‡ See *Works*, Vol. 13, p. 196.
§ See *Works*, Vol. 6, pp. 32, 222; Vol. 14, pp. 445, 517.

Still another phase of human life and experience is here unfolded before us:

"It is a poor centre of a man's action, himself. . . . it is a desperate evil in a servant to a prince or a citizen in a republic; for whatsoever affairs pass such a man's hands, he crooketh them to his own ends, which must needs be often eccentric to the ends of his master or state: therefore let princes or states choose such servants as have not this mark; except they mean their service should be made but the accessory. That which maketh the effect more pernicious is, that all proportion is lost: it were disproportionate enough for the servant's good to be preferred before the master's; but yet it is a greater extreme, when a little good of the servant shall carry things against a great good of the master's; and yet that is the case of bad officers, treasurers, ambassadors, generals, and other false and corrupt servants; which set a bias upon their bowl,* of their own pretty ends and envies to the overthrow of their master's great and important affairs; and for the most part, the good such servants receive is after the model of their own fortune; but the hurt they sell for that good is after the model of their master's fortune; and certainly it is the nature of extreme self-lovers, as they will set a house on fire, an it were but to roast their eggs."—*Of Wisdom for a Man's Self.*

It is obvious that had the Poet made Antonio accomplish his usurpation by the aid of his own minions, without bending Milan to such "ignoble stooping," this phase of human nature would have been left comparatively undeveloped and the lesson less pointedly taught.

---

* "Commodity, the bias of the world;
  The world, who of itself is piesèd well,
  Made to run even, upon even ground;
  Till this advantage, this vile drawing bias,
  This sway of motion, this commodity,
  Makes it take head from all indifferency,
  From all direction, purpose, course, intent."
  —*King John II., 2.*

"*Mir.*　　　　　O the heavens!
Pros. Mark his condition;* and the event;† then
　　tell me,
If this might be a brother."

" And even when the ties of relationship (which are as
the sacraments of nature) or of mutual good services come
in to aid, yet in most cases all are too weak for ambition
and interest and the license of power : the rather because
princes can always find plenty of plausible pretexts (not
being accountable to any arbiter) wherewith to justify and
veil their cupidity and bad faith."— *Wisdom of the Ancients, V.*

" *Mir.*　　　　　I should sin
　　To think but nobly of my grandmother :
　　Good wombs have borne bad sons."

See note to " a good parent," *ante*, page 44.

" *Pros.*　　　　　Now the condition.
This king of Naples being an enemy
To me inveterate, ‡ hearkened my brother's suit ; §
Which was, that he, in lieu o' the premises —"

In this concise, lawyer-like statement of the contract,

---

* See *Works*, Vol. 13, pp. 18, 64, 111, 212.

† See *Works*, Vol 3, p. 371 ; Vol. 8, pp. 356, 357, 383 ; Vol.
14, p. 494.

‡ The following from *Enc. Brit.*, Article ITALY—*History.*—
Age of Invasions, 1492,—would seem to indicate a close familiarity with the History of Italy on the part of the Poet: " Ludovico resolved to become Duke of Milan. The King of Naples was his *natural enemy*, and he had cause to suspect that
Piero de' Medici might abandon his alliance." See also *Works*,
Vol. 6, p. 208.

§ See *Works*, Vol. 8, p. 193.

its consideration, the condition of its performance, and its
fulfilment in the event, the appropriate use of this technical legal phrase will be recognized at once by every attorney. Moreover, it is evidently handled with that ease
and freedom which accompany a mastery of *technique*.

"Of homage, and I know not how much tribute,—
Should presently extirpate me and mine
Out of the dukedom; * and confer fair Milan,
With all the honors on my brother; whereon,
A treacherous army levied, one midnight
Fated to the purpose,† did Antonio open
The gates of Milan; and, i' the dead of darkness, ‡
The ministers for the purpose hurried thence
Me, and thy crying self."

The deep insight of the Poet into the heart of things,
and even into the occult sympathies existing between an action and its natural environment, here manifested in cloth-
ing this deed in the shroud of night, needs but to be mentioned to be appreciated.

After his fall, Bacon addressed the Bishop of Winches-
ter in these remarkable words; revealing his greatness,
even in the midst of his ruin:

"In this kind of consolation I have not been wanting
to myself, though as a Christian I have tasted (through
God's great goodness) of higher remedies. Having therefore, through the variety of my reading, set before me
many examples, both of ancient and later times, my
thoughts (I confess) have chiefly stayed upon three particulars, as the most eminent and the most resembling.
All three persons that had held chief places of authority

* See *Works*, Vol. 8, p. 133.
† See *Works*, Vol. 4, pp. 92, 320.
‡ See *Works*, Vol. 5, p. 496; Vol. 9, p. 110; Vol. 10, p. 185.

in their countries ; all three ruined, not by war, or by any
other disaster, but by justice and sentence, as delinquents
and criminals : all three famous writers, insomuch as the
resemblance of their calamity is now as to posterity but
as a little picture of *night-work*, remaining amongst the
fair and excellent tables of their acts and works ; and all
three (if that were anything to the matter) fit examples
to quench any man's ambition of rising again ; for that
they were every one of them restored with great glory,
but to their further ruin and destruction, ending in a violent death. The men were Demosthenes, Cicero, and
Seneca; persons that I durst not claim affinity with, except the similitude of our fortunes had contracted it.
When I had cast mine eyes upon these examples, I was
carried on further to observe how they did bear their fortunes, and principally how they did employ their times,
being banished and disabled for public business : to the
end that I might learn by them ; and that they might be
as well my counsellors as my comforters. . . . These examples confirmed me much in a resolution (whereunto I
was otherwise inclined) to spend my time wholly in writing ; and to put forth that poor talent, or half talent, or
what it is, that God hath given me, not as heretofore to
particular exchanges, but to banks or mounts of perpetuity, which will not break."

> "*Mir.*   Alack, for pity!
> I, not remembering how I cried out then,
> Will cry it o'er again : it is a hint
> That wrings mine eyes to 't."

Wright, and some critics following him, interpret the
word "hint" as meaning "subject, theme," while other
critics say "suggestion."

But there can be no doubt as to the meaning of the
word, or of its exquisite adaptation to the thought expressed, after reading the following :

"*Pity* causeth sometimes tears, and a flexion or cast of

the eye aside. Tears come from *the same cause* that they
do in grief: for pity is but grief in another's behalf."—
Natural History, 719.

"*Pros.*   Hear a little further,
And then I'll bring thee to the present business
Which now's upon us; without the which, this story
Were most impertinent."

" This were a large field to enter into, and therefore I
will only choose such a walk in it as leadeth *pertinently*
to the *question in hand:* wherein I will stand only on prerogatives that did beget this writ." — *Case of the Rege
Inconsulto.*

" Although therefore I had wholly sequestered my
thoughts from civil affairs, yet because it is a new case
and concerneth my country infinitely, I obtained of myself
to set down (out of long continued experience in business
of estate, and much conversation in books of policy and
history) what I thought *pertinent to this business.*"—
Considerations Touching a War With Spain.

" For if it be time to talk of this now, it is either because *the business now in hand* cannot proceed without
it, or because in time and order this matter should be
precedent."—*Speech on Union of Laws.*

"*Mir.*   Wherefore did they not
That hour destroy us?
Pros.   Well demanded, wench;
My tale provokes that question. Dear, they durst
        not,*—
So dear the love my people bore me,— not set
A mark so bloody on the business;† but
With colors fairer painted their foul ends."

---

* For this colloquialism see *ante* page 69.
† See *Works*, Vol. 6, p. 424; Vol. 7, p. 101; Vol. 12, p. 308.

" Color is, when men warily and skillfully make and prepare a way for themselves, for a favorable and convenient construction of their faults or wants ; as proceeding from a better cause, or intended for some other purpose than is commonly imagined." — *De Augmentis*, Eighth Book, Chap. II.

" And that if the king should have occasion to break up his Parliament suddenly there may be more civil color to do it."—*Advice Touching the Calling of Parliament*.

" Many a cruzado hath the Bishop of Rome granted to him and his predecessors upon that color, which have all been spent upon the effusion of Christian blood. And now this present year, the levies of Germans which should have been made underhand for France were colored with the pretence of war upon the Turk."— *Observations on a Libel.**

---

*(" *Des.* Believe me, I had rather have lost my purse
Full of *cruzadoes*."—*Othello, III., 4.*

  " and as the only means
To stop effusion of our Christian blood."
    —*I., Henry VI., V., 1.)*

" I have advertised him by secret means,
 That if, about this hour he make his way,
 Under the *color* of his usual game,
 He shall here find his friends, with horse and men
 To set him free from his captivity."
    —*III., Henry VI., IV., 5.*

(" I would be glad to hear often from you, and to be *advertised* how things pass, whereby to have some occasion to think some good thoughts."—*Letter to Sir John Davis.* See *Sonnet LXXXV.)*

" *Q. Mar.* Henry my lord is cold in great affairs,
 Too full of foolish pity: and Gloster's show
 Beguiles him as the mournful crocodile
 With sorrow snares relenting passengers. . . .
 Cardinal. That he should die is worthy policy:
 But yet we want a color for his death."
    —*II., Henry VI., III., 1.*

"So as the opinion of so great and wise a man doth seem unto me a good warrant both of the possibility and worth of this matter. . . . But because there be so many good painters both for hand and colors, it needeth but encouragement and instruction to give life and light to it."—*Letter to the Lord Chancellor.*

"Now pass to the excellencies of her person. The view of them wholly and not severally do make so sweet a wonder as I fear to divide them again. . . . For the beauty and many graces of her presence, what colors are fine enough for such a portraiture?"—*Discourse in Praise of the Queen.**

("It is the wisdom of crocodiles, that shed tears when they would devour."— *Of Wisdom for a Man's Self.*

"Neither do you deny, honorable Lords, to acknowledge safety, profit, and power to be of the substance of *policy*, and fame and honor rather to be as flowers of well ordained actions than as good ends."— *Gesta Grayorum.*

"Never did base and rotten policy.
Color her workings with such deadly wounds."
—*I., Henry IV., I., 3.*

"Wherein it must be confessed, that heaven was made too much to bow to earth, and religion to policy."—*History of Henry VII.)*

These things indeed you have articulated,
Proclaimed at market-crosses, read in churches,
To face the garment of rebellion
With some fine color that may please the eye.

. . . .

And never yet did insurrection want
Such water-colors to impaint his cause."
—*I., Henry IV., V., 1.*

* *Claud.* Disloyal?
D. John. The word is too good to *paint* out her wickedness."
—*Much Ado, III., 2.*

"And this I shall do, my Lords, *in verbis masculis; no flourishing or painted* words, but such words as are fit to go before deeds."--*Speech on Taking his Seat in Chancery.*

"Good lord Boyet, my beauty, though but mean,

"In few,* they hurried us aboard a bark;
Bore us some leagues to sea; where they prepared
A rotten carcase of a boat,† not rigg'd,
Nor tackle, sail, nor mast;"

See the lengthy description of a ship's rigging in *History of the Winds*.

"the very rats
Instinctively have quit it;"

"Wisdom for a man's self is, in many branches thereof, a depraved thing: it is the wisdom of rats, that will be sure to leave a house somewhat before it fall."—*Of Wisdom for a Man's Self*.

"there they hoist us,
To cry to the sea that roar'd to us; to sigh
To the winds, whose pity, sighing back again,
Did us but loving wrong.‡
Mir.   Alack! what trouble
Was I then to you!
Pros.   O! a cherubim §
Thou wast that did preserve me! Thou didst smile,
Infused with a fortitude from heaven,"

Needs not the painted flourish of your praise."
—*L. L. L., II.,* 1.

"Lend me the flourish of all gentle tongues,—
Fie, painted rhetoric! O, she needs it not."—*Id. IV., 3.*

* See *Works*, Vol. 6, p. 388; Vol. 13, pp. 68, 203; Vol. 14, p. 494.

† See *Works*, Vol. 14, pp. 322, 437.

‡ See *Works*, Vol. 2, p. 390. And for a like figure: "implying as if the King slept out the sobs of his subjects, until he was awaked with the thunderbolt of a parliament."—*Report of Salisbury's Answer to the Merchants.*

§ See *Works*, Vol. 3, pp. 152, 296.

" And it leadeth us to fortitude, for it teacheth us that we should not too much prize life which we cannot keep, nor fear death which we cannot shun ; that he which dies nobly doth live forever, and he that lives in fear doth die continually ; that pain and danger be great only by opinion, and that in truth nothing is fearful but fear itself."
—*Advice to Rutland on his Travels.**

" But to speak in a mean, the virtue of prosperity is temperance, the virtue of adversity is fortitude, which in morals is the more heroical virtue."—*Of Adversity.*

" Wherein you have well expressed to the world, that there is *infused* in your sacred heart *from God* that high principle and position of government."—*On Pacification and Edification of the Church.*

" When I have deck'd the sea with drops full salt; †
Under my burden groan'd ; which raised in me
An undergoing stomach, to bear up
Against what should ensue."

" There is shaped a tale in London's forge,‡ that beat-

---

* " Cowards die many times before their deaths;
  The valiant never taste of death but once.
  Of all the wonders that I yet have heard,
  It seems to me most strange that men should fear;
  Seeing that death, a necessary end,
  Will come when it will come."—*Julius Cæsar II., 3.*

† For another extravagant reference to tears see *Works*, Vol. 7, p. 141.

‡ " But now behold,
In the quick forge and working-house of thought,
How London doth pour out her citizens ! "
           —*Henry V., V., Chorus.*

" *Mrs. Page.* Come to the forge with it then ; shape it: I would not have things cool."—*Mer. Wives of Wind., IV., 2.* (See context.)

" Here he comes: to beguile two hours in a sleep, and then to return and swear the lies he *forges.*"—*All's Well. IV., 1.*

eth apace at this time. That I should deliver opinion to the Queen in my Lord of Essex' cause; first, that it was *praemunire;* * and now last, that it was high treason; and this opinion to be in opposition and encounter of the Lord Chief Justice's opinion and the Attorney-General's. My Lord, I thank God my wit serveth me not to deliver any opinion to the Queen, which my *stomach* serveth me not to maintain; one and the same conscience guiding and *fortifying* me. But the untruth of this fable God and my sovereign can witness, and there I leave it; knowing no more remedy against lies, than others do against libels."—*Letter to Howard.*

" This wrought in the earl, as in a haughty stomach it useth to do; for the ignominy printed deeper than the grace."

" And being a man of stomach and hardened by his former troubles refused to pay a mite."—*History of Henry VII.*†

---

* Possibly upon another occasion, he actually handled this intricate matter, over which he had such thorough command:

"So in 'King Henry VIII.' we have an equally accurate statement of the omnivorous nature of a writ of *praemunire.* The Duke of Suffolk, addressing Cardinal Wolsey, says:

" Lord Cardinal, the King's further pleasure is,
Because all those things you have done of late,
By your power legative within this kingdom,
Fall into the compass of a *praemunire,*
That therefore such a writ be used against you,
To forfeit all your goods, lands, tenements,
Chattles, and whatsoever, and to be
Out of the King's protection."
—Lord Campbell's *Shakespeare's Legal Acquirements.*

If the reader will consult Bacon's *Works,* Vol. 7, p. 741; Vol. 11, p. 270; Vol. 12, p. 388, and then read *Henry VIII.,* III., 2, he will more clearly apprehend the complexity of this *praemunire,* Bacon's mastery of it, and the aptness of its application to Wolsey's ecclesiastical offences.

† "Rather proclaim it, Westmoreland, through my host,

"*Mir.*   How came we ashore?

Pros.   By Providence divine."

The following, from a multitude of examples, may well command present attention, coming from a man of such deep insight, who was anything but a fanatic:

" In this fourteenth year also, *by God's wonderful providence*, that boweth things unto his will, and hangeth great weights upon small wires, there fell out a trifling and untoward accident, that drew on great and happy effects."—*History of Henry VII.**

" A matter that we cannot ascribe to the skill or temper of our own carriage, but to the guiding and conducting of God's holy providence and will, the true author of all unity and agreement."—*Consultation Concerning the Union of England and Scotland.*†

That he which hath no stomach to this fight,
Let him depart."—*Henry V., IV., 3.*
" High-stomached are they both and full of ire."
　　　　　　　　—*Richard II., I., 1.*
" Of an unbounded stomach, ever ranking
　Himself with princes."—*Henry VIII., IV., 2.*
* " He that of greatest works is finisher
　Oft does them by the weakest minister:
　. . . . . .　Great floods have flown
　From simple sources; and great seas have dried,
　When miracles have by the greatest been denied."
　　　　　　　　—*All's Well, II., 1.*

† "The third part, which is History of Providence, has indeed been handled by the pens of some pious writers, but not without partiality. Its business is to observe that divine correspondence which sometimes exists between God's revealed and secret will. For though the judgments and counsels of God are so obscure that to the natural man they are altogether inscrutable, yea, and many times hidden from the eyes of those that behold them from the tabernacle, yet at sometimes it pleases the Divine Wisdom, for the better establishment of his people and the confusion of those who are without God in the world, to write it and report it to view in such capital letters that (as the prophet

"Some food we had and some fresh water,
A noble Neapolitan, Gonzalo,

saith) 'He that runneth by may read it'; that is, that mere
sensual persons and voluptuaries, who hasten by God's judgments, and never bend or fix their thoughts upon them, are
nevertheless, though running fast and busy about other things,
forced to discern them. Such are late and unlooked for judgments; deliverances suddenly and unexpectedly vouchsafed;
divine counsels, through tortuous labyrinths and by vast cir-
cuits, at length manifestly accomplishing themselves; and the
like; all which things serve not only to console the minds of
the faithful, but to strike and convince the consciences of the
wicked."—*De Augmentis*, Second Book, Chap. XI.

"The hinge of Shakespeare's plays, that upon which they turn,
is God's providential order. . . . It is commandingly ethical, blazing forth the truth that the government of this moral sphere is
set against selfishness, against treachery, against hypocrisy,
against the madness of lust and the unwisdom of jealousy. . .
Nowhere outside of the Scriptures are the sins of men revealed
with more astonishing and terrific power as acts committed
against the divine moral order."—Address on *The World of
Shakespeare*, by Rev. Dr. John Henry Barrows.

"God's secret judgment."—*II., Henry VI., III., 2.*

"O God! I fear thy justice will take hold
    On me, and you, and mine, and yours, for this."
            —*Richard III., II., 1.*

"That high All-Seer, which I dallied with,
    Hath turn'd my feigned prayer on my head,
    And given in earnest what I begg'd in jest.
    Thus doth He force the swords of wicked men
    To turn their own points on their master's bosoms;

. . . .
    Come, lead me, officers, to the block of shame,
    Wrong hath but wrong, and blame the due of blame."
            —*Id., V., 1.*

"O God! if my deep prayers cannot appease thee,
    But thou wilt be avenged on my misdeeds,
    Yet execute thy wrath on me alone."
            —*Richard III., I., 4.*

"Take heed; for He holds vengeance in his hand,

Out of his charity *— being then appointed
Master of this design — did give us;"

We are reminded of Bacon's *mot*, found in the report
of his *Speech against the repeal of the Statute of Charitable Trusts:*

"That the last Parliament there were so many bills for
the relief of the poor that he called it a Feast of Charity."

Again, in a flame of poetic fervor, bursting forth even
amidst the dry husks of the law:

"Then I do wish that this rude mass and chaos of a
good deed were directed rather to a solid merit and durable charity than to a blaze of glory, that will crackle a
little in talk and quickly extinguish."—*Advice Concerning Sutton's Estate.*

And again, in the enunciation of a vital truth:

"But these be heathen and profane passages, which

To hurl upon their heads that break his laws."
—*Richard III.*, I., 4.

" *Edgar.* What means this bloody knife?
Gent.   'T is hot, it smokes;
It came even from the heart of — O, she's dead.
Albany. Who dead? speak, man.
Gent. Your lady, sir, your lady: and her sister
By her is poison'd; she confesses it.
Edmund. I was contracted to them both; all three
Now marry in an instant.
Albany. Produce the bodies, be they alive or dead! —
This judgment of the heavens, that makes us tremble,
Touches us not with pity."— *King Lear*, V., 3.

"Our indiscretion sometimes serves us well,
When our dear plots do pall; and that should teach us
There's a divinity that shapes our ends
Rough-hew them how we will."—*Hamlet*, V., 2.

* "That he would confirm and ratify all just privileges. —
This his bounty and amity; as a king, royally; as King James,
sweetly and kindly, *out of his good nature.*"— *Note of Report
on Compromise Suggested by the King.*

grasp at shadows greater than the substance; but the true religion and holy Christian faith lays hold of the reality itself, by imprinting upon men's souls, Charity, which is excellently called 'the bond of perfection,' because it comprehends and fastens all virtues together. . . . So certainly if a man's mind be truly inflamed with charity, it raises him to a greater perfection than all the doctrines of morality can do; which is but a sophist in comparison of the other. Nay, further, as Xenophon truly observed, 'that all other affections though they raise the mind, yet they distort and disorder it by their ecstasies and excesses, but love only at the same time exalts and composes it'; so all the other qualities which we admire in man, though they advance nature, are yet subject to excess; whereas Charity alone admits of no excess." — *De Augmentis,* Seventh Book, Chap. III.

Is not the word "charity," in the text, used in this higher sense? Bacon says:

" And for an example of this kind, I did ever allow the discretion and tenderness of the Rhemish translation in this point; that finding in the original the word ἀγάπη and never ἔρως, do ever translate *Charity* and never Love, because of the indifferency and equivocation of that word with impure love."—*Pacification and Unification of the Church.*

"with
Rich garments, linens, stuffs, and necessaries,*
Which since have steadied much; so, of his gentleness,
Knowing I loved my books, he furnish'd me,
From mine own library, with volumes that
I prize above my dukedom."

" Again for the pleasure and delight of knowledge and learning, it far surpasseth all other in nature. . . . We

* See *Works,* Vol. 6, p. 150; Vol. 8, p. 158; Vol. 14, p. 544.

see in all other pleasures there is satiety, and after they
be used their verdure departeth; . . . But of knowledge
there is no satiety, but satisfaction and appetite are perpetually interchangeable; and therefore appeareth to be
good in itself simply, without fallacy or accident. . . .
But the images of men's wits and knowledges remain in
books, exempted from the wrong of time and capable of
perpetual renovation. Neither are they fitly to be called
images, because they *generate* still, and cast their seeds in
the minds of others, provoking and causing infinite actions
and opinions in succeeding ages."—*Advancement of
Learning*, First Book.

> "*Mir.*   Would I might
> But ever see that man!
> *Pros.* Now I arise:—[*Resumes his mantle.*
> Sit still, and hear the last of our sea-sorrow.*
> Here in this island we arrived; and here
> Have I, thy schoolmaster, made thee more profit
> Than other princess' can, that have more time
> For vainer hours, and tutors not so careful."

"But what I mean is, that princes educated in courts,
as the undoubted heirs of a crown, are corrupted by indulgence, and thence generally rendered less capable and
less moderate in the management of affairs."—*In Memory
of Queen Elizabeth.*

> "Courts are but superficial schools,
>   to dandle fools."
>   —*Parody on a Greek Epigram.*

"*Mir.* Heavens thank you for't! And now, I pray
    you, Sir,
(For still 't is beating in my mind,) your reason
For raising this sea-storm?"

---

* See *Works*, Vol. 11, p. 200; Vol. 14, p. 489.

" I am now beating my brains (among many cases of his Majesty's business) touching the redeeming the time in this business of cloth."—*Letter to Villiers.*

" If he be not apt to beat over matters, and to call up one thing to prove and illustrate another, let him study the lawyer's cases."—*Of Studies.*

" So all opinions and doubts are beaten over, and then men, having made a taste of all, wax weary of variety." —*Of the Interpretation of Nature.**

" *Pros.*   Know thus far forth,
By accident most strange, bountiful Fortune,—
Now my dear lady—hath mine enemies
Brought to this shore:"

" All wise men, to decline the envy of their own virtues, use to ascribe them to Providence and Fortune; for so they may the better assume them : and besides, it is greatness in a man to be the care of higher powers. . . . and it hath been noted that those who ascribe openly too much to their own wisdom and policy end unfortunate. It is written that Timotheus, the Athenian, after he had, in the

---

* " Sir, my liege,
Do not infect your mind with beating on
The strangeness of this business."
                    —*Tempest, V., 1.*

" This something-settled matter in his heart;
    Whereon his brains still beating, puts him thus
    From fashion of himself."—*Hamlet, III., 1.*

" Which is a point not much stirred, though Sir Lionel Cranfield hath ever beaten upon it in his speech with me."— *Letter to the King.*

                    " I 'll presently
Acquaint the queen of your most noble offer ;
Who, but to-day, *hammer'd* of this design,
But durst not tempt a minister of honor,
Lest she should be denied."
                    —*Winter's Tale, II., 2.*

account he gave to the state of his government, often
interlaced this speech, 'and in this Fortune had no part,'
never prospered in anything he undertook afterwards."—
Of Fortune.[*]

"I now come to the causes of these errors, and of so
long a continuance in them through so many ages; which
are very many and very potent;—that all wonder how
these considerations which I bring forward should have
escaped men's notice till now, may cease; and the only
wonder be, how now at last they should have entered into
any man's head and become the subject of his thoughts;
which truly I myself esteem as the result of some happy
accident, rather than of any excellence of faculty in me;
a birth of Time rather than a birth of Wit."— *Novum
Organum, I.,* 78.[†]

And again, for it was a favorite theme:

"For otherwise, if it be believed as it soundeth, and
that a man entereth into a high imagination that he can
compass and fathom all accidents, and ascribeth all successes to his drifts and reaches, and the contrary to his

---

[*] "*K. Henry.* O God, thy arm was here,
   And not to us, but to thy arm alone,
   Ascribe we all,— where, without stratagem,
   But in plain shock and even play of battle,
   Was ever known so great and little loss,
   On one part and on the other?—take it, God!
   For it is none but thine!
   Exeter.   'Tis wonderful!
   K. Henry. Come, go we in procession to the village:
   And be it death proclaimed through our host,
   To boast of this, or take that praise from God
   Which is his only."—*Henry V., IV.,* 8.

[†] "As it is, however,— my object being to open a new way
for the understanding, a way by them untried and unknown,—
the case is altered; party zeal and emulation are at an end;
and I appear merely as a *guide* to point out the road; an office
of small authority, and depending more upon a kind of *luck*,
than upon any ability or excellency." — *Preface to Novum
Organum.*

errors and sleepings, it is commonly seen that the evening fortune of that man is not so prosperous, as of him that without slackening of his industry attributeth much to felicity and providence above him."—*Discourse Touching Helps for the Intellectual Powers.*

" Thus scorning all the care that Fate or Fortune brings,
He makes the Heaven his book, his wisdom heavenly things ;
Good thoughts his only friends, his life a well-spent age,
The earth his sober inn,— a quiet pilgrimage."
—*Verses made by Mr. Francis Bacon.*[*]

"and by my prescience"

" Therefore it [the union of England and Scotland] seemed a manifest work of Providence and case of reservation for these times ; insomuch as the vulgar conceived that there was now an end given and a consummation to superstitious prophesies, *the belief of fools, but the talk sometimes of wise men*, and to an ancient tacit expectation which had by tradition been infused and inveterated into men's minds. But as the best divinations and predictions are *the politic and probable foresight and conjectures of wise men*, so in this matter the providence of King Henry the Seventh was in all men's mouths, who, being one of the deepest and most prudent princes of the world, upon the deliberation concerning the marriage of his eldest daughter in Scotland, had by some speech uttered by him showed himself sensible and almost *prescient* of this event."— *Fragment of History of Great Britain.*[†]

_____

[*] *Works,* Vol. 7, p. 269.

[†] The like profound philosophy, based upon close observation, is embodied in the following, regarding another historic prophecy :

" *K. Henry.* You, cousin Nevil, as I may remember—
When Richard, with his eye brimful of tears,
Then check'd and rated by Northumberland,
Did speak these words, now proved a prophecy :

" I find my zenith doth depend upon
  A most auspicious star; whose influence "

" The third is, that the two stars which have always been propitious to me — the greater and the lesser — are now shining in the world; and may thereby, being reinforced by the auxiliary and benignant rays of your love towards me, gain influence enough to put me in some position not unbefitting my former fortune. . . . His Majesty addressed me not as a criminal, but as a man overthrown by a *tempest.*"—*Letter to Count Gondomar in Spain.**

" ' Northumberland, thou ladder, by the which
  My cousin Bolingbroke ascends my throne ';—
Though then, heaven knows, I had no such intent,
But that necessity so bow'd the state
That I and greatness were compell'd to kiss:—
' The time shall come,' thus did he follow it,
' The time will come, that foul sin gathering head,
Shall break into corruption ':—so went on,
Fortelling this same time's condition,
And the division of our amity.
War. There is a history in all men's lives,
Figuring the nature of the times deceased;
The which observed, a man may prophesy,
With a near aim, of the main chance of things
As yet not come to life: which in their seeds,
And weak beginnings, lie intreasured.
Such things become the hatch and brood of time;
And by the necessary form of this,
King Richard might create a perfect guess,
That great Northumberland, then false to him,
Would, of that seed, grow to a greater falseness;
Which should not find a ground to root upon,
Unless on you."—*II., Henry IV., III., 1.*

* Incidentally: In another letter to Count Gondomar, Bacon expresses the warmth of his affection with truly poetic fervor:

" For me, what can I do? I will at least be yours, if not in use and fruit, yet in desire and wish. Beneath the ashes of my fortune the sparks of love shall ever remain alive."

" And therefore I shall say no more of this point : but as you (Mr. Speaker) did well note, that when the King sits in Parliament, and his Prelates, Peers, and Commons attend him, he is in the exaltation of his orb ; so I wish things may be so carried, that he may be in greatest serenity and benignity of aspect ; shining upon his people both in glory and grace."—*Reply to the Speaker's Oration.*

" I see your Majesty is a star, that hath benevolent aspect and gracious influence upon all things that tend to a general good. This work [*Novum Organum*] which is for the bettering of men's bread and wine, which are the characters of temporal blessings and sacraments of eternal, I hope by God's holy providence will be ripened by Cæsar's star."—*Letter to King James.**

" So likewise hath he been in his government a benign or benevolent planet towards learning ; by whose influence

---

And in his *Notes for an Interview with the King,* he again introduces this figure, with but slight variations :

" Ashes are good for somewhat, for lees, for salts. But I hope I am rather embers than ashes, having the heat of good affections under the ashes of my fortunes."

The same figure, with slight modification, is employed in *Antony and Cleopatra, V., 2:*

" The gods ! It smites me
Beneath the fall I have.— Pr'thee, go hence ;
Or I shall show the cinders of my spirits
Through the ashes of my chance."

* " Some praises come of good wishes and respects, which is a form due in civility to kings and great persons, *laudando praecipere ;* (To instruct by praising) when by telling men what they are, they represent to them what they should be."— *Of Praise.*

" Henry, the fifth ! thy ghost I invocate ;
Prosper this realm, keep it from civil broils !
Combat with adverse planets in the heavens !
A far more glorious star thy soul will make
Than Julius Cæsar."—*I., Henry VI., 1., 1.*

those nurseries and gardens of learning, the Universities, were never more in flower nor fruit."—*Charge against St. John.*

"Now did the sign reign, and the constellation was come, under which Perkin should appear."—*History of Henry VII.**

"If now I court not, but omit, my fortunes
Will ever after droop.—Here cease more question;
Thou art inclined to sleep; 'tis a good dulness,†
And give it way;—I know thou canst not choose.—
　　　　　　　　　　　　[*Miranda sleeps.*"

"In the third place I set down reputation, because of

---

* "Happy star, reign now!"—*A Winter's Tale*, I., 2.
　　"I know thy constellation is right apt
　　For this affair."—*Twelfth Night*, I., 4.
　　　　"There's some ill planet reigns:
　　　　I must be patient, till the heavens look
　　　　With an aspect more favorable."
　　　　　　　　—*A Winter's Tale*, II., 1.
"And therefore is the glorious planet, Sol,
　　In noble eminence enthroned and sphered
　　Amidst the other; whose med'cinable eye
　　Corrects the ill aspects of planets evil."
　　　　　　　　—*Troil. and Cress.*, I., 3.
"Under the allowance of your great aspect,
　　Whose influence, like the wreath of radiant fire
　　On flickering Phoebus' front."—*King Lear*, II., 2.
"This is the excellent foppery of the world, that, when we are sick in fortune, (often the surfeit of our own behavior,) we make guilty of our disasters the sun, the moon, and stars: as if we were villains on necessity; fools by heavenly compulsion; knaves, thieves, and treachers by spherical predominance; drunkards, liars, and adulterers by an enforced obedience of planetary influence; and all that we are evil in, by a divine thrusting on."— *Id.*, I., 2.

† See *Works*, Vol. 2, pp. 263, 580; Vol. 5, pp. 278, 313.

the preemptory tides and currents it hath ; which if they be not taken in their due time are seldom recovered, it being extremely hard to play an after-game of reputation."—*Advancement of Learning*, Second Book.

"And if you had not been short-sighted in your own fortune (as I think) you might have had more use of me. But that tide is passed."— *Letter to Sir Edward Coke.*

"that the riches of any occasion, or the tide of any opportunity can possibly minister or offer . . . and that you are as well seen in the periods and tides of estates, as in your own circle and way."—*Letter to Cecil.*

"And thirdly, particular conspiracies have their periods of time, within which if they be not taken, they vanish."— *Charge Against Owen.*

"Yet because the opportunity of your Majesty's so urgent occasion flieth away."—*Advice Touching the Calling of Parliament.*

"For the time, if ever Parliament was to be measured by the hour-glass, it is this ; in regard of the instant occasion flying away irrevocably."—*Reply to the Speaker's Oration.*

"For occasion (as it is in the common verse) 'turneth a bald noddle after she hath presented her locks in front, and no hold taken ;' or, at least, turneth the handle of the bottle first to be received, and after the belly, which is hard to clasp."—*Of Delays.**

---

* "To take the saf'st occasion by the front
To bring you in again."—*Othello, III., 1.*
"Let's take the instant by the forward top."
—*All's Well, V., 3.*

"and, if he found her accordant, he meant to take the present time by the top, and instantly break with you of it."—*Much Ado, I., 2.*

("And to Geo. Raleigh the Sergeant Major, to whom he did use the like discountenances in public, who took it more tenderly and complained and *brake* with him about it, he did open himself more plainly." — *Declaration Concerning Sir W. Raleigh.*)

(Over.)

Prospero here concludes his narrative ; and in review-
ing the work, the Seventy-sixth *Sonnet* is brought forcibly
to mind.   How applicable the Poet's words, how deeply
significant, and how true !

> " Why is my verse so barren of new pride,
> So far from variation or quick change?
> Why with the time do I not glance aside
> To new-found methods and to compounds strange?
> Why write I still all one, ever the same,
> And keep invention in a noted *weed*,
> *That every word doth almost tell my name,*
> *Shewing their birth, and where they did proceed?*"

The word " weed," so prominent in the verse, one member in the comparison, is obviously a *symbol*, standing for

---

> " And are enforced from our most quiet sphere
> By the rough torrent of occasion."
> —*II., Henry IV., IV., 1.*

> " For this,
> I'll never follow thy pall'd fortunes more.—
> Who seeks and will not take, when once 'tis offered,
> Shall never find it more."—*Ant. and Cleo., II., 7.*

> " I cannot, lord; I have important business,
> The tide whereof is now."—*Troil. and Cres., V., 1.*

> " Yea, watch
> His pettish lunes, his ebbs, his flows, as if
> The passage and whole carriage of this action
> Rode on his tide."—*Ib., II., 3.*

(" But my Lord Coke floweth according to his own tides,
and not according to the tides of business." — *Letter to the
King.*)

> " There is a tide in the affairs of men,
> Which, taken at the flood, leads on to fortune;
> Omitted, all the voyage of their life
> Is bound in shallows and in miseries.
> On such a full sea are we now afloat;
> And we must take the current when it serves,
> Or lose our ventures."—*Julius Cæsar, IV., 3.*

some literary work of the Poet of greater invention * than the Sonnets. Bacon uses the identical symbol in his celebrated prayer, found in manuscript among his papers after his death :

" The state and bread of the poor and oppressed have been precious in mine eyes : I have hated all cruelty and hardness of heart : I have (though in a despised *weed*) procured the good of all men."

In his *Advancement of Learning*, Second Book, he has given us an adequate interpretation of the symbol :

" In this third part of learning, which is Poetry, I can report no deficiency. For being as a plant that cometh of the lust of the earth, without a formal seed, it hath sprung up and spread abroad more than any other kind. But to ascribe unto it that which is due ; for the expressing of affections, passions, corruptions, and customs, we are beholden to poets, more than to philosophers' works ; and for wit and eloquence not much less than to orators' harangues."

And again in the Sixth Book :

" As to poetry, both with regard to its fable and its verse, it is like a luxuriant plant, sprouting not from seed, but by the mere vigor of the soil ; whence it everywhere creeps up, and spreads itself so wide that it were endless to be solicitous about its defects."

And so it appears that after all we have but exemplified the Poet's own thought ; tracing in this " weed " the origin of almost every word,

" Shewing their birth, and where they did proceed."

If the reader will presently but attempt to thus annotate any other verse, of any period, from any prose, either of its author or of any contemporary, for example one of

* " The invention of young men is more lively than that of old, and imaginations stream into their minds better, and, as it were, more divinely."—*Of Youth and Age.*

Lowell's poems, not excepting his noted *Bigelow Papers* (first published under a *pseudonym*), his experience of its utter impossibility will perhaps give him a keener apprehension of the wherefore, the occasion, and the unique propriety of the Poet's declaration regarding the plays,

"That every word doth almost tell my name."

It certainly will quicken, if need be, his discernment of the profound significance of the foregoing annotations, taken in their entirety.*

---

* Incidentally: the possible difference between prose and poetry by the same author is admirably illustrated in Milton. The following is the first passage selected from Milton's prose by Taine, in his *History of English Literature*, to which the reader is referred for further examples.

"What advantage is it to be a man, over it is to be a boy at school, if we have only escaped the ferula, to come under the fescue of an imprimatur? If serious and elaborate writings, as if they were no more than the theme of a grammar-lad under his pedagogue, must not be uttered without the cursory eyes of a temporizing and extemporizing licenser? He who is not trusted with his own actions, his drift not being known to be evil, and standing to the hazard of law and penalty, has no great argument to think himself reputed in the commonwealth wherein he was born for other than a fool or a foreigner. When a man writes to the world, he summons up all his reason and deliberation to assist him; he searches, meditates, is industrious, and likely consults and confers with his judicious friends; after all which done, he takes himself to be informed in what he writes, as well as any that wrote before him; if in this, the most consummate act of his fidelity and ripeness, no years, no industry, no former proof of his abilities, can bring him to that state of maturity, as not to be still mistrusted and suspected, unless he carry all his considerate diligence, all his midnight watchings, and expense of Palladian oil, to the hasty view of an unleisured licenser, perhaps much his younger, perhaps far his inferior in judgment, perhaps one who never knew the labor of book writing; and if he be not repulsed, or slighted, must appear in print like a puny with his guardian, and his censor's hand on the back of his title to be his bail and surety, that he is no idiot or seducer; it cannot be but a dishonor and derogation to the author, to the book, to the privilege and dignity of learning."—*Areopagitica.*

The following are brief selections from Milton's best poetry:

In the briefest statement: There is here developed a *phenomenon*, unique in literary history and in human expe-

> "Haste thee, nymph, and bring with thee
> Jest, and youthful jollity,
> Quips and cranks and wanton wiles,
> Nods and becks and wreathèd smiles,
> Such as hang on Hebe's cheek,
> And love to live in dimple sleek;
> Sport that wrinkled care divides,
> And laughter holding both his sides.
> Come, and trip it, as you go,
> On the light fantastic toe."—*L'Allegro.*

> "Can any mortal mixture of earth's mould
> Breathe such divine enchanting ravishment?
> Sure something holy lodges in that breast,
> And with these raptures moves the vocal air
> To testify his hidden residence.
> How sweetly did they float upon the wings
> Of silence, through the empty-vaulted night,
> At every fall smoothing the raven down
> Of darkness till it smiled!"—*Comus.*

> "The sun, now fallen . . .
> Arraying with reflected purple and gold
> The clouds that on his western throne attend:
> Now came still evening on, and twilight gray
> Had in her sober livery all things clad.
> Silence accompanied; for beast and bird,
> They to their grassy couch, these to their nests,
> Were slunk, all but the wakeful nightingale:
> She all night long her amorous descant sung.
> Silence was pleased.   Now glowed the firmament
> With living saphires; Hesperus, that led
> The starry host, rode brightest, till the Moon,
> Rising in clouded majesty, at length
> Apparent queen, unveiled her peerless light,
> And o'er the dark her silver mantle threw."
> —*Paradise Lost.*

One unaware of the truth well might ask, with complacent confidence: "How can both be the productions of the same author, when there is such an obvious and integral difference both in the style and in the mode of thought?"   But nevertheless, such is the fact; and evidently the explanation is to be sought in a more intimate knowledge of the manifold capacity of the human intellect.

rience; precisely the phenomenon which the Poet himself
appears to have remarked,—for else are his words incapable of explanation.

It certainly demands a solution. And as with all other
phenomena, induction, rather than logic, is the efficient
instrument. Experience has taught us that in such matters the scientific method is the only safe and reliable
pathway to the truth; leading us to the adoption of that
interpretation which best explains the facts because of its
entire consistency with all the details.

In this case, the phenomenon is manifestly the development in the verse and in the prose writings of an identity
in the workings of the intellect which therein find expression; unfolded continuously throughout a very wide range
of topics; comprising both the personally accumulated
materials of thought and their distinctive elaboration;
even to the evolution of the same ideas out of the like
observations of nature and humanity, and their expression
in the self-same vocabulary, metaphor, and illustration.

There is one explanation which obviously is perfectly
consistent with all the details, and which, moreover, is an
adequate interpretation, viz., *that the whole is indeed the
product of one mentality.* And yet from this we would
find some way of escape. But personally, we have been
unable to find any other explanation which is at all satisfactory. We can no longer resort to *Chance* as a theory
of explanation; for it is entirely inadequate, and in fact
has ceased to be applicable. While a moment's consideration makes it equally manifest that *Plagiarism*, as a
theory of explanation, is utterly untenable; where upon so
many and so varied themes, thought and its phraseology;
metaphor and simile; wit and wisdom; poetic insight,
feeling, and expression; knowledge of the human heart;
philosophy, politics, and statecraft; legal, scientific, and
classical lore; mental attributes, characteristics, and pecu-

liarities; in a word, all the elements that enter into the composition are so inextricably interwoven. The " music " is indeed full, rich, harmonious — not a jar or a discord. The most diverse elements successively blend together in that union and perfect concord, that continuity and congruity which characterize the work of the individual, and which is the very sign-manual of the soul. We not only find it impossible to distinguish any manifestation of two distinct individualities, but everywhere we sense the presence, feel the subtle influence, and breathe, as it were, in the atmosphere of a single, unique, wonderful personality, —an atmosphere made up of the views, the reflected experience, the associations, the memories, the learning and the philosophy of this one personality.

In the light of such a manifestation, and in its continued reflection, argument, in its ordinary acceptation, would appear to be inopportune and out of place; as inappropriate as would be a resort to logic to prove that gold is heavy, or that water, ice, and steam are of one and the same substance.

Syllogisms may perhaps be useful to one groping in the dark, but vision is vastly more welcome and satisfying. Argument never yet convinced one that the rainbow is beautiful — its visible glory alone does the work.

And here we behold, in deed and in truth, and as in his very lineaments, the " myriad-minded " man, truly " universal " in the scope and range of his genius. Though we have considered but a fragment of one of the plays, we are already conscious that hitherto we had not appreciated one-half of the richness, the depth, the fulness, and the subtlety of the thought present in the mind of their writer as he composed them, or of the tremendous resources from which they were drawn. His " princely trunk," of vigorous growth, was so deeply and widely rooted, it put forth so many branches clothed in enduring verdure, blossomed in such profusion, and bore so rich, so varied, and such abundant fruit; in short, the man was so immeasurably greater than his work, that any adequate discussion of even the phases already disclosed would fill a volume, while the chapter already exceeds its allotted length.

All this must, perforce, be left to the reader, to his insight, his candor, and his courage, and " to the liberty and faculty of every man's judgment." *

One or two fresh matters, closely related, may serve as side-lights upon the subject. We have observed how many rootlets, reaching down into the classic sub-soil, drew thence nourishment that gave to flower and fruit borne upon this tree a distinctive fragrance and a richer flavor. The amazing fact is developed that the plays are indeed a storehouse, wherein are garnered the choicest thoughts of the brightest intellects of the ages; priceless gems, into which he so infused the interior fire of his genius that in their new setting they glow with a radiance far surpassing their pristine beauty.

Take a single example for illustration. We quote from Richard Grant White's scholarly Essay on the *Genius of Shakespeare*:

" But when, in *Henry the Fifth*, the Bishop of Exeter makes his comparison of government to the subordination and harmony of parts in music,—

> 'For government, though high and low and lower,
> Put into parts, doth keep in one consent;
> Congruing in a full and natural close,
> Like music.'—

---

* It is indeed a cheering sign, full of promise, that in these closing hours of the Nineteenth century, people, *individually*, are rapidly learning to think for themselves, asking only for the materials; more and more determined in the exercise of this sacred prerogative of personality—a supreme regality inherent in liberty. O Liberty! what joys are enfolded within thy substance!

it were more than superfluous to seek, as some have sought, in Cicero's *De Republica*, the origin of this simile; for that book was lost to literature, and unknown except by name, until Angelo Mai discovered it upon a palimpsest in 1822. Cicero very probably borrowed the fancy from Plato; but it was not Shakespeare's way to go so far for that which lay near at hand. Music, and particularly vocal part-music, was much cultivated by our forefathers in Shakespeare's time; and he *seems* to have been a proficient in the art. The comparison is one that might well occur to any thoughtful man who is also a musician, but it is not every such man who would use it with so much aptness and make it with so much beauty."

We are no longer peering into darkness, through a wilderness of conjecture; for we have seen in clear vision where and how Bacon caught the key-note of this ancient melody, as it came echoing through the ages, though many of its strains were lost to the ear. And we know and appreciate with what wondrous skill this Master Composer could adapt and develop the theme, striking new chords and creating beautiful variations, in magnificent harmonies; for he was both a proficient in music and "perfected" in the arts of government.*

Paraphrasing freely: As Nero, in government, wound up the pins too high or let them down too low, winding them high and low and lower, so Bacon, having full reference to one consent but working contrariously, besought the King to tune his instrument to that consent where heart-strings not tongue-strings make the music, that harmony might not end in discord, and that the music might be the fuller; admonishing, that not the stringing of the harp nor the tuning of it would serve, except it be well played on from time to time; for government, *put into parts*, doth keep in one consent—as it doeth well in church music when the greatest part of the hymn is sung by one

* See *ante*, page 40.

voice, and then the quire at times falls in sweetly and solemnly—so the same harmony sorteth well in monarchy between the King and his Parliament; congruing in a full and natural close; like to a diapason in music, the eighth rise or reach, a good number and accord for a close.

If such were the preludes developed in tuning the harp of the muses and reducing it to perfect harmony, where is the one who can thereafter touch the strings into sweeter strains, with a better hand or a better quill? Certainly it is not every thoughtful man, also a musician, who would use the comparison so aptly, in such comprehensive but perfectly congruent harmony, or make it with so much beauty.

Again, viewing the narrative as a whole, we perceive that though feigned, it is essentially a history, and as such a masterpiece. Every action, without exception, is traced to its source and efficient cause. Even the act of the subordinate character, Gonzalo, arises " out of his charity " and " of his gentleness."[*] Not an incident happens but its origin is disclosed, either in human conduct, or when beyond this, in Providence, or in Fortune or Fate, which to Bacon were but other names for Providence.[†] And in the accomplishment of these ends there is afforded a masterly delineation of the play of motives, the growth of ambition, and the workings of the human heart as they were developed under the extraordinary circumstances. In ef-

---

[*] See *History of Great Britain. ante.* page 51.

[†] See *Novum Organum. II., 2.*

And this also reveals the *philosopher.* We are reminded of this by an incidental remark of Charles Waldstein, in his admirable *Essays on the Art of Pheidias:* " I shall do this, even at the risk of being taxed with *philosophising,* by attempting to account for the origin of phenomena and their effect, instead of merely remaining content with a statement of dead facts, which, indeed, from being merely stated can hardly be at once recognized as facts."

feet, we are given a perfect comprehension of the whole matter ; even better than if we had been merely eye-witnesses ; while throughout the reader is left, just as in life, to do for himself the moralizing. All in all, it would appear to be the very *beau-ideal* of a perfect history.

We ought now to appreciate, perhaps as never before, the narrowness and the stupidity of persons, evidently well-meaning but deficient in artistic instincts, who have severely censured Bacon for writing his History upon this unique and admirable method—notably Sir James Mackintosh.

Prof. Minto, in his *Manual of English Prose Literature*, gives us an insight into the situation. Of Bacon's *History of Henry VII.* he says:

"Considered on its own claims as an explanation of events by reference to the feelings and purposes of the chief actor, it is perhaps a better model than any history that has been published since. 'He gives,' says Bishop Nicholson, ' as sprightly a view of the secrets of Henry's council as if he had been President of it.' In one respect Bacon's history is in strong contrast to Macaulay's. In relating the schemes and actions of such a king as Henry, Macaulay would have overlaid the narrative with strong expressions of approval or disapproval. Bacon writes calmly, narrating facts and motives without any comment of a moral nature. . . . On this ground he is visited with a sonorous declamation by Sir James Mackintosh—as if his not improving the occasion were a sign that he approved of what had been done. Bacon wrote upon a principle that is beginning to be pretty widely accepted as regards personal histories claiming to be impartial—namely, that ' It is the true office of history to represent the events themselves together with the counsels, and to leave the observations and conclusions thereupon to the liberty and faculty of every man's judgment.' He does not seek to seal up historical facts from the useful office of pointing

7

a moral; he only held that the moralizing should not interfere with the narrative." *

Spedding says of Bacon's History:

" To educe a living-likeness of the man and the time, to
detect the true relations of events, and to present them to
the reader in their proper succession and proportions, was
the task which he now undertook. In this, which under
such conditions was all he could attempt, he succeeded so
well that he has left later historians little to do. . . . The
facts he was obliged, for the reasons above stated, to take
and leave almost as he found them; but the effect of his
treatment was like that of bringing a light into a dark
room: the objects are there as they were before, but now
you can distinguish them."

And again: " Every history which has been written
since has derived all its light from this, and followed its
guidance in every question of importance . . . as a study
of character in action and a specimen of the art of historical narrative, it comes nearer to the merit of Thucydides
than any English history that I know."

He concludes a vigorous defence of Bacon's work against
the charge of Sir James Mackintosh in these forcible
words:

" It is enough to say that in that book which all who
profess and call themselves Christians are bound to acknowledge as the highest authority, the most odious of all
treasons, the most unjust of all judgments, the most pathetic of all tales of martyred innocence, is related four
times over without a single indignant comment or a single
vituperative expression."

---

* " The historian we are told must not leave his readers to
themselves. He must not only lay the facts before them: he
must tell them what he himself thinks. In my opinion, this is
precisely what he ought not to do. Bishop Butler says somewhere that the best book which could be written would be a
book consisting only of premises, from which the readers should
draw conclusions for themselves."—*Froude*.

Truly, things need but to be portrayed in their simple reality to be read aright, in their true significance, and in an unapproachable power over the soul.

"Truth needs no color with his color fix'd;
Beauty no pencil, beauty's truth to lay;
But best is best, if never intermix'd."
—*Sonnet CI.*[*]

Bacon himself said in the beginning what may prove to be the final word: "But for a man who is professedly writing a Perfect History to be everywhere introducing political reflections, and thereby interrupting the narrative, is unreasonable and wearisome. For though every wise history is pregnant, as it were, with political precepts and warnings, yet the writer himself should not play the midwife."

These words of the Master of his Art bespeak the originality, the imperative artistic impulse reaching forth towards perfection, the implicit confidence in man's inherent power of discernment and the limitless patience in awaiting its development, that were so characteristic of his mighty genius: and they are also a sufficient answer to the same criticism made by Birch and others upon the plays,—those illumined histories of human life in its manifold experiences.[†]

---

[*] " For it is the true office of history to represent the events themselves together with the counsels, and to leave the observations and conclusions thereupon to the liberty and faculty of every man's judgment. But *mixtures* are things irregular, whereof no man can define."—*Advancement of Learning*, Second Book.

[†] Regarding the historical plays, the historian, Froude, significantly remarks: "The most perfect English history which exists is to be found, in my opinion, in the historical plays of Shakespeare. . . . Shakespeare's object was to exhibit as faithfully as he possibly could, the exact character of the great actors in the national drama — the circumstances which surrounded them, and the motives, internal and external, by which they

Bacon evidently patterned after the art of the Almighty, whose works are indeed revelations to opened eyes, though often meaningless to the stupid.

And now, in closing the chapter, one request is made of the reader, to whom these data have been presented almost without comment, and who is thus thrown, as was the writer, directly upon the exercise of his own powers, in untrammeled freedom of thought. He is asked, in all earnestness, however he may be inclined, to refrain from coming to an immediate conclusion, holding his judgment still in suspense. Many important aspects of the matter yet remain to be considered; and if, in passing them in review, abundant confirmation be found on every hand; if all the elements, as they are successively developed, continue to fit together integrally; harmonious both within and without, in perfect consistence with each other and in continuation of the actual at every point, the mind will then come happily to a final conviction, in a more enduring stability and rest. We had almost said, *In cœlum festina lente,* for so here the joy will be the deeper and the fuller.

If he be so disposed, let him regard this merely as the presentation of what lawyers formally term " a *prima facie* case "; as a platform upon which he will mount and from thence survey the opening prospect; or rather, as a vestibule, through which he enters and engages in the exploration of what possibly may prove to be a very Parthenon of human greatness.

----

were influenced. To know this is to know all. The reader can form his own theories. . . . No such directness of insight, no such breadth of sympathy, has since been applied to the writing of English history."

CHAPTER II.

Bacon's " new birth " into the higher intellectual life is thus graphically outlined by Spedding, in his luminous narrative in Vol. VIII. of his edition of Bacon's Works:

"There is no reason to suppose that he was regarded as a wonderful child. Of the first sixteen years of his life indeed nothing is known that distinguished him from a hundred other clever and well disposed boys. . . . When the temperament is quick and sensitive, the desire of knowledge strong, and the faculties so vigorous, obedient, and equally developed that they find almost all things easy, the mind will commonly fasten upon the first object of interest that presents itself, with the ardor of a first love. Now these qualities, which so eminently distinguished Bacon as a man, must have been in him from a boy; and if we would know the source of those great impulses which began to work in him so early and continued to govern him so long, we must look for it among the circumstances by which his boyhood was surrounded. What his mother taught him we do not know; but we know that she was a learned, eloquent, and religious woman, full of affection and puritanical fervor, deeply interested in the condition of the church, and perfectly believing that the cause of the Nonconformists was the whole cause of Christ. Such a mother could not but endeavor to lead her child's mind into the temple where her own treasure was laid up, and the child's mind, so led, could not but follow thither with awful curiosity and impressions not to be effaced. Neither do we know what his father taught him; but he appears to have designed him for the service of the state, and we need not doubt but that the son of Elizabeth's Lord Keeper, and nephew of her principal Secretary,

early imbibed a reverence for the mysteries of statesman-
ship and a deep sense of the dignity, responsibility, and
importance of the statesman's calling. . . . It is certain
that he was more than once in the immediate presence of
the Queen herself, smiled on by the countenance which
was looked up to by all the young and all the old around
him with love and reverence. . . . So situated, it must
have been as difficult for a young and susceptible imagination not to aspire after civil dignities as for a boy bred
in camps not to long to be a soldier. But the time for
these was not yet come. For the present his field of ambition was still in the school-room; where, perhaps from
the delicacy of his constitution, he was more at home than
in the play-ground. His career there was victorious; new
prospects of boundless extent opening on every side; till
at length, just about the age at which an intellect of quick
growth begins to be conscious of original power, he was
sent to the University, where he hoped to learn all that
men knew. By the time, however, that he had gone through
the usual course and heard what the various professors
had to say, he was conscious of a disappointment. It
seemed that towards the end of the Sixteenth century men
neither knew nor aspired to know more than was to be
learned from Aristotle; a strange thing at any time; more
strange than ever just then, when the heavens themselves
seemed to be taking up the argument in their own behalf,
and by suddenly lighting up within the very region of the
Unchangeable and Incorruptible, and presently extin-
guishing, a new fixed star as bright as Jupiter—(the new
star Cassiopeia shone with full lustre on Bacon's fresh-
manship)—to be protesting by signs and wonders against
the cardinal doctrine of the Aristotleian philosophy. It
was then that a thought struck him, the date of which deserves to be recorded, not for anything extraordinary in
the thought itself, which had probably occurred to others
before him, but for its influence upon his after life. If
our study of nature be thus barren, he thought, our method
of study must be wrong; might not a better method be

found? The suggestion was simple and obvious. The singularity was in the way he took hold of it. With most men such a thought would have come and gone in a passing regret; a few might have matured it into a wish; some into a vague project; one or two might perhaps have followed it out so far as to attain a distinct conception of the better method, and hazard a distant indication of the direction in which it lay. But in him the gift of seeing in prophetic vision what might be and ought to be was united with the practical talent of devising means and handling details. He could at once imagine like a poet and execute like a clerk of the works. Upon the conviction, This may be done, followed at once the question, *How* may it be done? Upon that question answered, followed the resolution to try and do it.

"Of the degrees by which the suggestion ripened into a project, the project into an undertaking, and the undertaking unfolded itself into distinct proportions and the full grandeur of its total dimensions, I can say nothing. But that the thought first occurred to him during his residence at Cambridge, therefore before he had completed his fifteenth year, we know upon the best authority — his own statement to Dr. Rawley. I believe it ought to be regarded as the most important event in his life; the event which had a greater influence than any other upon his character and future course. From that moment there was awakened within his breast the appetite which cannot be satisfied and the passion which cannot commit excess. From that moment he had a vocation which employed and stimulated all the energies of his mind, gave a value to every vacant interval of time, and interest and significance to every random thought and casual accession of knowledge; an object to live for as wide as humanity, as immortal as the human race; an idea to live in vast and lofty enough to fill the soul forever with religious and heroic aspirations. From that moment, though still subject to interruptions, disappointments, errors, and regrets, he could never be without either work or hope or consolation."

Spedding was right. It was a moment of clear vision, of profound conviction, developing into high resolve, in a mighty faith and in a spirit of intense consecration; the most momentous in his career, both to himself and to mankind.

Ever since the days of Plato, man had been looking within for the truth, searching his intellect for the *ideals* of things, seeking to develop them from its recesses by the workings of its processes, and shutting his eyes to the realities of existence, of which knowledge is power. The result had been centuries of dreary waste and barrenness.

By God's gift, Bacon saw, as by a flash of inspiration, the fatal error in which mankind had been involved, with such disastrous consequences; and he discerned likewise the certainty of inestimable blessings following the adoption of the contrary course. This thought, so obviously vital in its bearing upon the destiny of the race, set his soul on fire, and though he was but a youth of fifteen, he determined to effect a revolution, by thus turning the whole tide of thought and of human affairs.

This mighty resolve was perhaps the birth of that universality, which distinguishes him from all others. His purpose is the measure of a man, and its accomplishment the measure of his growth. With Bacon all humanity was embraced within its scope and the universe was its subject-matter. The efficient prosecution of a design of such magnitude and the intense mental activity involved developed his powers to a corresponding compass, until he attained to an enormous breadth of comprehension, and a vision at once telescopic and microscopic in its range.

Deeming it necessary to the accomplishment of his purpose, he applied himself to the acquisition of all that was then known upon every subject, and in fact very little escaped him. In his own words, he 'made all knowledge his province': his bark " sailed round the whole circumference of the old and new world of sciences"; he traversed the highways and by-ways of its continents; and the vast extent of his acquirements is abundantly evidenced upon almost every page of his works. The profusion of his classical quotations and allusions, introduced in apt expression or enforcement of his thought, reveals his mastery of the ancient lore, with its accumulated wealth of wit, fable, and illustration, while his occasional quotations from French, Italian, and Spanish authors show his familiarity with mediaeval literature. The resources of history, both ancient and modern, were added to his acquirements, including both a knowledge of the course of events and an insight into the springs of action underlying them, together with a notable comprehension of the character, motives, and mould of the principal actors.

His intent centered in mankind, with whom he had also to deal, and by close observation and study he attained to an unrivalled knowledge of human nature; illustrated especially in his *Essays*, of which it is the substance, the warp and woof of their texture.

He not only encompassed the "old world" of science, but he drew the boundary line and opened the expanse of its "new world." He regenerated it, breathing into modern science its first breath of vital life, and infusing the spirit which now animates it. He cradled its infancy, opened its understanding through the avenues of the senses, gave initial development to its newly awakened powers, and enlisted the interest of mankind in its growth, so that in after years Newton, Faraday, and Franklin, and a host of colaborers of every nationality eagerly ministered to its further development, until now its stalwart arms are sustained by the multitude.

Man and Nature were his inspiring themes; and nature for man, for his interpretation, his comprehension, and his consequent dominion,—as God's own vineyard, divinely ordained, planted, and watered for man's abundant sustenance and enjoyment, and only awaiting his entry into its complete possession.

And to this end, he besought man to cease from his search after truth within the recesses of his own mind, and to turn his attention outward, to the study of the world of his abode, in its actual realities, and with a due 'submission of the mind unto things.' He also opened up and definitely unfolded the new way of dealing effectively with nature; substituting for the prevalent Aristotleian and scholastic Logic, with its reverence for "the first notions of the mind," and its inevitable imposition of them upon nature, his *Interpretation of Nature* by orderly Induction; which should educe or draw forth her meaning out of and directly from her phenomena, and which was therefore based upon the close, minute, and persistent *observation* of her manifestations,—all of which is set forth at length in his *Great Instauration.** The following brief quotation will afford the reader a glimpse of the especial emphasis he placed upon " observation," and of the spirit and intent of his work; though we can hardly appreciate its truly revolutionary character, in its antagonism to the then dominant scholastic philosophy; now that the Baconian spirit has been so long in supremacy, and we have become so accustomed to the enjoyment of its fruits. Having outlined his " Art of Interpreting Nature," he continues:

---

* Our present wonder was fully shared by him, in his vivid realization of the situation at that time. In his *Novum Organum*, he observes:

" For it is sufficient to astonish any reflecting mind, that nobody should have cared or wished to open and complete a way for the understanding, setting off from the senses, and regular, well-conducted experiment; but that everything has been abandoned either to the mists of tradition, the whirl and confusion of argument, or the waves and mazes of chance, and desultory, ill-combined experiment."

" But as we propose not only to pave and show the way, but also to tread in it ourselves, we shall next exhibit the phenomena of the universe ; that is, such experience of all kinds, and such a natural history, as may afford a foundation to philosophy. For as no fine method of demonstration or form of explaining nature can preserve the mind from error, and support it from falling ; so neither can it hence receive any matter of science. Those, therefore, who determine not to conjecture and guess, but to find out and know ; not to invent fables and romances of worlds, but to look into and dissect the nature of this real world, *must consult only things themselves.* Nor can any force of genius, thought, or argument be substituted for this labor, search, and inspection ; not even though all the wits of men were united : this, therefore, must either be had or the business be deserted forever."

Strange as it now may seem, this was a radical departure from the methods then in vogue and for centuries past ; inaugurating a new era for mankind.

Incidentally, it may be noted that in applying his philosophy Bacon studied things in nature and human experience so closely that he caught their spirit ; a vital element in their adequate interpretation, especially in the important phase of poetical treatment, of which it is the very essence. This is made strikingly apparent in succeeding sentences, where his thought is clothed, as in a garment, in the imagery of nature and man's surroundings, with the characteristic addition of a bit of mythological garniture drawn from the classics. He continues :

" Our natural history is not designed so much to please by its variety, or benefit by gainful experiments. as to afford light to the discovery of causes, and hold out the breasts to philosophy ; for though we principally regard works, and the active parts of the sciences, yet we wait for the time of harvest, and would not reap the blade for the ear. We are well aware that axioms, rightly framed, will draw after them whole sheaves of works : but for that untimely and childish desire of seeing fruits of new works before the season, we absolutely condemn and reject it, as the golden apple that hinders the progress."

And again : " For as we have greater hopes from our constant conversation with nature, than from our force of genius, the discoveries we shall thus make may serve as inns on the road, for the mind to repose in, during its progress to greater certainties."

The garb perfectly fits the thought ; for this student of nature and experience had become familiar with her language, in the comprehension of the subtle thoughts and delicate shades of meaning expressed in her works, and had thus at command a whole wardrobe of appropriate vestments ; having only to make choice of that which had been ordained for the expression of meanings analogous or identical with his own. Bacon truly entered into converse with nature, " interrogating " her, listening attentively to her voice, and catching the very tones and accent of " the mother tongue."

He concludes his announcement in these impressive words :

" We design no contemptible beginning to the work ; and anticipate that the fortune of mankind will lead it to such a termination as is not possible for the present race to conceive. The point in view is not only the contemplative happiness, but the whole fortunes, and affairs, and powers, and works of men. For man being the minister and interpreter of nature, acts and understands so far as he has observed of the order, the works, and mind of nature, and can proceed no further ; for no power is able to loose or break the chain of causes, nor is nature to be conquered but by submission ; whence those twin intentions, human knowledge and human power, are really coincident ; and the greatest hindrance to works is the ignorance of causes.

" The capital precept for the whole undertaking is this,

that the eye of the mind be never taken off from things themselves, but receive their images truly as they are. And God forbid that ever we should offer the dreams of fancy for a model of the world ; but rather in his kindness vouchsafe to us the means of writing a revelation and true vision of the traces and moulds of the Creator in his creatures.

" May thou, therefore, O Father, who gavest the light of vision as the first fruit of creation, and who hast spread over the fall of man the light of thy understanding as the accomplishment of thy works, guard and direct this work, which issuing from thy goodness, seeks in return thy glory ! When thou hast surveyed the works which thy hands had wrought all seemed good in thy sight and Thou restedst. But when man turned to the works of his hands, he found all vanity and vexation of spirit, and experienced no rest. If, however, we labor in thy works, Thou wilt make us to partake of thy vision and sabbath ; we, therefore, humbly beseech Thee to strengthen our purpose, that Thou mayst be willing to endow thy family of mankind with new gifts, through our hands, and the hands of those in whom Thou shalt implant the same spirit."

Three centuries have rolled their course since Francis Bacon uttered that prayer. The world has been borne onward, with ever accelerating velocity, in the trend of a mighty revolution. The eye can scarcely penetrate with clear vision into the remote regions of that age, where darkness prevailed, and where for centuries the lot of man had been one of discomfort, privation, and poverty of resource. Earth has entered the bounds of brighter realms, in whose enlightenment man has indeed been endowed with new gifts of comfort and enjoyment, and with enlarged powers and opportunities.

We dwell, to-day, at the dawning of the Twentieth century, in a truly palatial environment : we are tasting the sweets of regal power, in our newly acquired dominion over the forces of nature. The lightning's flash has been arrested in its course and made to glow in an enduring and steady light, to minister to our comfort. It is already an old story of its employment as a Mercury, to carry our thoughts and even our voices to friends at a distance : it is rather as a Jove, in its personification of power, that its performances now daily astonish us. Light, heat, electricity, indeed all the subtle forces of nature, are being brought into harness and to the pole, to give increased impetus to the forward movement, expending their energies in a thousand services to mankind.

Invention has lit its torch in every hamlet, and the Arts, utilizing nature's forces by its aid, have attained a development surpassing in accomplishment all that was ever attributed to the fabled Genii, summoned at the call of the magician. And even Medicine, instead of bleeding, cupping, and torturing its victims, now ministers intelligently to man, in reinforcement of nature, arousing her latent powers and stimulating them to throw off the disease.

And Science, the parent tree, of which these developments are the fruits, has grown to such proportions that its branches fill the earth, and whatever is, is embraced within its scope ; while its accumulations have become so vast that almost a lifetime is required to master a single department. Bacon's spirit has been an inspiration to the race, " the same spirit " now animating all ; and by the patient observance of his cardinal precept, of 'fastening the eye of the mind upon things themselves, to receive their images truly as they are,' in complete submission, man has been brought from afar to the very threshold of the inner court of nature's sanctuary, with a hope of even penetrating the cloud of her mystery. Submission is effecting the conquest, and in this subtler than a Jacob's wrestling, man is prevailing over nature, despoiling her of her secrets, and appropriating her powers to his service.

And all the while, in a thousand channels, Science, in fulfilment of its true function and end, and because of the
coincidence of knowledge and power, is continually ministering to the welfare of man, in an affluence of benefactions,— bounty upon bounty, a never-ceasing stream of
bounties.

Surely, here is an advancement in "the whole fortunes,
and affairs, and powers, and works of men," beyond any
conception that could possibly have been entertained three
hundred years ago. Such was Bacon's anticipation ; and
ours is the day of the realization of his prophetic vision,
in the fulfilment of a faith in the unseen that was truly
sublime.

But there are centuries yet to come. They will roll on,
bearing the world into those heavens whose light is the
effulgence of the glory of God ; made manifest in the comprehension of His works, and in their complete utilization
and enjoyment by man ; where the accomplishment of
these works will be attained in man's understanding of
Him ; and when the labor which shall have wrought this
shall end in a participation in His rest and sabbath. Then,
and not till then, will the full intent of Bacon's thought
be compassed, as it found expression in his prayer.

This prayer also reveals the man, in its unfolding of
his sincere desire. It was the cry to the Almighty of a
great heart burdened with the fateful import of his message to mankind, which, in his belief, was to effect materially the fortunes, the welfare, and the happiness of the
race through all coming generations, to the end of time.
Standing alone, and about to cast the die, in the solemnity
of the moment when such a destiny was at stake, he turned
instinctively to the Father, imploring Him to strengthen
his purpose, to guard and direct the work, and to endow
his family of mankind with new gifts at his hands, "and
the hands of those in whom Thou shalt implant the same
spirit."

Bacon's prayer has been likened to the devotion of an angel: it was the far more precious utterance of a mortal, sounding from the depths unto the heavens, benign in intent, and inspired by a faith which was the likeness and reflection of the vision of the Almighty.

In his profound wisdom, Bacon found a place and a function for prayer. He believed in its efficacy. His trust in an overruling Providence was serene and unfaltering. And who can say that his earnest petition in behalf of mankind did not find a lodgment in the ear and heart of the Almighty; that it did not comply with the conditions of some spiritual law under which the cry of the mortal can move the arm of the Father; and that His directing guidance, thus implored, was not an efficient instrumentality in effecting the marked turn in the tide of human affairs which followed, and which has secured to us such an enlargement of life, through its endowment with the " new gifts " we so abundantly enjoy?

Francis Bacon was deeply touched with human infirmity. While his iniquity was far less than that into which Jacob and David and Solomon unfortunately lapsed, yet it drew upon him the chastisement of an overwhelming retribution. His sin bore heavily upon him : he felt the burning imprint of its ugly brand, the agony of its painful stain. He could only apply the divinely healing balm of deep contrition. He washed it with the tears of his repentance, and wiped it with the hope that his example might prove a bulwark to others in like temptation, and he covered it with the white mantle of his beneficence to man. Let no cruel hand, in the basest ingratitude, now seek to uncover his nakedness.

Mankind can never discharge its indebtedness to Bacon : but we are lost to charity, and to magnanimity as well, if in our hearts there be found no chords responsive to the spirit of his Prospero's final and touching appeal :

"Now I want
Spirits to enforce, art to enchant;
And my ending is despair,
Unless I be relieved by *prayer;*
Which pierces so, that it assaults
Mercy itself, and frees all faults.
As you from crimes would pardoned be,
Let your indulgence set me free."

It may be that there are those, who, in their consciousness of rectitude and their few shortcomings, are strangers
to any sympathetic indulgence for their fellow men, and
so without mercy either for the living or the dead. But
surely, in their acute sense of the binding force of obligation, they will not withhold their acknowledgment, long
since due, of what we owe to Bacon: they will join in its
grateful recognition; or at least, they will do him simple
justice:

He was at once, and in each in the highest sense, the
Prophet of progress, the Interpreter of nature, the reverent Worshipper of the Father, and the world's great Bene-
factor.

CHAPTER III.

"'Two gates the entrance of sleep's house adorn,
  Of ivory one, the other simple horn;
  Through horn a crowd of real visions streams,
  Through ivory portals pass delusive dreams."

THE above lines from Virgil, so beautifully translated by
Spedding, were quoted by Bacon in his *De Augmentis*,
Seventh Book, in answer to a possible criticism that his
work upon a given topic had been " but to collect into an
art or science that which had been omitted by other writers as matter of common sense, and sufficiently clear and
self-evident." He continues: "Great no doubt is the
magnificence of the ivory gate, but the true dreams pass
through the gate of horn."

This gate of simple horn was to Bacon 'the fastening
of the eye of the mind upon things themselves, to receive
their images truly as they are,' in vigilant, painstaking
industry,—the homely portal through which alone streams
the real vision of the truth behind the fact. Indeed, this
faithful observation of the realities, even in their most
commonplace and apparently trivial details, was Bacon's
cardinal principle, underlying his whole work.

It led him to base his *Great Instauration* upon the
groundwork of a proposed *Natural History*, which should
be an accurate record of man's observations and experiments, throughout the whole range of nature and humanity; thereby affording the requisite materials for the more
difficult work of induction. Just as in our day, Charles
Darwin, working in a narrower but broad field, spent five
years of his life in the arduous work of collecting from

all over the world all sorts of facts bearing, however remotely, upon "Species"; as a preliminary to the working
out, during further years of observation, of the mighty
inductions given to the world in his *Origin of Species.**
To us, with our extended knowledge, Bacon's project
seems a colossal enterprise, impossible of accomplishment,
though a thousand pens were employed ; but in Bacon's
day, when so little was accurately known, it seemed, to
him at least, a feasible undertaking, though obviously involving immense toil and the severest drudgery. Moreover, he had in view the ultimate development of a *philosophia prima*, unfolding the principles that underlie all
phenomena, in their common unity.

He, therefore, applied himself with characteristic energy
to the performance of the task, though it involved a seeming neglect of higher matters. In opening his *Natural
and Experimental History*, he announces this purpose in
an eloquent plea for the cause ; perhaps, within its brief
compass, the most exalted appeal to the higher motives to
be found in any literature outside of the Bible :

"If, therefore, there be any humility towards the Creator, any reverence for or disposition to magnify His
works, any charity for man and anxiety to relieve his sorrows and necessities, any love of truth in nature, any
hatred of darkness, any desire for the purification of the
understanding, we must entreat men again and again to
discard, or at least set apart for a while, those volatile and
preposterous philosophies, which have preferred theses to

* "On my return home it occurred to me, in 1837, that something might perhaps be made out of this question by patiently
accumulating and reflecting on all sorts of facts which could
possibly have any bearing on it. After five years' work I
allowed myself to speculate on the subject, and drew up some
short notes ; these I enlarged in 1844 into a sketch of the conclusions which then seemed to me probable ; from that period
to the present day [1859] I have steadily pursued the same
object."—*Introduction to the Origin of Species.*

hypotheses, led experience captive, and trampled over the works of God; and to approach with humility and veneration to unroll the volume of Creation, to linger and meditate therein, and with minds washed clean from opinions to study it in purity and integrity. For this is that sound and language which went forth into all lands,* and did not incur the confusion of Babel; this should men study to be perfect in, and becoming again as little children, condescend to take the alphabet of it into their hands and spare no pains to search and unravel the interpretation thereof, but pursue it strenuously and persevere even unto death.

"Having therefore in my Instauration placed the Natural History — such a Natural History as may serve my purpose—in the third part of the work, I have thought it right to make some anticipation thereof, and to enter upon it at once. For although not a few things, and those among the most important, still remain to be completed in my Organum, yet my design is rather to advance the universal work of Instauration in many things, than to perfect it in a few; ever earnestly desiring, with such a passion as we believe God alone inspires, that this which has been hitherto unattempted may not now be attempted in vain. . . . May God, the Founder, Preserver, and Renewer of the universe, in His love and compassion to men, protect and rule this work, both in its ascent to His glory and in its descent to the good of men, through His only Son, God with us."

He tried also to enlist the help of others in this great work; even appealing to the King for the aid of his influence in this direction; writing, in reply to his acknowledgment of the receipt of a presentation copy of the *Novum Organum:*

"This comfortable beginning makes me hope further that your Majesty will be aiding to me, in setting men on work for the collecting of a natural and experimental his-

---

* Psalm XIX., 1–4.

tory; which is *basis totius negotii;* a thing which I assure myself will be from time to time an excellent recreation for you; I say, to that admirable spirit of yours, that delighteth in light: and I hope well that even in your times many noble inventions may be discovered for man's use. For who can tell, now this Mine of Truth is once opened, how the veins go, and what lieth higher and what lieth lower?"

But King James would do nothing, as indeed might have been expected from one who had shown himself so sharply obtuse, in his remark about the *Novum Organum,* that it was "like the peace of God, that passeth all understanding"; and so Bacon was left to work alone.

Dr. Rawley, his chaplain and biographer, in his preface to Bacon's *Natural History,* gives us a glimpse of the severity of the situation:

"And in this behalf, I have heard his lordship speak complainingly, that his lordship (who thinketh he deserveth to be an architect in this building) should be forced to be a workman and a laborer, and to dig the clay and burn the brick; and more than that (according to the hard condition of the Israelites at the latter end), to gather the straw and stubble over all the fields to burn the bricks withal. For he knoweth that except he do it, nothing will be done: men are so set to despise the means of their own good."

This reference to the crude materials, to clay, brick, straw, and stubble, was peculiarly felicitous; and we cannot give the reader a better insight into the character of the work than by following Dr. Rawley's example, in the recital of Bacon's own words. In his *Novum Organum,* CXIX., he says:

"There will be met with also in my history and experiments many things which are trivial and commonly known: many which are mean and low; many, lastly, which are too subtle and merely speculative, and that seem to be of no use; which kind of things may possibly avert and alienate men's interest.

"And first for those things which seem common : let men bear in mind that hitherto they have been accustomed to do no more than refer and adopt the causes of things which rarely happen to such as happen frequently ; while of those which happen frequently they never ask the cause, but take them as they are for granted. And therefore they do not investigate the causes of weight, of the rotation of the heavenly bodies, of heat, cold, light, hardness, softness, rarity, density, liquidity, solidity, animation, inanimation, similarity, dissimilarity, organization, and the like ; but admitting these as self-evident and obvious, they dispute and decide on other things of less frequent and familiar occurrence.

"But I, who am well aware that no judgment can be passed on uncommon or remarkable things, much less anything new brought to light, unless the causes of common things, and the causes of those causes, be first duly examined and found out, am of necessity compelled to admit the commonest things into my history. Nay, in my judgment philosophy has been hindered by nothing more than this,—that things of familiar and frequent occurrence do not arrest and detain the thoughts of men, but are received in passing without any inquiry into their causes ; insomuch that information concerning things which are not known is not oftener wanted than attention concerning things which are."

Bacon sought, first and foremost, to get at " the power and the mystery of common things "; and in his *Preparation towards a Natural and Experimental History*, he summarizes as follows :

" In this place also is to be resumed that which in the 99th, 119th, and 120th Aphorisms of the first, book I treated more at large, but which it may be enough here to enjoin shortly by way of precept ; namely, that there are to be received into this history, first, things the most ordinary, such as might be thought superfluous to record in writing, because they are so familiarly known ; secondly, things mean, illiberal, filthy (for 'to the pure all things are pure,' and if money obtained from Vespasian's tax smelt well, much more does light and information from whatever source derived); thirdly, things trifling and childish (and no wonder, for we are to become again as little children); and lastly, things which seem over subtle, because they are in themselves of no use. For the things which will be set forth in this History are not collected (as I have already said) on their own account ; and therefore neither is their importance to be measured by what they are worth in themselves, but according to their indirect bearing upon other things, and the influence they may have upon philosophy."

This allusion to filthy things awakens the suggestion, that possibly the Poet may have been actuated by the same principle of absolute fidelity to the realities, in his insertion in the plays of details so grossly offensive, in the midst of so much that is beautiful and inspiring. May he not have touched upon these matters, in common with all phases of humanity, in that breadth of interpretation which comprehends an infolded meaning in every function and development of man's being, and which seeks to give expression to nature's language in its whole vocabulary and in its every mood and tense?

All his biographers agree that Bacon was a pure man ; which gives the greater strength to his position upon this point, stated even more forcibly in the 120th Aphorism :

" And for things that are mean or even filthy,—things which (as Pliny says) must be introduced with an apology, — such things, no less than the most splendid and costly, must be admitted into natural history. Nor is natural history polluted thereby ; for the sun enters the sewer no less than the palace, yet takes no pollution. And for myself, I am not raising a capital or pyramid to the pride of man, but laying a foundation in the human understanding for a holy temple after the model of the world. That model, therefore, I follow. For whatever deserves to exist deserves also to be known, for knowledge is the image of existence; and things mean and splendid exist alike. Moreover, as from certain putrid substances — musk for instance, and civit—the sweetest odors are sometimes generated, so too from mean and sordid instances emanate excellent light and information. But enough and more than enough of this; such fastidiousness being merely childish and effeminate."

Regarding the scope of the work, the 127th Aphorism, in its breadth of view, is even applicable to the conditions to-day:

" It may also be asked (in the way of doubt rather than objection) whether I speak of natural philosophy only, or whether I mean that the other sciences, logic, ethics, and politics should be carried on by this method. Now I certainly mean what I have said to be understood of them all; and as the common logic, which governs by the syllogism, extends not only to natural but to all sciences; so does mine also, which proceeds by induction, embrace everything. For I form a History and tables of discovery for anger, fear, shame, and the like; for matters political; and again for the mental operations of memory, composition and division, judgment and the rest; not less than for heat and cold, or light, or vegetation, or the like. But nevertheless since my method of interpretation, after the history has been prepared and duly arranged, regards not the working and discourse of the mind only (as the common logic does) but the nature of things also, I supply the mind with such rules and guidance that it may in every case apply itself aptly to the nature of things. And therefore I deliver many and diverse precepts in the doctrine of Interpretation, which in some measure modify the method of invention according to the quality and condition of the subject of the inquiry."

And finally, regarding the style of the work, in his *Preparation*, etc., Bacon says :

"Nor is this all. For in a great work it is no less necessary that what is admitted should be written succinctly than that which is superfluous should be rejected ; though no doubt this kind of chastity and brevity will give less pleasure both to the reader and the writer. But it is always to be remembered that this which we are now about is only a granary and storehouse of matters, not meant to be pleasant to stay or live in, but only to be entered as occasion requires, when anything is wanted for the work of the Interpreter, which follows."

Bacon himself, in fulfilment of his capital precept, was a close observer of everything. Through this life-long habit, he was enabled to gather at first hand a store of materials that was unequalled in its variety and almost boundless in extent, as is evidenced in his works. In the words of Macaulay : "The Essays contain abundant proofs that no nice feature of character, no peculiarity in the ordering of a house, a garden, or a court masque, could escape the notice of one whose mind was capable of taking in the whole world of knowledge."

He drew from this vast fund of information in writing his Natural Histories, availing himself also of many observations noted by the ancients. He left a *Natural and Experimental History*, comprising a *History of the Winds*, a *History of Life and Death*, a *History of Dense and Rare*, and Introductions to others of like character ; also a *Sylva Sylvarum* or *Natural History*, consisting of a thousand paragraphs, divided into ten centuries, containing observations upon a great variety of matters. The value of these collections lay in their use, and as our knowledge is vastly more complete, they have generally been regarded as useless lumber, cumbering the library shelves, though fortunately for us they have been preserved.

And now the reader well may ask, what possible rela-

tion could such collections of the dry details of things
have to Poetry, or the Poet's plays?

The answer is simple, direct, significant. The close
study of Bacon in his works has led us to the recognition
of a vital principle, possibly of far-reaching consequence.
While in both Science and Poetry there are far higher
departments with their richer treasures of truth; as in
Science these observations of things themselves, "truly
as they are," are, to use Bacon's figure, the alphabet out
of which the whole structure is drawn and framed; so the
same materials, industriously gathered and personally as-
similated, are alike the alphabet of true Poetry—the best
and most enduring, such as is found in the plays — and
indeed of all literature whose aim is revelation or interpretation, the evolution of the universal out of the particular, the translation of fact into truth.

This exalted realm is the common domain of modern
science and the truest poetry, in whose lofty perspective
the parallel lines meet and blend together: it is the arch
connecting the two pillars at their top, yea, the dome sur-
mounting the entire Pantheon of human learning, covering the whole structure. Its solid foundation is in the
realities: and throughout, the only gate opening to the
entrance of true visions is the gate of homely horn.

This cardinal principle was with Bacon a standard
canon, expressed in the tributes he incidentally pays to
the best poets from time to time. Thus, in brief:

"The south wind with us is rainy, the north wind clear;
the former collects and nurtures clouds, the latter breaks
and dissipates them. Poets, therefore, in their descriptions of the deluge represent the north wind as at that
time imprisoned, and the south wind let loose with full
force."

Again: "We should not altogether neglect the testimony of Virgil, seeing he was by no means ignorant of

natural philosophy: 'At once the winds rush forth, the east, and the south, and south-west, laden with storms,' and again, 'I have seen all the battles of the winds meet together in the air.'"

"To conclude, therefore : as certain critics are used to say hyperbolically,—*That if all sciences were lost they might be found in Virgil ;*—so certainly this may be said truly, there are the prints and footsteps of learning in those few speeches which are reported of this prince."

And again : "So likewise I find some particular writings of an elegant nature touching some of the affections ; as of anger, of comfort upon adverse accidents, of tenderness of countenance, and other. But the poets and writers of history are the best doctors of this knowledge ; where we may find painted forth with great life, how affections are kindled and incited ; and how pacified and refrained ; and how again contained from act and further degree ; how they disclose themselves, how they work, how they vary, how they gather and fortify, how they are inwrapped one with another, and how they do fight and encounter one with another, and other the like particulars."

That we may fully recognize the dominance of this principle, let us now enter these storehouses of Bacon's observations, his *Natural Histories*, and with the plays in hand scrutinize closely these primary elements, or letters of the alphabet ; noting with what fidelity and wondrous skill this " architect " wrought them into beautiful structures, " after the model of the world," and which will endure as long as there is a world. Let us enter as into his workshop, humbly, reverently, and with studious mien, as is becoming to those who would observe the methods of this great Master of his art.

Let us proceed, not at random, but more comprehensively, by topics ; and as the only difficulty arises from an embarrassment of riches, we will begin at the end of all things — Death.

"THE PORCHES OF DEATH.*

" I now come to the inquiry concerning the porches of death ; that is, of the things which happen to men both a little before and a little after the point of death ; that seeing that there are so many paths which lead to death, we may know what are the common issues of them all."

" The immediate signs which precede death are, great restlessness and tossing of the body, fumbling of the hands, hard clutching and grasping, teeth firmly set, a hollow voice, trembling of the lower lip, pallor of the face, a confused memory, loss of speech, cold sweats, elongation of the body, raising up of the whites of the eyes, alteration of the whole countenance (as the nose becoming sharp, the eyes hollow, and the cheeks sinking in), contraction and rolling of the tongue, coldness of the extremities, in some a discharge of blood or seed, a shrill cry, thick breathing, falling of the lower jaw, and the like."

(For brevity, we leave to the reader the pleasure of tracing out in this " alphabet" the numerous details in the following quotations from the plays.)

" *K. Hen.* Set me the crown upon my pillow here.
  Cla. His eye is hollow and he changes much."
                    II., *King Henry IV.*, IV., 4.

" A needy, hollow-eyed, sharp-looking wretch,
  A living dead man."—*Com. of Err.*, V., 1.

" Not so, even through the hollow eyes of death
  I spy life peering."—*K. Richard II.*, II., 1.

" O farewell, dear Hector,
  Look, how thou diest! look, how thy eye turns pale!"
                    Troil. and Cress., V., 3.

" My arm shall give thee help to bear thee hence;
  For I do see the cruel pangs of death
  Right in thine eye."—*K. John*, V., 4.†

---

* *History of Life and Death.*

† " I know many wise men that fear to die; for the change is bitter, and flesh would refuse to prove it: besides, the expectation brings terror, and that exceeds the evil. But I do not

"*War.* See how the pangs of death do make him grin!
Sal. Disturb him not, let him pass peaceably."
—*II., Henry IV., III., 3.*

"The king I fear is poisoned by a monk:
I left him almost speechless and broke out
To acquaint you with this evil."—*K. John, V., 3.*

"O, I could prophecy
But that the earthly and cold hand of death
Lies on my tongue."—*I., K. Henry IV., V., 4.*

"*Quint.* My sight is very dull, whate'er it bodes.
I am surprised with an uncouth fear;
A chilling sweat o'erruns my trembling joints;
My heart suspects more than mine eye can see.
Mart. To prove thou hast a true *divining* heart,
Aaron and thou look down into this den,
And see a fearful sight of blood and death."
—*Tit. Andron., II., 4.*

"*Patience.*   Do you note
How much her grace is altered on the sudden?
How long her face is drawn? how pale she looks,
And of an earthly cold?   Mark her eyes!
Grif. She is going, wench; pray, pray."
—*K. Henry VIII., IV., 2.*

"Ah, Warwick, Montague hath breathed his last;
And to the latest gasp cried out for Warwick,
And said, 'Commend me to my valiant brother.'
And more he would have said; and more he spake,
Which sounded like a cannon in a vault,
That mought not be distinguished: but at last,

---

believe that any man fears to be dead, but only *the stroke of death.*"—*On Death.*

"Dar'st thou die?
The sense of death is most in apprehension;
And the poor beetle that we tread upon,
In corporal sufferance finds a pang as great
As when a giant dies."—*Measure for Measure, III., 1.*

"*Bolingbroke.* See them deliver'd over
To execution and the hand of death.
Bushy. More welcome is the stroke of death to me
Than Bolingbroke to England."—*Richard II., III., 1.*

I well might hear, delivered with a groan,
  'O farewell, Warwick.' "--*III., K. Kenry VI., V., 2.*

" It is too late ; the life of all his blood
  Is touched corruptibly ; and his pure brain
  (Which some suppose the soul's frail dwelling house)
  Doth by the idle comments that it makes,
  Foretell the ending of mortality."—*K. John, V., 7.*

(The words " some suppose " exactly express Bacon's attitude, frankly avowed in his *Advancement of Learning,* Fourth Book : " But among those doctrines of union, or consent of soul and body, there is none more necessary than an inquiry into the proper seat and habitation of each faculty of the soul in the body and its organs. Some, indeed, have prosecuted this subject ; but all usually delivered upon it is either controverted or slightly examined, so as to require more pains and accuracy. The opinion of Plato, which seats the understanding in the brain, courage in the heart, and sensuality in the liver, should neither be totally rejected nor fondly received.")*

The following is Dame Quickly's account of Falstaff's death :

" 'A made a finer end, and went away, an it had been any christom child ; 'a parted just between twelve and one, e'en at the turning o' the tide : for after I saw him fumble with the sheets, and play with flowers, and smile upon his finger ends, I know there was but one way ; for his nose was as sharp as a pen, and 'a babbled of green fields.

---

* " — when liver, brain, and heart,
These sovereign thrones, are all supplied and fill'd — "
                                —*Twelfth Night, I., 1.*
" *Ford.* Love my wife !
  Pistol. With liver burning hot."
                                —*Merry Wives of Windsor, II., 1.*
" *Biron.* This is the liver vein which makes flesh a deity."
                                —*L. L. L., IV., 3.*
" *Ferdinand.* I warrant you, sir ;
  The white cold virgin snow upon my heart
  Abates the ardor of my liver."—*Tempest. IV., 1.*

So 'a cried out—God, God, God! I hoped there was no need
to trouble himself with any such thoughts yet: so 'a bade
me lay more clothes on his feet: I put my hand into the
bed and felt them, and they were as cold as any stone ;
then I felt to his knees, and so upward, and upward, and
all was as cold as any stone."—*K. Henry V., II., 3.*

Dr. J. C. Bucknell's elegant comment on this passage,
in his *Medical Knowledge of Shakespeare*, is pertinent :

"There is no small amount of medical knowledge in
Mistress Quickly's account of Sir John's exit from the
stage of life ; knowledge, indeed, conveyed in language so
quaintly humorous that it might easily be overlooked.
. . . What a fine touch of nature there is in the repro-
bate old knight ' babbling on green fields ' in his last delirium ; the impressions of early years, of innocent happiness flitting through his brain ; the last of life's memories
fading into the first, as the twilight of eve sometimes
touches that of morn. It is remarkable what good sense
and exact observation Shakespeare constantly puts into
the mouths of his vulgar characters."

May we not also remark the entrance of this real vision
through the gate of horn ? Indeed, have we not at last
within tangible grasp one of the *sources* of the Poet's
power ? The foliage put forth upon this " princely trunk "
was developed out of primal nutriment, drawn from the
hard subsoil, through patient, painstaking drudgery, and
therefore, with unshrivelled verdure, it has withstood the
withering blast of centuries, not a leaf falling to the
ground.

Bacon continues his observations : " Death is succeeded
by deprivation of all sense and motion, as well of the *heart
and arteries* as of the nerves and limbs, by inability of
the body to support itself upright, by stiffness of the
nerves and parts, by loss of all warmth, and soon after by
putrefaction and stench."

" Death, death, O amiable, lovely death !
Thou odoriferous stench!"—*K. John, III., 4.*

"Ha! let me see her:—out, alas! she's cold;
Her blood is settled, and her joints are stiff;
Life and these lips have long been separated:
Death lies on her, like an untimely frost
Upon the sweetest flower of all the field."
—*Romeo and Juliet, IV., 5.*

"Oft have I seen a timely-parted ghost,
Of ashy semblance, meagre, pale and bloodless,
Being all descended to the laboring heart;
Who, in the conflict that it holds with death,
Attracts the same for aidance 'gainst the enemy;
Which with the heart there cools and ne'er returneth
To blush and beautify the cheek again."
—*II., Henry VI., III., 2.*

"Take thou this phial, being then in bed,
And this distilled liquor drink thou off:
When, presently, through all thy veins shall run
A cold and drowsy humor; for no pulse
Shall keep his native progress, but surcease;
No warmth, no breath, shall testify thou livest;
The roses in thy lips and cheeks shall fade
To paly ashes; thy eyes' windows fall,
Like death, when he shuts up the day of life;
Each *part*, deprived of subtle government,
Shall, stiff, and stark, and cold, appear like death:
And in this borrow'd likeness of shrunk death
Thou shalt continue two and forty hours,
And then awake as from a pleasant sleep."
—*Romeo and Juliet, IV., 1.*

He continues: "There have been many instances of men who have been left for dead, laid out, and carried forth to burial; nay, of some who have been actually buried, that have come to life again. . . . A physician still alive told me that by the use of *frictions and warm baths he had recovered* a man who had hung himself and had been suspended for half an hour."

"Death may usurp on nature many hours,
And yet the fire of life kindle again
The o'erpress'd spirits. I have heard of an Egyptian
That had nine hours lien dead,

Who was *by good appliances recovered."*
—*Pericles, III., 2.*

And in the same connection: "I remember *to have heard* of a gentleman who, being curious to know what the sensation of hanging was, hung himself, by mounting on a stool and jumping off, thinking, of course, that he would be able to regain the stool as soon as he liked; but this he was unable to do, and he was only released by a friend who was present. On being asked what he had suffered, he said that he felt *no pain*, but that at first he saw around him the appearance of fire burning, which was succeeded by an intense blackness or darkness, and then by a kind of pale or sea-green color, such as is also seen by fainting persons."

Out of the jaws of death (so narrowly escaped in a foolish "experiment") Bacon drew honey, gathering therefrom "light and information." The "sweet" in the following verse is the riddle: its solution gives us the secret of his strength:

"*Luc.* Art thou sorry for these heinous deeds?
Aaron. Ay, that I had not done a thousand more."

"*Luc.* Bring down the devil, for he must not die
So sweet a death as hanging presently."
—*Tit. Andron., V., 1.*

"The death that is most *without pain* hath been noted to be upon taking the portion of hemlock; which in humanity was the form of execution of capital offenders in Athens. The poison of the Asp, that Cleopatra used, hath some affinity with it. The cause is, for that the *torments* of death are chiefly raised by the strife of the spirits; and these vapors quench the spirits by degrees; like to the death of an extreme old man."—*Natural History*, 643.

"*Cleopatra.* Hast thou the pretty worm of Nilus there,
That kills and *pains not?*"

"Peace, peace!
Dost thou not see my baby at my breast,

9

That sucks the nurse asleep?
As sweet as balm, as soft as air, as gentle,—"
" *Cæsar.*   Most probable
That so she died; for her physician tells me
She hath pursued conclusions infinite
Of *easy ways* to die."—*Ant. and Cleo., V., 2.*

We conclude with one of nature's occasional notes from a song of a sweeter cadence, whose subtle, evanescent melody Bacon caught and recorded in his *Wisdom of the Ancients:*

" And this part of the allegory has a further meaning which is striking and noble; namely, that in the case of persons who suffer for religion, the words which they speak at their death, like the song of the dying swan, have a wonderful effect and impression upon men's minds, and dwell longer in their memory and feelings ":

" Holy men at their death have good inspirations."
—*Mer. of Ven., I., 2.*

" O, but they say the tongues of dying men
Enforce attention, like deep harmony:
Where words are scarce, they are seldom spent in vain;
For they breathe truth, that breathe their words in *pain.*
He, that no more must say, is listen'd more
Than they whom youth and ease have taught to glose;
More are men's ends marked, than their lives before:
The setting sun and *music at the close,*
(As the last taste of sweets is sweetest) last,
Writ in remembrance, more than things long past;
Though Richard my life's counsel would not hear,
My death's sad tale may yet *undeaf his ear.*"
—*Richard II., II., 1.*[*]

---

[*] In the closing scene of *Othello,* when Emilia would convince the Moor of Desdemona's innocence, dying, she cries:

" Hark, canst thou hear me?   I will play the swan,
And die in music: '*Willow, willow, willow.*'—
Moor, she was chaste; she lov'd thee, cruel Moor;
So come my soul to bliss, as I speak true;
So speaking as I think, I die,—I die. |*Dies.*"

The wretched Moor, all doubt dispelled, wounds Iago and then kills himself.

CHAPTER III.—Continued.

OLD AGE.

THE following is from Bacon's *History of Life and Death:*

"Lastly, since it is convenient to know the character and form of old age; which will be done best *by making a careful collection of all the differences in the state and functions of the body between youth and old age,* that by them you may see what it is that branches out into so many effects."

"The differences between youth and old age are these: A young man's skin is even and smooth, an old man's dry and wrinkled, especially about the eyes and forehead; a young man's flesh is soft and tender, an old man's hard; youth has strength and activity, old age decay of strength and slowness of motion; youth has a strong, old age a weak digestion; a young man's bowels are soft and succulent, an old man's salt and parched; in youth the body is erect, in old age bent into a curve; a young man's limbs are firm, an old man's weak and trembling; in youth the humors are billious and the blood hot, in old age the humors are phlegmatic and melancholy, and the blood cold; a young man's sexual passions are quick, an old man's slow; in youth the juices of the body are more roscid, in old age more crude and watery; in youth the spirit is plentiful and effervescent, in old age poor and scanty; in youth the spirit is dense and fresh, in old age dull and impaired; a young man's teeth are strong and perfect, an old man's weak, worn, and falling out; a young man's hair is colored, an old man's (whatever color it formerly was) white; youth has hair, old age baldness; in youth the pulse beats stronger and quicker, in old age weaker and slower, a young man's illnesses are more acute and curable, an old man's chronic and hard to cure; in youth, wounds heal fast, in old age slowly; a young man's cheeks are fresh colored, an old man's pale or rubicund, and the blood thick; youth is less troubled with rheums, age more so. Neither, as far as I know, does age bring any improvement to the body unless it be sometimes in fatness."

(Note also in the following exemplifications the continued antithesis between old age and youth.)

"A good leg will fall; a straight back will stoop; a black beard will turn white; a curled pate will grow bald; a fair face will wither; a full eye will wax hollow."—*Henry V., V., 2.*

"*Falstaff.* You that are old consider not the capacities of us that are young: you measure the heat of our livers with the bitterness of your galls: and we that are in the vanward of our youth, I must confess, are wags too.

" *Ch. Justice.* Do you set down your name in scroll of youth, that are written down old with all the characters of age? Have you not a moist eye? a dry hand? a yellow cheek? a white beard? a decreasing leg? an increasing belly? Is not your voice broken? your wind short? your chin double? your wit single? and every part about you blasted with antiquity? And will you yet call yourself young? Fie, fie, Sir John."—*II., Henry IV., 1., 2.*

"*Falstaff.* Your lordship, though not clean past your youth, hath yet some smack of age in you, some relish of the *saltness* of time."—*Id.*

> "why I desire thee
> To give me secret harbor, hath a purpose
> More grave and wrinkled than the aims and ends
> Of burning youth."—*Measure for Measure, I., 4.*

> "Thou art Hermione; or, rather thou art she
> In thy not chiding; for she was as tender
> As infancy and grace,— But yet, Paulina,
> Hermione was not so much wrinkled; nothing
> So aged as this seems."— *Winter's Tale, V., 3.*

> "And for an old aunt, whom the Greeks held captive,
> He brought a Grecian queen, whose youth and freshness

Wrinkles Apollo's, and makes stale the morning."
— *Troil. and Cress.*, *II.*, *2.*

"Let it stamp wrinkles in her brow of youth."
—*K. Lear*, *I.*, *4.*

"Thou bring'st happiness and peace, Sir John;
But health, alack, with youthful wings is flown
From this bare withered trunk."
—*II., Henry IV.*, *IV.*, *4.*

"To shake all cares and business from our age;
Conferring them on younger strength, while we
Unburden'd crawl towards death."—*K. Lear*, *I.*, *1.*

"Son of sixteen,
Pluck the lined crutch from thy old limping sire." *
—*Tim. of Athens*, *IV.*, *1.*

"that stale old mouse-eaten dry cheese, Nestor,"
—*Troil. and Cress.*, *V.*, *4.*

"I will now take my leave of these six dry, round, old withered knights."—*II., Henry IV.*, *II.*, *4.*

"We had like to have had our two noses snapped off with two old men without teeth."—*Much Ado*, *V.*, *1.*

"*Nurse.* I'll lay fourteen of my teeth —
And yet, to my teen be it spoken, I have but four —
She is not fourteen."—*Romeo and Juliet*, *I.*, *3.*

"*Dromio.* There's no time for a man to recover his hair, that grows bald by nature.

Ant. May he not do it *by fine and recovery?*

Dromio. Yes, to pay a fine for a periwig, and recover the lost hair of another man. . . .

---

* "The scale or succession of stages in the human body is this; conception, . . . gray hairs and baldness, cessation of the menstrua and of the generative power, tendency to decrepitude and *a three-legged animal*, death. In the meantime the mind also has its periods, though they cannot be described by years; as a failing memory and the like, of which hereafter."—*History of Life and Death.*

"Last scene of all,
That ends this strange eventful history,
Is second childishness and mere oblivion;
Sans teeth, *sans* eyes, *sans* taste, *sans* everything."
—*As You Like It*, *II.*, *7.*

Ant. But your reason was not substantial, why there is no time to recover.

Dromio. Thus I mend it: Time himself is bald, and therefore, to the world's end, will have bald followers."— *Com. of Errors, II., 2.*

" Thou canst help time to furrow me with age,
But stop no wrinkle in his pilgrimage."
—*Richard II., I., 3.*

" To let the wretched man outlive his wealth,
To view with hollow eye and wrinkled brow,
An age of poverty."—*Merchant of Venice, IV., 1.*

" That so his sickness, age, and impotence."
—*Hamlet, II., 2.*

" When sapless age, and weak unable limbs,
Should bring thy father to his drooping chair."
—*I., Henry VI., IV., 5.*

" That he is old (the more the pity) his white hairs do witness it."—*I., Henry IV., II., 4.*

" Why, how now, Kate? I hope thou art not mad;
This is a man, old, wrinkled, faded, wither'd;
And not a maiden, as thou say'st he is."
—*Taming of the Shrew, IV., 5.*

" *Hamlet.* Slanders, sir: for the satirical slave says here, that old men have gray beards; that their faces are wrinkled; their eyes purging thick amber, or plum-tree gum; and that they have a plentiful lack of wit, together with weak hams: all which, sir, though I most powerfully and potently believe, yet I hold it not honestly to have it thus set down; for you yourself, sir, should be old as I am, if, like a crab, you could go backward.

Polonius. Though this be madness, yet there is method in it."
—*Hamlet, II., 2.*

Bacon continues the record of his observations:

" Next in order comes the consideration of the affections of the mind. I remember when I was a young man at Poictiers in France that I was very intimate with a young Frenchman of great wit, but somewhat talkative, who afterwards turned out a very eminent man. He used to inveigh against the manners of old men, and say that if their minds could be seen as well as their bodies, they would appear no less deformed; and further indulging his fancy, he argued that the defects of their minds had some parallel and correspondence with those of the body. To dryness of the skin he opposed impudence; to hardness of the bowels, hardness of the heart; to blear eyes,* envy, and the evil eye; to sunken eyes and bowing of the body to the ground, atheism (for they no longer, he says, look up to heaven); to the trembling of the limbs, vacillation of purpose and inconstancy; to the bending and clutching of the fingers, rapacity and avarice; to the tottering of the knees, timidity; to wrinkles, cunning and crooked ways; and other parallels which do not now occur to me. But to be serious; youth has modesty and a sense of shame, old age is somewhat hardened; a young man has

---

* "*Bru.* All tongues speak of him, and the bleared sights
   Are *spectacled* to see him."—*Coriolanus, II., 1.*

A characteristic blunder. Spectacles were not invented till towards the close of the thirteenth century. See *Enc. Brit.*, Article, *Spectacles.* In his Essay, *Of Friendship*, Bacon says: "It was well said by Themistocles to the King of Persia, 'That speech was like the cloth of Arras, opened and put abroad; whereby the imagery doth appear in figure; whereas in thoughts they lie but as in packs.'"

In Bohn's edition of the Essays, Devey, the editor, says in a note: "Speaking hypercritically, Lord Bacon commits an anachronism here, as Arras did not manufacture tapestry till the middle ages."

For other mistakes see also the same edition, pages 101, 118, 172, 173, 175, 180, 182, 184, 189.

Abbott, Bacon's biographer, says of him: "We have absolute proof that he was eminently inattentive to details. His scientific works are full of inaccuracies. King James found in this defect of his Chancellor the matter for a witticism: '*De Minimis non curat lex.*' [The law cares not for trifles.]"

In his *Notes for a Conference with Buckingham*, Bacon gracefully accepts the joke, in these words: "You know the King was wont to do me the honor as to say of me *de minimis non curat lex;* if good for anything for great volumes. I cannot thridd needles so well."

kindness and mercy, an old man has become pitiless and callous; youth has a praiseworthy emulation, old age an ill-natured envy; youth is inclined to religion and devotion by reason of its fervency and inexperience of evil, in old age piety cools through the lukewarmness of charity and long intercourse with evil, together with the difficulty of believing; a young man's wishes are vehement, an old man's moderate; youth is fickle and unstable, old age more grave and constant; youth is liberal, generous, and philanthropic, old age is covetous, wise for itself, and self-seeking; youth is confident and hopeful, old age diffident and distrustful; a young man is easy and obliging, an old man churlish and peevish; youth is frank and sincere, old age cautious and reserved; youth desires great things, old age regards those that are necessary; a young man thinks well of the present, an old man prefers the past; a young man reverences his superiors, an old man finds out their faults; and there are many other distinctions which belong rather to manners than the present inquiry. Nevertheless as old men in some respects improve in their bodies, so also in their minds, unless they are quite worn out. For instance, though less ready in invention, yet they are more powerful in judgment, and prefer a safe and sound to a specious course. They increase likewise in talkativeness and ostentation; for being less fit for action they look for fruit of speech; so it was not without reason that the poets represented Tithonus as transformed into a grasshopper."

A sad picture, truly, of old age, as here mirrored from life! For Bacon was a close, keen observer of human nature, as it was developed in the characteristics of those about him; religiously determined upon the observation of things themselves, "to receive their images truly as they are." We must therefore, perforce, accept these observations as a correct transcript of life, especially as they are repeatedly interwoven in the fabric of the plays, forming a part of the coloring of their pattern.

But if we are not mistaken, in our day, and especially in America,—due perhaps to the marked amelioration of the conditions of life, the broadening of its interests, the better developing and more widely extended culture, and above all, to the growing recognition of ethical principles and their better observance,—old age is now more attractive, sweeter, mellower, and in many ways more expressive of nature's analogy in the rich, golden autumn of the seasons.

If this be so, then are Bacon's observations invaluable: they stand forth as a landmark or milestone, by whose bearings we may note the moral progress of the race.

The following are a few examples of their utilization in the plays:

"*Falstaff.* A man can no more separate age and covetousness, than he can part young limbs and lechery."—*II., Henry VI., I., 2.*

"*Verg.* Yes, I thank God, I am as honest as any man living, that is an old man, and no honester than I.

Leon. Neighbors, you are *tedious.*"—*Much Ado, III., 5.*

" and I begin to love, as an old man loves money, with no stomach."—*All's Well, III., 2.*

"Banish your dotage; banish usury,
That makes the senate ugly."—*Timon of Athens, III., 5.*

" And, for I know your reverend ages love security,
I'll pawn my victories, all my honor to you,
Upon his good returns."—*Id.*

" Pity not honor'd age for his white beard.
He's an usurer."—*Id., IV., 3.*

" Well, thou shalt see, thy eyes shall be the judge,
The difference of *old* Shylock and Bassanio."
—*Merchant of Venice, II., 5.*

" Where Hotspur's father, old Northumberland,
Lies crafty-sick."—*II., Henry IV., Induction.*

" That villainous abominable misleader of youth,
Falstaff, that old white-bearded Satan."—*Id., II., 4.*

"I know thee not, old man : fall to thy progress ;
How ill white hairs become a fool and jester !
I have long dreamed of such a kind of man,
So surfeit swell'd, so old, and so profane."—*Id.*, *V.*, *5.*

"*Page.* Old, cold, withered, and of intolerable entrails?
Ford. And one that is as slanderous as Satan?"
                              —*Merry Wives, V., 5.*

"Hast thou forgot
The foul witch Sycorax, who, with age and envy,
Was grown into a hoop?"—*Tempest, I., 2.*

"Old I do wax ; and from my weary limbs
Honor is cudgell'd."—*Henry V., V., 2.*

"I do see the bottom of Justice Shallow. How subject we
old men are to the vice of lying! This same starved justice
hath done nothing but prate to me of the wildness of his youth,
and the feats he hath done about Turnbull Street ; and every
third word a lie, duer paid to the hearer than the Turk's tribute."—*II., Henry IV., III., 2.*

"*Flavius.* They answer in *a joint and corporate* voice
That now they are at fall, want treasure, cannot
Do what they would ; . . .
Timon.   You Gods reward them !
Pr'ythee, man, look cheerily ! These old fellows
Have their ingratitude in them hereditary :
Their blood is caked, 't is cold, it seldom flows,
'T is lack of kindly warmth, they are not kind ;
And nature, as it grows again towards earth,
Is fashioned for the journey, dull and heavy."
                              —*Timon of Athens, II., 2.*

"And thy unkindness be like crooked age."
                              —*Richard II., II., 1.*

"And let them die that age and sullens have ;
For both hast thou, and both become the grave."—*Id.*

"*Pandarus.* A tisick, a rascally tisick so troubles me, and
the foolish fortunes of this girl ; and what one thing, what another, that I shall leave you one o' these days : and I have a
rheum in mine eyes too ; and such an ache in my bones, that
unless a man were cursed, I cannot tell what to think on 't."—
Troil. and Cress., V., 3.

The Nurse, in *Romeo and Juliet,* is an admirable illustration of garrulity in old age; and to quote briefly from Mrs. Jamison: "Her low humor, her shallow garrulity, mixed with dotage and petulancy of age — her subserviency, her secrecy, and her total want of elevated principle, or even common honesty — are brought before us like a living palpable truth."

(Bacon further observes, in his *History of Life and Death:* " And certainly as old men are generally talkative and garrulous, so talkative persons very often grow to a great age; for it betokens a light contemplation, and one that does not greatly distress or vex the spirits: whereas subtle, acute, and eager inquisition shortens life; for it fatigues and preys upon the spirits."

> " *Gratiano.* You look not well, signior Antonio:
> You have too much respect upon the world:
> They *lose* it that do buy it with much care.
> Believe me, you are marvelously changed.
>
> *Antonio.* I hold the world but as the world, Gratiano;
> A stage, where every man must play a part,
> And mine a sad one.*
>
> *Gratiano.*   Let me play the Fool: †

* See *ante,* page 62.

† " Moreover the course of life should, if possible, be so ordered that it may have many and various restorations; and the spirits may not grow torpid by perpetual intercourse with the same things. For though Seneca said well, ' A fool is always beginning to live,' yet this folly, like many others, *contributes to longevity."—History of Life and Death.*

" I am sure care 's an enemy to life."—*Twelfth Night, I., 3.*

> "*Ros.* You 'll ne'er be friends with him; he kill'd your sister.
> *Kath.* He made her melancholy, sad, and heavy;
> And so she died: had she been *light*, like you,
> Of such a merry, nimble, stirring spirit,
> She might have been a grandam ere she died:
> And so may you; *for a light heart lives long."*
> —*L. L. L., V., 2.*

> " And frame your mind to mirth and merriment,
> Which bars a thousand harms, and *lengthens life."*
> — *Taming of the Shrew, Induction.*

With mirth and laughter let old wrinkles come;
And let my liver rather heat with wine,
Than my heart cool with mortifying groans.
Why should a man, whose blood is warm within,
Sit like his grandsire cut in alabaster?
Sleep when he wakes? and creep into the jaundice
By being peevish."—*Merchant of Venice, I., 1.*

" Though I look old, yet am I strong and lusty:
For in my youth I never did apply
Hot and rebellious liquors in my blood:
Nor did not in unbashful forehead woo
The means of weakness and debility;
Therefore my age is as a lusty winter,
Frosty but kindly."—*As You Like It, II., 3.*[*])

" You cannot call it love: for at your age
The hey-day in the blood is tame, it's humble,
And waits upon the *judgment.*"—*Hamlet, III., 4.*

" *Othello.* Give me your hand: this hand is moist, my lady.
Desd. It yet has felt no age, nor known no sorrow.
Oth. This argues fruitfulness and *liberal heart:*
Hot, hot, and moist: this hand of yours requires
A *sequester* from liberty, fasting and prayer,
Much castigation, exercise devout;
For here's a young and sweating devil here,
That commonly rebels. 'Tis a good hand,
A *frank* one."—*Othello, III., 4.*

" The brain may devise laws for the blood; but a hot temper leaps o'er a cold decree: such a hare is madness, the youth, to skip o'er the meshes of good counsel, the cripple."—*Merchant of Venice, I., 2.*

---

[*] " As therefore strong drink, spices, and the like, *inflame the spirits and shorten life*, so, on the other hand, nitre composes and restrains the spirits and tends to longevity."

" Now the spirits are continued in the same state by restraint of the affections, temperance of diet, abstinence from sexual intercourse, refraining from labor, and moderate rest. They are overpowered and altered by the contrary; namely, by violent affections, profuse feasting, immoderate indulgence of the sexual appetite, arduous labors, intense study and business."—*History of Life and Death.*

"Had she affections and warm youthful blood,
She would be as swift in motion as a ball;
My words would bandy her to my sweet love,
And his to me.
But old folks, many feign as they were dead;
Unwieldy, slow, heavy and pale as lead."
—*Romeo and Juliet*, II., 5.

"for youth no less becomes
The light and careless livery that it wears,
Than settled age his sables, and his weeds,
Importing health and graveness."—*Hamlet, IV., 7.*

"There is not a white hair on your face but should have his effect of gravity."—*II., Henry IV., I., 2.**

"To approve my youth further I will not: the truth is, I am old in judgment and understanding."—*Id.*

"Old folks you know have discretion, as they say, and know the world."—*Merry Wives, II., 2.*

"though I now be old and of the peace."—*Id., II., 3.*

"As you are old and reverend, you should be wise."
—*King Lear, I., 4.*

"*Polonius.* It seems it is as proper to our age
To cast beyond ourselves in our opinions,
As it is common for the younger sort
To lack discretion."—*Hamlet, II., 1.*

"Young in limbs, in judgment old."
—*Merchant of Venice, II., 7.*

"I never knew so young a body with so old a head."
—*Id., IV., 1.*

"As venerable Nestor, hatch'd in silver,
Should with a bond of air, strong as the axle-tree
On which the heavens ride, knit all Greeks' ears
To his experienced tongue."—*Troil. and Cress., I., 3.*

---

* "*Shallow.* I have lived fourscore years and upward; I have never heard a man of his place, gravity, and learning, so wide of his own respect."—*Merry Wives of Windsor, III., 1.*

("Be not, Sir, a mean to prefer to those places for any by-respect; but only such as for their learning, gravity, and worth are deserving."—*Letter to Villiers.*)

" *Met.* O let us have him ; for his silver hairs
Will purchase us a good opinion,
And buy men's voices to commend our deeds :
It shall be said his judgment ruled our hands ;
Our youths and wildness, shall no whit appear,
But all be buried in his gravity.

Brutus. O, name him not ; let us not break with him ; *
For he will never follow anything
That other men begin."—*Julius Cæsar, II., 1.*

We close with an appropriate refrain, from the Poet's *Passionate Pilgrim :*

" Crabbed age and youth
　　Cannot live together ;
Youth is full of pleasance,
　　Age is full of care :
Youth is like summer morn,
　　Age like winter weather ;
Youth like summer brave,
　　Age like winter bare.
Youth is full of sport,
Age's breath is short ;
　　Youth is nimble, age is lame :
Youth is hot and bold,
Age is weak and cold ;
　　Youth is wild and age is tame.
Age, I do abhor thee,
Youth, I do adore thee ;
　　O, my love, my love is young !
Age, I do defy thee ;
O, sweet shepherd, hie thee,
　　For, methinks thou stay'st too long."

---

* See *ante,* page 87, note.

NOTE.—Hope, one of the trinity of man's spiritual blessings, is another subject that receives peculiar treatment in many passages in the plays :

" The ample proposition that hope makes
In all designs begun on earth below,
Fails in the promised largeness."
　　　　　　　　　—*Troil. and Cress., I., 3.*

" But, by your leave, it never yet did hurt,
To lay down likelihoods, and forms of hope."
—*II., Henry IV., I., 3.*

" I will despair, and be at enmity
With cozening hope ; he is a flatterer,
A parasite, a keeper back of death,
Who gently would dissolve the bands of life,
Which false hope lingers in extremity."
—*Richard II., II., 2.*

" Do not satisfy your resolution with hopes that are fallible."
—*Measure for Measure, III., 1.*

" Hope is a curtal dog in some affairs."
—*Merry Wives, II., 1.*

" Even here I will put off my hope, and keep it
No longer for my flatterer."—*Tempest, III., 3.*

" Thoughts speculative their unseen hopes relate ;
But certain issue, strokes must arbitrate."— *Macb., V., 4.*

" Oft expectation fails, and most oft there
Where most it promises ; and oft it hits
Where hope is coldest, and despair most fits."
—*All's Well, II., 1.*

" And hope to joy is little less in joy
Than hope enjoyed."—*Richard II., II., 3.*

" *Duke.* So then you hope of pardon from Lord Angelo?
Claud. The miserable have no other medicine,
But only hope :
I have hope to live, and am prepared to die.
Duke. Be absolute for death ; either death or life,
Shall thereby be the sweeter."— *Meas. for Meas., IV., 1.*

But Bacon gives valid reasons for this peculiar view of hope.
In his Meditation, *Of Earthly Hope,* he says :

" The sense which *takes everything simply as it is* makes a
better mental condition and estate than those imaginations and
wanderings of the mind. . . . But in hope there seems to be
no use. For what avails that anticipation of good? If the
good turn out less than you hoped for, good though it be, yet
because it is not *so* good, it seems to you more like a loss than
a gain, by reason of the overhope. If neither more nor less, but
so ; the event being equal and answerable to the hope : yet the

flower of it having been by that hope already gathered, you find it a stale thing and almost distasteful. If the good be beyond the hope, then no doubt there is a sense of gain: true: yet had it not been better to gain the whole by hoping not at all, than the difference by hoping too little? . . . Certainly in all delay and expectation, to keep the mind tranquil and steadfast by the good government and composure of the same, I hold to be the chief firmament of human life; but such tranquility as depends upon hope I reject, as light and unsure. Not but it is fit to see and presuppose upon sound and sober conjecture good things as well as evil, that we may the better fit our actions to the probable event: only this must be the work of the understanding and judgment, with a just inclination of the feeling. But who is there whose hopes are so ordered that when once he has concluded with himself out of a vigilant and steady consideration of probabilities that better things are coming, he has not dwelt upon the very anticipation of good, and indulged in that kind of thought as in a pleasant dream? And this it is which makes the mind light, frothy, unequal, wandering. Therefore all hope is to be employed *upon the life to come* in heaven: but here on earth, by how much purer is the sense of things present, without infection or tincture of imagination, by so much wiser and better is the soul.

> Long hope to cherish in so short a span
> Befits not man."

(See also *Works*, Vol. 4, p. 382; Vol. 5, pp. 48, 203, 279; Vol. 6, p. 751.)

And among his *Apothegms* is the following: "There were fishermen drawing the river at Chelsea: Mr. Bacon came thither by chance in the afternoon, and offered to buy their draught: They were willing. He asked them what they would take? They asked thirty shillings. Mr. Bacon offered them ten. They refused it. 'Why then,' saith Mr. Bacon, 'I will be only a looker on.' They drew and catched nothing. Saith Mr. Bacon: 'Are you not mad fellows now, that might have had an angel in your purse, to have made merry withal, and to have warmed you thoroughly, and now you must go home with nothing.' 'Ay but,' said the fishermen, 'we had hope then to make a better gain of it.' Saith Mr. Bacon: 'Well, my masters, then I'll tell you, hope is a good breakfast, but it is a bad supper.'"

THE FLOWERS IN THEIR SEASONS.

Many other like topics might be presented in further illustration, but their effect would be merely cumulative. There is room for but one more, presented in somewhat different form because of its threefold guise. Bacon's observations of the Flowers in their Seasons appear unadorned in his *Natural History*, clothed in sober prose in his Essay, *Of Gardens*, and in the bright garb of poetry in *The Winter's Tale*. The Essay and the Poem are Literature, and the three, taken together, form an unique object lesson in its study. We can only present them in order, leaving to the reader to note their characteristic variations.

Natural History, § 577 : "*Experiment in consort touching the seasons in which plants come forth:* There be some flowers, blossoms, grains, and fruits, which come more early, and others which come more late in the year. The flowers that come early with us are primroses, violets, anemones, water-daffodillies, crocus vernus, and some early tulippas. And they are all cold plants; which therefore (as it should seem) have a quicker perception of the heat of the sun increasing than the *hot* herbs have; as a cold hand will sooner find a little warmth than a hot. And those that come next after are wall-flowers, cowslips, hyacinths, rosemary flowers, etc. ; and after them pinks, roses, flower-de-luces, etc. ; and the latest are gilly-flowers, holly-oaks, larks-foot, etc. The earliest blossoms are the blossoms of peaches, almonds, cornelians, mezerions, etc. ; and they are of such trees as have much moisture, either watery or oily. And therefore crocus vernus also, being an herb that hath an oily juice, putteth forth early ; for those also find the sun sooner than the drier trees." "§ 592 : Of plants, some are green all winter ; others cast their leaves. There are green all winter, holly, ivy, box, fir, yew, cypress, juniper, bays, rosemary, etc. The cause of the holding green is the close and compact substance of their leaves, and the pedicles of them."

Essay, *Of Gardens:* "God Almighty first planted a
Garden. And indeed it is the purest of human pleasures.
It is the greatest refreshment to the spirits of man; without which buildings and palaces are but gross handy-
works: and a man shall ever see that when ages grow to
civility and elegancy, men come to build stately sooner
than to garden finely; as if gardening were the greater
perfection. I do hold it, in the royal ordering of gardens,
there ought to be gardens for all the months in the year;
in which severally things of beauty may be then in season.
For December, and January, and the latter part of November, you must take such things as are green all winter: holly; ivy; bays; juniper; cypress-trees; yew; pine
apple-trees: fir-trees; rosemary; lavender; periwinkles,
the white, the purple, and the blue; germander; flags;
orange-trees; lemon-trees; and myrtles, if they be stoved;
and sweet majorum, warm set. There followeth, for the
latter part of January and February, the mezereon-tree,
which then blossoms; crocus vernus, both the yellow and
the grey; primroses; anemones; the early tulippa; hya-
cinthus orientalis; chamaïris; fritellaria. For March,
there come violets, specially the single blue, which are the
earliest; the yellow daffodil; the daisy; the almond-tree
in blossom; the peach-tree in blossom; the cornelian-tree
in blossom; sweet-briar. In April follow the double
white violet; the wall-flower; the stock-gilliflower; the
cowslip; flower-de-luces, and lilies of all natures; rose-
mary-flowers; the tulippa; the double piony; the pale daffodil; the French honeysuckle; the cherry-tree in blossom;
the dammascene and plum-trees in blossom; the white thorn
in leaf; the lilac-tree. In May and June come pinks of
all sorts, specially the blush-pink; roses of all kinds, except the musk, which comes later; honeysuckles; straw-
berries; bugloss; columbine; the French marigold; flos
Africanus; cherry-tree in fruit; ribes; figs in fruit; rasps;
vine-flowers; lavender in flowers; the sweet satyrian, with
the white flower; herba muscaria; lilium convallium; the
apple-tree in blossom. In July come gilliflowers of all

varieties; musk-roses; the lime-tree in blossom; early pears and plums in fruit; genitings, codlins. In August come plums of all sorts in fruit; pears; apricots; barberries; filberds; musk-melons; monks-hoods, of all colors. In September come grapes; apples; poppies of all colors; peaches; melocotones; nectarines; cornelians; wardens; quinces. In October come services; medlars; bullaces; roses cut or removed to come late; holly-oaks; and such like. These particulars are for the climate of London; but my meaning is perceived, that you may have *ver perpetuum*, as the place affords. And because the breath of flowers is far sweeter in the air (where it comes and goes like the warbling of music) than in the hand, therefore nothing is more fit for that delight, than to know what be the flowers and plants that do best perfume the air," etc.

A Winter's Tale, IV., 3:

> "*Perdita. (To Polixenes).* Sir, welcome!
> It is my father's will I should take on me
> The hostess-ship o' the day.—*(To Camillo)*
> You're welcome, sir!—
> Give me those flowers there, Dorcas.—Reverend sirs,
> For you there's rosemary, and rue; these keep
> Seeming, and savor, *all the winter long:*
> Grace, and remembrance be to you both,
> And welcome to our shearing!
> *Pol.*   Shepherdess,
> (A fair one are you) well you fit our ages
> With flowers of winter.
> *Per.*   Sir, the year growing ancient,—
> Not yet on summer's death, nor on the birth
> Of trembling winter,— the fairest flowers o' the season
> Are our carnations, and streak'd gillyvors,
> Which some call nature's *bastards:* o' that kind
> Our rustic garden's barren; and I care not
> To get slips of them."

("Take gilly-flower seed, of one kind of gilly-flower, (as of the clove-gilly-flower, which is the most common), and sow it; and there will come up gilly-flowers, some of

one color and some of another, casually, as the seed meeteth nourishment in the earth; so that the gardeners find
that they may have two or three roots amongst an hundred that are rare and of great price; as purple, *carna-
tion of several stripes:* the cause is (no doubt) that in
earth, though it be contiguous and in one bed, there are
very several juices; and *as the seed doth casually meet
with them*, so it cometh forth."—*Natural History*, § 510.)

> " *Pol.*   Wherefore, gentle maiden,
> Do you neglect them?
> *Per.*   For I have heard it said,
> There is an *art* which, in their piedness, shares
> With great creating nature."

("Amongst curiosities I shall place coloration, though it
be somewhat better; for beauty in flowers is their pre-
eminence. It is observed by some, that gilly-flowers,
sweet-williams, violets, that are colored, if they be neglected, and neither watered, nor new moulded, nor trans-
planted, will turn white. *And it is probable that the
white with much culture may turn colored.* For this is
certain, that the white color cometh of scarcity of nourishment; except in flowers that are only white, and admit
of no other colors.* It is good, therefore, to see what
natures do accompany what colors; for by that you shall
have light *how to induce colors, by producing those natures.*"—*Natural History*, § 506–7.)

> " *Pol.*   Say, there be;
> Yet nature is made better by no mean,
> But nature makes that mean: so, over that art,

---

* " She, in my judgment, was as fair as you;
But since she did neglect her looking-glass,
And threw her sun-expelling mask away,
The air hath *starved* the roses in her cheeks."
—*Two Gentlemen of Verona, IV.*, 4.

(" So blue violets and other flowers, if they be starved, turn
pale and white."—*Natural History*, § 93.)

> Which, you say, adds to nature, is an art
> That nature makes."

("All I mean is, that nature, like Proteus, is forced by art to do that which without art would not be done; call it which you will,—force and bonds, or help and perfection. . . . As for instance, when a man makes the appearance of a rainbow on a wall by the sprinkling of water, nature does the work for him, just as much as when the same effect is produced in the air by a dripping cloud; and on the other hand when gold is found pure in sands, nature does the work for herself just as much as if it were refined by the furnace and human appliances. Sometimes again the ministering office is by the law of the universe deputed to other animals; for honey, which is made by the industry of the bee, is no less artificial than sugar, which is made by man; and in manna (which is a thing of like kind) nature asks no help, but does all herself. Therefore, as nature is one and the same, and her power extends through things, nor does she ever forsake herself, these three things should by all means be set down as all alike subordinate only to nature; namely, the course of nature; the wandering of nature; and art, or nature with man to help."—*Description of the Intellectual Globe.*) *

> "You see, sweet maid, we marry
> A gentle scion to the wildest stock;
> And make conceive a bark of baser kind
> By bud of nobler race: this is an art
> Which does mend nature,—change it rather: but
> The art itself is nature."

("As grafting doth generally advance and meliorate fruits, above that which they would be if they were set of kernels or stones, in regard the nourishment is better concocted; so (no doubt), even in grafting, for the same cause, the choice of the stock doth much; *always pro-*

---

* The attentive reader will discern that, not only observations, but inductions therefrom, or in other words, sound philosophy, is an element properly entering into the composition of the truest poetry.

vided that it be somewhat inferior to the scion; for otherwise, it dulleth it.   They commend much the grafting of pears or apples upon a quince."— *Natural History*, § 467.

"For art, which is meant by Alanta, is in itself, if nothing stand in the way, far swifter than nature, and, as one may say, the better runner, and comes sooner to the goal.   For this may be seen in almost everything; you see that fruit grows *slowly from the kernel, swiftly from the graft;* you see clay hardens slowly into stones, fast into baked bricks: so also in morals, oblivion and comfort of grief comes by nature in length of time ; but philosophy (which may be regarded as the art of living) does it without waiting so long, but forestalls and anticipates the day."— *Wisdom of the Ancients*, XXV.) *

> "*Per.*   So it is.
> *Pol.* Then make your garden rich in gillyvors,
> And do not call them bastards.
> *Per.*   I'll not put
> The dibble in earth to set one slip of them:
> No more than, were I *painted*, I would wish
> This youth to say, 't were well; and only therefore
> Desire to breed by me."

(A delicate touch : see above "the white with much culture may turn *colored*.")

>   — "Here's flowers for you;
> *Hot* lavender, mints, savory, marjoram;

---

* "*Brutus.* O Cassius, I am sick of many griefs.
Cassius. Of your *philosophy* you make no use,
If you give place to accidental evils.
Brutus. No man bears sorrow better:—Portia is dead. . . .
Why, farewell, Portia,—We must die, Messala :
With meditating that she must die once,
I have the patience to endure it now.
Mes. Even so great men great losses should endure.
Cassius. I have as much of this in *art* as you,
But yet my *nature* could not bear it so."
                          — *Julius Cæsar, IV., 3.*

The marigold, that goes to bed with the sun,
And with him rises weeping; "

("Some of the ancients and likewise divers of the
modern writers that have labored in natural magic, have
noted a sympathy between the sun, moon, and some principal stars, and certain herbs and plants. And so they
have denominated some herbs 'solar' and some 'lunar':
and such like toys put into great words. It is manifest
that there are some flowers that have respect to the sun;
in two kinds; the one by opening and shutting, and the
other by bowing and inclining the head. For *marygolds*,
tulippas, pimpernal, and indeed most flowers, do open
or spread their leaves abroad when the sun shineth serene
and fair: and again (in some part) close them or gather
them inward, either towards night, or when the sky is
overcast. Of this there needeth no such solemn reason
to be assigned, as to say that they rejoice at the presence
of the sun, and mourn at the absence thereof. For it is
nothing else but a little loading of the leaves and swelling them at the bottom with the *moisture* of the air;
whereas the dry air doth extend them."— *Natural History*, § 493.)

" these are the flowers
Of *middle summer*, and, I think, they are given
To men of middle age: you are very welcome.
Cam. I should leave grazing, were I of your flock,
And only live by gazing.
Per.   Out, alas!
You'd be so lean, that blasts of January
Would blow you through and through.—
      Now, my fairest friend,
I would I had some flowers o' the spring, that might
Become your time of day; and yours, and yours;
That wear your virgin branches yet,
Your maidenheads growing: O, Proserpina,
For the flowers now, that, frighted, thou let'st fall
From Dis's wagon! "

(" Seizing his opportunity therefore, while Proserpina,
daughter of Ceres, a fair virgin, was gathering flowers of

Narcissus in the Sicilian meadows, he [Pluto] rushed
suddenly upon her and carried her off in his *chariot* to
the subterranean regions.   Great reverence was paid her
there: so much that she was even called the Mistress or
Queen of Dis."— *Wisdom of the Ancients—Proserpina.*

   " And it was a beautiful thought to choose the flower
of *spring* as an emblem of characters like this: characters
which in the opening of their career flourish and are talked
of, but disappoint in maturity the promise of their *youth*."
—*Id.—Narcissus.*)

<blockquote>
" daffodils,
That come before the swallow dares, and take
The winds of *March* with beauty ; violets dim
But sweeter than the lids of Juno's eyes,
Or Cytherea's breath ; "
</blockquote>

(" That which, *above all others*, yields the sweetest smell
in the air is the violet, especially the *white* double violet,
which comes twice a year, about the middle of April, and
about Bartholomew-tide."— *Of Gardens.*)*

---

* " That breathes upon a bank of violets,
   Stealing and giving odor."
                    —*Twelfth Night, I., 1.*
" The violet smells to him as it doth to me."
                    —*Henry V., IV., 1.*
" A violet in the *youth* of primy nature,
   Forward, not permanent, sweet, *not lasting*,
   The perfume and suppliance of a minute."
                    —*Hamlet, I., 3.*
" To gild refined gold, to paint the lily,
   To throw a perfume on the violet,"
                    —*King John, IV., 2.*

" But purposing to be at Chiswick (where I have taken a
house) within this seven nights, I hope to wait upon your Lordship, and to gather some violets in your garden."—*Letter to
the Lord Treasurer.*

Bacon was not only a lover of flowers and music, but his sensitive organization was so highly attuned, that his chaplain, Dr.
Rawley, relates of him what seems almost incredible:

" It may seem the moon had some principal place in the figure

" pale primroses,
That die unmarried, ere they can behold
Bright Phœbus in his strength, a malady
Most incident to maids ; "

(" The general color of plants is green, which is a color
that no flower is of. There is a greenish primrose, but it
is *pale*, and scarce a green."—*Natural History*, § 512.)

" bold oxlips, and
The crown imperial; lilies of all kinds,
The flower-de-luce being one! Oh! these I lack,
To make you garlands of ; and my sweet friend,
To strew him o'er and o'er."

That this poetic picture may appear all the brighter by
contrast, we complete its sober frame by a return to prose ;
quoting, " to point a moral," the following terse exposition of a higher order of gardening, the comparative value
of which cannot be over-estimated :

" Our bodies are our gardens ; to the which our wits
are gardeners : so that if we will plant nettles, or sew let-
tuce ; set hyssop, and weed up thyme ; supply it with one
gender of herbs, or distract it with many ; either to have
it sterile with idleness, or manured with industry ; why,
the power and corrigible authority of this lies in our wills."*

of his nativity : for the moon was never in her passion, or
eclipsed, but he was surprised with a sudden fit of fainting ; and
that, though he observed not nor took any previous knowledge
of the eclipse thereof; and as soon as the eclipse ceased, he
was restored to his former strength again."—Dr. Rawley's *Life
of Bacon.*

Of this, Spedding says, in a note:

" Of course Rawley's statement is not sufficient to prove
the reality of any such connection (between the eclipse and his
fainting) ; but the fact of the fainting-fits need not be doubted,
and may be fairly taken, I think, as evidence of the extreme
delicacy of Bacon's temperament, and its sensibility to the skyey
influences."

* " How weary, stale, flat, and unprofitable
Seems to me all the uses of this world !
Fie on 't ! O fie ! 't is an unweeded garden,

That grows to seed; things rank, and gross in nature,
Possess it merely."—*Hamlet, I., 2.*

" Oh! what pity is it,
That he had not so trimm'd and dress'd his land,
As we this garden!   We at time of year
Do wound the bark, the skin of our fruit-trees;
Lest, being over-proud with sap and blood,
With too much riches it confound itself:
Had he done so to great and growing men,
They might have lived to bear, and he to taste
Their fruits of duty.   Superfluous branches
We lop away, that bearing boughs may live:
Had he done so, himself had borne the crown,
Which waste and idle hours hath quite thrown down."
                     —*Richard II., III., 4.*

One other brief example must be added, peculiarly significant, because it embodies a bit of Bacon's original philosophy
of plant life.   In his *Natural History,* he observes:

" This we see manifestly, that there be certain cornflowers
which come seldom or never in other places, unless they be set,
but only amongst corn: as the blue-bottle, a kind of yellow mary-
gold, wild poppy, and fumitory. Neither can this be by reason of
the culture of the ground, by ploughing or furrowing; as some
herbs and flowers will grow but in ditches new cast; for if the
ground lie fallow and unsown, they will not come: *so as it
should seem to be the corn that qualifieth the earth, and pre-
pareth it for their growth.*"

This observation is utilized in *King Lear, IV., 4:*

" Alack, 'tis he; why he was met even now
As mad as the vex'd sea: singing aloud;
With harlocks, hemlock, nettles, cuckoo-flowers,
Darnel, and all the idle weeds that grow
In our sustaining corn."

Indeed, as to these "works of the alphabet," Bacon's words
regarding "fame" are alike applicable:

" There be a thousand such like examples, and the more they
are the less they need to be repeated, because a man meeteth
with them everywhere."

(It may be well to note that Bacon's *Natural History* was
not published until after his death.)

CHAPTER IV.

HAVING studied, all too briefly, the alphabet of the plays, let us now advance a step and take up their *Primer;* leaving the successive Readers to their orderly development. For this purpose we have chosen the subject of Envy, to which Bacon, an experienced courtier, gave especial attention.

Nowadays, we look upon what we call envy rather disdainfully; regarding it as odious indeed, something from which we would personally be exempt; as base, unseemly, and belittling; but taking small pains to guard ourselves against it in others. We even speak admiringly of another, as " occupying an enviable position." But to Bacon, envy was a baneful *activity*, the incarnation of malice, the very apple of the " evil eye "; emitting a subtle, malign influence, whose venomous ray was to be warded off, even as one would guard against the machinations of the devil. It is needless to add that this view is continually reflected in the plays. In brief, in the italics of Dr. W. J. Rolfe, the eminent Shakespearean scholar : " *Envy* has here the sense often borne by the Latin *invidia*, or nearly the same with *hatred* or *malice*,— the sense in which it is almost always used by Shakespeare."

> " As is the bud bit with an envious worm,
> Ere he can spread his sweet leaves to the air,
> Or dedicate his beauty to the sun."

In his Essay, *Of Envy*, Bacon utilized his observations in the development of its *science;* unfolding the principles underlying its activity. In the play of *Julius Cæsar*, these same principles are given *representation* in operation ; the original observations being wrought into new creations, that are faithful reproductions of the life they mirror. The play partakes of the complexity of life, with its intricate interplay of many motives, and is therefore almost as great a puzzle.

But the Essay is the key to its mysteries: it fits perfectly the tumblers in the lock. By its use we are ushered at once into its innermost recesses, where we discern that Envy is its dominant chord, its quickening spirit, indeed the baneful fire kindling the whole conflagration, and that *Cassius* is its embodiment.

As is unavoidable in the study of a primer, we must first spell out its sentences : all the rest is then easy, and the task at length becomes a joy. Accordingly, we will take up *seriatim* the salient principles as they are successively developed in the Essay, and, in each instance, look into the play for their corresponding representation in the action.

The Essay opens with a general introduction defining the nature of envy :

" There have been none of the affections which have been noted to *fascinate* or *bewitch*, but love and envy. They both have vehement wishes ; they frame themselves readily into imaginations and suggestions ; and they come easily into the eye, especially upon the presence of the objects : which are the points that conduce to fascination, if any such thing there be.* We see likewise the scrip-

---

* " *Fascination* is the power and act of imagination intensive upon the body of another (for of the power of imagination upon the body of the imaginant I have spoken above) ; wherein the school of Paracelsus and the disciples of pretended natural magic have been so intemperate, that they have exalted the power and apprehension of the imagination to be much one with the power of miracle-working faith. Others that draw nearer to probability, looking with a clearer eye at the secret workings and impressions of things, the irradiations of the senses, the passage of contagion from body to body, the conveyance of magnetic

ture calleth envy an *evil eye ;** and the astrologers call
the evil influences of the stars evil aspects ; so that still
there seemeth to be acknowledged in the *act* of envy, an
ejaculation or irradiation of the eye. Nay, some have been
so curious as to note, that the times when the stroke or
percussion of an envious eye doth most hurt, are when the
party envied is *beheld in glory or triumph ;* for that sets
an edge upon envy : and besides, at such times the spirits of the person envied do come forth most into the outward parts, and so meet the blow."†

---

virtues, have concluded that it is much more probable there
should be impressions, conveyances, and communications from
spirit to spirit (seeing that the spirit is above all other things
both strenuous to act and soft and tender to be acted on) ; whence
have arisen those conceits (now become as it were popular) of
the mastering spirit, of men unlucky and ill omened, of the
glances of love, envy, and the like."— *De Augmentis.* Fourth
Book.

" But more than that, he [Perkin] had such a crafty and be-
witching fashion, both to move pity, and to induce belief, as
was a kind of fascination and enchantment to those that saw
him or heard him."—*History of Henry VII.*

" And yet boldness is a child of ignorance and baseness, far
inferior to other parts : but, nevertheless, it doth fascinate, and
bind hand and foot those that are either shallow in judgment
or weak in courage, which are the greatest part ; yea, and prevaileth with wise men at weak times."—*Of Boldness.*

"So that they seem to have spoken either figuratively, or
under the influence of fascination ; the stronger impression carrying the rest with it."—*On Principles and Origins.*

See also *Advancement of Learning,* Second Book, and the
whole of Century X.. *Natural History.*

* See *Proverbs* 23, 6–8 ; *Mark* 7, 21, 22.

† " Forth at your eyes your spirits wildly peep."
—*Hamlet, III., 4.*

" Your spirits shine through you."—*Macbeth, III., 1.*

" Her wanton spirits look out
At every joint and motive of her body."
—*Troil. and Cress., IV., 5.*

Julius Cæsar, *Act I.*, *Scene 1*:

"*Flavius.* Is this a holiday?"

"*Citizen.* But, indeed, sir, we make holiday, to see Cæsar, and to rejoice in his *triumph*."

"*Mar.* And do you now put on your best attire?
And do you now cull out a holiday?
And do you now strew flowers in his way,
That comes in *triumph* over Pompey's blood?"

"*Flav.* Go you down that way towards the Capitol;
This way will I : disrobe the images,
If you do find them deck'd with ceremonies.
Mar. May we do so?
You know it is the feast of Lupercal.
Flav. It is no matter; let no images
Be hung with Cæsar's trophies.   I'll about,
And drive away the vulgar from the streets;
So do you too, where you perceive them thick,
These growing feathers pluck'd from Cæsar's wing
Will make him fly an ordinary pitch;
*Who else would soar above the view of men,
And keep us all in servile fearfulness.*"

"*Brutus.* What means this shouting?   I do fear the people
Choose Cæsar for their king."

"*Brutus.* Another general shout!
I do believe that these applauses are
For some new honors that are heap'd on Cæsar."

                                        —*Id.*, *I.*, *2.*

The Essay continues: "But leaving these curiosities (though not unworthy to be thought on in fit place)* we will handle, what persons are apt to envy others; what persons are most subject to be envied themselves; and what is the difference between public and private envy.

"A man that hath no virtue in himself, ever envieth virtue in others.   For men's minds will either feed upon their own good or upon other's evil; and who wanteth the one will prey upon the other; and whoso is out of hope to attain to another's virtue, will seek to come at even hand by depressing another's fortune."

* See especially, *Natural History*, § 944.

In the play, Cassius' character is disclosed in a few effective touches:

> "*Brutus.* Let me tell you, Cassius, you yourself
> Are much condemn'd to have an itching palm:
> To sell and mart your offices for gold
> To undeservers."

> "The name of Cassius honors this *corruption*,
> And chastisement doth therefore hide his head."

> "What, shall one of us,
> That struck the foremost man of all this world,
> But for supporting robbers, shall we now
> Contaminate our fingers with base bribes,
> And sell the mighty space of our large honors,
> For so much trash as may be grasped thus?—
> I had rather be a dog and bay the moon
> Than such a Roman."

> "Go, show your slaves how choleric you are,
> And make your bondmen tremble. Must I budge?
> Must I observe you? Must I stand and crouch
> Under your testy humor? By the gods,
> You shall digest the venom of your spleen,
> Though it do split you! for, from this day forth,
> I'll use you for my mirth, yea, for my laughter,
> When you are waspish."

> "I did send
> To you for gold to pay my legions,
> Which you denied me: was that done like Cassius?
> Should I have answer'd Caius Cassius so?
> When Marcus Brutus grows so *covetous*,
> To lock such rascal counters from his friends,
> Be ready, gods, with all your thunderbolts,
> Dash him to pieces!
> *Cassius.*   I denied you not.
> *Brutus.* You did.
> *Cassius.* I did not:—he was but a fool
> That brought my answer back."—*Id., IV., 3.*

> "*Cassius.* You know that I hold Epicurus strong,
> And his opinion:* now I change my mind,

---

* "But Epicurus, accommodating and subjecting his natural to his moral philosophy (as appears from his own words), would

And partly credit things that do presage.
Coming from Sardis, on our former ensign
Two mighty eagles fell; and there they perch'd,
Gorging and feeding from our soldiers' hands,
Who to Philippi have consorted us;
This morning are they fled away and gone;
And in their steads do ravens, crows, and kites,
Fly o'er our heads, and downward look on us,
As we were sickly prey; their shadows seem
A canopy most fatal, under which
Our army lies, ready to give up the ghost.*
(*Brutus advancing.*)
Cassius.   Now, most noble Brutus,
The gods to-day stand friendly; that we may.
Lovers in peace, lead on our days to age!"—*Id., V., 1.*

" *Brutus.* [*Speaking of Cassius*]. Thou hast described
A hot friend cooling; ever note, Lucilius,
When love begins to sicken and decay,
It useth an enforced ceremony.
There are no tricks in plain and simple faith:
But *hollow* men, like horses hot at hand,
Make gallant show and promise of their mettle:
But when they should endure the bloody spur,
They fall their crests, and, like deceitful jades,
Sink in the trial."—*Id., IV., 2.*

" *Cassius.* Casca, be sudden, for we fear prevention.—
Brutus, what shall be done? If this be known,

not willingly admit any *opinion* that depressed or hurt the
mind, and troubled or disturbed that *Euthumia* of his, which
he had adopted from Democritus. And so being more fond of
enjoying the sweets of thought than patient of the truth, he
fairly threw off the yoke, and rejected both the necessity of
Fate and the fear of the gods."—*De Augmentis,* Second Book.
See also *Works,* Vol. 3, p. 241; Vol. 5, pp. 13, 18.

* " Divination hath been anciently and fitly divided into artificial and natural; whereof artificial is when the mind maketh
a prediction by argument, concluding upon signs and tokens;
. . . such as were the heathen observations upon the inspection
of sacrifices, *the flight of birds,* the swarming of bees; and
such as was the Chaldean Astrology, and the like."—*Advancement of Learning,* Second Book.

Cassius or Cæsar never shall turn back,
For I will slay myself.
Brutus.   Cassius, be constant:
Papilius Lena speaks not of our purposes."
                                    — *Id., III., 1.*

"*Cassius.* When Cæsar lived he durst not thus have moved me.
Brutus. Peace, peace! you durst not so have tempted him.
Cassius. I durst not?
Brutus. No.
Cassius. What? durst not tempt him?
Brutus. For your life you durst not."—*Id., IV., 3.*

' *Cassius.* Pardon, Cæsar: Cæsar, pardon:
As low as to thy foot does Cassius fall,
To beg enfranchisement for Publius Cimber."
                                    — *Id., III., 1.*

"*Cassius.* Why now, blow, wind; swell billow; and swim, bark!
The storm is up, and all is on the hazard."—*Id., V., 1.*

"*Cassius.* Go, Pindarus, get higher on that hill,
My sight was ever thick; regard Titinius,
And tell me what thou not'st about the field.—
This day I breathed first: time is come round,
And where I did begin there shall I end;
My life is run his compass."

"*Cassius.* Come down, behold no more.—
O, coward that I am, to live so long,
To see my best friend ta'en before my face!"

"*Tit.* These tidings will well comfort Cassius.
Mes. Where did you leave him?
Tit.   All disconsolate,
With Pindarus, his bondsman, on this hill.
Mes. Is not that he that lies upon the ground?
Tit.   No, this was he, Messala,
But Cassius is no more."

"*Mes.* Mistrust of good success hath done this deed."
                                    —*Id., V., 3.*

"*Octavius.*   So I hope;
I was not born to die on Brutus' sword.
Brutus. O, if thou wert the noblest of thy strain,
Young man, thou couldst not die more honorable.
Cassius. A peevish school-boy, worthless of such honor,

Join'd with a masker and a reveller.
Antony. Old Cassius still!"—*Id., V., 1.*

"A man that is busy and inquisitive is commonly envious. For to know much of other men's matters cannot be because all that ado may concern his own estate; therefore it must needs be that he taketh a kind of play-pleasure in looking upon the fortunes of others. Neither can he that mindeth but his own business find much matter for envy. For envy is a gadding passion, and walketh the streets, and doth not keep home: *Non est curiosus, quin idem sit malevolus:* (There is no curious man but has some malevolence to quicken his curiosity.)"

"*Flavius.* Speak, what trade art thou?
Mar. Where is thy leather apron, and thy rule?
What dost thou with thy best apparel on? —
You, sir; what trade are you?"

"But what trade art thou? Answer me directly."

"What trade thou knave? thou naughty knave, what trade?"

"*Flavius.* Thou art a cobbler, art thou?"

"But wherefore art not in thy shop to-day?
Why dost thou lead these men about the streets?"

"*Mar.* Wherefore rejoice? What conquest brings he home?
What tributaries follow him to Rome,
To grace in captive bonds his chariot wheels?"—*Id., I., 1.*

"*Brutus.* The games are done, and Cæsar is returning.
Cassius. As they pass by, pluck Casca by the sleeve;
And he will, after his sour fashion, tell you
What hath proceeded worthy note to-day."

"*Casca.* You pulled me by the cloak: would you speak with me?
Brutus. Ay, Casca; tell us what hath chanced to-day,
That Cæsar looks so sad?
Casca. Why, you were with him, were you not?
Brutus. I should not then ask Casca what had chanced.
Casca. Why, there was a crown offered him: and being offered him, he put it by with the back of his hand, thus; and then the people fell a shouting.
Brutus. What was the second noise for?
Casca. Why, for that too.

Cassius. They shouted thrice: what was the last cry for?
Casca. Why, for that too.
Brutus. Was the crown offered him thrice?
Casca. Ay, marry, was 't, and he put it by thrice, every time gentler than other; and at every putting by, mine honest neighbors shouted.
Cassius. Who offered him the crown?
Casca. Why, Antony.
Brutus. Tell us the manner of it, gentle Casca.
Casca. I can as well be hanged as tell the manner of it: it was mere foolery; I did not mark it . . . and still as he refused it, the rabblement shouted, and clapped their chapped hands, and threw up their *sweaty* night-caps, and uttered such a deal of *stinking breath* because Cæsar refused the crown, that it had almost choked Cæsar; for he swooned, and fell down at it; and for mine own part, I durst not laugh, for fear of opening my lips and receiving the bad air.*
Cassius. But, soft, I pray you: what? Did Cæsar swoon?

---

* "Out of question, if such foul smells be made by art and by the hand, they consist chiefly of man's flesh or *sweat* putrified; for they are not those stinks which the nostrils straight abhor and expel, that are most pernicious; but such airs as have some similitude with man's body, and, so insinuate themselves, and betray the spirits. There may be great danger in using such compositions in great meetings of people within houses; as in churches, at arraignments, at plays and solemnities, and the like: for poisoning of air is no less dangerous than poisoning of water, which hath been used by the Turks in the wars, and was used by Emanuel Comneus towards the Christians, when they passed through his country to the Holy Land. And these empoisonments of air are the more dangerous in meetings of people, because the much *breath* of people doth further the reception of the infection; and therefore, where any such thing is feared, it were good those public places were perfumed, before the assemblies." *Natural History,* § 915. (See *Antony and Cleopatra, V., 2.*) "It hath long been confirmed by divers trials, that the root of the male piony dried, tied to the neck, doth help the *falling sickness;* and likewise the incubus, which we call the mare. The cause of both these diseases, and especially of the epilepsy from the stomach, is *the grossness of the vapors which rise and enter into the cells of the brain.*"—§ 966.

Casca. He fell down in the market-place, and foamed at the mouth, and was speechless.

Brutus. 'T is very like : he hath the falling-sickness.

Cassius. No, Cæsar hath it not; but you and I,
And honest Casca, we have the falling sickness."

" *Brutus.* What said he when he came unto himself?

Casca. Marry, before he fell down, when he perceived the common herd was glad he refused the crown, he plucked me ope his doublet, and offered them his throat to cut,—. . .

Brutus. And after that he came thus sad away?

Casca. Ay.

Cassius. Did Cicero say anything?

Casca. Ay, he spoke in Greek.

Cassius. To what effect?

Casca. Nay, an I tell you that I 'll ne'er look you i' the face again : . . . There was more foolery yet, if I could remember it.

Cassius. Will you sup with me to-night, Casca?"—*Id.*, *I.*, *2.*

" *Cassius.* Who 's there?

Casca. A Roman.

Cassius. Casca, by your voice.

Casca. Your ear is good. Cassius, what night is this?

Cassius. A very pleasing night to honest men.

Casca. Who ever knew the heavens menace so?

Cassius. Those that have known the earth so full of faults.
For my part, *I have walked about the streets,*
Submitting me unto the perilous night."—*Id.*, *I.*, *3.*

" Men of noble birth are noted to be envious towards new men when they rise. For the distance is altered ; and it is like a deceit of the eye, that when others come on they think themselves go back. Deformed persons,* and eunuchs, and *old* men and bastards † are envious."

" *Antony.* [*Speaking of Cassius.*]
Fear him not, Cæsar, he 's not dangerous ;
He is a noble Roman, and well given."—*Id.*, *I.*, *2.*

" *Cassius.* Now in the names of all the gods at once,
Upon what meat doth this our Cæsar feed,
That he is *grown* so great? Age, thou art shamed !

---

* See *King Richard III.*, *I.*, *1.*

† See *Edmund*, in *King Lear.*

Rome, thou hast lost the breed of noble bloods!
When went there by an age, since the great flood,
But it was famed with more than with one man?
When could they say, till now, that talk'd of Rome,
That her wide walks encompass'd but one man?
Now is it Rome indeed, and room enough,
When there is in it but one only man."—*Id.. I., 2.*

" *Cassius.* Those that with haste will make a mighty fire
Begin it with weak straws: what trash is Rome,
What rubbish, and what offal, when it serves
For the base matter to illuminate
So *vile* a thing as Cæsar!"—*Id., I., 3.*

" Lastly, near kinsfolks, and fellows in office, and those
that have been *bred together*, are more apt to envy their
equals when they are raised. For it doth upbraid unto
them their own fortunes, and pointeth at them, and cometh oftener into their remembrance, and incurreth likewise more into the note of others; and envy ever re-
doubleth from speech and fame."

" *Cassius.* For once upon a raw and gusty day,
The troubled Tiber chafing with her shores,
Cæsar said to me, ' Dar'st thou, Cassius, now
Leap in with me into this angry flood,
And swim to yonder point?'— Upon the word,
Accoutred as I was, I plunged in,
And bade him follow: so, indeed, he did.
The torrent roar'd; and we did buffet it
With lusty sinews; throwing it aside,
And stemming it with hearts of controversy.
But ere we could arrive the point proposed,
Cæsar cried, ' Help me, Cassius, or I sink.'
I, as Æneas, our great ancestor,
Did from the flames of Troy upon his shoulder
The old Anchises bear, so, from the waves of Tiber
Did I the tired Cæsar: and this man
Is now become a god; and Cassius is
A wretched creature, and must bend his body,
If Cæsar carelessly but nod on him.
He had a fever when he was in Spain,
And, when the fit was on him, I did mark

How he did shake : 't is true, this god did shake :
His *coward* lips did from their color fly ;
And that same eye, whose bend doth awe the world,
Did lose his lustre : I did hear him groan :
Ay, and that tongue of his that bade the Romans
Mark him, and write his speeches in their books,[*]
' Alas !' it cried, 'give me some drink, Titinius,'
As a sick girl.   Ye gods, it doth amaze me,
A man of such a *feeble* temper should
So get the start of the majestic world,
And bear the palm *alone*."—*Id., I., 2.*

"Concerning those that are more or less subject to
envy : First, persons of eminent virtue, when they are
advanced, are less envied. For their fortune seemeth but
due unto them ; and no man envieth the payment of a
debt, but *rewards and liberality* rather.   Again, *envy is
ever joined with the comparing of a man's self;* and where
there is no comparison, no envy ; and therefore kings are
not envied but by kings."

"Persons of noble blood are less envied in their rising.
For it seemeth but due to their birth. Besides, *there
seemeth not much added to their fortune;* and envy is as
the sunbeams, that beat hotter upon a bank or *steep rising* ground, than upon a flat.   And for the same reason
those that are advanced by degrees are less envied than
those that are advanced suddenly and *per saltum*."

(See *ante*, "new honors that are heap'd on Cæsar.")

" *Cassius.* I cannot tell what you and other men
Think of this life ; but for my single self,
I had as lief not be as live to be
In awe of such a thing as I myself.
I was born free as Cæsar; so were you :
We both have fed as well ; and we can both

---

[*] " They that desire to excel in too many matters, out of levity
and vain glory, are ever envious.   For they cannot want work :
it being impossible but many in some one of those things should
surpass them.   Which was the character of Adrian the Emperor ; that mortally envied poets and painters and artificers,
in works wherein he had a vein to excel."—*Id.*

Endure the winter's cold as well as he:"

" Why, man, he doth bestride the narrow world,*
Like a Colossus; and we petty men
Walk under his huge legs, and peep about
To find ourselves dishonorable graves.
Men at sometime are masters of their fates:
The fault, dear Brutus, is not in our stars,
But in ourselves, that we are *underlings*.
' Brutus,' and ' Cæsar': what should be in that ' Cæsar'?
Why should that name be sounded more than yours?
Write them together, yours is as fair a name;
Sound them, it doth become the mouth as well;
Weigh them, it is as heavy; conjure with them,
' Brutus ' will start a spirit as soon as ' Cæsar.' "

—*Id., I., 2.*

" *Cassius.* Now could I, Casca, name to thee a man
Most like this dreadful night;
That thunders, lightens, opens graves, and roars
As doth the lion in the Capitol;
A man no mightier than thyself, or me,
In personal action; yet prodigious *grown*
And fearful, as these strange eruptions are.''—*Id., I., 3.*

" Above all, those are most subject to envy, which carry
the greatness of their fortunes in *an insolent and proud
manner;* being never well but while they are shewing
how *great* they are, either by outward pomp, or by tri-
umphing over all opposition or competition."

" *Cæsar.* I rather tell thee what is to be feared
Than what I fear, for always I am Cæsar."—*Id., I., 2.*

" *Cæsar.* Cæsar shall forth: the things that threaten'd me
Ne'er looked but on my back; when they shall see
The face of Cæsar, they are vanquished."

" *Cæsar.*   Danger knows full well
That Cæsar is more dangerous than he.
We are two lions litter'd in one day,
And I the elder and more terrible;
And Cæsar shall forth."

" *Cæsar.*   Shall Cæsar send a lie?

---

* " For this giant bestrideth the sea; and I would take him
by the foot on this side."—*Charge Touching Duels.*

Have I in conquest stretch'd mine arm so far,
To be afraid to tell greybeards the truth?
Decius, go tell them Cæsar will not come."

" The cause is in my will, I will not come;
That is enough to satisfy the senate."—*Id., II., 2.*

" *Cæsar.*   I must prevent thee, Cimber,
These couchings, and these lowly courtesies,
Might fire the blood of ordinary men,
And turn *pre-ordinance,* and *first decree,**
Into the law of children.   Be not fond,
To think that Cæsar bears such rebel blood,
That will be thawed from the true quality
With that which melteth fools; I mean sweet words,
Low crooked curtsies, and base spaniel-fawning.
Thy brother by decree is banished;

---

* " I believe . . . that out of his eternal and infinite goodness and love, purposing to become a Creator, and to communicate with his creatures, he *ordained in his eternal counsel,* that one person of the Godhead should in time be united to one nature and to one particular of his creatures: that so in the person of the Mediator the true ladder might be fixed, whereby God might descend to his creatures, and his creatures ascend to God."—*Confession of Faith.*

" As surely as my soul intends to live
With that dread King, *that took our state upon him.*
To free us from his Father's wrathful curse."
                              —*II., Henry VI.. III.. 2.*

" I charge you, as you hope to have redemption
By Christ's dear blood, shed for our grievous sins."
                              —*Richard III., I., 4.*

(Of this confession Spedding says: " To criticise the theology of it would be beyond my province.   But if anyone wishes to read a *summa theologiæ* digested into seven pages of the finest English of the days when its tones were finest, he may read it here.")

"—suffering him to foreknow some things as an unconcerned looker on, which he does not *predestine and preordain;* a notion not unlike the figment which Epicurus introduced into the philosophy of Democritus, to get rid of fate and make room for fortune."—*Meditation, Of Heresies.*

If thou dost bend, and pray, and fawn, for him,
I spurn thee like a cur, out of my way.
Know, Cæsar doth not wrong: nor without cause
Will he be satisfied."
" *Cæsar.* I could well be moved if I were as you;
If I could pray to move, prayers would move me;
But I am constant as the northern star,
Of whose true-fix'd and resting quality
There is no fellow in the firmament.
The skies are painted with unnumbered sparks,
They are all fire,* and every one doth shine;
But there's but one in all doth hold his place:
So, in the world: 't is furnish'd well with men,
And men are flesh and blood, and apprehensive;
Yet, in the number, I do know but one,
That unassailable holds on his rank,
Unshaked of motion: and, that I am he,
Let me a little show it,— even in this,
That I was constant Cimber should be banish'd
And constant do remain to keep him so."—*Id., III., 1.*

" Lastly to conclude this part; as we said in the beginning that the act of envy had somewhat in it of witchcraft, so, there is no other cure of envy but the cure of witchcraft; and that is, to remove the ' lot ' (as they call it) and to lay it upon another. For which purpose, the wiser sort of great persons bring in ever *upon the stage*

---

* " Another question is, are the stars true fires? a question however which requires some care to understand it rightly. For it is one thing to say that the stars are true fires; and another thing to say that the stars (admitting them to be true fires) exert all the powers and produce the same effects which common fire does. For the fire of the stars is pure, perfect, and native; whereas our fire is degenerate, like Vulcan thrown from heaven and halting with the fall. For if a man observe it, fire as we have it here is out of its place, trembling, surrounded by contraries, needy, depending for sustenance upon fuel and fugitive. Whereas in heaven fire exists in its true place, removed from the assault of any contrary body, *constant,* sustained by itself, and things like itself, and performing its proper operations freely and without molestation."--*Description of the Intellectual Globe.*

somebody upon whom to derive the envy that would come upon themselves; sometimes upon ministers and servants; sometimes upon *colleagues and associates;* and the like; and for that turn there are never wanting some persons of violent and undertaking natures, who, so they may have power and business, will take it at any cost."

" *(Exit Lepidus.)*
 Antony. This is a slight unmeritable man,
Meet to be sent on errands: is it fit,
The three-fold world divided, he should stand
One of the three to share it?
 Octavius.   So you thought him;
And took his voice, who should be prick'd to die,
In our black sentence and proscription.*
 Antony. Octavius, I have seen more days than you:
And though we lay these honors on this man,
To ease ourselves of divers slanderous loads,
He shall but bear them as the ass bears gold,
To groan and sweat under the *business,*
Either led or driven, as we point the way;
And having brought our treasure where we will,
Then take we down his load, and turn him off,
Like to the empty ass, to shake his ears,
And graze in commons.
 Octavius.   You may do your will;
But he's a tried and valiant soldier."—*Id., IV., 1.*

" We will add this in general, touching the affection of envy; that of all other affections it is the most importune and continual. For of other affections there is occasion given but now and then; and therefore it was well said, *Invidia festos dies non agit:* (Envy keeps no holidays:) for it is ever working upon some other. And it is also noted that love and envy do make a man *pine,* which other affections do not, because they are not so continual."

---

* * " For nothing increaseth envy more than an unnecessary and ambitious engrossing of business. And nothing doth extinguish envy more than for a great person to preserve all other inferior officers in their full rights and pre-eminences of their places. For by that means there be so many screens between him and envy."—*Id.*

" *Cæsar*. Let me have men about me that are *fat;*
Sleek-headed men, and such as sleep o' nights:
Yond' Cassius has a *lean* and hungry look;
He thinks too much: such men are dangerous.
Would he were *fatter;* — but I fear him not:
Yet if my name were liable to fear,
I do not know the man I should avoid
So soon as that *spare* Cassius. He reads much;
He is a great observer, and he looks
Quite through the deeds of men: he loves no plays,
As thou dost, Antony: he hears no music:
Seldom he smiles; and smiles in such a sort
As if he mock'd himself, and scorn'd his spirit
That could be moved to smile at anything.
*Such men as he be never at heart's ease
Whiles they behold a greater than themselves;*
And therefore are they very dangerous."—*Id.*, I., 2.

" It is also the vilest affection, and the most depraved ;
for which cause it is the proper attribute of the devil, who
is called ' The envious man, that soweth tares among the
wheat by night;' as it always cometh to pass, that envy
worketh *subtilly*, and *in the dark;* and to the prejudice
of good things, such as is the wheat."

" *Cassius*. Brutus, I do observe you now of late
I have not from your eyes that gentleness,
And show of love, as I was wont to have:
You bear too stubborn and too strange a hand
Over your friend that loves you."

" *Cassius*. Then, Brutus, I have mistook your passion ;
By means whereof this breast of mine hath buried
Thoughts of great value, worthy cogitations.
Tell me, good Brutus, can you see your face?
Brutus. No, Cassius: for the eye sees not itself,
But by reflection, by some other things.
Cassius. 'Tis just:
And it is very much lamented, Brutus,
That you have no such mirrors as will turn
Your hidden worthiness into your eye,
That you might see your shadow. I have heard,
That many of the best respect in Rome,
(Except immortal Cæsar), speaking of Brutus,

And groaning underneath this age's yoke,
Have wish'd that noble Brutus had his eyes.
Brutus. Into what dangers would you lead me, Cassius,
That you would have me seek into myself
For that which is not in me?
Cassius. Therefore, good Brutus, be prepared to hear:
And, since you know you cannot see yourself
So well as by reflection, I, your glass,
Will modestly discover to yourself
That of yourself which you yet know not of." *

" *Brutus.* But wherefore do you hold me here so long?
What is it that you would impart to me?
It it be aught toward the general good,
Set honor in one eye, and death i' the other,
And I will look on both indifferently:
For, let the gods so speed me as I love
The name of honor more than I fear death.
Cassius. I know that virtue to be in you, Brutus,
As well as I do know your outward favor.
Well, honor is the subject of my story,—"

" *Brutus.* That you do love me, I am nothing jealous;
What you would *work me to*, I have some aim;
How I have thought of this, and of these times,
I shall recount hereafter; for this present,
I would not, so with love I might entreat you,
Be any further moved.   What you have said,
I will consider; what you have to say,
I will with patience hear: and find a time
Both meet to hear and answer such high things.
Till then, my noble friend, chew upon this;
Brutus had rather be a villager,
Than to repute himself a son of Rome
Under these hard conditions, as this time
Is like to lay upon us.
Cassius. I am glad that my weak words

---

* " For who can by often looking in the glass discern and judge so well of his own favor, as another with whom he converseth? "—*Letter to Essex.*

" Yet nevertheless, I believe well that this your Lordship's absence will rather be a glass unto you to shew you many things whereof you may make use hereafter."—*Letter to Buckingham.*

Have struck but thus much show of fire from Brutus."
"*Brutus.* For this time I will leave you:
  To-morrow, if you please to speak with me,
  I will come home to you; or, if you will,
  Come home to me, and I will wait for you.
  Cassius. I will do so;—till then, think of the world.
                       [*Exit Brutus.*
  Well, Brutus, thou art noble; yet I see
  Thy honorable metal may be wrought
  From that it is disposed: therefore it is meet
  That noble minds keep ever with their likes:
  For who so firm that cannot be *seduced?*
  Cæsar doth bear me hard? but he loves Brutus:
  If I were Brutus now, and he were Cassius,
  He should not humor me.*   I will *this night,*
  In several hands, in at his window throw,
  As if they came from several citizens,
  Writings, all tending to the great *opinion*
  That Rome holds of his name; wherein obscurely
  Cæsar's ambition shall be *glanced* at;
  And, after this, let Cæsar seat him sure;
  For we will shake him, or worse days endure."
                       —*Id.,* I., 2.

("But certain it is, whether it be believed or no, that as *the most excellent of metals,* gold, is of all other the most pliant and most enduring to be *wrought;* so of all living and breathing substances, the perfectest (Man) is the most susceptible of help, improvement, impression, and alteration. . . . And as to the will of man, it is that which is most *maniable* and obedient; as that which admitteth most medicines to cure and alter it. The most sovereign of all is Religion, which is able to change and transform it in the deepest and most inward inclinations and motions. And next to that is *Opinion* and *Apprehension;* whether it be infused by tradition and institution, or wrought in by disputation and persuasion. And

---

* "The meaning seems to be, If I were in his position (a favorite with Cæsar), and he in mine (disliked by Cæsar), he should not cajole, or turn and wind me, as I now do him."—Craik's *The English of Shakespeare,* Rolfe's edition.

the third is *Example*, which transformeth the will of man into the similitude of that which is much observant and familiar towards it. And the fourth is, when one affection is healed and corrected by another; as when cowardice is remedied by shame and dishonor, or sluggishness and backwardness by *indignation and emulation;* and so of the like. And lastly, when all these means, or any of them, have *new framed or formed* human will, then doth custom and habit corroborate and confirm all the rest." —*Helps for the Intellectual Powers.)* *

"*Casca.* It is the part of men to fear and tremble
When the most mighty gods, by tokens, send
Such dreadful heralds to astonish us.

"*Cassius.* You are *dull*, Casca; and those sparks of life
That should be in a Roman you do want,
Or else you use not. You look pale and gaze,
And put on fear, and cast yourself in wonder,
To see the strange impatience of the heavens:
But if you would consider the true cause
Why all these fires, why all these gliding ghosts,
Why birds and beasts, from quality and kind;
Why old men, fools, and children calculate;
Why all these things change from their ordinance,
Their natures, and pre-formed faculties,
To monstrous quality; — why you shall find,
That heaven hath infused them with these spirits,
To make them instruments of fear and warning
Unto some monstrous state. . . .
Casca. 'Tis Cæsar that you mean; is it not, Cassius?"
"*Cassius.*　　　　　　　　But, O, *grief!*
Where hast thou led me? I, perhaps, speak this
Before a willing bondman: then I know
My answer must be made: but I am arm'd,
And dangers are to me indifferent.

---

* "And as in negotiation with others, men are *wrought by cunning, by importunity, and by vehemency;* so in this negotiation within ourselves men are undermined by Inconsequences, solicited and importuned by Impressions or Observations, and transported by Passion."—*Advancement of Learning,* Second Book.

Casca. You speak to Casca; and to such man
There is no fleering tell-tale. Hold my hand:
Be factious for redress of all these griefs:
And I will set this foot of mine as far
As who goes farthest.

Cassius.   There's a bargain made.
Now know you, Casca, *I have moved already*
Some certain of the noblest-minded Romans,
To undergo with me an enterprise
Of honorable-dangerous consequence,
And I do know by this they stay for me
In Pompey's porch: for now, this fearful *night*,
There is no stir or walking in the streets;
And the complexion of the element
Has favors, like the work we have in hand,
Most *bloody*, fiery, and most terrible."

" *Cinna.*   O, Cassius, if you could
But win the noble Brutus to our party —
Cassius. Be you content. Good Cinna, take this paper,
And, look you, lay it in the prætor's chair,
Where Brutus may but find it; and throw this
In at his window: set this up with wax
Upon old Brutus' statue; all this done.
Repair to Pompey's porch, where you shall find us.
Is Decius Brutus, and Trebonius there?
Cinna. All, but Metellus Cimber; and he's gone
To seek you at your house. Well, I will hie,
And so bestow these papers as you bade me.
Cassius. That done, repair to Pompey's theatre.
Come, Casca, you and I will yet, *ere day*,
See Brutus at his house: three parts of him
Is ours already; and the man entire,
Upon the next encounter, yields him ours.
Casca. O, he sits high in all the people's hearts:
And all that which would appear offence in us,
His countenance, like richest alchemy,
Will change to virtue and to worthiness.
Cassius. Him, and his worth, and our great need of him,
You have right well conceited. Let us go,
For *it is after midnight;* and ere day
We will awake him, and be sure of him."—*Id., 1., 3.*

This concludes the Essay : and the play closes with an unmistakable declaration of the dominant motive in the action, in Antony's luminous words over Brutus' body :

> " This was the noblest Roman of them all :
> All the conspirators, save only he,
> Did that they did in *envy* of great Cæsar ;
> He only, in a general honest thought,
> And common good to all, made one of them."

Our patient study of this Primer of the play has indeed brought us a rich reward.   In effect, this Master Architect has here opened to us his studio ; permitting us to enter and inspect his original plans and specifications, and to trace their fulfilment in the finished structure.   We are thus enabled to comprehend, perhaps as never before, the bearing and peculiar significance of this detail, and that, and the other, " the reason for their existence," and their essential relation to the whole, as directly contributory to the development of the theme.

We have grasped the underlying thought of the Poet ; and manifestly, the key to the mysteries of the play is now in our possession : and henceforward, our delightful study of its intricacies will be prosecuted from within, rather than from without its portals.

But while all is now so clear, we are confronted by the astonishing fact, readily verified, that the critics generally, wanting the key, have utterly failed to comprehend the true import of this play ; discerning neither its dominant motive, nor the principles underlying the development of its action.* The eminent German critic, A. W. Schlegel, a recognized authority in Dramatic Literature, whose ap-

---

* With the possible exception of Gervinus, the one great commentator upon the plays, who exhibits a thorough mastery of Bacon's prose, and in accordance, has shown the deepest insight into the Shakespeare.

preciative criticism did so much to awaken the admiration and love of the German people for the plays, is a good example. In his Lectures on *Dramatic Art and Literature*, he speaks thus intelligently :

" It was, generally speaking, the prevailing tendency of the time which preceded our own (and which has showed itself particularly in physical science), to consider everything having life as a mere accumulation of dead parts, to separate what exists only in connection and cannot otherwise be conceived, instead of penetrating to the central point and viewing all the parts as so many irradiations from it. Hence nothing is so rare as a critic who can elevate himself to the comprehensive contemplation of a work of art. Shakespeare's compositions, from the very depth of purpose displayed in them, have been especially liable to the misfortune of being misunderstood."

And yet, in his discussion of *Julius Cæsar*, in the same work, he does not mention envy, nor even hint at the possibility of its influence on Cassius ; whom he eulogizes as follows :

" After the overthrow of the external splendor and greatness of the conqueror and ruler of the world, *the intrinsic grandeur* of character of Brutus and Cassius is all that remains to fill the stage and occupy the minds of the spectators : suitably to their name, as the last of the Romans, they stand there, in some degree alone ; and the forming of a great and hazardous determination is more powerfully calculated to excite our expectation, than the supporting the consequences of the deed with heroic firmness."

And regarding the significance of the display of Cæsar's arrogance, he says :

" In the part of Cæsar several ostentatious speeches have been censured as unsuitable. But as he never appears in action, we have no other measure of his greatness than the impression which he makes upon the rest of the characters, and his peculiar confidence in himself."

Another and more recent example is equally illustrative.

The world is to-day graced by the presence of an artist
who confessedly stands foremost in his profession; a position won by arduous labor, diligent cultivation of his
talents, and a conscientious devotion to his work. Henry
Irving is an ardent admirer of the plays, giving to their
interpretation the closest study : and yet, in his recent edition of the Shakespeare—a model of elegance, culture, and
scholarship—in the analysis of *Julius Cæsar*, written by
Messrs. Adams and Marshall, accomplished Shakespearean critics, no mention whatever is made of envy, nor any
suggestion of its bearing upon the action. The significance of Cæsar's demeanor also remains a mystery. A
single brief quotation must suffice :

" The treatment of the living Cæsar by the poet, however, has been a puzzle to many of the critics. . . . If
he is to impress us as verily ' great Cæsar,' it must be by
what he says, not by what he does, and by what he says
when there is no occasion for grand or heroic utterance.
Under the circumstances, a little boasting and bravado appears to be necessary to his being recognized as the Roman
Dictator."

But who of us can throw any stones at these " glass
houses " ? Were we not also upon the outside, until we
gained entrance through Bacon's gate of horn; following the pathway he so kindly blazoned for us?

The explanation is not far to seek. Life's problem is
a far greater puzzle, with its thousand intricacies of interfering motives, passions and affections. And we begin
to realize that this master of the human heart, alone, in
all the world, had resolved the particular enigma of envy ;
unravelling its strand from the tangled skein, and becoming familiar with its characteristics, its color, its peculiar
texture, and its wonted combinations and ramifications.
With this strand thus in hand, he was enabled to inter-
weave it in a new fabric of his own creation ; and in such

perfect similitude to life's pattern, that, for three centuries, its really simple intricacies have been equally puzzling to the world. It was only because he had solved the greater problem, that he was enabled to puzzle us with the lesser.

And how wonderfully has he cleared up for us somewhat of the mystery of Art! showing us, by his methods, its legitimate domain, its limitations, and its essential principles! In brief, he takes out of the universe a real thing, in this case, one of man's "affections," and embodies it in a creation of his own; an organism, in which this entity is given growth, development, and expansion, according to the laws of its nature.

His work, in an important sense, is a *revelation*. It is not a photograph of nature. The thousand and one extraneous matters, that would fill such a picture, are dropped out of sight, and only those are utilized which contribute towards the designed development. All the elements are true to life, because they are drawn directly from it; but over and beyond this, they are each given that specific form, that peculiar cast, which will contribute its essential shade of expression to the thing represented, — in what Taine calls the whole of Art: "concentration of manifestation."

The thing given representation is a fragment of nature's kingdom; reëmbodied in the similitude of its original connections; put under a magnifying glass, if you please, that we may the more clearly discern its essential characteristics; just as the microscopist puts the wing of a fly under a lens, whose exaggerations disclose the reality, and delight him with a more comprehensive vision of its inherent glories.

And in its further development, in the delightful exercise of this wonderful creative power, new combinations are formed out of these original elements; exhibiting more distinctly their mutual relations, their characteristic actions and reactions, and their bearing upon the evolution of the whole; even as the new combinations of the primary elements made by the chemist in his laboratory reveal to him, by their "conduct," the forces at work in nature and their mode of operation. And especially, in this development, is the operation of these forces quickened and intensified, in the more effective revelation of their existence and potency; that we may be impressed with their reality, and ofttimes delighted by the recognition of their action.

The whole is indeed a new creation, complete in itself, and instinct with a beauty drawn directly from nature's fount. And throughout, what we call "the ideal," he finds in and develops out of the real.

"Great no doubt is the magnificence of the *ivory* gate, but the true dreams pass through the gate of horn."

CHAPTER V.

WE are now enabled also to appreciate more adequately
the Dramatic Art of the play. It is truly a masterpiece;
one in which the dominant motive is given complete expression, in all its phases. Its development commences
amid the circumstances which naturally contribute to its
evolution; and with ever-increasing interest, it is continued through the specific manifestations marking its progress, until it comes to a culmination in the thrilling scenes
of the central climax. Here, immediately, its fulfilling
counter-motive is brought into prominence and is developed through its inevitable course, " to a full and natural
close"; the whole forming the unity of a completely
rounded, well-finished structure; embellished here and
there with subtle touches of exquisite beauty.

The opening notes sound a prelude appropriate to the
theme. The exultant tones of celebration are the first
chord that strikes the ear: "We make holiday, to see Cæsar,
and to rejoice in his triumph," are the words of the citizens, who appear upon the scene in holiday attire. Their
very jokes give a more vivid coloring; indicating that the
jubilation is so great that laboring men, dependent upon
their earnings, are idling in the streets. It is manifestly
just the occasion when envy is especially set on edge.

The effect is further intensified by the exhibition of the
malevolence engendered in the hearts of the old-time adherents of Pompey. In their newly-fired hatred, they disperse the crowd, and maliciously tear down the trophies
with which Cæsar's images are decked. For this they

were afterwards put to death, which is reported to Cassius : who, be it noted, had also been an adherent of Pompey, in command of his fleet, but had surrendered to Cæsar, who had forgiven his enmity and advanced him to honors. Though with consummate art, this significant fact is hidden from view, or thus merely shadowed forth, since envy, and not revenge, is to be the dominant motive of the action.

In the midst of this jubilee, Cassius and Brutus appear upon the scene. And it now quickly becomes manifest that Cassius' envy (in the full Baconian sense of the word) is indeed set on edge. He is unmistakably operating upon Brutus ; not idly or at random, but intelligently, in the persistent prosecution of a definite purpose. After the interview he says to Cinna :

> "See Brutus at his house: three parts of him
>   Is ours already; and the man entire,
>   Upon the next encounter yields him ours."

To what end? *Cæsar's death!* Manifestly, premeditated murder is enthroned in Cassius' heart, directing all his energies. Unlike Brutus, there are no evidences of internal conflict; no struggles with reason or conscience. His purpose has complete possession of the man. Small vices are little devils, but murder is a fiend. The great Goethe opens his dramatic masterpiece, *Faust*, with the mediæval " fantasy" of the devil appearing in person to a *blasé* old man and buying his soul, by the welcomed proffer of personal service and unlimited pleasures. But Bacon, dealing directly with realities, in their immeasurable depths, has here portrayed the far more awful spectacle, of humanly incarnate malevolence, not seducing guileless innocence or toppling old age, but through the exercise of its terrible power, actually beguiling into crime a mature man, strong, virtuous, generous, of noble aspirations and disinterested purpose, the very personification of magnanimity :

> " His life was gentle; and the elements
> So mix'd in him that Nature might stand up
> And say to all the world, *This was a man.*"

It is all the more terrible because of its truth to the life about us. As Cassius, in the foretaste of victory, coolly observes:

> "therefore it is meet
> That noble minds keep ever with their likes:
> For who so firm that cannot be *seduced?*"

Indeed, the portrayal is so absolutely faithful to life, where in such proceedings, the real animus and intent are usually cloaked under the specious garb of normal, virtuous instincts, that the glamour falls even upon our eyes, and these " depths of Satan " had well-nigh escaped our observation.

In his *Advancement of Learning*, Second Book, Bacon aptly says: " For as the fable goeth of the Basilisk, that if he see you first you die for it, but if you see him first he dieth; so is it with *deceits and evil arts;* which if they be first espied they leese their life, but if they prevent they endanger. So that we are much beholden to Machiavel and others, that write what men do, and not what they ought to do.* For it is not possible to join

---

* " I 'll drown more sailors than the mermaid shall;
I'll slay more gazers than the basilisk;
I 'll play the orator as well as Nestor;
Deceive more slily than Ulysses could;
And, like a Sinon, take another Troy:
I can add colors to the cameleon;
Change shapes with Proteus, for advantages,
And set the murderous Machiavel to school."
　　　　　　　　—III., Henry VI., III., 2.

" Make me not sighted like the basilisk:
I have look't on thousands, who have sped the better
By my regard, but kill'd none so."
　　　　　　　　—A Winter's Tale, I., 2.

" Am I politic? am I subtle? am I a Machiavel?"
　　　　　　　　—Merry Wives, III., 1.

serpentine wisdom with the columbine innocency, except
men know exactly all the conditions of the serpent; his
baseness and going upon his belly, his volubility and
lubricity, his envy and sting, and the rest; that is, all
forms and natures of evil. For without this, virtue lieth
open and unfenced. Nay an honest man can do no good
upon those that are wicked to reclaim them, without the
help of the knowledge of evil."

Let us here also follow in his footsteps, tracing out, to
use his words, " the roots of good and evil, and the strings
of those roots."

Bacon opens his Essay with the pregnant words:
" There be none of the affections which have been noted
to fascinate or bewitch, but love and envy;" a hint which,
in its expansion, inducts us at once into the mode of the
action. In a word, strange as at first blush it may appear,
it becomes plainly manifest, through a comparison of all
the details in their express significance, that Cassius, in his
malevolence, exercises over Brutus that awful power of
Fascination (often ignored, but none the less real) which,
in such satanic use, is essentially the base perversion to
evil of Love's transcendent power; in fine, the pollute and
polluting energy of the " evil eye," " the proper attribute
of the devil."

Strong man that he was, Brutus flutters like a bird,
under this serpent's charm :

> " Into what dangers would you lead me, Cassius,
> That you would have me seek into myself
> For that which is not in me?"

> " But wherefore do you hold me here so long?
> What is it that you would impart to me?"

> " That you do love me, I am nothing jealous;
> What you would work me to I have some aim:
> How I have thought of this and of these times
> I shall recount hereafter; for this present,
> I would not, so with love I might entreat you,
> Be any further moved."

"For this time I will leave you:
To-morrow, if you please to speak with me,
I will come home to you; or, if you will
Come home to me, and I will wait for you."

And to our now opened eyes, Cassius' animus quickly becomes manifest. Does he discourse to Brutus of Liberty? Of its sacredness, or its peril? Of the Republic, or of the responsibility of its citizens? Or even of the welfare of the state, or of the common good? Not at all. Surely these are the things, bespeaking a noble intent, that would strongly move a man of Brutus' mould. But such considerations are alien to Cassius' purpose. His theme is personal, and insidious wiles are his method.

Envy frames itself " readily into Imaginations and Suggestions." He 'obscurely glances at Cæsar's ambition'; thereby most effectually inciting in Brutus the inward working power of Apprehension. He cunningly directs upon him the force of Opinion, with the light touch of a glittering generality:

"I have heard,
Where many of the best respect in Rome,
(Except immortal Cæsar), speaking of Brutus,
And groaning underneath this age's yoke,
Have wish'd that noble Brutus had his eyes."

But first of all, with exquisite subtlety, he creates the genial atmosphere of affection; through expressions of tender solicitude, of an injured grief, that vanishes at the word of explanation — the sun shining warmer after the storm-bearing cloud has cleared. And " your friend that *loves* you" follows up the advantage, by working the giddy spell wrought through the intoxicating power of delicious flattery; savoring of Opinion and piquant with Suggestion.

"And it is very much lamented, Brutus,
That you have no such mirrors as will turn
Your hidden worthiness into your eye,
That you might see your shadow."

> "Therefore, good Brutus, be prepared to hear:
> And since you know you cannot see yourself
> So well as by reflection, I, your glass,
> Will modestly discover to yourself
> That of yourself, which you yet know not of."

Cassius strengthens the dose by the infusion of a sense of its sincerity and exceptional value, sweetening it with a tincture of affection:

> "And be not jealous on me, gentle Brutus:
> Were I a common laugher, or did use
> To stale with ordinary oaths my love
> To every new protester; if you know
> That I do fawn on men, and hug them hard,
> And after scandal them; or if you know
> That I profess myself in banqueting
> To all the rout, then hold me dangerous."

Nor is the spell wrought in vain. 'The charm works apace,' and the subtle stimulant mounts quickly to the brain, producing the usual exhilaration. Brutus shows that this high opinion of himself is not unfounded: he is equal to any demand that may be made upon him. Rising to the full height of conscious greatness and nobility of soul, he speaks of himself in impassioned tones; giving utterance to the innermost thought of his heart, and to its inspiration:

> "What is it that you would impart to me?
> If it be ought toward the general good,
> Set honor in one eye, and death i' the other,
> And I will look on both indifferently:
> For, let the gods so speed me as I love
> The name of honor more than I fear death."

But all unconsciously to himself, the meshes are even now tightening around him. In this moment of heroic exaltation and excitement, he has at one blow swept away the protecting barriers of self-restraint and prudent reserve—the safeguards of personality—and has bared his bosom to the attack. Cassius, seizing the opportunity,

for which he has so cunningly wrought, instantly responds
with words of personal appreciation,—of his consciousness
of this greatness. He is thoroughly *en rapport* with him:
responsive in thought and word, in the sweet harmony of
perfect accord :

> "I know that virtue to be in you, Brutus,
> As well as I do know your outward favor.
> Well, honor is the subject of my story.—"

In this, Cassius is more than adroit ; for as Bacon profoundly observes, in his Essay, *Of Praise:* " If he be a
cunning flatterer, he will follow the arch-flatterer, which is
a man's self, and wherein a man thinketh best of himself,
therein the flatterer will *uphold* him most."

And here follows the effective work in the action, the
consummation of the spell.

In his study of Fascination *(Natural History*, Century
X.) Bacon says : " The fifth is the emissions of spirits ;
and this is the principal in our intention to handle now in
this place ; namely, the operation of the spirits of the
mind of man upon other spirits : and this is of a double
nature ; the operations of the affections, if they be vehement ; and the operation of the imagination, if it be *strong*.
But these two are so coupled, as we shall handle them together : for when an envious or amorous aspect doth infect the spirits of another, there is joined both affection
and imagination."

And again : " Certainly it is agreeable to reason, that
there are at the least some light effluxions from spirit to
spirit, when men are in the presence one with another, as
well as from body to body. . . . Audacity and confidence
doth, in civil business, so great effects, as a man may reasonably doubt that, besides the very daring and earnestness
and persisting and importunity, there should be *some secret
binding and stooping* of other men's spirits to such persons. The affections (no doubt) do make the spirits more
powerful and active ; and especially those affections which
draw the spirits into the eyes : which are two : love, and

envy, which is called *oculus malus*. . . . But yet if there
be any such infection from spirit to spirit, there is no
doubt but that it worketh by presence, and not by the eye
alone; yet most forcibly by the eye. Fear and shame are
likewise infective; for we see that the starting of one will
make another ready to start: and, when one man is out
of countenance in a company, others do likewise blush in
his behalf."

Taking up the thread, in the light of Bacon's explana-
tions: The sight of Cæsar's *relative greatness*, 'steeply
rising,' and its aggravating contemplation, had enraged
Cassius, even unto venom. Determined upon Cæsar's
death, he is now striving with all his might to " infect "
Brutus with this poison; — to " whet " him against Cæsar
personally. To this end, he now exerts upon him that
supreme enchantment wrought by Example; displaying
before him openly, shamelessly, with hot vehemence and
impassioned words, the workings of this poison within
himself; fanning into sheets of flame the fire raging in
his own heart and tingling in his veins. For infection,
like fire, is communicated by contact, through its manifestation.

Or to put it more directly, translating Bacon's words
into the language of modern thought: Cassius is thereby
exerting upon Brutus a positive force; expending upon
him personal energy, in the accomplishment of " work."
In the rhythm of being, our souls are attuned to exquisite
vibration; and in the atmosphere of Love, whose spell
Cassius had already wrought, these vibrations are communicated; coalescing by sweet compulsion into harmony,
wherein is satisfaction; communicating, through their
translation into manifestation and their re-translation
through impression, in this universal telephone. And thus
by the very laws of existence, a chord sharply struck in
one determined heart, and sounding forth loudly, vehe-

mently, persistently, and as here, concentrated in its manifestations upon another, loving, highly strung, and in a
receptive mood, *is* a powerful force, tending almost inevitably to awaken in that heart like chords in sympathetic
vibration.

And now, while the word "honor" is still sounding in
Brutus' soul, all tumultuous with heroic emotion, Cassius
bursts forth in a subtly coalescing peal of true musical
quality, loudly ringing; in whose vibrations we feel
instinctively the impress of a determined, concentrated
will-power; which must have thrilled Brutus, penetrating
him to the core:

> "I cannot tell what *you* and other men
> Think of this life; but, for my single self,
> I had as lief not be, as live to be
> In awe of such a thing as I myself."

We can almost hear the responding, "Amen," to such a
clear proposition, so involved in "honor." But the key-
note is struck; and thence the theme is developed in continuous strains, stealing into Brutus' soul their poisonous
thrill. "Envy is ever joined with the comparing of a
man's self; and where there is no comparison, no envy."
Cassius purposes to thoroughly initiate Brutus into this
mode of thought, already subtly engendered. He accordingly prolongs the strain into the definite enunciation of a
comparison—one of self-evident truth,—gently interweaving Brutus within its terms; thus 'secretly binding and
stooping his mind,' *making* him to think the same thoughts
at the same time:

> "I was born free as Cæsar; so were you:
> We both have fed as well; and we can both
> Endure the winter's cold as well as he."

Although this needs no demonstration, Cassius continues in its exemplification; binding Brutus into closer
assent, and accustoming him in this trend of thought. He

recounts the swim with his old comrade in the Tiber; where Cæsar had been ignominiously worsted in this contest of physical strength and endurance,—the especial pride of the Romans:

"Cæsar cried, 'Help me, Cassius, or I sink.'
I, as Æneas, our great ancestor,
Did from the flames of Troy upon his shoulders
The old Anchises bear, so, from the waves of Tiber
Did I the tired Cæsar."

And now he works upon Brutus the mightiest spell of all; whose mystery is almost inscrutable. By virtue of the hold already acquired, and through the operation of subtle but potent forces directed upon him, he would actually carry Brutus off his moorings; taking the helm himself, and shaping the course; binding Brutus' mind into consonance with his will; enforcing his thoughts upon him, in their entirety; making them Brutus' own; and imprinting them so deeply that they must eventually warp him to their inevitable conclusion. Brutus' honorable metal, " of all other the most pliant and enduring to be wrought," must indeed " be wrought from that it is disposed"; but such working could only be performed under the fire of Imagination.

Bacon informs us that " Fascination is the power and act of Imagination, intensive upon the body of another." And in his *Natural History*, he relates, " not for the weight thereof, but because it doth handsomely open the nature of the question"; the explanation given him by a gentleman of the artifice whereby a juggler could tell a man what card he thought; to wit, " It was not the knowledge of the man's thought (for that is proper to God) but it was *the enforcing of a thought upon him, and binding his imagination by a stronger*, that he could think no other card. . . . for if the man had thought first, his thought had been fixed; but the other imagining first, bound his thought." Bacon pertinently remarks: " The inquisition of this subject in our way (which is by induction) is wonderful hard: for the things that are reported are full of fables; and new experiments can hardly be made but with extreme caution, for the reason which we will hereafter declare." He says: " Imagination in this place, I understand to be, *the representation of an individual thought.* Imagination is of three kinds: the first joined with belief of that which is to come: the second joined with memory of that which is past: and the third is of things present, or as if they were present; for I comprehend in this imaginations feigned and at pleasure; as if one should imagine such a man *to be in the vestments of a Pope, or to have wings.*"

Cassius, utilizing this principle, gives representation to his individual thought in a Titanic sweep of the imagination, of terribly enforcing power:

> "and this man
> *Is now become a God;* and Cassius is
> A wretched creature, and must bend his body,
> If Cæsar carelessly but nod on him."

He continues the figure, charging his words with venom:

> "He had a fever when he was in Spain,
> And when the fever was on him, I did mark
> How he did shake: *'t is true, this god did shake:*
> His *coward* lips did from their color fly;
> .   .   .   .   . Ye gods, it doth amaze me,
> A man of such a *feeble temper* should
> So get the start of the majestic world,
> And bear the palm *alone.*"

The Dramatist ever lays heavy odds against himself. Brutus *loves* Cæsar. And love is ever alert to any possible offence against the loved one. But though there is here afforded an opportunity to protest against the venomous implication inherent in the words " coward " and " feeble," so manifestly unjust in their application to Cæsar, Brutus is so wrought upon, so " spell-bound," that he is wholly unconscious of the insidious poison he is im-

bibing: which, in reality, is vitiating his love; gradually
but surely transforming his personal attitude towards
Cæsar. But instead, as a peal of acclamation is borne in
upon them, Brutus responds:

> "Another general shout!
> I do believe that these applauses are
> For some new honors that are *heap'd on Cæsar.*"

Bacon continues: "The experiments which may certainly demonstrate the power of imagination upon other
bodies, are few or none: . . . We shall, therefore, be
forced in this inquiry to resort to new experiments;
wherein we can give only directions of trials, and not any
positive experiments. . . . We find in the art of memory,
that *images visible* work better than other conceits: as if
you would remember the word 'philosophy,' you shall
more surely do it by imagining that such a man (for men
are the best places) is reading upon Aristotle's Physics;
than if you should imagine him to say, 'I'll go study philosophy.' And therefore this observation would be translated to the subject we now speak of: *for the more lustrous the imagination is, it filleth and fixeth the better.*
And therefore I conceive that you shall, in that experiment (whereof we spake before) of *binding* of thoughts,
less fail, if you tell one that such an one shall name one
of twenty men, than if it were one of twenty cards."

This enables us to appreciate the intent, the tremendous force and binding power, of the lustrous figure Cassius now pictures into Brutus' mind; there to remain forever a vivid imprint; of the very substance of his mental
conception of Cæsar:

> "Why, man, he doth bestride the narrow world,
> *Like a Colossus:* and we petty men
> Walk under his huge legs, and peep about
> To find ourselves dishonorable graves."

Seemingly conscious that this part of his work had been
fully accomplished,—"the stronger impression carrying
the rest with it,"— Cassius now closes in upon Brutus;

laying hold upon the springs of action, and putting them into operation. Brutus is a strong man, thoroughly self-reliant, resolute, a man of decision and action. And Cassius, by a subtle stroke, arouses these very energies, directing them against Cæsar; Brutus' very greatness making him here especially pliant, and inevitably responsive to the touch.

In his *Advancement of Learning*, Second Book, Bacon says: " But yet nevertheless these positions, *Faber quisque fortunæ suæ; Sapiens dominabitur astris; Invia virtuti nulla est via ;* (Every man is the maker of his fortune; the wise man will command his stars; No path is impervious to virtue); and the like, being taken and used as *spurs* to industry, and not as stirrups to insolency, rather for resolution than for presumption or outward declaration, have been ever thought sound and good, and are no question imprinted in the greatest minds; who are so sensible of this opinion as they can scarce contain it within."

Cassius now strikes forcibly upon this chord, well knowing that it will continue to vibrate in Brutus, until it is silenced by resolve :

> "Men at some time are *masters of their fates:*
> The fault, dear Brutus, is not *in our stars,*
> But in *ourselves*, that we are *underlings.*"

In his Essay, *Of Cunning*, Bacon says: " Another [point of cunning] is, that when you have anything to obtain of present dispatch, you entertain and amuse the party with whom you deal with some other discourse, *that he be not too much awake to make objections.*" Cassius here makes analogous use of the underlying principle. Sheathing the spur for a moment, he hides from immediate view the awful consequences necessarily involved in this Suggestion, by the instant display, in rapid sequence, of a series of delusive conceptions ; centering the comparison on Brutus alone ; and dazzling his vision by the iridescent play of brilliant fancies :

" *Brutus* and *Cæsar:* what should be in that *Cæsar?*
Why should that name be sounded more than yours?
Write them together, yours is as fair a name;
Sound them, it doth become the mouth as well;
Weigh them, it is as heavy; conjure with them,
Brutus will start a spirit as soon as *Cæsar.*"

And finally, Bacon says *(De Augmentis,* Fifth Book):
" And again, it is no small dominion which Imagination
holds in persuasions that are wrought by eloquence; for
when by arts of speech men's minds are soothed, inflamed,
and carried hither and thither, it is all done by stimulating the imagination till it becomes ungovernable, and not
only sets reason at naught, but offers violence to it, partly
by blinding, partly by incensing it."

And in climax, Cássius employs this dominating power
to effectually clinch his binding hold upon Brutus; firing
his imagination into an ungovernable flame ; in whose intensity Brutus' soul is subtly incensed against Cæsar;
whose glare blinds his vision, and whose impetus whirls
him irretrievably into the vortex of crime.   This Cassius
accomplishes by the concentration of all his energies into
one sustained, melodious strain of impassioned eloquence;
ringing all possible changes upon the theme of " one man "
filling Rome till there is no room; and rising upon the
tide of swelling emotion to a culmination, in the thrilling
appeal to Brutus' just pride in his great ancestor, and an
irresistible implication of shame upon a possibly degenerate son :

" Now in the names of all the gods at once,
Upon what meat doth this our Cæsar feed,
That he is grown so great?   Age, thou art shamed!
Rome, thou hast lost the breed of noble bloods!
When went there by an age, since the great flood,
But it was famed with more than with one man?
When could they say, till now, that talk'd of Rome,
That her wide walks encompass'd but one man?
Now is it Rome indeed, and room enough,

> When there is in it but one only man.
> O! you and I have heard our fathers say,
> There was a Brutus once that would have brook'd
> The eternal devil to keep his state in Rome,
> As easily as a king."

The spell is wrought; and Brutus is lost. Imagination, not reason, is at the helm; and the tremendous forces of good within him, the mighty motive powers, under full pressure, are driving him straight into crime. It is but a question of hours when this fiend incarnate can claim him as his own:

> "three parts of him
> Is ours already; and the man entire,
> Upon the next encounter, yields him ours.
> . . . . Let us go,
> For it is after midnight; and ere day
> We will awake him, and be sure of him."

How profoundly Brutus is moved; how that it is all that he can endure; his implicit confidence throughout in Cassius' good intent; his dawning consciousness that Cæsar's death is the awful deed to which he is being worked; his poignant apprehension of the hard conditions likely to come upon them in Rome, "when there is in it but one only man"; his gentle pride; his strong, laconic reticence; his instinctive aversion to external constraint; his habitual self-reliance, even under the severest strain; his purposed deliberation; his resolute determination, facing squarely the issue, to be equal to the occasion; and the first flaming of the fire now enkindled within him, are all disclosed in his response to Cassius:

> "That you do love me, I am nothing jealous;
> What you would work me to, I have some aim;
> How I have thought of this, and of these times,
> I shall recount hereafter; for this present,
> I would not, so with love I might entreat you,
> Be any further moved. What you have said,
> I will consider; what you have to say,

> I will with patience hear; and find a time
> Both meet to hear and answer such high things.
> Till then, my noble friend, chew upon this:
> Brutus had rather be a villager,
> Than to repute himself a son of Rome
> Under these hard conditions as this time
> Is like to lay upon us."

Cassius is content. He comprehends the man, his perturbed condition, the trend of his thoughts, and the conclusion to which they will inevitably lead him. And so he simply upholds Brutus in this bent by an expression of warm approval; cunningly removing any sense of outward constraint, and in effect, complimenting him, by strongly depreciating his own effort:

> "I am glad that my weak words
> Have struck but this much show of fire from Brutus."

Though in this subtle touch, Cassius is but fanning the incipient fire into flame, by the gentlest wafture; for Brutus must have been conscious that if *such* words were indeed "weak," it was because they were inadequate to the situation.

In his study of Fascination (*Natural History*, Century X.) Bacon continues:

"It is good to consider upon what things imagination hath most force: and the rule (as I conceive) is, that it hath most force upon things that have the lightest and easiest motions. And therefore above all, upon the spirits of men; and in them, upon such affections as move lightest; as upon procuring of love; binding of lust, which is ever with imagination; upon men in fear; or men in irresolution; and the like." And again: "The body passive and to be wrought upon (I mean not of the imaginant), is better wrought upon (as hath been partly touched) at some times than at others." And he notes "choice of the hour" as among the things that have "been used in magic (if there be in these practices anything that is purely natural)."

The embodiment of these principles in the scene makes the representation complete. In the beginning, upon the exit of Cæsar's triumphal procession, Cassius finds Brutus in a disturbed condition, disquieted, troubled, anxious; evidently regarding the state of affairs in Rome:

> " I am not gamesome: I do lack some part
> Of that quick spirit that is in Antony.
> . . . . . if I have veil'd my look,
> I turn the trouble of my countenance
> Merely upon myself. Vexed I am,
> Of late, with passions of some difference,
> Conceptions only proper to myself,
> Which give some soil, perhaps, to my behavior:
> But let not therefore my good friends be grieved ;
> (Among which number, Cassius, be you one) ;
> Nor construe any further my neglect,
> Than that poor Brutus, with himself at war,
> Forgets the shows of love to other men."

And all through the hour of their conversation, shouts of acclamation, heard in applause of Cæsar, are tingling in their ears. And at this juncture, Cæsar and his train, returning from the course, flash across the scene, and

> "The angry spot doth glow on Cæsar's brow."

And as though Fate, that awful mystery to the Romans, were indeed an invisible actor, behind the scene, playing now directly into Cassius' hand, and crowding Cæsar to his doom, Brutus is told that, this day, a crown has been thrice offered to Cæsar; put by " every time gentler than other."

The relation of the incident of Cæsar's " falling sickness " also enables Cassius to quicken Brutus' Apprehension by a home thrust:

> " No, Cæsar hath it not; but you and I
> And honest Casca, we have the falling sickness."

Cassius likewise takes advantage of the departure of Casca, and of the usual conversation about him between those left behind, to give Brutus' mind a push in the direction of its present bent; and this by the subtlest Intimation of the formation and execution of a concerted design:

> *Brutus.* What a blunt fellow is this grown to be!
> He was quick mettle when he went to school.
> *Cassius.* So he is now, *in execution*
> *Of any bold or noble enterprise,*
> However he puts on this tardy form."

Brutus also departs; and Cassius, left alone, opens his heart to our scrutiny. Richard III., that fiend incarnate in a misshapen body, through this terrible power of Fascination, wins a betrothal of marriage from the widowed Lady Anne, in the very presence of the bleeding body of her late beloved husband, whom she knew Richard had murdered: and now, we can almost hear his satanic " Ha, ha," ringing in the undertones of Cassius' soliloquy, as he chuckles to himself over his beguilement of Brutus, plans its continuance, and anticipates the wreaking of his hatred upon Cæsar:

> " Well, Brutus, thou art noble; yet I see
> Thy honorable metal may be wrought
> From that it is disposed: therefore it is meet
> That noble minds keep ever with their likes:
> For who so firm that cannot be seduced?
> Cæsar doth bear me hard: but he loves Brutus:
> If I were Brutus now, and he were Cassius,
> He should not humor me. I will this night,
> In several hands, in at his windows throw,
> As if they came from several citizens,
> Writings, all tending to the great opinion
> That Rome holds of his name; wherein obscurely
> Cæsar's ambition shall be glanced at;
> And, after this, let Cæsar seat him sure;
> For we will shake him, or worse days endure."

CHAPTER VI.

AND now, while we pause for a moment's rest, ere we resume with Brutus, let us fill in the time in noting how cleverly Cicero is handled in the play.

Bacon's exposition of Divination, from which a brief quotation is given, *ante*, page 160, note, is substantially a condensation from Cicero's treatise, *On Divination*. In the first part of this work, Cicero argues quite plausibly in its favor, as worthy of credence ; but in the concluding portion he turns about and argues much more strongly against it. To freshly roast a still savory " chestnut ": This was like Rufus Choate appearing in court successively upon opposite sides of the same question, and replying to the quizzing judge, " Yesterday I thought I was right ; to-day I *know* I am." And it is told that he used often to argue with his cronies upon one side of some subject until he had convinced them, and then upon the other side until he had convinced them back again. But this sort of mental gymnastics, like the ground and lofty tumbling of the well-oiled acrobat, though highly entertaining to the audience, is inevitably weakening to the *backbone* of the performer. It makes him very flexible indeed, but unduly loosens the joints ; for sincerity and fidelity to conviction are the vertebræ in the spinal column of character, coalescing in unity of thought and action. And somehow, there is in this very flexibility of a highly developed reason, trained to the discernment and constant balancing of a great variety of opposing considerations, a marked tendency to make one excellent indeed in contemplation, but negative or irresolute in action.

This seems to have been Cicero's characteristic weakness, or at least, such was Bacon's conception of the man. For in his *Advancement of Learning*, First Book, he mentions his example in this regard as one of those through whose penetration learning may " minister to a mind diseased ":

" And for those particular seducements or indispositions of the mind for policy and government, which learning is pretended to insinuate ; if it be granted that any such thing be, it must be remembered withal, that learning ministereth in every of them greater strength of medicine or remedy, than it offereth of indisposition or infirmity. . . . And these medicines it conveyeth into men's minds much more forcibly by the quickness and penetration of examples. For let a man look into the errors of Clement the Seventh, so lively described by Guicciardine, who served under him, or into the errors of Cicero, painted out by his own pencil in his epistles to Atticus, and *he will fly apace from being irresolute.*"

And in the play, though a less consummate artist might have omitted him altogether, in accord with the strict rules of dramatic construction, he has thrown Cicero into prominence, though merely as a " looker on," highly interested ;

> " and Cicero
> Looks with such ferret and such fiery eyes,
> As we have seen him in the Capitol,
> Being cross'd in conference by some senators";

but nevertheless taking no part whatever in the action. Though we may rest assured that his portrayal contributes to the development of the central theme.

Regarding Cicero's *On Divination*, it may be noted that his treatment of divination by the observation of the flight of birds, " once considered of so much consequence in military expeditions," and his early argument that "every other philosopher, *except Epicurus*, who talks so childishly about the nature of the gods, has sanctioned a belief in divination," throw light upon Cassius' utterance in Act V., scene 1. (See *ante*, page 159.) But the following brief extract from his concluding argument, where he evidently "knows" that he is right, is especially significant, embodying the essence of his philosophy, even as it is developed in the play.

"But you will say that in the entrails of the fat bull Cæsar offered, there was no heart, and since it was not possible that this animal could have lived without a heart, we must suppose that the heart was annihilated at the instant of immolation. How is it that you think it impossible that its heart could vanish so suddenly, nobody knows whither? For myself, I know not how much vigor in a heart is necessary to carry on the vital function, and suspect that if afflicted by any disease, the heart of a victim may be found so withered, and wasted, and small as to be quite unlike a heart. But on what argument can you build an opinion that the heart of this same fat bullock, if it existed in him before, disappeared at the instant of immolation? Did the bullock behold Cæsar in a heartless condition even while arrayed in the purple, and thus lose its own heart by mere force of sympathy? . . . It was announced to the senate that it had rained blood, that the river had become blackened with blood, and that the statues of the immortal gods were covered with sweat. Do you imagine that Thales or Anaxagoras, or any other natural philosopher, would have given credence to such news? Blood and sweat only proceed from the animal body; there might have been some discoloration caused by some contagion of earth very like blood, and some moisture may have fallen on the statues from without, resembling perspiration, as we see sometimes in plaster during the prevalence of a south wind; . . . Are we, then, alarmed if at any time any unnatural productions are reported as having proceeded from man or

beast? Any one of which occurrences, to be brief, may
be accounted for on one principle. Whatever is born, of
whatever kind it may be, *must have some cause in nature*,
so that even though it may be contrary to custom, it cannot possibly be contrary to nature. Investigate, if you
can, *the natural cause* of every novel and extraordinary
circumstance: even if you cannot discover the cause, still
you may feel sure that nothing can have taken place without a cause; and, by the principles of nature, drive away
that terror which the novelty of the thing may have occa-
sioned you. Then neither earthquakes, nor thunder-
storms, nor showers of blood and stones, nor shooting
stars, nor glancing torches will alarm you any more."

Bacon must have written the play with Cicero's *On
Divination* at his hand; for he has condensed the whole
substance and spirit of the foregoing powerful reasoning
into a single line, making it the point of Casca's reproach-
ful fling at Cicero in the next scene.

Casca, we are informed, had been a boy of "quick
mettle," of "that temperament which is susceptible of high
excitement." (Webster.) Through what chilling experiences he had passed we know not, but in manhood, as
developed in Scene 2, he has evidently become callous,
hard-crusted, and imperturbable, even under the excitement of the most momentous events. He is "a blunt
fellow," of good wit, but rude, cynical, and of "tardy
form," careless of the thoughts and feelings of others,
even scornful of their infirmities, and keenly observant of
the worst side of everything,—a sharp, bold, unmagnani-
mous, forceful man.

But in the next scene, a metamorphosis has apparently
taken place, and Casca is so completely transformed that
we recognize him only by name. His Religion is superstition, and it is the touch of what he regards as the
supernatural that has wrought the marvelous change. He
is now the creature of excitement, pale, breathless, star-

ing. He has "put on fear" and is "cast in wonder."
His imagination, highly wrought, wholly dominates the
man. Soaring aloft, it views the sway of earth, rides upon
the wind, and crests the mountain wave, in its exalted
flight. Meeting Cicero, in answer to his questionings, he
says:

> "Are you not moved, when all the sway of earth
> Shakes like a thing unfirm? O Cicero,
> I have seen tempests, when the scolding winds
> Have rived the knotty oaks; and I have seen
> The ambitious ocean swell, and rage, and foam,
> To be exalted with the threatening clouds:
> But never till to-night, never till now,
> Did I go through a tempest dropping fire.
> Either there is a civil strife in heaven;
> Or else the world, too saucy with the gods,
> Incenses them to send destruction."

Cicero, whose imagination is thoroughly subject to his
reason, evidently discerning in all this nothing but the
operation of natural causes, coolly asks:

> "Why, saw you anything more wonderful?" *

Casca then narrates the prodigies mentioned by Plutarch:

> "A common slave (you know him well by sight)
> Held up his left hand, which did flame and burn,
> Like twenty torches join'd; and yet his hand,
> Not sensible of fire, remain'd unscorch'd.
> Besides, (I have not since put up my sword,)
> Against the Capitol I met a lion,
> Who glared upon me, and went surly by

---

* "Therefore a diviner and interpreter of prodigies being
consulted by a man who informed him, as a great prodigy, that
he had discovered in his house a serpent coiled around a bar,
answered very discreetly, that there was *nothing very wonderful
in this*, but if he had found the bar coiled around the serpent,
this would have been a prodigy indeed. By this reply, he
plainly indicated that nothing can be a prodigy which is consistent with the nature of things."—Cicero's *On Divination*.

Without annoying me: and there were drawn
Upon a heap a hundred ghastly women,
Transformed with their fear; who swore they saw
Men all in fire walk up and down the streets.
And, yesterday, the bird of night did sit,
Even at noon-day, upon the market place,
Hooting and shrieking."

And then he gives Cicero the home-thrust, to which
reference has been made:

" When these prodigies
Do so conjointly meet, let not men say,
'These are their reasons,— they are natural;'
For, I believe, they are portentous things
Unto the climate that they point upon."

Cicero, however, meets the issue with a fresh instalment of the same philosophy, likewise embodying the
spirit of his argument against the portentous interpretation of apparent prodigies (see *On Divination*, Bohn's
edition, pp. 222–227), and immediately turns the conversation:

" Indeed, it is a strange-disposed time:
But men may construe things, after their fashion,
Clean from the purpose of the things themselves.
Comes Cæsar to the Capitol to-morrow?" *

---

* Incidentally, we also learn from Cicero's *On Divination*
the philosophy of the Romans regarding lightning, and can
thus better appreciate the "local coloring" in Brutus' words:

" The exhalations, whizzing in the air,
Give so much light, that I may read by them."
                              —*Act II., 1.*

" For the opinion of the Stoics on this point is, that the *exhalations* of the earth, which are cold, when they begin to flow
abroad, become winds; and when they form themselves into clouds
and begin to divide and break up their fine particles by repeated
and *vehement gusts*, then thunder and lightning ensue; and
that when by the conflict of the clouds the heat is squeezed out
so as to emit itself, then there is *lightning*. Can we, then,
look for any intimation of futurity in a thing which we see

With the departure of Cicero, Cassius enters upon the scene, and taking advantage of Casca's excited condition, moulds him to his design. He operates directly upon Casca's already inflamed imagination, stimulating it to yet greater intensity, and turns the whole power of his superstition against Cæsar; holding him up as the very object against which the gods were incensed to such manifestations of their displeasure; and supplementing his work with *vehement protestations* and the power of his own Example. And thus, at one interview, by his infernal arts, he converts this formerly active adherent of Cæsar into a deadly enemy, pledged to the conspiracy against him.

Regarding Cicero, it should be observed, that though it is made strikingly apparent that reason is paramount in his mental constitution, nevertheless, his weakness, manifested in his irresolute inactivity, or negative attitude in this momentous crisis, is shown to have brought upon him the inexorable Nemesis of destruction. He is put to death upon the success of Antony and Octavius, as is told in Act IV., scene 3.

Meanwhile, he is utilized in the play, incidentally, in the representation of one of the lighter phases of Envy. In his *De Augmentis*, Eighth Book, Bacon says : "There is added the envy of nobles, who are secretly displeased

---

brought about by the mere force of nature, without any regularity or any determined period?"—*On Divination.*

This also lends additional force to Gervinus' interpretation, that "Brutus is born to be a *Stoic,* and practices the principles of that school, which prescribes the passive use of life and enjoins the power of endurance."

It is perhaps worthy of note, that although in Bacon's time Cicero's *On Divination* had been published on the Continent, it was not translated into English, or even published in England in Latin, till a century later. (See Ebert's *Bibliographical Dictionary.*)

with the issue though fortunate and prosperous, because it did not originate in themselves." This phase is developed in the play, in Act II., scene 1 :

> "*Cassius.* But what of Cicero?   Shall we sound him?
> I think he will stand very strong with us.
> *Casca.* Let us not leave him out.
> *Cinna.*   No, by no means.
> *Metellus.* O let us have him ; for his silver hairs
> Will purchase us a good opinion,
> And buy men's voices to commend our deeds :
> It shall be said his judgment ruled our hands ;
> Our youths, and wildness, shall no whit appear,
> But all be buried in his gravity.
> *Brutus.* O, name him not ; let us not break with him ;
> For he will never follow anything
> That other men begin.
> *Cassius.*   Then leave him out.
> *Casca.* Indeed he is not fit."

And in this connection, we may note the portrayal of still another phase of Envy, or rather of a marked indication of its absence in Brutus.   In his Essay, Bacon profoundly observes : "Those that have joined with their honor great travels, cares, or perils, are less subject to envy.   For men think that they earn their honors hardly, and pity them sometimes ; and *pity ever healeth envy.*"

In the play, Brutus, striving to convince Antony of the purity of his intent in the assassination, makes this fundamental principle the very substance of his protestation :

> "Though now we must appear bloody and cruel,
> As, by our hands and this our present act,
> You see we do ; yet see you but our hands,
> And this the bleeding business they have done :
> Our hearts you see not, they are *pitiful;*
> And *pity* to the general wrong of Rome
> (As fire drives out fire, so pity, pity) *
> Hath done this deed on Cæsar."

---

* A peculiar philosophy :

  "One fire drives out one fire ; one nail, one nail ;

But advancing a step, let us study more closely the methods whereby Bacon was enabled to give to the theme of the play the broadest, and at the same time, the most artistic development.

Mr. Hamilton W. Mabie says of Corot, the great " creative " landscape painter:

" I have read somewhere that Corot was in the habit of going into the fields at the earliest dawn ; and there, pipe in hand, in the silence of the creative hour he watched the birth of the day. These morning vigils held the secret of his marvelous interpretation of the most spiritual and poetic of all the material processes. Aurora touched his pencil ; and who can look on these morning skies, so divinely transparent in revelation, without the sudden rush of adoration ! "

With our eyes opened by this touch of the critic, we look upon one of Corot's pictures with new appreciation and a before unfelt delight. We discern, in every stroke, an expression and revelation of the *joyousness* that pervades all nature in this creative hour, " the birth of the

---

Rights by rights fouler, strengths by strengths do fail."
—*Coriolanus, IV.*, 7.

" Even as one heat another heat expels,
Or as one nail by strength drives out another."
—*Two Gentlemen of Verona, II.*, 4.

" Neither does all heat cherish heat, for when two heats differ many degrees from one another, either kills and destroys the other no less than cold ; one having its proper actions, and thwarting and opposing the actions of the other ; so that Telesius makes lesser heats to be as traitors and deserters towards great ones, and as conspiring with cold. Therefore the feeble heat which creeps in water destroys the lively heat which vibrates in fire ; and in like manner the preternatural heat of putrid humors in the human body suffocates and extinguishes the natural heat."—*On Principles and Origins.*

" *Clavum clavo pellere* " [To drive out a nail with a nail.]
Promus of Formularies and Elegancies.

day." This is manifested not only in the glowing light
that gladdens the morn, and in the physical atmosphere,
which is made so perceptible, but in what is sometimes
termed the subtler, artistic "atmosphere" of the piece.
Thus in one picture, the dancing nymphs are there sporting in the grove, and in another, Orpheus is attendant
with his lyre; to give collateral, contributory expression
to the joyousness which is the central theme; and thus
every detail contributes essentially to its unfolding development.

This illustration from a kindred Art enables us to better
appreciate the like consummate art here displayed by the
Dramatist. Moreover, we have abundant evidence, attendant upon every detail of the work, that this was the
fruitage of the like close, attentive study of his theme,
both directly and in its collateral manifestations. And
through a corresponding study of his work in this light,
we may perhaps attain, in the end, to a better comprehension both of his methods and of the sources of his power.

And first, we note that it was preëminently characteristic of Bacon to view things in their entirety; comprehending a vast body of intricate relations, which ofttimes
wholly escape our observation, but which were to his vision
luminous with the radiance from a central unity.

Thus, in dealing with Envy, he observes, among other
things, its remarkable power "to fascinate or bewitch."
This opens up the whole subject of Fascination in general;
and in its discussion, he grasps the fundamental fact that
it is essentially "the power or act of Imagination intensive upon the body of another." But instantly, under the
flash of this light, whole congeries of cognate matters enter
the field of his vision. Note a few of them, stated in the
succeeding sentence:

"Others that draw nearer to probability, looking with
a clearer eye at the secret workings and impressions of

things, the irradiations of the senses, the passage of contagion from body to body, the conveyance of magnetic virtues, have concluded that it is much more probable there should be impressions, conveyances, and communications from spirit to spirit (seeing that the spirit is above all other things both strenuous to act and soft and tender to be acted on) ; whence have arisen those conceits (now become as it were popular) of the mastering spirit, of men unlucky and ill-omened, of the glances of love, envy, and the like."

Moreover, he devotes the whole of Century X. of his *Natural History* to the exploration of these occult, but closely allied relations ; treating successively, as indexed :

" Of the Transmission and Influx of Immateriate Virtues, and the force of Imagination."

" Of the Emission of Spirits in Vapor, or Exhalation, Odor-like."

" Of Emissions of Spiritual Species which affect the senses."

" Of Emission of Immateriate Virtues from the Minds and Spirits of Men, by Affections, Imagination, or other Impressions."

" Of the Secret Virtue of Sympathy and Antipathy."

" Of Secret Virtues and Proprieties."

" Of the General Sympathy of Men's Spirits."

Through his laborious mastery of the resources of this inner, occult world, and by their happy utilization in the play, Bacon was enabled to give his theme the amplest, most artistic representation, in almost its entirety ; giving it embodiment in an organic structure, complete in itself, having a natural environment appropriate to its theme, and an " atmosphere " luminous with its rays. Indeed, one must read the play with this Century of Bacon's *Natural History* at hand, and with eyes opened to the discernment of the subtle relations binding together its mass of apparently heterogeneous particulars, in what he termed

11

their " secret order," if he would thoroughly comprehend the unity, the variety, and the exquisite fitness of the " coloring " given the details of the play, contributory to the " concentrated manifestation " of its central theme.

It is needless to remind the reader of the direct utilization of these resources in the development of Cassius' work upon Brutus, unfolded in the preceding chapter. But regarding the introduction into that scene of Casca's detailed account of the baleful effect upon Cæsar of the foul air, poisoned by the emanations from the rabblement,—as they " shouted, and clapped their chapped hands, and threw up their sweaty night-caps, and uttered such a deal of stinking breath," that even Casca " durst not laugh, for fear of opening his lips and receiving the bad air," and when Cæsar " swooned and fell down at it ";—and considering this in connection with Bacon's observations, out of which it is developed (see *ante*, page 163, note), wherein he observes that these pernicious effects are worked by " such airs as have some similitude with man's body ; and so *insinuate themselves and betray the spirits*"; and that the cause of the falling sickness " is the grossness of the vapors which rise and enter into the cells of the brain ";— it is worthy of remark that these observations are recorded in this Century of his *Natural History*, under the heads respectively of " Experiments in consort touching emission of spirits in vapor or exhalation, odor-like," and " Experiments in consort touching the secret virtue of sympathy and antipathy "; all under the general head of " *Experiments in consort touching transmission and influx of immateriate virtues, and the force of imagination.*" And with our knowledge of his mental grasp of the analogous relations, binding this great variety of agencies into the unity of a complex entirety, may we not discern, in this incidental portrayal, in the context of the play, of one of these analogies in nature, the designed creation of an exquisitely harmonious environment, contributing its moiety towards the complete manifestation of the noxious influence, so deadly to Cæsar, which Cassius is then exerting upon Brutus; insinuating into his soul the subtlest poison, and paralyzing, or at least, beclouding his reason,—which is the dominant interest in the scene?

Just as, conversely, he employs the like analogy, in the portrayal of the dissolution of the "enchantment" wrought by Prospero on his visitors, in *The Tempest;* condensing it into a metaphor, in the beautiful lines :

> "The charm dissolves apace ;
> And as the morning steals upon the night,
> Melting the darkness, so their rising senses
> Begin to chase the ignorant *fumes* that mantle
> Their clearer reason."

And it may be there is the same breadth of artistic treatment displayed in the succeeding Act, in the words of Portia addressed to Brutus, immediately following the early morning visit of the conspirators at his house :

> " Is Brutus sick? and is it physical
> To walk unbraced, and *suck up the humors*
> *Of the dank morning?* What, is Brutus sick ;
> And will he steal out of his wholesome bed,
> To dare the *vile contagion* of the night,
> And tempt the rheumy and unpurged air,
> To add unto his sickness? No, my Brutus ;
> You have some *sick offense* within your mind,
> Which by the right and virtue of my place,
> I ought to know of. . . . .
> Why are you heavy ; and what men to-night
> Have had resort to you : for here have been
> Some six or seven, who did hide their faces
> Even from darkness."

We know the associations uniting these matters in Bacon's mind ; for in the same connection in this Century, he treats of " contagion " in its various forms, touching also upon the effect of wholesome and of " pestilent " airs.

And possibly, there is discernible, in his introduction of the foregoing passage, the purposed impartation of a richer coloring, giving a more intense or ampler manifestation to the baneful influences operating upon Brutus; by their incidental expression in one of nature's subtlest analogies, in the delicious harmony of a formless metaphor,—as truly existent as if it had been crystalized into a formal figure or an extended simile, and infinitely more artistic. It is less conventional; more in accord with the methods of expression of the Supreme Artist, whose manifestations, voicing formlessly unutterable depths of significance, are the originals of man's similitudes, alike the pattern, the substance and the inspiration of his Art, and whose interpretative reproduction is its especial function. Certainly, it is well to know that even this higher department of poetry has also its indispensable "Natural History," its alphabet and its Primer; accumulated through observation and induction, and by patient toil. For such seems to have been the method of its recognized Master; and it is perhaps one of the secrets of the supremacy of his work.

Again, in the same Century, Bacon observes: "There be many things that work upon the spirits of men by secret sympathy and antipathy. . . . But it is manifest that light, above all things, excelleth in comforting the spirits of men." *

---

* "O weary night, O long and tedious night,
    Abate thy hours: shine, *comforts*, from the *east*."
                —*Midsummer-Night's Dream, III., 2.*

"I have been troubled in my sleep this night,
    But dawning day new *comfort* hath inspired."
                —*Tit. And., II., 2.*

"We'll rest us, Hermia, if you think it good,
    And tarry for the *comfort* of the day."
                —*Midsummer-Night's Dream, II., 2.*

This subtle influence upon the spirits of men is given manifestation in the play, in the portrayal of the meeting of the conspirators at Brutus' house, where, in the anxious moment while they are awaiting his decision, they turn instinctively towards the dawning light, searching for its presence, and finding comfort even in its discussion :

" *Decius.* Here lies the east: doth not the day break here?
Casca. No.
Cinna. O, pardon, sir, it doth ; and you gray lines
That fret the clouds are messengers of day.
Casca. You shall both confess that you are deceived.
Here, as I point my sword, the sun arises ;
Which is a great way growing on the south,
Weighing the youthful season of the year.
Some two months hence, up higher toward the north
He first presents his fire ; and the *high east* ⁎
Stands, as the Capitol, directly here."

A truly luminous element in this peculiar "atmosphere" of occult influences, in which the action is clothed as in its own emanations !

A like atmospheric effect is produced by the portrayal of another of these secret influences upon the spirits of men. In the same Century, Bacon makes the following remarkable observation :

" The relations touching the force of imagination and the secret instincts of nature are so uncertain, as they require a great deal of examination ere we conclude upon them. I would have it first thoroughly inquired, whether there be any secret passages of sympathy between persons of near blood ; as parents, children, brothers, sisters, nurse-children, husbands, wives, etc. There be many reports in history, that upon the death of persons of such nearness, men have had an inward feeling of it. I myself remember, that being in Paris, and my father dying in London, two or three days before my father's death I

* " Nay, Cadwal, we must lay his head to the *east :*
My father hath a reason for 't."—*Cymbeline. IV., 2.*

had a dream, which I told to divers English gentlemen, that my father's house in the country was plastered all over with black mortar."

And in consonance, in the play, the night before Cæsar's death, his wife, Calphurnia, dreams:

> " She dreamt to-night she saw my statua,
>   Which like a fountain, with a hundred spouts,
>   Did run pure blood; and many lusty Romans
>   Came smiling, and did bathe their hands in it.
>   And these does she apply for warnings, and portents,
>   And evils imminent; and on her knee
>   Hath begg'd that I will stay at home to-day."

And as if to emphasize the potency of these secret influences, this dream is given almost literal fulfilment in the awful scene of the assassination. In the frenzy of the moment, Brutus cries:

> " So are we Cæsar's friends, that have abridged
>   His time of fearing death.— Stoop, Romans, stoop,
>   And let us bathe our hands in Cæsar's blood
>   Up to the elbows, and besmear our swords."

And Cassius also cries: "Stoop then, and wash." *

Again, in his Essay, *Of Friendship*, Bacon says: " With Julius Cæsar, Decimus Brutus had obtained that interest, as he set him down in his testament for heir in remainder after his nephew; and this was the man that had power with him to draw him forth to his death: for

---

* And as if by one of " the secret instincts of nature," and in a like contribution towards the sympathetic atmosphere of the play, Cinna, the poet, after the assassination, and the night before his death, dreams ominously:

> " I dreamt to-night that I did feast with Cæsar,
>   And things unlucky charge my fantasy:
>   I have no will to wander forth of doors,
>   Yet something leads me forth."

> " Before the days of change, still is it so:
>   By a divine *instinct*, men's minds mistrust
>   Ensuing danger."—*Richard III., II., 3.*

when Cæsar would have discharged the Senate, in regard
of some ill presages, and specially a dream of Calphurnia,
this man lifted him gently by the arm out of his chair,
telling him he hoped he would not dismiss the Senate till
his wife had dreamt a better dream ; and it seemeth his
favor was so great, as Antonius, in a letter which is re-
cited verbatim in one of Cicero's Philippics, called him
' venefica,'—' witch '; as if he had enchanted Cæsar."

And in this Century, under the head of "*Experiment
solitary touching the general sympathy of men's spirits,*"
Bacon profoundly observes : " The delight which men
have in popularity, fame, honor, submission and subjection
of other men's minds, wills, or affections, (although these
things may be desired for other ends), seemeth to be a
thing in itself, without contemplation of consequence,
grateful and agreeable to the nature of man. This thing
(surely) is not without some signification, as if all spirits
and souls of men came forth out of one divine limbus ;
*else why should men be so much affected with that which
others think or say ?* "

And in the like harmony, not only is this ' enchantment ' of Cæsar given representation in the play, but in
its portrayal, its spell is manifestly wrought through the
operation of these subtle influences :

" *Cæsar.* Decius, go tell them Cæsar will not come.*

---

* In North's translation of Plutarch, with which the English
public was then familiar, the Latin name " Decimus " had been
Anglicized into " Decius "; and obviously, under the circumstances, it was not unadvisable to conform in such details to the
English version. The same remark applies to " Antonius "
Anglicized into " Antony," " Octavianus " into " Octavius," and
to the name " Calphurnia," which is thus spelled in Bohn's edition of the Essays, but is spelled " Calpurnia " in Spedding's
edition. We can hardly attribute the adoption of these names
in the play to its author's ignorance of Latin ; for Cicero's
philosophy, so deftly expressed in the text, was not given by
Plutarch, and was only to be found in the original tongue. If,

Decius. Most mighty Cæsar, let me know some cause,
Lest I be laugh'd at when I tell them so."

Cæsar then relates Calphurnia's dream, to which Decius Brutus gives a favorable interpretation, worthy of Cicero's wit, and then continues:

"the senate have concluded
To give, this day, a crown to mighty Cæsar.
If you shall send them word you will not come,
Their minds may change. Besides it were a *mock*
Apt to be render'd, for some one to say,
'Break up the senate till another time,
When Cæsar's wife shall meet with better dreams.'
If Cæsar *hide* himself, shall they not whisper
'*Lo, Cæsar is afraid?'*
Pardon me, Cæsar: for my *dear, dear love*
To your proceeding bids me tell you this;
And *reason to my love is liable.*
Cæsar. How foolish do your fears seem now, Calphurnia!
I am ashamed I did yield to them. —
Give me my robe, for I will go; —"

And it is noticeable that previously, at the meeting of the conspirators, when doubt is expressed,

"Whether Cæsar will come forth to-day or no:"

Decius displays absolute "confidence" in himself and his powers, itself a power (see *ante*, page 187), and reveals, in part, the subtle forces, through whose 'witchery' he sways Cæsar's powerful will:

"Never fear that: if he be so resolved.
I can o'ersway him: for he loves to hear
That unicorns may be betray'd with trees,
And bears with glasses, elephants with holes,
Lions with toils, and men with flatterers:
But when I tell him he hates flatterers,
He says he does; being then most flatter'd.
Let me work:

---

however, it be regarded as a careless blunder, see *ante.* page 135, note.

For I can give his humor the true bent;
And I will bring him to the Capitol."

Again, in Act V., Scene 1, there is portrayed a brief but striking episode:

"[*Enter a messenger.*]
Messala.   Prepare you, generals;
The enemy comes on in gallant show;
Their bloody sign of battle is hung out,
And something to be done immediately.
Antony. Octavius, lead your battle softly on,
Upon the left hand of the even field.
Octavius. Upon the right hand I; keep thou the left.
Antony. Why do you cross me in this exigent?
Octavius. I do not cross you; *but I will do so.* [*March.*"

At first, we may fail to see the reason for the introduction of this contest of will between the equal Triumvirs, in which Octavius so summarily crushes Antony, or its bearing upon the theme of the play; but it was evidently a purposed touch, giving further development to its distinctive atmosphere.

In the same Century, under the head of "*Experiments in consort touching emission of immateriate virtues from the minds and spirits of men, either by affections, or by imaginations, or by other impressions,*" Bacon observes: "There was an Egyptian soothsayer, that made Antonius believe that his Genius * (which otherwise was brave and confident) was, in the presence of Octavianus Cæsar, poor and cowardly: therefore he advised him to absent himself as much as he could, and remove far from him. This soothsayer was thought to be suborned by Cleopatra, to make him live in Egypt, and other remote places from Rome. Howsoever the conceit of *a predominant or mas-*

---

* "The Genius and the mortal instruments
Are then in council;" —*II., 1.*
        "There is none but he
Whose being I do fear: and under him
My Genius is rebuked; as, it is said,
Mark Antony's was by Cæsar."—*Macbeth III., 1.*

tering spirit of one man over another is ancient, and received still, in vulgar opinion." *

In the play, in Mark Antony's case, this is merely shadowed forth in the significance of the foregoing brief episode; in conformity with the artistic requirement of a due proportion between the several parts. But this slight touch was here sufficient for atmospheric effect: for the

---

* This may be supplemented with Bacon's remark, already quoted: "Whence have arisen those conceits (now become as it were popular) of the mastering spirit, of men *unlucky* and ill-omened, of the glances of love, envy, and the like." And the whole is given complete representation in *Antony and Cleopatra*, II., 3:

"*Antony.* Say to me,
Whose fortunes shall rise higher, Cæsar's or mine?
Soothsayer. Cæsar's.
Therefore, O Antony, stay not by his side:
Thy dæmon *(that thy spirit which keeps thee)* is
Noble, courageous, high, unmatchable,
Where Cæsar is not; but near him thy angel
Becomes a Fear, as being o'erpowered; therefore
Make space enough between you.
Antony.   Speak this no more.
Soothsayer. To none but thee; no more, but when to thee.
If thou dost play with him at any game,
Thou art sure to lose; and, of that *natural luck*,
He beats thee 'gainst the odds; thy lustre thickens
When he shines by: I say again, thy *spirit*
Is all afraid to govern thee near him;
But, he away, 'tis noble.
Antony.   Get thee gone:
Say to Ventidius, I would speak with him:
                                   [*Exit Soothsayer.*
He shall to Partia.— Be it art, or hap,
He hath spoken true: the very dice obey him:
And in our sports my better cunning faints
Under his chance: if we draw lots, he speeds:
His cocks do win the battle still of mine,
When it is all to nought; and his quails ever
Beat mine, inhoop'd, at odds.   I will to Egypt."

distinctive workings of this "predominant or mastering spirit of one man over another" are given abundant manifestation in the play, in unmistakable strokes, in the portrayal of Brutus himself. Thus, in the delineation of the meeting of the conspirators at Brutus' house, when some of them propose that Cicero's adhesion be procured, note how distinctly it is made apparent that they succumb, at the instant, to Brutus' determination to the contrary. (See *ante*, page 206.)

And again, when Cassius forcibly urges the death of Antony, pointing out its necessity, Brutus' opposing will is dominant, and Antony is spared, to their ruin. And when Antony requests permission to speak at Cæsar's funeral, notwithstanding the strenuous opposition of Cassius,—

"You know not what you do ; do not consent,"—

the headstrong Brutus maintains his masterful sway, and the fateful blunder is committed. And the like occurs when Cassius, with better generalship, opposes the forward march to meet the enemy, but is compelled to yield :

"Then, with your will, go on :
We 'll along ourselves, and meet them at Philippi."

Always and everywhere, in any conflict, Brutus' will prevails : while the masterful sway of one man's spirit over another is given marked exemplification in his case, in the episode of Ligarius' visit ; of whom Brutus had declared,

"He *loves* me well, and I have given him reasons ;
Send him but hither, and I 'll fashion him,"

in a confidence amply justified in the event :

"*Ligarius.* By all the gods that Romans bow before,
I here discard my sickness ! Soul of Rome !
Brave son, derived from honorable loins !
Thou, like an exorcist, hast conjured up
My mortified spirit. Now bid me run,
And I will strive with things impossible ;

Yea, get the better of them.   What's to do?
Brutus. A piece of work that will make sick men whole.
Ligarius. But are not some whole that we must make sick?
Brutus. That must we also.   What it is, my Caius,
I shall unfold to thee, as we are going;
To whom it must be done.
Ligarius.   Set on your foot;
And, with a heart new fired, I follow you,
To do I know not what: but it sufficeth
That Brutus leads me on."

And again, the " no small dominion which imagination
holds in persuasions wrought by eloquence," effected " by
stimulating the imagination till it becomes ungovernable
and not only sets reason at nought, but offers violence to
it, partly by blinding, and partly by incensing it," is given
the most striking manifestation, in the portrayal of the
effect produced upon the Roman citizens by Antony's powerful eloquence.   Under its potent influence, they are
wrought to a pitch of ungovernable fury.   They cry:

" Revenge!   About!—seek!—burn!—fire!—kill!—slay!—
let not a traitor live!"

Reason is dethroned, and in their rage, they tear to pieces
the poet Cinna, merely because he bears the name of one
of the conspirators; while Brutus, Cassius, and the rest,
are compelled to flee the city to escape the storm.

The play of *Julius Cæsar* is a two-fold tragedy, whose
common core is a Crime.   Its outward, tangible tragedy
is the murder of Cæsar: its inner, spiritual tragedy is
the shipwreck of Brutus' noble soul.   The two are given
complete representation, the one within the other, in a
grandeur of conception and execution that is one of the
sublimities which attend the heights of man's creative
power.   It is the embodiment of the intangible within the
tangible, of the spiritual in the material, of a soul within
a body.   The spiritual tragedy, as in life, is of paramount

interest, and all things are made to work together towards
its adequate expression. Its primal elements are the invisible forces, " that work upon the spirits of men "; and
these are so inwrought into the action, and given such tangible manifestation in things visible, that we are actually
brought within their realm, and made to feel their power.
Though, as in nature, we can only comprehend their underlying principles, or " mode of operation," through the
closest study of their manifestations ; wherein also the
play is fashioned " after the model of the world," and upon
the pattern of the Highest Art.

The mightiest forces are ever the subtlest ; both in nature in general, and in their action upon man. This is
equally true in Art. And these apparently casual, unre-
lated manifestations, we have been considering, are in
reality integral developments of that invisible world enshrined in the play, whose consistent portrayal is a principal source of its subtle charm. They are strains from
out of that world, consonant with the dominant tones ;
blending with them into rich chords, which contribute materially towards that magnificent harmony, which in its
total effect so delights us, though we may be unconscious
of the cause. It is the harmony inherent in an artistic
whole, with every part expressive of its theme, in its complete development. And in this respect, and in its interpretative revelation of the inner, invisible world through
its outward manifestations, the play is one of the triumphs
of man's creative art.

In our study of the material universe, we are ever approaching a clearer apprehension of its essential unity.
Prof. Lodge, the distinguished English scientist, in his
Modern Views of Electricity, after recounting the famous
experiments of Dr. Hertz, which demonstrate the identity
of light and electricity, gives expression to the present
attitude of scientific men in these beautiful words :

"An old and trite subject is seen to have in the light of theory an unexpected charm and brilliancy. So it is with a great number of old, familiar facts at the present time. The present is an epoch of astounding activity in physical science. Progress is a thing of months and weeks, almost of days. The long line of isolated ripples of past discovery seems blending into a mighty wave, on the crest of which one begins to discern some oncoming magnificent generalization. The suspense is becoming feverish, at times almost painful. One feels like a boy who has been long strumming on the silent keyboard of a deserted organ, into the chest of which an unseen power begins to blow a vivifying breath. Astonished, he now finds that the touch of a finger elicits a responsive note, and he hesitates, half delighted, half affrighted, lest he be deafened by the chords which it would seem he can now summon forth almost at will."

We have tried the experiment of the recognition of Bacon's authorship of the plays. We have been working upon the hypothesis of the identity of origin of his prose and of this poetry. We have put it to the test, in the direct application of the thoughts, the observations, and the inductions set forth in that prose to the illuminative interpretation of the play. And may it not justly be said, that this old, familiar drama, the precious heritage of three centuries, is seen to have, in the light of this "theory," thus applied, a depth, a richness, a power, a magnificence of harmony never before apprehended? And above and beyond all, have we not been gaining distinct glimpses of the fundamental methods of the Master?

CHAPTER VII.

BRUTUS, like most remarkable men, is a psychological study. He is, however, a creation, and is therefore best studied from the standpoint of his author, and through the medium of his peculiar Psychology. This is briefly summarized in the following, from *De Augmentis*, Second Book; where it will be observed that its distinctive characteristic is the exceptional importance attributed to the imagination, in its correlation with reason and the will:

" The doctrine concerning the Intellect (most excellent King), and the doctrine concerning the Will of man, are as it were twins by birth. For purity of illumination and freedom of will began and fell together ; and nowhere in the universal nature of things is there so intimate a sympathy as between truth and goodness. The more should learned men be ashamed, if in knowledge they be as the winged angels, but in their desires as crawling serpents ; carrying about with them minds like a mirror indeed, but a mirror polluted and false.

" I come now to the knowledge which respects the use and objects of the faculties of the human soul. It has two parts, and those well known and by general agreement admitted ; namely, Logic and Ethic. . . . Logic discourses of the understanding and Reason ; Ethic of the Will, Appetite, and Affections: the one produces determinations, the other actions. It is true, indeed, that the Imagination performs the office of an agent or messenger or proctor in both provinces, both the judicial and the ministerial. For Sense sends all kinds of images over to Imagination for Reason to judge of ; and Reason again, when it has made its judgment and selection, sends them over to Imagination before the decree be put in execution. For voluntary motion is ever preceded and incited by imagination ; so that imagination is as a common instrument to both,— both reason and will ; saving that this Janus of imagination has two different faces ; for the face toward reason has the print of truth, and the face towards action has the print of goodness ; which nevertheless are faces,

— quales decet esse sororum.

["— Such as sisters' faces should be.—*Ovid. Met. II., 14.*"]

Neither is the imagination simply and only a messenger ; but it is either invested with or usurps no small authority in itself, besides the simple duty of the message. For it was well said by Aristotle, ' That the mind has over the body that commandment which the lord has over a bondman ; but that reason has over the imagination that commandment which a magistrate has over a free citizen,' who may come also to rule in his turn. For we see that in matters of faith and religion our imagination raises itself above our reason ; not that divine illumination resides in the imagination ; its seat being rather in the very citadel of the mind and understanding ; but that the divine grace uses the motions of the imagination as an instrument of illumination, just as it uses the motions of the will as an instrument of virtue ; which is the reason why religion ever sought access to the mind by similitudes, types, parables, visions, dreams." (Here follows the statement, already quoted, of the dominion exercised by the imagination when stimulated by eloquence, when at times it " not only sets reason at nought, but offers violence to it, partly by blinding and partly by incensing it.")

These principles afford us the key to the adequate comprehension of Brutus ; enabling us, through their application to his mental constitution, as it is developed in the play, to lay hold upon its very substance, and to understand it; both in its complex unity, and in its distinctly marked details. And thereby, perhaps, we may come very close to one of the secrets of the Dramatist's Art; how he was enabled to make a character "universal," a representative type, while at the same time, it is distinctively an individual portrait.

Upon close study of the "manifestations" for that which is manifested, it becomes very clear that in Brutus the imagination is very ardent; smouldering, indeed, under a reserved exterior, but ever ready to leap into flame upon occasion offered; that his will is powerful; and that his reason is weak; its function being continually usurped and exercised by the imagination. That his will is powerful, the reader must have already recognized; and the rest will, perhaps, become equally manifest.

It is strikingly significant that his conclusions are uniformly unsound, the product of his imagination, and contrary to the fact.

Thus, upon his first introduction to our acquaintance, and while he is talking with Cassius, sounds of applause are borne in upon him, through his "Sense." And out of these impressions, his imagination immediately fashions a scene without, wherein the people are heaping honors upon Cæsar, and possibly choosing him for their king:

> "I do *believe* that these applauses are
> For some new honors that are heap'd on Cæsar."

> "I do fear the people
> Choose Cæsar for their King."

When, on the contrary, as appears from Casca's report, "there was a crown offered him; and being offered him, he put it by with the back of his hand, thus; and *then* the people fell a shouting"; "and at every putting by, mine honest neighbors shouted"; "and still as he refused it, the rabblement shouted, and clapped their chapped hands."

He believes also in Cassius; putting implicit faith in his protestations of love, and of his kindly intent:

"That you do love me, I am nothing jealous."

When, in fact, Cassius is utterly unmindful of Brutus' welfare; seeking only to mould him into the furtherance of his own envious ends:

"Cæsar doth bear me hard: but he loves Brutus;
If I were Brutus now, and he were Cassius,
He should not humor me."

And when, at his instigation, writings, in several hands, are thrown into Brutus' window,

"all tending to the great opinion
That Rome holds of his name; wherein obscurely
Cæsar's ambition shall be glanced at,"

Brutus' imagination pieces out these obscure hints; picturing, in what is to him a vivid reality, all Rome looking to him for its redress; and thereby awakening in himself an impulse that is irresistible:

"Am I entreated
To speak and strike? O Rome! I make thee promise,
If the redress will follow, thou receivest
Thy full petition at the hand of *Brutus!*"

When, as matter of fact, not only did these several writings proceed from a single designing hand, but there was absolutely no demand whatever from the public for redress.

"The baseless fabric of this vision," conjured up by Cassius, existed only in Brutus' imagination. Beautiful in theory, expressive of a lofty ideal of the state, but, in the existing conditions, as chimerical as Plato's republic, it was totally at variance with the facts. As subsequently appears, the conspirators were but the fingers of one man, only eight in number, and upon Cæsar's death they were compelled by the angered populace to flee for their lives.

Cuvier, we are told, could, by the "scientific use of the

imagination," reconstruct an extinct animal from a single bone. And Brutus, likewise, given one or two facts, or sense impressions, was wont to develop therefrom a complete structure. But Cuvier's work was based upon close observation of instance after instance in nature. It was the outcome of induction from a vast accumulation of facts, and was, therefore, in close contact with the actual at every point; and, as was subsequently shown, it was thoroughly reliable. While, on the other hand, Brutus' supposed cognizance was a sort of hurried "divination" from insufficient data, a "jumped conclusion," the product of his imagination, and a manifest delusion. Nevertheless, it was to him as vivid and as real as the actual; and as potent in effecting his determinations.

Indeed, in his conduct of affairs throughout, and especially in his soliloquy, Brutus shows himself to be closely allied to the class whom Bacon aptly termed "intellectualists": whose methods in the study of nature he so strongly condemned, and against whose tendencies he labored continually to warn and guard mankind.

The following is the passage referred to, from his *Advancement of Learning*, First Book; though there are many like utterances, with much pertinent detail, that should all be read, if one would catch Bacon's spirit and intent, and adequately comprehend the full amplitude of his thought, in its practical bearing upon "the whole fortunes, and affairs, and powers, and works of men":

"Another error hath proceeded from too great a reverence, and a kind of adoration of the mind and understanding of man; by means whereof men have withdrawn themselves too much from the contemplation of nature and the observations of experience, and have tumbled up and down in their own reason and conceits. Upon these *intellectualists*, Heraclitus gave a just censure, saying, 'Men sought truth in their own little worlds, and not in the

great and common world '; for they disdain to spell, and
so by degrees to read in the volume of God's works ; and
contrariwise, by continual meditation and agitation of wit
do urge and as it were invocate their own spirits to divine
and give oracles unto them, whereby they are deservedly
deluded."

In fact, Brutus, as by design, from his very constitution, seems to have been one of the noble family of " ideal-
ists," in the popular acceptation of the term. Pure and
unselfish, with Appetite under dominion and the Affections predominant, a lover of music and of books, and
attuned to self-devotion, he rose above the coarseness of
material things and dwelt largely in an ideal world, far
superior to the actual, and ofttimes out of touch with it.

Thus, when Cassius proposes that the conspirators be
bound to secrecy by the sanctity of an oath, Brutus fairly
scorns the thought,—so contrary is it to his conception of
human nature, and especially of the Roman character :

> "To think that, or our cause, or our performance,
> Did need an oath ; when every drop of blood
> That every Roman bears, and nobly bears,
> Is guilty of a several bastardy,
> If he do break the smallest particle
> Of any promise that hath pass'd from him."

And as usual the conspirators bow to his will.

But in Act II., Scene 3, which is apparently introduced
solely to make Brutus' error manifest, Artemidorus enters
reading the following paper :

> "Cæsar, beware of Brutus ; take heed of Cassius ; come not
> near Casca ; have an eye to Cinna ; trust not Trebonius ; mark
> well Metellus Cimber ; Decius Brutus loves thee not ; thou hast
> wronged Caius Ligarius. There is but one mind in all of these
> men, and it is bent against Cæsar. If thou beest not immortal,
> look about you ; security gives way to conspiracy. The mighty
> gods defend thee ! Thy lover, Artemidorus."

The distinct particularity with which each of the conspirators is mentioned by name, in this declaration of their

purpose against Cæsar, indicates that the information came
from "inside sources." But for the barest chance, which
prevented its reading, not Cæsar but the conspirators
would have been put to death. And here again, we may
discern the presence and movement of that mysterious
actor, Fate, which is ever looming up in the background,
playing its part in human affairs.

Again, Brutus is wofully mistaken in Antony. Viewing him from his own lofty standpoint, and observing him
to be a voluptuary, "a masker and a reveller," "that
revels long o' nights," and is apparently given over to the
dominion of Appetite, Brutus is instinctively contempt-
uous of such a creature. Out of this insufficient date, he
fashions an Antony that is pictured before him, in vivid
outlines, as a weakling, irresolute, reckless, void of stam-
ina, and unworthy of consideration; who is a mere "limb
of Cæsar," impotent after the head is cut off:

> "And for Mark Antony, think not of him;
> For he can do no more than Cæsar's arm,
> When Cæsar's head is off."

Cassius furnishes additional data:

> "we shall find of him
> A shrewd contriver; and you know his means,
> If he improve them, may well stretch so far
> As to annoy us all."

And he urges as a further consideration:

> "Yet I do fear him,
> For the ingrafted love he bears to Cæsar, — "

But Brutus, impatient, interrupts:

> "Alas, good Cassius, all that he can do
> Is to himself,— take thought, and die for Cæsar:
> And that were much he should; for he is given
> To sports, to wildness, and much company."

And with idealistic practical wisdom, the outcome of a
kindly heart, which was also exceedingly sensitive to the
good opinion of others, he would spare Antony, because

" Our course will seem too bloody, Caius Cassius,
  To cut the head off, and then hack the limbs;
  Like wrath in death and envy afterwards; "

not realizing that, once their hands were imbued in Cæsar's
blood, self-preservation and the success of the cause made
Antony's death a political necessity.

Indeed, viewed closely, there is something inexpressi-
bly horrible in this attempt of a noble soul to conduct an
assassination upon ideal principles :

" Let us be *sacrificers*, but not butchers, Caius,
We all stand up against the *spirit* of Cæsar;
And in the spirit of men there is no blood :
O, that we then could come by Cæsar's spirit,
And not dismember Cæsar ! But, alas,
Cæsar must bleed for it."

And he puts De Quincey to the blush, in his depiction
of " Murder as a Fine Art ":

" And gentle friends,
Let 's kill him boldly, but not wrathfully;
Let 's carve him as a dish fit for the gods,
Not hew him as a carcase fit for hounds:
And let our hearts, as subtle masters do,
Stir up their servants to an act of rage,
And after seem to chide them. This shall make
Our purpose necessary, and not envious :
Which so appearing to the common eyes,
We shall be call'd purgers, not murderers."

He does violence to his own instincts ; sharing in Cæsar's
murder, in

" The deep damnation of his taking off,"

utterly oblivious of its essential enormity ; when all the
while he is fairly choked with loathing, by the mere breath
of the vileness that is its native atmosphere ; though he
would mask it under the genial influence of a gracious
affability :

" O Conspiracy !
Sham'st thou to show thy dangerous brow by night,

When *evils* are most free?   O then, by day
Where wilt thou find a cavern dark enough
To mask thy monstrous visage?   Seek none, Conspiracy;
Hide it in smiles and affability :
For if thou put thy native semblance on,
Not Erebus itself were dim enough
To hide thee from prevention."

And again, at Cæsar's assassination, when Antony comes forward and shakes the bloody hands of the conspirators, in pretended friendship, asking that he be permitted to speak at Cæsar's funeral, and promising not to blame them, Brutus, overruling Cassius' protest, freely consents. Surely, he may safely yield to the prompting of humanity,

"when every drop of blood
That every Roman bears, and nobly bears,
Is guilty of a several bastardy,
If he do break the smallest particle
Of any *promise* that hath pass'd from him."

But we all know the disastrous consequences.*

And yet again, at the camp near Sardis, when their fate is involved in the decision of a vital question of military strategy; one requiring the exercise of calm, clear judgment and the utmost discretion; when Cassius ad-

---

* Brutus' error arose from his persistent judgment of others by himself; ganging all by the high standard of his own native nobility, and his accustomed honor and integrity. As Bacon warningly puts it:

" Let us consider again the false appearances imposed upon us by every man's own individual nature and custom, in that feigned supposition that Plato maketh of the cave : for certainly if a child were continued in a grot or cave under the earth until maturity of age, and come suddenly abroad, he would have strange and absurd imaginations; so, in like manner, although our persons live in view of heaven, yet our spirits are included in the caves of our own complexions and customs; which minister unto us infinite errors and vain opinions, if they be not recalled to examination."—*Advancement of Learning*, Second Book.

vances cogent reasons why they should not march to Philippi, Brutus, as in Antony's case, meets them with inferior reasons. He is impatient of discussion, refusing to listen to Cassius, and waxing warm, his imagination usurps control; transforming hope into certainty, and picturing their hosts advancing to assured victory upon an imaginary tide whereon they float:

> " There is a tide in the affairs of men,
>   Which taken at the flood, leads on to fortune;
>   Omitted, all the voyage of their life
>   Is bound in shallows and in miseries.
>   And we must take the current when it serves,
>   Or lose our ventures."

Cassius bows to the inevitable:

> " Then, with your will, go on:
>   We'll along ourselves, and meet them at Philippi."

And well might Octavius say to Antony:

> " Now, Antony, our hopes are answered,"

for the conspirators advance to predestined defeat and to death.

Let us now turn directly to the consideration of the tragedy wrought in Brutus, wherein the seed sown by Cassius was developed to a maturity, which ripened into such a terrible harvest.

An ardent patriot, we find him, in the beginning, greatly troubled over the condition of affairs in Rome. He is out of sympathy with their trend, and cares not to " see the order of the course."

> " I am not gamesome: I do lack some part
>   Of that quick spirit that is in Antony."

> " If I have veil'd my look,
> I turn the trouble of my countenance
> Merely upon myself. Vexed I am,
> Of late, with passions of some difference,
> Conceptions only proper to myself."

> " Nor construe any further my neglect,

Than that poor Brutus, with himself at war,
Forgets the shows of love to other men."

These warring passions were, undoubtedly, his love of
Cæsar and his affection for Rome:

"Not that I loved Cæsar less, but that I loved Rome
more," was the burden of his subsequent speech to the
Romans.

As Cæsar's devoted lover, his heart would rejoice at
any honors, even the highest, that might cluster upon him.
But as a lover of Rome, he would not have him crowned
king. Hence the turmoil in his soul, and his manifest
distaste for the present proceedings, tending toward that
issue. But he is still faithful to both loves; and, as is inevitable in a true heart, there is a struggle for some possible basis of reconciliation, whereby both loves may continue their sway. A truly loyal friend, when from the
applause without he infers that possibly the feared consummation is already being effected, it is not to Cæsar,
but to the people, that he imputes the act:

"I do fear the people
Choose Cæsar for their King."

And again, when renewed applause is heard:

"I do believe that these applauses are
For some new honors that are heap'd on Cæsar."

Cassius, with malign intent, makes of this an opening
wedge:

"Ay, do you fear it?
Then must I think you would not have it so."

To which Brutus frankly replies:

"I would not, Cassius; yet I love him well:—"

And then Cassius, with blow after blow, widens this
"rift in the lute." He projects into Brutus' mind, in
vivid outlines, a distorted image of Cæsar, which rapidly
develops into what becomes to him an awful reality. His
eyes are opened, as he believes, and he beholds in this

man, whom he has been loving so dearly, a monstrous, abnormal, and ever-growing greatness, that is filling Rome
to the suppression of all else:

> "Now in the name of all the gods at once,
>   Upon what meat doth this our Cæsar feed,
>   That he is grown so great?"
> "Why, man, he doth bestride the narrow world,
>   Like a Colossus; and we petty men
>   Walk under his huge legs, and peep about
>   To find ourselves dishonorable graves."
>   "this man
> Is now become a god:"
>   "whose bend doth awe the world."

This "monstrous visage," thus indelibly impressed upon
Brutus' mind, and with such burning intensity, becomes
thenceforward his mental representation of Cæsar, and
is, in effect, one of the realities of the world in which he
dwells. A little later, we behold its reflection in his impulsive utterance:

> "Shall Rome stand under one man's awe?
> What! Rome?"

Brutus' honorable metal, truly, has been " wrought from
that it is disposed"; for his whole attitude towards Cæsar
has undergone a radical change. In one fell sweep, the
idol has been thrown from its pedestal, transformed into
a monster, and is now become an object of instinctive
aversion, rapidly ripening into deadly hostility. His
former devoted affection for Cæsar has been literally
" murdered," deadened for the time by violence; while
his love for Rome is become a consuming fire. Their conflict is ended; and henceforward, the struggle is of altogether another sort.

There remains, indeed, a lingering regret, a fond remembrance of the Cæsar of his former knowledge, which
Brutus idealizes into love for the present Cæsar; but it is
love without influence, illusive and delusive, the spirit-

less spectre of its former self ; without a spark of vitality,
a single prompting towards salvation, or even a reminder
of the obligations of friendship.

There was a foundation of truth in the worldling Antony's impassioned words :

> " This was the most unkindest cut of all :
> For when the noble Cæsar saw *him* stab,
> Ingratitude, more strong than traitor's arms,
> Quite vanquish'd him : then burst his mighty heart."

Having thus effectually " whet " Brutus against Cæsar,
Cassius' remaining task is easy. He has but to suggest,
the more remotely the better, and Brutus' imagination
does all the rest.

And here let it be observed that Cassius' effort to
mould Brutus to his design by awakening in him a personal envy of Cæsar was a total failure. Bacon has given
us an infallible test : " Again, envy is ever joined with
the comparison of a man's self ; and where there is no
comparison, no envy." We apply this test, and while
Cassius' animus thus becomes plainly manifest, the closest scrutiny of Brutus fails to reveal, either in thought
(soliloquy) or in utterance, the slightest comparison of
himself with Cæsar ; and this is decisive of the matter.

Nevertheless, Cassius' efforts do most assuredly accomplish his ulterior purpose, and are, in fact, exquisitely
adapted to that end. For Brutus is a man peculiarly under the sway of any noble Affection. In him, love of self
is wholly subordinate to his awakened love for Rome.
And every appeal made by the ignoble Cassius to his supposed baser nature * acts instead, and with tenfold force,

---

* For Cassius also is made illustrative of this source of error
in human judgment, in pursuance of the broad method of treatment before mentioned. Just as the painter repeats, in minor
details, the colors which appear in mass in his picture : or as
Gervinus more adequately puts it, in his *résumé* of the Plays :

upon his more generous instincts ; awakening alarm, quickening his love for the "general" to a flame of devotion, and inciting him to decisive action.

Cassius' vivid portrayal of Cæsar's inordinate greatness :

"Age, thou art shamed!
Rome, thou hast lost the breed of noble bloods!
When went there by an age, since the great flood,
But it was famed with more than with one man?
When could they say, till now, that talk'd of Rome,
That her wide walls encompass'd but one man?
Now is it Rome indeed, and room enough,
When there is in it but one only man,"

subtly enforced by the whole power of his personality concentrated upon Brutus, awakens in him no spark of envy, no thought of its effect upon himself individually, but what is much more effective, it enkindles his anxious solicitude for Rome into immediate and intense alarm, an acute and really overpowering Apprehension. This is, in effect, the work of his highly excited imagination ; producing a mental condition which the specialist, skilled in medical jurisprudence, will clearly understand.

And in this state, Cassius' obscure hints, wherein

"Cæsar's ambition shall be *glanced* at,"

are as torches to Brutus' heated imagination ; kindling it into an ungovernable flame, that envelops all his powers, consuming his affection for Cæsar, blinding and incensing his reason, and becoming the illumination of his will.

In his concentrated effort, Cassius' nearest approach to a suggestion of action is in these concluding words :

"There was a Brutus once that would have brook'd
The eternal devil to keep his state in Rome,
As easily as a *king*."

"Just as Shakespeare went from instance to instance in his judgment of moral actions, and never founded a law *on a single experience*, so did Bacon in natural science avoid leaping from one experience of the senses to general principles."

Brutus' imagination lays hold upon this hint, so subtly appealing to his nobler instincts, his pride, and his patriotism, and makes it the corner-stone of the whole edifice of his excited thought; developing therefrom a complete structure, the exalted embodiment of what he conceives to be his personal and imperative *duty;* and of which we catch a glimpse in his later outburst:

> "Shall Rome stand under one man's awe?
> What! Rome?
> My ancestors did from the streets of Rome
> The Tarquin drive, when he was call'd a *king.*"

Beneath the surface, the sure foundation upon which his reason rests, there lies the settled conviction that Cæsar is absolutely determined to become king in Rome.[*]

---

[*] And with consummate art, and almost limitless patience as well, Brutus is shown to have received, immediately following Cassius' utterance, and through his senses, Impressions which are so apparently decisive as to Cæsar's inner and determined purpose, that to him they must have been " confirmations strong as proofs of holy writ."

And first, as to the experience of the eye: Now more alert even than Cassius, when Cæsar and his train return from the course, Brutus notes and calls Cassius' attention to their peculiar appearance:

> " But look you, Cassius,
> The angry spot doth glow on Cæsar's brow,
> And all the rest look like a chidden train:
> Calphurnia's cheek is pale; and Cicero
> Looks with such ferret and such fiery eyes,
> As we have seen him in the Capitol,
> Being cross'd in conference by some senators."

Plucking Casca by the sleeve, at Cassius' instigation, he is foremost in their eager questionings as to what had happened. He then *hears* the narrative of an eye-witness, whose account, obviously, is profusely colored with his own personal opinions and deductions; shrewd, cynical, and doubtless discerning.

He hears from Casca that this day, Antony, Cæsar's devoted

This neither receives nor admits of any discussion. It is now beyond question ; the one clearly recognized and established fact. But this, most assuredly, calls for *prevention*. And there is heard, in his inner consciousness, the voice of his great ancestor, thus evoked from the shades, summoning him to action ; if indeed, he be not the degenerate son of such a worthy sire. It incites him to a like act of heroic devotion. And thence the idea takes possession of him, that death — Cæsar's violent death — is the one preventive remedy, the bounden duty to which he is called. And this also becomes a settled conviction, attaining over him what is known as the dominating power of the *fixed idea ;* entertained in that dreadful certainty that partakes of madness.* He is caught in the mad whirl of this vor-

---

friend, thrice offered him the crown : that " he put it by thrice, every time gentler than other ": that "he put it by once ; but for all that, he would fain have had it. Then he offered it to him again ; then he put it by again ; but to my thinking, he was very loth to lay his fingers off it. And then he offered it the third time ; he put it the third time by : and still as he refused it, the rabblement shouted, and clapped their chapped hands, and threw up their sweaty night-caps, and uttered such a deal of stinking breath, because Cæsar refused the crown, that it had almost choked Cæsar ; for he swooned and fell down at it ": and there was the end of the matter.

Brutus' precipitate conclusion brings forcibly to mind Bacon's earnest caution to mankind, in his *Novum Organum*, First Book :

" But by far the greatest hindrance and aberration of the human understanding proceeds from the dulness, incompetency, and deceptious of the senses ; in that things *which strike the sense* outweigh things which do not immediately strike it, though they be more important. Hence it is that speculation commonly ceases when sight ceases ; insomuch that of things invisible there is little or no observation."

* " *Antony.*   And 't was I
    That the *mad* Brutus ended."
                            —*Antony and Cleopatra, III., 9.*

tex, and all his thoughts circle continually round its centre : while the vision of the heroism that lies at its core
so entrances him that he seeks no escape. Egotism unconsciously finds supreme expression in this almost unparalleled act of devotion ; the impending sacrifice of both
himself and his loved one upon the altar of his country.
His moral perceptions are dazed and bewildered in the
overshadowing presence of such dazzling splendor. The
cup is intoxicating in its sweetness : and we can now understand, perhaps as never before, how the Nihilist, for
example, can eagerly, aye joyously, throw the bomb, whose
explosion must inevitably ingulf himself in the destruction purposed for his Czar.

Under the tension of this morbid excitement, when
such a mighty destiny is felt crowding upon him, Brutus
is evidently wrought up to the highest pitch of mental and
spiritual exaltation ; as witness his horrible travesty of
murder :

"Let's carve him as a dish fit for the gods."

And further, it should be remembered that though a
man of inflexible will, Brutus, when himself, is naturally
of the sweetest disposition, tender-hearted, sympathetic,
and forbearing. "His life was gentle"; full of loving
kindness and delicate attentions to the comfort and happiness of even his attendants :

"*Brutus.* I pray you, sirs, lie in my tent, and sleep;
It may be I shall raise you by and by
On business to my brother Cassius.
Var. So please you, we will stand, and watch your pleasure.
Brutus. I will not have it so : lie down, good sirs ;
It may be I shall otherwise bethink me.—

. . . .

[*To Lucius.*]
It was well done; and thou shalt sleep again ;
I will not hold thee long : if I do live,
I will be good to thee. [*Music and a Song.*

> This is a sleepy tune: — O murderous slumber!
> Lay'st thou thy leaden mace upon my boy,
> That plays thee music? — Gentle knave, good night;
> I will not do thee so much wrong to wake thee.
> If thou dost nod, thou break'st thy instrument;
> I 'll take it from thee; and, good boy, good night."—

But now, an ominous change makes itself distinctly manifest. He is continuously *sleepless*. He becomes sullenly dumb, morose, irritable, and impatient; ungentle even to his devoted wife, "musing and sighing," and moodily self-absorbed:

> "You have ungently, Brutus,
> Stole from my bed: and yesternight, at supper,
> You suddenly arose, and walk'd about,
> Musing and sighing, with your arms across:
> And when I asked you what the matter was,
> You *stared* upon me with ungentle looks:
> I urged you further; then you scratch'd your head,
> And too impatiently stamp'd with your foot:
> Yet I insisted, yet you answer'd not;
> But, with an angry wafture of your hand,
> Gave sign for me to leave you: so I did;
> Fearing to strengthen that impatience
> Which seemed too much enkindled. . . .
> It will not let you eat, nor talk, nor sleep;
> And, could it work so much upon your shape
> As it hath much prevail'd on your condition,
> *I should not know you*, Brutus."

All too plainly, Brutus is for the time distracted, — drawn away from himself. And as he muses, his weary brain is overrun with "figures" and "fantasies." Nature and experience, as is seen in his soliloquy, are continually affording him subtle analogies, which feed and strengthen his delusion. From the first inception of this dreadful thing, till its final enactment, all the interim is one prolonged mental delirium, a disordered conclave of "the Genius and the mortal instruments," like unto "a phantasma, or a hideous dream":

"Since Cassius first did *whet* me against Cæsar,
I have not slept.
Between the acting of a dreadful thing
And the first motion, all the interim is
Like a phantasma, or a hideous dream:
The Genius and the mortal instruments
Are then in council; and the state of man,
Like to a little kingdom, suffers then
The nature of an insurrection."

When reason, even temporarily, is set at naught, de-throned, and her province usurped, then indeed does the little kingdom of man suffer "*the nature of an insurrection.*" And in this "council," Brutus' unregulated powers act in unison, as if they were allied in a conspiracy to enforce this "fixed idea." Affection is clamoring for its satisfaction, in this supreme act of self-devotion. Imag-ination pictures its entrancing glories, and presents no other alternative. Reason, subjected, is forced to lend its tottering aid: while the Will, awaiting determination, is subtly enforcing the affirmative.*

---

* The following, from Bacon's *Advancement of Learning,* Second Book, are material aids to our comprehension of Brutus:

"Secondly, there is a seducement that worketh by the strength of the impression and not by the subtilty of the illaquea-tion [sophism]; not so much perplexing the reason, as *overrul-ing it by power of the imagination.* But this part I think more proper to handle when I shall speak of Rhetoric. But lastly, there is a yet much more important and profound kind of falla-cies in the mind of man, which I find not observed or inquired at all, and think good to place here, as that which of all others appertaineth most to rectify judgment; the force whereof is such, as it doth not dazzle or snare the understanding in some particulars, but doth more generally and inwardly infect and corrupt the state thereof. For the mind of man is far from *the nature of a clear and equal glass,* wherein the beams of things should reflect according to their true incidence; nay, it is rather like an enchanted glass, full of superstition and imposture, if it be not delivered and reduced. For this purpose, let us consider

In this 'negotiation within himself' Brutus thinks aloud; thus affording us an exemplification of its general character and course of procedure. And it is the especial province of this soliloquy to enable us, as far as may be, to "think over his thoughts after him," in their painful development; to follow them in their circuitous round, as it is unrolled before us. For as Bacon profoundly observes, in his *De Augmentis*, Sixth Book:

"Certainly it is possible for a man in a greater or less degree to revisit his own knowledge, and trace over again the footsteps both of his cognition and consent; and by that means to transplant it into another mind, just as it grew in his own."

"It must be by his death":

Brutus' bewildered mind is involved in the intricacies of a labyrinthine maze. This is the centre from which he starts, and to which he always returns. He is bound to it by chords of the heart, whose pull is stronger than magnetic earth's upon the needle. The sane mind, indeed,

---

the false appearances that are imposed upon us by the general nature of the mind, beholding them in an example or two; as first in that instance which is the root of all superstition, namely, *That to the nature of the mind of all men it is consonant for the affirmative or active to affect more than the negative or privative.*" (Bacon's italics.) And again:

"The duty and office of Rhetoric is to apply Reason to Imagination for the better moving of the Will. For we see Reason is disturbed in the administration thereof by three means: by Illaqueation or Sophism, which pertains to Logic; by Imagination or Impression, which pertains to Rhetoric; and by Passion or Affection, which pertains to Morality (Ethic.) And as in negotiation with others men are *wrought* by cunning, by importunity, and by vehemency; so in this negotiation within ourselves, men are undermined by Inconsequences, solicited and importuned by Impressions or Observations, and transported by Passions."

can scarcely comprehend his absolute " possession " by
this idea ; wrought through the spell of its horrible fascination.

The ideas, the representative conceptions, aye the realities of Home, Country, Humanity, and God, are intrenched
in the citadel of man's soul ; held there by the strong
grasp of his affections. In supreme moments, it becomes
manifest that they are dearer to him than life itself. And
the saner the man, the more dominant they are over him.
He is " possessed " by them : they influence and ofttimes
determine his conduct. And these "fixed ideas" are sound
and sane, because they are cognitions of basic *realities.*
It is only when they are in whole, or in part, delusive —
illusions of the imagination—that their presence raises the
question of insanity, or of partial or temporary aberration.
Galileo's conception was the recognition of a reality ; and
the world justly regards him as a genius. Had it been in
fact a delusion, the world, as justly, would have pronounced him a crank. The difference was due to his
" purity of illumination," through the clear, " dry light "
of reason.

Looking through this glass into an abnormal condition,
we gain a faint glimpse of the nature and essential characteristics of Brutus' hallucination. For it is a development of defective vision, literally, " the perception of
things which have no reality." In a word, he is the unconscious victim of a chimera of his inflamed imagination.
The idea, or mental conception, of Cæsar's violent death,
as the one and only prevention of the apprehended danger, is to him the vision, intensely vivid, of a reality. It
has become one of the verities of his " little kingdom."
And this idea quickly expands and develops into a form-
ulated *Act.* Putting Cæsar to death, becomes his meditation, or as the lawyers would say, his " premeditation."
This " dreadful thing," whose *animus* is the spirit of fan-

aticism, insensibly entwines itself around all his powers, becomes seated in his affections, and is at length as strongly, as surely intrenched in the citadel, as are any of the sanctities mentioned. The outward manifestations justly alarm his wife; and within,— between its final acting and the first motion,—

> "all the interim is
> Like a phantasma, or a hideous dream."

During this mild delirium, it even dawns upon him that the killing of Cæsar is not a butchery but a " sacrifice ": and his benighted mind, under the lurid illumination of his imagination, discerns in this act the enshrinement of all these sanctities, their concrete crystallization, their embodied essence,— and need we wonder at its dazzling, intoxicating power? Or that it insensibly develops into the *choice* of his noble soul?

Indeed, looking closely, we can perceive on his part no effort to escape this act; nor even the desire. But strange to say, in all his gropings, though perhaps unconsciously, *he is ever seeking after its adequate justification;* centering his efforts on the discovery and upbuilding of a reasonable vindication of his choice : nor will he be balked by any difficulties encountered. Nevertheless, he would be thoroughly honest with himself,

> "and, for my part,
> I know no personal cause to spurn at him,"

In Cæsar personally, aside from his purpose, he finds no fault. However it may be with Cassius, for his part, he has no personal ground. The cause, the occasion, lies not in this,

> " But for the general. He would be crowned:
> How that might change his nature, there's the question":

Clearly, the virtual gravamen in the matter, a fundamental and unquestionable grievance, is *oppression*, in the state and of the people. It goes without saying, that Tyranny—Cæsar's apprehended tyranny—"his arbitrary rule, responsible only to himself, and without holding himself to responsibility," is the monstrous evil that must be prevented, even " by his death." Conscience and reason alike rest contentedly upon this secure foundation.

But he is also well aware, as soon appears, that Cæsar, in the past, notably, has shown no tendency to rule without holding himself to responsibility, but rather the contrary.

He finds, and finds again, that there is here no material that can be builded upon this foundation. But how far the exercise of the kingly prerogative might change his nature, "*There's the question.*" For if Cæsar's rule would not be tyrannical, then, certainly, his death would be unwarranted ; without adequate cause or occasion. But if, on the contrary, his nature would change, and he would become a tyrant, then, that it must be prevented by his death is self-evident. (To Brutus.) And reason, though almost blinded in this lurid light, would seem for the moment to be assuming her lawful sway. A debatable question is here submitted to its consideration ; whose point becomes thenceforth the focus of the whole discussion.

But thereupon, instantly, imagination, as if " retained " by some unknown power, pictures before him a killing analogy :

> " It is the bright day that brings forth the adder :
> And that craves wary walking. Crown him — that — "

Here a link is missing. Imagination breaks down : it is unable to complete the figure. Cæsar is no adder, bearing an envenomed sting !

But reason rises triumphantly. It discerns in this broken analogy what may prove to be a restful premise :

> " And then, I grant, we put a sting in him,
> That at his will he may do danger with."

It advances a further step ; discerning clearly an applicable principle :

"The abuse of greatness is when it disjoins
Remorse from power : "

Here we have the legitimate " Interpretation "; unfolding the genesis of this abuse, its origin and source. As outlined by Bacon, it " closes with nature and comes at the very brink of operation, if it does not actually deal with it." Such " are not empty notions, but well defined, and such as nature would really recognize as her first principles, and such as lie at the heart and marrow of things."

Power, indeed, divorced from a poignant sense of responsibility—whose sanction is in the reason—is lawless. " Ought " is naught, liberty license, and will caprice : and this is the very essence of tyranny. Remorse (as here used, — the pagan expression for the christian " conscience,") is the whip-cord of self restraint, the stinging compunction, the remedial punishment, that enforces the sway of responsibility ; and its absence breeds monsters —of which tyranny, in its utter contempt of self-restraint, is the foremost example.

The next step is the application of this fundamental principle to Cæsar *individually ;* and in the light afforded by observation :

"and, to speak truth of Cæsar,
I have not known when his affections sway'd
More than his reason." *

* To fully comprehend the occasion, the force, and the bearing of this " observation," we must turn again to Bacon's Psychology :

" Again, if the affections in themselves were pliant and *obedient to reason,* it were true there should be no great use of persuasions and insinuations to the will, more than of naked propositions and proofs ; but in regard of the continual *mutinies and seditions of the affections,*

A priori, and *a posteriori* as well, Cæsar is thus pre-eminently a safe man to be entrusted with power,—unless, indeed, all kings be tyrants, which, *a posteriori*, is preposterous. And Brutus would appear to be approaching a reasonable conclusion,—even upon his own premises.

But instantly, again, imagination, as if suborned by desire, comes to the rescue; projecting before him, graphically, the fatal picture of young ambition climbing upon the ladder of lowliness into the clouds, and then turning his back in scorn upon the base rounds on which he has risen:

> " But 'tis a common proof
> That lowliness is young ambition's ladder,
> Whereto the climber-upward turns his face:
> But when he once attains the upmost round,
> He then unto the ladder turns his back,
> Looks in the clouds, scorning the base degrees
> By which he did ascend."

This is essentially what Bacon terms an " Anticipation," as distinguished from an " Interpretation." *

> *Video meliora, proboque;*
> *Deteriora sequor:*

[" whereby they not only see the better course, but approve it also, nevertheless follow the worse,"] reason would become captive and servile, if Eloquence of Persuasions did not practice and win the Imagination *from the Affection's part*, and contract a confederacy between the Reason and Imagination *against the Affections*. For the affections themselves carry ever an appetite to good, as reason doth; the difference is, that, *the affection beholdeth merely the present; reason the future and sum of time;* [Bacon's italics] and therefore the present filling the imagination more, *reason is commonly vanquished;* but after that force of eloquence and persuasion hath made things future and remote appear as present, then upon the revolt of the imagination *reason prevaileth."* — *Advancement of Learning*, Second Book.

* " And to make my meaning clearer, and to familiarize the thing by giving it a name, I have chosen to call one of these methods or ways *Anticipation of the Mind*, the other *Interpre-*

It is a glittering generality, " confused and ill-defined and
hastily and irregularly drawn from reality ": it is commonly approved " upon certain rumors and vague fumes
and airs of experience ": it means almost anything, and
embraces everybody, and therefore Cæsar. Divested of
its dazzling glamour, this oracular " dictum," * thus en-

tation of Nature." " For the one just glances at experiment
and particulars in passing, the other dwells duly and orderly
among them. The one, again, begins at once by establishing
certain abstract and useless generalities ; the other rises by grad-
ual steps to that which is prior and better known in the order
of nature." " The one flies from the senses and particulars to
the most general axioms, and from these principles, the truth
of which it takes for settled and immovable, proceeds to judgment." " For though your direction seems to be certain and
free by pointing you to a nature that is inseparable from the
nature you inquire upon, yet if it do not carry you a degree or
remove nearer to action, operation, or light to make or produce,
it is but superficial and counterfeit." And again: "I call Anticipations the voluntary collection that the mind maketh of
knowledge ; _which is every man's reason."—Novum Organum,_
and _Of the Interpretation of Nature._

* " Now let any man soberly and diligently consider what the
way is by which men have been accustomed to proceed in the
investigation and discovery of things ; and in the first place he
will no doubt remark a method of discovery very simple and in-
artificial ; which is the most ordinary method, and is no more
than this. When a man addresses himself to discover something, he first seeks out and sets before him all that has been
said about it by others ; then he begins to meditate for himself ;
and so by much agitation and working of the wit solicits and
as it were evokes his own spirit to give him oracles: which
method has no foundation at all, but rests only upon opinions
and is carried about with them."

" The human understanding is moved by those things most
which strike and enter the mind simultaneously and suddenly,
and so fill the imagination ; and then it feigns and supposes all
other things to be somehow, though it cannot see how, similar
to those few things by which it is surrounded."

And again: " The human understanding when it has once

forced upon Brutus' reason, so far as it means anything
specifically, is to the effect that it is commonly known that
this habit of character, which he has recognized as being
so pronounced in Cæsar, is but an assumed bearing, affected as a means to further an ambitious end : and that
when one thus attains the highest power, he spurns this
scaffolding, changes front, throws off the mask, and becomes a tyrant.

> "so Cæsar may :
> Then lest he may, prevent."

Brutus' understanding is indeed " colored and infected";
" blinded and incensed." Were he in his sober senses,
his vision undazzled, he would realize, in utter abhorrence,
the plain import of this judgment, in its last analysis.
For its whole fabric rests upon the basis, and is to the
effect, that the quality which he has just recognized in
Cæsar, in itself a virtue, the surest foundation of safety
in the exercise of power, *may be* in him a falsity, a base
artifice, the fair outward development of an inward du-
plicity and insidious treachery : and upon this *possibility*
he dooms him to assassination.

But he has found what all the while he was uncon-

---

adopted an opinion (either as being the received opinion, or as
being agreeable to itself) draws all things else to support and
agree with it . . . in order that by this great and pernicious
predetermination the authority of its former conclusions may
remain inviolate."

" For what a man had rather were true he more readily believes. Therefore he rejects difficult things from impatience of
research ; sober things, because they narrow hope ; the deeper
things of nature, from superstition ; the light of experience,
from arrogance and pride, lest his mind should seem to be occupied with things mean and transitory ; things not commonly
believed, out of deference to the opinion of the vulgar. Numberless in short are the ways, and sometimes imperceptible, in
which *the affections color and infect the understanding*."—
Novum Organum. First Book.

sciously seeking—an adequate justification for his death.
And he would clinch it beyond peradventure:

> "And since the quarrel
> Will bear no color for the thing he is,
> Fashion it thus: that what he is, augmented,
> Would run to these and these extremities:
> And therefore *think* him as a serpent's egg,
> Which hatch'd, would as his kind grow mischievous
> And kill him in the shell."

Here the awful bias imposed upon Brutus fully asserts
its predominant sway. By the subtlest cunning, he utterly
befools himself. "*May be*" is imperceptibly moulded
into "*is.*" And reason, by violence, is made to fashion
it thus; and thus to arrive at a reasonable conclusion,—
dazzling in its brilliancy, and clearly, an absolute vindication.

In the giddy whirl of his bewildered brain, overborne
by the mutinies, seditions, and insurrections of his excited
powers, and under the illumination of these lightning
flashes of the imagination, he now beholds in this imaged
serpent the vivid reality, in the hideous phantasma of a
distracted mind. He actually "thinks" Cæsar an un-
hatched serpent. He is treading in an endless maze: he
has rounded the circle, and is come again to the starting
point, "It must be by his death"; now intensified into
"*kill him in the shell.*" The little excursion has but en-
meshed him the tighter in the web; adding stupefaction
to intoxication. His reason, blinded, now rests contentedly in established security; conscience is seemingly satisfied, and Brutus is "honest" in his conviction:

> "and what other oath,
> Than honesty to honesty engaged,
> That this shall be, or we will fall for it?"

But one thing more remains to complete his determination. At this moment Lucius brings him the missive,
which Cinna had thrown in at the window, at Cassius'

instigation. And by the illumination of the "exhalations," the uncertain, fitful light of the lurid lightnings, he reads:

> "Brutus, thou sleep'st: awake, and *see thyself.*
> Shall Rome, etc. Speak, strike, redress!
> Brutus, thou sleep'st: awake!"

He is called. *Brutus!* All Rome is calling upon *him;* to awake from his torpor; to *see himself*—the son of that glorious ancestor, who once before redeemed her. Rome looks to *him;* to speak! to strike! to *redress!* And he will not, can not fail her. Brutus is thus exalted, his understanding completely enravished. The last slender moorings that anchored him to the solid earth are snapped asunder; and he is fully launched upon that dread, shoreless ocean of a crime-breeding delusion. A flood-tide of deepest emotion sweeps him onward in its resistless surge: imagination, usurping from reason the guidance, holds him in the current; and the sweetest, purest, holiest affections of the soul drive him headlong into the glad consecration of himself, unreservedly, to the execution of this murderous design:

> "'*Shall Rome, etc.*' Thus must I piece it out;
> Shall Rome stand under one man's awe?
>   What! Rome?
> My ancestors did from the streets of Rome
> The Tarquin drive, when he was call'd a king.
> '*Speak, strike, redress!*'— Am I entreated
> To speak and strike? O Rome! I make thee promise,
> If the redress will follow, thou receivest
> Thy full petition at the hand of Brutus."

The spiritual tragedy is wrought: and poor Brutus, completely enthralled, is delivered over to the destinies, to the working out of an awful fate.

NOTE. — Were Brutus now on trial for his life, for example in Germany, under its enlightened code, his case would "fall into the compass" of the following liberal provision (R. G.

B. §51), "the result of very careful discussion both by physicians and lawyers ":

"There is no criminal act when the actor at the time of the offence is in a state of unconsciousness or morbid disturbance of the mind, through which *the free determination of the will is excluded.*"

The question of his guilt, in its subtler windings, would touch closely upon the principle tersely put by Bacon in his opening paragraph: "For purity of illumination and freedom of the will began and fell together." And the world may yet be driven to accept Bacon's conclusion; developed didactically in his Psychology, and in concrete representation, in Brutus.

CHAPTER VIII.

ATHWART the murky atmosphere, so appropriately environing the action in the play, and which is indeed its native element, there streams a beam of sunshine. It is as if a gilded ray from heaven were penetrating the lurid, perverted light that emanates from hell; and the contrast enables us to distinguish both their likeness and their difference.

When that fiend in human form, Richard III., was exercising his satanic fascination over Lady Anne, winning her for his bride, even while they were standing before the bleeding corpse of her beloved husband, whom he had murdered,—

> " What! I that kill'd her husband and his father,
> To take her in her heart's extremest hate;
> With curses in her mouth, tears in her eyes,
> The bleeding witness of her hatred by;
> Having God, her conscience, and these bars against me,
> And I no friends to back my suit withal,
> But the plain devil, and dissembling looks,
> And yet to win her, — all the world to nothing!
> Ha!"—

the final, transcendent effort which enchained her is thus set forth:

> " Lo! here I hand thee this sharp-pointed sword;
> Which if thou please to hide in this true breast,
> And let the soul forth that adoreth thee,
> I lay it naked to the deadly stroke,
> And humbly beg the death upon my knee.
> [*He lays his breast open; she offers at it with his sword.*

Nay, do not pause; for I did kill King Henry; —
But 't was thy beauty that provoked me,
Nay, now dispatch; 't was I that stabbed young Edward; —
[*She again offers at his breast.*
But 't was thy heavenly face that set me on.
[*She lets fall the sword,*"

and a moment later accepts the ring of espousal.

And again, in the "quarrel scene" between Brutus and
Cassius, when Brutus, in his intense anger, shows himself implacable, and deaf to threats, Cassius finally subdues
him by the like supreme effort:

"There is my dagger,
And here my naked breast; within a heart
Dearer than Pluto's mine; richer than gold:
If that thou beest a Roman, take it forth;
I, that denied thee gold, will give my heart:
Strike, as thou didst at Cæsar; for, I know,
When thou didst *hate* him worst thou lov'd'st him better
Than ever thou *lov'st Cassius.*"

Brutus instantly succumbs:

"Sheathe your dagger:
Be angry when you will, it shall have scope;
Do what you will, dishonor shall be humor.
   O Cassius, you are yoked with a lamb
That carries anger as the flint bears fire;
Who, much enforcèd, shows a hasty spark,
And straight is cold again. . . .
Cassius. Do you confess so much? Give me your hand.
Brutus. And my heart too."

But there is a legitimate fascination; tender, true, potent, — of which this satanic fascination is the base perversion. It is the sweet, benign influence of real love.
In its grateful exercise, it touches the heart of man,
moves the springs of action within him, and gently, but
effectually, prevails over his will. This sane, rightful fascination is given appropriate exemplification in the play,
in the sway of the loving Portia over Brutus.

Portia is the personification of the noble woman, the devoted wife,

> "tender offspring of that rib, *refin'd*
> *By God's own finger*, and by Him assign'd
> To be a help and not a hurt to man."

She is wrapped up in Brutus, become again one with him, in an united life. And when her regardful eye notes with alarm his evident distraction, moved by her intense solicitude, she concentrates herself upon him; presses him with tender but urgent importunity to disclose to her the cause; for, woman-like, she would share the burden. And Brutus resisting, she thus gently pulls upon the chords that bind them together:

> "No, my Brutus;
> You have some sick offense within your mind,
> Which, by the right and virtue of my place,
> I ought to know of: and, upon my knees,
> I charm you, by my once commended beauty,
> By all your vows of love, and that great vow
> Which did incorporate and make us one,
> That you unfold to me, *yourself, your half,*
> Why you are heavy; and what men to-night
> Have had resort to you: for here have been
> Some six or seven, who did hide their faces
> Even from darkness. . . . .
> Within the bond of marriage, tell me, Brutus,
> Is it excepted I should know no secrets
> That appertain to you? Am I yourself
> But, as it were, in sort or limitation;
> To keep with you at meals, comfort your bed,
> And talk to you sometimes? Dwell I but in the suburbs
> Of your good pleasure? If it be no more,
> Portia is Brutus' harlot, not his wife."

Brutus still proving obdurate, even under such an appeal, Portia, divining the occasion of his resistance, finally vanquishes him by a like supreme effort, in a manifestation both of her constancy and her devotion that is irresistible. But, mark you, this time, it is by the exhibition of *a real wound, self-inflicted upon her own person:*

" I grant I am a woman; but, withal,
A woman that Lord Brutus took to wife:
I grant I am a woman; but, withal,
A woman well reputed,— Cato's daughter.
Think you I am no stronger than my sex,
Being so father'd, and so husbanded?
Tell me your counsels, I will not disclose them:
I have made strong proof of my constancy,
Giving myself a voluntary wound
Here, in the thigh: can I bear that with patience,
And not my husband's secrets?"

Brutus is melted, subjected: as what mortal would not be, under such an exhibition of devotion? He cries:

"O ye gods,
Render me worthy of this noble wife!"

And then and there, interrupted, he gives her the sacred promise:

"Portia, go in a while;
And by and by thy bosom shall partake
The secrets of my heart.
All my engagements I will construe to thee,
All the charactery of my sad brows."

If we penetrate to the heart of this truly worthy fascination, that thus subjects Brutus' will, we find that it is wrought through love's potent spell, and that its efficient means is *manifestation*.

This is true of even the Supreme Love:

" *And I, if I be lifted up from the earth, will draw all men unto me.*"

This mighty manifestation of love divine touches forever the heart of humanity; melts and subdues it; and prevails over the will of the individual soul. But it is through the legitimate workings of his imagination, quickened into activity by this sight, that man attains to its actual "realization"; which awakens the answering impulse, and procures the surrender of his will. As Bacon profoundly observes: "Not that divine illumination re-

sides in the imagination ; its seat being rather in the very
citadel of the mind and understanding ; but that the divine
grace uses the motions of the imagination as an instrument of illumination ; just as it uses the motions of the
will as an instrument of virtue."

Love enkindles love : it is self-propagating ; begetting
itself in its answering likeness. It is the Holy Spirit, that
quickening Power, that illuminates and comforts the soul.
It is God. And manifestation is love's torch ; the embodiment, the enshrinement of its living, propagating
flame ; blazing forth towards the loved one. And in the
receptive mind, its presence kindles the imagination into
a glow of illumination ; into a vision and revelation of its
unutterable depths, in a faith that lays hold upon its very
substance. An " attachment " is thereby effected, and by
divine grace, there is engendered a " new birth " into a
corresponding love.

And human love is patterned after the divine. It was
Portia's expressive manifestation of her devotion, firing
Brutus' imagination into its adequate realization,—in the
vision and revelation of its fathomless depths,—that wrung
from him his cry of adoration, and deprived him of all
power of further resistance.

This contrasting example also enables us to better comprehend the nature and operation of that false or satanic
fascination, which is such an important element in the action,—in its consistent development.

Manifestation is alike the efficient means, through which
its spell is wrought. But in difference, it is not love's
manifestation, but its *counterfeit presentment*, in its very
garb and lineaments. It is likewise an embodiment, but
one of which *deception* is the soul.

Richard III. and Cassius both speak in the accents of
love. Eye, voice, and " dissembling looks " all breathe
of its presence and dominating power. They *enact* its

17

manifestations, in perfect similitude. And in climax, they give devotion's supreme expression, in the tender of their lives in its exemplification. Their very audacity creates faith, instinctively; for daring is a belonging of sincerity and truth. It is the seeming reality, enacted before them, which dazzles the vision of their victims; exercising over them the tremendous power inherent in its genuine presence; firing their imagination, exactly as does love's manifestation; creating the same "motions" and emotions, and maintaining the same all-powerful sway. It is the work of the devil; only performed by one whose soul is on fire of hell.

Its immediate aim is the production of *illusion;* and therefore its efforts are centred upon the imagination; stimulating it into an activity which self-accomplishes their ulterior purpose. And we can now perhaps better understand the *modus operandi* of Cassius' work upon Brutus, before unfolded in detail. It was through the production of illusion in Brutus' mind that his delusion was effected.

In addition to its marvelous organic unity, the strength of this play, in great part, is in that it lays hold upon the very issues of life. And this is done, as we have seen, by virtue of their prior intelligent grasp by its author. And accordingly, we have but to follow in his plainly marked footsteps, to more adequately comprehend his truly magnificent work,—a two-fold revelation; incidentally, of his own world of thought, and comprehensively, of mankind unto itself.*

* Obviously also, the astonishing unity, which characterizes the play as a living organism,—wherein the several varied elements, interesting in themselves, are yet more interesting as the essential parts of one unfolding whole, — is itself the product and outcome of a prior, thorough mastery of such elements by one predisposed to the observation of the likeness and unity of things; and especially by one accustomed to the comprehension

But as Gervinus observes, he "never founded a law upon a single experience"; and accordingly, we are afforded another instance of love's influence, in Calphurnia's temporary sway over Cæsar. Upon her bended knees, she implores him not to go forth upon this fateful day; and for a time she prevails. Less noble than Portia, less "refin'd," she is yet thoroughly womanly in her tender solicitude. Her method is altogether different; but both

---

of the subtlest, most exquisite blendings of their characteristics and attributes, whereby they may partake of unity. But we are less astonished, the better we become acquainted with Bacon. For this temperament, or habit of thought, was one of the striking peculiarities of his personality. Macaulay even ridicules him on some of its manifestations. In his Essay on Bacon, he says:

"In the third book of *De Augmentis*, he tells us that there are some principles which are not peculiar to one science, but are common to several. That part of philosophy which concerns itself with these principles is, in his nomenclature, designated as *philosophia prima*. He then proceeds to mention some of the principles with which this *philosophia prima* is conversant. One of them is this. An infectious disease is more likely to be communicated while it is in progress than when it has reached its height. This, says he, is true in medicine. It is also true in morals; for we see that the example of very abandoned men injures public morality less than the example of men in whom vice has not yet extinguished all good qualities. Again, he tells us that in music a discord ending in a concord is agreeable, and that the same thing may be noted in the affections. (See *ante*, page 185.) Once more he tells us, that in physics the energy with which a principle acts is often increased by the antiperistasis of its opposite; and that it is the same in the contests of factions. If the making of ingenious and sparkling similitudes like these be indeed the *philosophia prima*, we are quite sure that the greatest philosophical work of the nineteenth century is Mr. Moore's *Lalla Rookh*. The similitudes which we have cited are very happy similitudes. But that a man like Bacon should have taken them for more, that he should have thought the discovery of such resemblances as these

tend to the same end, — the moving of the will through
the action of the imagination. As Bacon indicates, Superstition has its seat in the imagination ; and it is through
this avenue she approaches Cæsar ; portraying to him
her wonderful dream, of such ominous significance, and
relating graphically the fearful portents that had occurred.
And well she might : for it must have seemed as though
nature, voicing the will of the gods, was framing, in her

---

an important part of philosophy, has always appeared to us one
of the most singular facts in the history of letters."

That we may comprehend Bacon, it is but fair to give his
continuation of this passage : "Neither are all these which I
have mentioned, and others of this kind, only *similitudes* (as
men of narrow observation may perhaps conceive them to be),
but plainly the same footsteps of nature treading or printing
upon different subjects and matters. And it is a thing which
has not as yet been carefully handled. You may perhaps find
in the writings of the profounder sort of wits such axioms here
and there sparingly inserted for the use of the argument they
have in hand ; but for any body of such axioms, which should
tend primitively and summarily to the advancement of the sciences, no one has as yet collected one ; though it is a thing of
excellent use for displaying the *unity* of nature, which is supposed to be the true office of Primitive Philosophy."

And again, in his *Interpretation of Nature:* "And these are
no allusions but direct communities, the same delights of the
mind being to be found not only in music, rhetoric, but in moral
philosophy, policy, and other knowledges, and that obscure in
the one, which is more apparent in the other, yea and that discovered in the one which is not found at all in the other, and
so one science greatly aiding to the invention and augmentation
of another."

The truth is, Bacon was endowed with a vision, penetrating
into the heart of things, which overleaped the past three centuries, and discerned what is likely to be the *definite*, salient conception of the incoming Twentieth century ; in our dawning
recognition of the community of every department of knowledge and their underlying unity. Thus, for a single example :

malignant aspects, an appropriate setting for the enactment of some immediately impending and awful tragedy :

> " There is one within,
> Besides the things we have *heard* and *seen,*
> Recounts most horrid sights seen by the watch,
> A lioness hath whelped in the streets ;
> And graves have yawn'd and yielded up their dead :
> Fierce fiery warriors fought upon the clouds,
> In ranks and squadrons and right form of war,
> Which drizzled blood upon the Capitol :
> The *noise* of battle hurtled in the air,
> Horses did neigh, and dying men did groan,
> And ghosts did shriek and squeal about the streets.
> O Cæsar! these things are beyond all use,
> And I do fear them."

All this is supported by the report of the augurers :

> "Plucking the entrails of an offering forth,
> They could not find a heart within the beast."

Cæsar is susceptible to these influences :

> " For he is superstitious grown of late ;"

Bacon says in the passage referred to : " The quavering upon a
stop in music gives the same pleasure to the ear, as the playing
of light on water or a diamond gives to the eye ;

> *Splendet tremulo sub lumine pontus.*

[" Beneath the trembling light glitters the sea."—*Virg.*]

The common delight-producing element present in both is
rhythm, the substance of Harmony, the essence of all sensuous
Beauty,—that dynamic modulation of "energy" (the physical
expression of the Supreme Power) which, in its transmission
through the senses to the brain and in its effect upon the consciousness, is especially pleasurable,—and Harmony is the soul
of spiritual beauty. And we thus catch a glimpse of the wonderful unity of all beauty ; and even of the veil that hides
from us the actual unity of the spiritual and material universe.

Bacon dealt in something more than mere similitudes. He
put his fingers upon the keys of a mighty instrument, whence
there will yet proceed strains of sweetest unison, in an almost
overpowering harmony.

and this is manifested even upon his first entrance on the
stage :

> " Forget not, in your speed, *Antonius*,
>   To touch Calphurnia : for our elders say,
>   The barren touched in this holy chase,
>   Shake off their sterile course."

Calphurnia, thus, for the present, prevails over Cæsar's
powerful will, procuring the reversal of his avowed purpose : though loudly protesting his superiority to such
influences, he finally yields to her entreaty ; " denying,
he yet consents."

Incidentally, we are struck by the forceful, sententious
vigor of many of Cæsar's utterances ; revealing his lofty
imaginative power, his commanding intellect, and his imperious will.   Thus,

> " Cæsar shall forth : the things that threaten'd me
>   Ne'er looked but on my back ; when they shall see
>   The face of Cæsar, they are vanquished."
> " Cowards die many times before their deaths :
>   The valiant never taste of death but once."
> " Cæsar should be a beast without a heart,
>   If he should stay at home to-day for fear."
>   " Danger knows full well
>   That Cæsar is more dangerous than he.
>   We are two lions litter'd in one day,
>   And I the elder and more terrible."
> " Cannot is false ; and that I dare not falser."
> " The cause is in my will, I will not come."

We may know that his words are given this cast of purpose, with discriminating intent ; for Bacon notes especially, and with marked appreciation, this special characteristic of Cæsar.   In his *Advancement of Learning*,
First Book, he says of him :

" If I should enumerate divers of his speeches, as I did
those of Alexander, they are truly such as Solomon no-
teth, when he saith, *Verba sapientum tanquam aculei, et
tanquam clavi in altum defixi :* (the words of the wise are

as goads, and as nails fixed deep in :) whereof I will only recite three, not so delectable for elegancy, but admirable for vigor and efficacy. . . . The last speech which I will mention was used to Metullus ; when Cæsar, after war declared, did possess himself of Rome ; at which time entering into the inner treasury to take the money there accumulate, Metellus being tribune forbade him : whereto Cæsar said, ' That if he did not desist, he would lay him dead in the place ;' and presently taking himself up he added, ' Young man, it is harder for me to speak it than to do it.' *Adolescens, durius est mihi hoc dicere quam facere.* A speech compounded of the greatest terror and greatest clemency that could proceed out of the mouth of man."

But there is another quality, equally pronounced, which pervades these utterances ; purposely infused into them, because of its subtly significant bearing upon Cæsar's approaching fate ; affording us a key to his destiny, as it is unfolded in the play. They bespeak, unmistakably, an arrogant pride, an exultant, over-weening self-confidence and self-sufficiency. In his *De Augmentis*, Eighth Book, Bacon, after recounting Timotheus' lofty utterance, " And in this fortune had no part," and its unhappy sequel, continues :

" For this is too high and too arrogant, savoring of that which Ezekiel says of Pharaoh, ' Thou sayest, mine river is mine own, and I have made it for myself ;' or that which Habakkuk says, ' They exult and offer sacrifices to their net ;' or of that which the poet expresses of Mezentius, the despiser of the gods :—

' *Dextra mihi Deus, et telum quod missile libro*
Nunc adsint.'
[' My own right hand and sword assist my stroke,
These gods Mezentius will invoke.']

" Lastly, Julius Cæsar never, as far as I recollect, betrayed the weakness of his secret thoughts, except in a similar kind of speech. For when the augur brought him word that the entrails were not favorable, he murmured in a low voice, ' *They will be more favorable when I choose ;'* which speech did not long precede the misfortune of his death. *For this excess of confidence was ever as unlucky as unhallowed.*" *

---

* This was not superstition in Bacon, but the reverse. It was a judgment based upon the close observation of life in its workings, as disclosed in the events about him, in history, and in the Bible ; the comprehension of somewhat of that destiny which underlies human affairs, and which the Greeks made the controlling element in their mightiest Tragedies.

And even as we write, the principle has possibly received an exemplification in our own midst, though under a much milder provocation,— merely the public, confident assertion of a continued hold upon life, which is beyond the control of mortals. An incident attendant upon the death of Carter Harrison, late Mayor of Chicago, is at least worthy of record in this connection.

The Columbian Exposition was approaching its close. The city was in the full tide of exultation over its magnificent success, achieved by really herculean labors. It was an hour of triumph, not only for Chicago, but for the whole people—the awakening of a young nation to a consciousness of its hitherto undreamed of powers. Carter Harrison was an integral part of the city : he was serving his fourth term as its Mayor, elected the last time by an overwhelming majority. Naturally somewhat egotistical, of buoyant spirits, and about to wed again, he felt, perhaps more than others, the exhilaration attendant upon the occasion. He was uplifted by his exultant joy. And in an eloquent speech to the assembled Mayors of the American cities, he said :

" *I intend to live more than half a century,* and at the end of that half century, London will be trembling lest Chicago shall surpass it, and New York will say, ' Let it go to the metropolis of America.' "   And again: " *I myself have taken a new lease of life,* and I believe I shall see the day when Chicago will be the biggest city in America, and the third city on the face of the globe."

But that night, ' his soul was required of him.' He was shot

But now Decius Brutus enters upon the scene, in opposition to Calphurnia; and well does he fulfil his promise to the conspirators, to bring Cæsar forth. For the odds are against him. Calphurnia has prevailed, winning from Cæsar the promise,

> "Mark Antony shall say I am not well;
> And, for thy humor, I will stay at home."

And now Cæsar is as imperious in his assertion that he will not go, as before he was emphatic in his avowal that he would:

> "The cause is in my will, I will not come;
> That is enough to satisfy the senate."

But for Decius' "private satisfaction," and because of his love for him, he tells him the reason:

> "Calphurnia here, my wife, stays me at home:
> She dreamt to-night she saw my statua,
> Which like a fountain, with a hundred spouts,
> Did run pure blood; and many lusty Romans
> Came smiling, and did bathe their hands in it.
> And these does she apply for warnings, and portents,
> And evils imminent; and on her knee
> Hath begg'd that I will stay at home to-day."

But Decius, through his infernal arts, is equal to the occasion. He gives to Calphurnia's dream another and a favorable interpretation; exquisitely flattering to Cæsar, and which he cannot but accept:

> "And this way have you well expounded it."

He works subtly upon his inordinate pride, depicting vividly the *mockery* that is sure to be pointed at him. He

---

down, in his own home, by a miserable crank, to redress a fancied wrong, suffered in the Mayor's refusal of an appointment for which he was utterly unqualified. Chicago's exultation was dampened in her grief, and her joy was chastened to mourning: and possibly, in her Mayor's tragic death, she was saved from inviting upon herself a like awful fate.

applies the torch to his ambition, and allures him by the statement, that

> "the senate have concluded
> To give, this day, a crown to mighty Cæsar,"

though he purposes "this day" his death.*

By this serpent-like, beguiling "witchery," he "o'ersways" the "mighty Cæsar"; drawing him forth to his doom.

> "How foolish do your fears seem now, Calphurnia!
> I am ashamed I did yield to them.—
> Give me my robe, for I will go : —"†

And as though the hand of Fate were visibly pushing him forward into destruction, he then requests Trebonius, one of the conspirators, to be near him this day :

> "*Treb.* Cæsar, I will:—*(aside)* and so near will I be,
> That your best friends shall wish I had been further."

But wherefore this vacillation, so sharply outlined in Cæsar, of indomitable will,—this swaying to and fro, even as the weather-cock responds to the shifting breeze,—and which is exhibited again in his ineffectual dallying with the crown, thrice offered him by Mark Antony? Of what, in itself, is it a manifestation?

Vacillation bespeaks irresolution. And the truth is that

---

* Casca, however, mentions a material restriction, which would have been especially distasteful to Cæsar:

> "Indeed they say the senators to-morrow
> Mean to establish Cæsar as a king:
> And he shall wear his crown by sea and land,
> In every place *save here in Italy.*"

† It is interesting to observe that this disregard of ominous portents and warnings is a characteristic feature of the ancient Greek Tragedies: "The Greek poets frequently exhibited the indifference of prosperous persons to divine monitions. Cassandra's prophesies were not attended to ; the Delphic oracle spoke in vain ; and Teiresias [the soothsayer] is only honored when it is too late."— *Studies of the Greek Poets,* by John Addington Symonds. (Chapter on Sophocles.)

Cæsar, as revealed in the play, is for the time a rudderless ship. And this for the simple reason, that he is unable as yet to come to a definite *determination*.

Once before, earlier in his career, he confronted a like situation. The laws of Rome prohibited his crossing the Rubicon with his army. But after weighing every consideration and possible contingency, he finally came to a settled conclusion. And thereafter, his course was straightforward : he advanced unfalteringly, with constant, inflexible resolution.

But now his demeanor is altogether different. He eagerly covets the crown ; involving the absolute destruction of the republic. But for some potent reason — perhaps because of a reasonable doubt of success, or possibly owing to some subtle restraint—he hesitates : he is un-willing to resort to violence : he does not see his way clear to the attainment of his desire. He unmistakably falters.

His Desire is vehement. The crown is dangling just before him : and to be king in Rome is to be king of the known world, — an incomparable dignity. His actual power is tremendous, his will indomitable, imperious : but the vision which guides it is confused ; it cannot see the way to his gratification. He is balked : and yet he must obey his reason. Thus Cæsar also is "with himself at war": he is in a tumult within, under the boundings of his curbed desire.

He loses, in a measure, his equipoise. He who was wont to act from within, with self-originating, intelligently directed effort, under the clear-visioned guidance of his reason, now incited by his urgent desire, turns half-helplessly to the exterior world ; trusting that, somehow, the pathway will be opened to its gratification. But reliance upon the favorable concurrence of events differs but little, in its reflex action, from trust in " the chapter of accidents." And by a law of man's nature, such a depend-

ence tends, almost inevitably, to breed superstition. This
is why gamblers, as a class, are so invariably superstitious.
And conversely, Cæsar's pronounced *change* towards superstition indicates, almost unmistakably, this corresponding change in his mental attitude.

He turns to the people, in the hope that they will aid
him, — only to find that the populace of Rome does not
want a king. His judgment, which prevents his acceptance of the proffered crown, is thus possibly confirmed:
but his desire is baffled, and

     " The angry spot doth glow on Cæsar's brow; "
and in sympathy,

      "all the rest look like a chidden train."

Moreover, Cæsar's suppressed anger, Calphurnia's sympathetic paleness, and the " chidden " appearance of his
train, all bespeak a consciousness of weakness. Somehow
Cæsar is not master of the situation.

But there is yet another possible contingency: and
this fateful day, Cæsar is allured to the Capitol, in the
expectation that the *Senate* will grant him the crown.
And thenceforward, Cæsar rushing headlong to his doom,
is the *motive* in his further delineation.

The finger of Fate, in the very beginning, points the
way. Upon his first appearance, he hears in the throng
" a tongue, shriller than all the music," crying " Cæsar! "
and commands, " Speak! "

   " *Soothsayer.* Beware the ides of March!
   Cæsar. What man is that?
   Brutus. A soothsayer, bids you beware the ides of March.
   Cæsar. Set him before me; let me see his face.
   Casca. Fellow, come from the throng: look upon Cæsar.
   Cæsar. What say'st thou to me now? Speak once again.
   Sooth. Beware the ides of March.
   Cæsar. He is a dreamer; let us leave him; — pass."

This ominous date is again noted by Brutus, who says
to Lucius:

"Is not to-morrow, boy, the ides of March? [*15th.*]
Lucius. I know not, sir.
Brutus. Look in the calendar, and bring me word.
Lucius. I will, sir. . . . . . .
Sir, March is wasted fourteen days."

And on his way to the Capitol, Cæsar remarks:

"The ides of March are come.
Sooth. Ay, Cæsar, but not gone."

Meanwhile, the exterior forces that are to work his destruction have converged to a focus. The instruments are prepared: the sword is already poised for the blow. The malevolent Cassius, who originates the conspiracy, has been untiring in activity. Walking the streets at night, "keeping no holiday," working "subtilely and in the dark," he has at last, by his devilish arts, gained sufficient adherents for the accomplishment of his murderous purpose. And in addition, there is secured through Brutus the valued aid of Caius Ligarius, who

"doth bear Cæsar hard,
Who rated him for speaking well of Pompey."

The conspirators meet at night under the shadow of Pompey's porch, or as it is again called, "Pompey's theatre"; and again at Brutus' house, where they receive his formal adherence, and perfect their plans for the morrow. And now all but Cassius have assembled at Cæsar's palace, to accompany him to the Capitol.

Cæsar, utterly blinded to their deadly intent, greets these "friends" each kindly by name, with a gentle word even for Ligarius:

"Cæsar was ne'er so much your enemy,
As that same ague which hath made you lean."

He takes the blame for the delay upon himself, and generously bids them,

"Good friends, go in, and taste some wine with me;
And we, like friends, will straightway go together."

Even Brutus is touched: but his regret finds its surcease in his logic:

> "*(Aside.)* That every like is not the same, O Cæsar,
>   The heart of Brutus yearns to think upon,"

and they pass out to the Capitol.

"*Whom the gods would destroy they first make mad.*"
This was never better illustrated than in Cæsar, in his
portrayal in the play. He is entering, as he fondly believes, upon his hour of supreme triumph,—his enthrone-
ment upon the topmost pinnacle of earth. In the exhil-
eration accompanying such a culmination, he loses his
equipoise: he is exalted above himself; elevated to the
heights of a Titanic egotism, with its attendant intoxication.

And strange to say, excessive egotism, as physicians
tell us, is an inchoate form of madness,—the germ of
many of its developments. It is essentially an illusion, a
"fixed idea," engendered by a man's lofty imagination.
This peculiar work of the imagination is admirably exemplified in Cæsar's case,—even in the very manifestations
of his egotism. Thus Decius says:

> "When I tell him he hates flatterers,
>   He says he does; *being then most flattered.*"

Again, he is loudest in his lofty protestations of personal indifference to superstitious influences, at the very
moment when he yields to them,

> "For he is superstitious grown of late."

And yet again, the very morning when he exhibits such
marked vacillation, he imperiously declares to the Senate:

> "But I am *constant* as the northern star,
>   Of whose true-fix'd and resting quality
>   There is no fellow in the firmament."

Again, inordinate egotism is a subtle form of self-adula-
tion: it is "unhallowed," an idolatry that is especially
offensive to the Powers above. It somehow invites de-

struction,— ofttimes procuring it, through its very manifestations. And thus Cæsar, as if impelled by the gods, ministers directly to his ruin.

Many of us have witnessed, in actual life, instances where men have conducted themselves with such reckless foolishness or brazen effrontery that we have exclaimed, " He must be demented ": when, in fact, the very acts which called forth the exclamation were in themselves the initial workings of a rapidly approaching retribution. And in just such an apparent perversity — the irony of fate — Cæsar, in his hour of intoxication, by his very arrogance, nerves the conspirators to their task. In a boldness of conception quite unsurpassed, but which attests the transcendent genius of the Artist and his profound insight, Cæsar is made to " turn his back " upon his past, and the principles which heretofore had regulated his conduct, and to enact before the assembled conspirators the very role assigned him by Cassius and accepted by Brutus :

> " and this man
> Is now become a god."

They are now assembled in the Capitol, and Cæsar arrogantly inquires :

> " What is now amiss,
> That Cæsar and *his* Senate must redress ? "

Metellus Cimber, one of the conspirators, makes suit for the recall of his banished brother. Kneeling before Cæsar he commences :

> " Most high, most mighty, and most puissant Cæsar,
> Metellus Cimber throws before thy seat
> A humble heart : — "

But Cæsar interrupts :

> " I must prevent thee, Cimber.
> These couchings, and these lowly courtesies,
> Might fire the blood of ordinary men,
> And turn preordinance, and first decree,
> Into the law of children. Be not fond,

> To think that Cæsar bears such rebel blood,
> That will be thaw'd from the true quality
> With that which melteth fools; I mean, sweet words,
> Low-crooked curtsies, and base spaniel-fawning.
> Thy brother by decree is banished;
> If thou dost bend, and pray, and fawn, for him,
> I spurn thee, like a cur, out of my way.
> Know, *Cæsar doth not wrong:* nor without cause
> Will he be satisfied."

Brutus intercedes in vain, and Cassius also, to whom Cæsar replies:

> "I could be well mov'd if I were as you;
> If I could pray to move, prayers would move me:
> But I am constant as the northern star,
> Of whose true-fix'd and resting quality
> There is no fellow in the firmament.
> The skies are painted with unnumber'd sparks,
> They are all fire, and every one doth shine;
> But there's but one in all doth hold his place:
> So, in the world; 't is furnish'd well with men,
> And men are flesh and blood, and apprehensive;
> Yet, in the number, I do know but one
> That unassailable holds on his rank,
> Unshaken of motion: and, that I am he,
> Let me a little show it,— even in this,
> That I was constant Cimber should be banish'd,
> And constant do remain to keep him so."

Cinna also pleads; but Cæsar impiously cries:

> "Hence! *wilt thou lift up Olympus?*"

The infuriated conspirators press upon Cæsar; they stab him, Brutus last of all. Cæsar exclaims, "*Et tu Brute,*" and expires. Fate, that awful figure that all the time has been looming up in the dim background, now advances to the front, and as by a visible push of her arm, Cæsar is thrown at the base of Pompey's statue:

> "And, in his mantle muffling up his face,
> Even at the base of Pompey's statua,
> Which all the while ran blood, great Cæsar fell."

And Pompey, Cæsar's former friend and son-in-law, whom he had long before overthrown and driven to his death, is thus finally *avenged*.

In the excitement of the moment, Brutus' logic again runs riot. Cassius remarking,

> "Why, he that cuts off twenty years of life,
> Cuts off so many years of fearing death,"

Brutus replies:

> " *Grant that*, and then is death a benefit,
> So are we Cæsar's friends, that have abridged
> His time of fearing death."

The conspirators, in their drunken fury, bathe their hands in Cæsar's blood, "up to the elbows," and rush forth, crying, "*Peace, Freedom, and Liberty!*" a shout that later found its echo in the bloody drama of the French Revolution; drawing forth from Madame Roland, on her way to the guillotine, its appropriate answering cry, also ringing through the ages: "*O Liberty! what crimes are committed in thy name!*"

CHAPTER IX.

THE physical tragedy is wrought: and a less consummate artist would either have here ended the play, or else continuing it, have failed thereafter to sustain the interest. But to the mighty intellect that had conceived and developed Brutus' fatal error and crime as the direct outgrowth of his unfortified constitutional weakness, when assailed by a malignant force centred thereon, the action was as yet incomplete. The conspirators must be shown to have drawn upon themselves a fearful retribution.

Dante, indeed, looking through the ruby gate of imagination into the fires of hell, saw, last of all, and portrayed in an ideal retribution, Cassius and Brutus plunged into its lowermost pit and there held in the mouths of the three-faced Lucifer, in grinding torment:

"At every mouth he with his teeth was crunching
    A sinner, in the manner of a brake,
    So that he three of them tormented thus.
To him in front the biting was as naught
    Unto the clawing, for sometimes the spine
    Utterly stripped of all the skin remained.
'That soul up there which has the greatest pain,'
    The Master said, 'is Judas Iscariot;
    With head inside, he plies his legs without.
Of the two others, who head downward are,
    The one who hangs from the black jowl is Brutus;
    See how he writhes himself, and speaks no word.
And the other, who so stalwart seems, is Cassius.
    But night is reascending, and 't is time
    That we depart, for we have seen the whole.'"
        —*Inferno, Longfellow's Translation.*

But Bacon, as we have seen, by the very cast of his personality, and through the clarity of his vision, laid hold upon and gave expression to the life that now is—our life — in its complex realities, and in the subtle workings of the retributive forces that ofttimes shape its destinies. And it is upon these lines that the development of the play proceeds.

In the powerful Tragedies of ancient Greece, whose production marked its Golden Age, the controlling element in the action was *an irresistible destiny*, in whose coils man was infolded, and which, struggle as he might, he could not avert ; his very efforts ministering to the fatal end,—a doom decreed by the gods, in retribution for some former violent deed ; sometimes even one divorced from a guilty intent. (See Schlegel's *Dramatic Literature.*) This ancient Tragedy is thoroughly mastered, its agencies grasped and its spirit caught, long prior to its critical exposition in modern times ; and in this play, cast amid ancient scenes, it is grandly paralleled. Its spirit is reëmbodied, in this magnificent portrayal of Cæsar advancing inevitably, in disregard of portents and warnings, and with determined strides, straight to the doom prepared for him by the gods, in retribution for his former destruction of Pompey.

But over and beyond this, in the further development of the theme, in the unfolding of the destiny of Cassius, and of Brutus also, this modern masterpiece marks a distinct advance upon the conception and methods of the ancients,— an advance evincing a mightier grasp of life and its mystery, a clearer insight into its subtler workings, and a broader, keener comprehension of its realities.*

---

* Certainly as regards Æschylus : but as to Sophocles, the advance, though real, might be regarded by some as less distinctly marked. Thus, Symonds, in his luminous *Studies of the Greek Poets,* discussing Sophocles' *Œdipus Tyrannis,* con-

In its portrayal in the play, Cassius' righteous doom, enmeshing both himself and Brutus, is wrought through the direct instrumentality and operation of the very forces he employed so effectively, and with such malign intent, to accomplish Cæsar's death,— thus exemplifying, through its developments in this life, the fundamental fact,

"That sin in man the plague of sin must be."

The process commences, or at least, is distinctly foreshadowed, in the very hour of the consummation of his purpose, at the moment when Cæsar's life is in the balance. Bacon observes, as we remember, that, " Fascination is the power and act of Imagination intensive upon the body of another." This peculiar power had been utilized, most effectively, by Cassius, in moulding Brutus to his purpose. And this was accomplished, primarily, through the very intensity of his vivid imagination, whose force

tends, with much force, that he wrought out doom as "the natural consequence of moral, physical, and intellectual qualities"; that " he delights in exhibiting the blindness of arrogance and self-confidence, and in showing that characters determined by these qualities rush recklessly to their own doom"; and that " he made it clear that the characters of men constitute their fatality." But nevertheless, the fact remains, that the dominant *motive* in his tragedy, the theme given development, is the specific, and indeed marvellous fulfilment of the doom-pronouncing oracles emanating from the gods; one of them even before (Edipus' birth. And as Symonds afterwards candidly remarks : " Sophocles unfolds schemes and sequences of doomed events, where individual wills and passions play indeed their part, but where they are subordinated to the idea which the tragedian undertakes to illustrate. . . . The antique drama aims at the presentation of tragic situations, determined and controlled by some mysterious force superior to the agents. The modern aims at the presentation of tragic situations, immediately produced and brought about by the free action of the *dramatis personæ.*"

was centred upon Brutus. And now, when the conspirators are assembled before Cæsar, and Popilius, an outsider, advances and speaks to him privately, Cassius' imagination is awakened to its characteristic intense activity. He instantly associates Popilius' act with his preceding remark,

"I wish your enterprise to-day may thrive,"

and pictures to himself, in the vividness of a reality, Popilius disclosing to Cæsar their plot. A vision of the terrible consequences involved flashes before him. And the whole fabric wrought by his imagination is so awful, so appalling in its vivid realization, that, in expressive parlance, "he goes all to pieces," and threatens suicide upon the spot. The very intensity of Cassius' imagination,—the source of his malignant power,—by the working of a natural law, is becoming in him a disorganizing force, and its present manifestation is distinctly premonitory of the method of his ultimate destruction.

Again, Cassius envenoms Brutus against Cæsar, and thus procures his adherence to the conspirators, with the intent to utilize his established influence with the people to ensure their safety, after Cæsar's death:

"O, he sits high in all the people's hearts:
And that which would appear offense in us,
His countenance, like richest alchemy,
Will change to virtue and to worthiness."

But not only does he utterly fail them in this respect, but in the very hour of their success, he becomes, unwittingly, the direct instrumentality in effecting their rejection and overthrow by the people.

Indeed, Brutus' very blindness, which before was so serviceable to Cassius, now ministers to his ruin. And Cassius' own peculiar weapon is also turned against himself. Antony's servant enters, bearing a message from his master, addressed to *Brutus:*

"Brutus is noble, wise, valiant, and honest:

. . . .

If Brutus will vouchsafe that Antony
May safely come to him, and be resolv'd
How Cæsar hath deserv'd to lie in death,
Mark Antony shall not love Cæsar dead
So well as Brutus living, but will follow
The fortunes and affairs of noble Brutus
Through the hazards of this untrod state,
With all true faith."

Brutus is touched to the quick by this subtle appeal to his *recognized* nobility, "being then most flattered," and replies:

"Thy master is a wise and valiant Roman;
I never thought him worse.
Tell him, so please him, come unto this place,
He shall be satisfied; and, by my honor,
Depart untouch'd."

And he confidently exclaims,

"I know that we shall have him well to friend."

Antony appears, asking that he may speak at Cæsar's funeral, and Brutus makes haste to grant his request; overriding the strenuous opposition of Cassius, who finds, too late, that like the magician of old, he has summoned to his aid, as by enchantment, a Genii of powerful will, who is become his master, and is blindly leading him to destruction.

Later, the citizens are gathered at the funeral, and Brutus addresses them. In his *Advancement of Learning*, Second Book, Bacon keenly observes:

"So that there is no such artificer of dissimulation, nor no such commanded countenance (*cultus jussus*) that can sever from a feigned tale some of these fashions; either a more slight and careless fashion, or *more set and formal*, or more tedious and wandering, or coming from a man *more drily and hardly*."

And though Brutus is by no means consciously dissembling in his speech, the whole fabric of his thought is an ingrained *falsity.* He has deceived himself; and, in a word, he is now applying the same deception to the people.

> " And since the quarrel
> Will bear no color for the thing he is,
> *Fashion it thus:*"

> " And let our hearts, as subtle masters do,
> Stir up their servants to an act of rage,
> And after seem to chide them. This shall make
> Our purpose necessary, and not envious:
> Which so *appearing* to the common eyes,
> We shall be call'd purgers, not murderers."

Here we have the explanation of the hard, dry, set, formal, artificial quality of his sentences, so often noted by the commentators, and so apparent to the sensitive ear:

" Romans, countrymen, and lovers! hear me for my cause; and be silent, that you may hear: believe me for mine honor: and have respect to mine honor, that you may believe: censure me in your wisdom; and awake your senses, that you may the better judge. . . . As Cæsar loved me, I weep for him; as he was fortunate, I rejoice at it; as he was valiant, I honor him; but as he was ambitious, I slew him. There is tears for his love; joy for his fortune; honor for his valor; and death for his ambition. . . . The question of his death is enrolled in the Capitol; his glory not extenuated, wherein he was worthy; nor his offences enforced, for which he suffered death."

Brutus' influence, from which so much had been expected, was thus, in reality, paralyzed, poisoned at its fountain head; and his speech, by the operation of natural causes, was a *predestined* failure.*

---

* " And so on the other hand, it is no less truly said of the wicked, ' His own manners will be his punishment.' Secondly, men in projecting their schemes and diffusing their thoughts abroad on every side, in order to forecast and advance their fortunes, ought, in the midst *of these flights of the mind,* to look

Its momentary, evanescent influence upon the
> "Inconstant people, never constant known,"

resulting in their impulsive proffer of Cæsar's mantle to
Brutus "*crown'd*," both reveals the quixotic character of
his enterprise, and suggests, indeed, the bare possibility
of the conspirator's salvation, but for Brutus' fatal blunder in permitting Antony to speak.

Mark Antony, whom Brutus had so blindly underrated,
has been awakened from his seeming lethargy, by the
shock of his beloved Cæsar's atrocious murder.* Its direct
consequence is the quickening of all his powers into intense
activity. He becomes the Nemesis of the conspirators;
and "Cæsar's arm" avenges Cæsar's death.

In the prosecution of his purpose, he becomes, in a two-
fold sense, an *actor* upon the stage. He employs Cassius'
own arts against Cassius. Like him, and with like intent,
he deals in "intensive" manifestations.

To accomplish his purpose, he must first gain a *pou
sto :* he must win from the conspirators the opportunity
to address the people. And to this end, he follows up his
cajoling message to Brutus, by appearing before them in
person, even while they are under the most intense excitement. He makes the like supreme, and supremely effective manifestation, by the proffer of his own life:

---

up to the Eternal Providence and Divine Judgment, which often
overthrows and brings to naught the machinations and evil designs of the wicked, however deeply laid; according to that
Scripture, 'He hath conceived mischief, and shall bring forth
a vain thing.' "—*De Augmentis*, Eighth Book.

"Next, your Lordship goeth against three of the unluckiest
vices of all others, Disloyalty, *Ingratitude*, and Insolency; which
three offences, in all examples, *have seldom their doom ad-
journed to the world to come.*"—*Advice to Essex.*

* "Wars also undertaken for a just revenge have almost always been successful; as the war against Brutus and Cassius to
avenge the *murder* of Cæsar." — *De Augmentis*, Second Book.

" I know not, gentlemen, what you intend,
Who else must be let blood, who else is rank:
If I myself, there is no hour so fit
As Cæsar's death hour; nor no instrument
Of half that worth as these your swords, made rich
With the most noble blood of all this world.
I do beseech ye, if ye bear me hard,
Now, whilst your purpled hands do reek and smoke,
Fulfil your pleasure.   Live a thousand years,
I shall not find myself so apt to die:
No place will please me so, no mean of death,
As here by Cæsar, and by you cut off,
The choice and master spirits of this age.'

Brutus is melted:

" O, Antony, beg not your death of us.
.   .   .   .   .   For your part,
To you our swords have leaden points, Mark Antony:
Our arms no strength of malice, and our hearts,
Of brothers' temper, do receive you in
With all kind love, good thoughts, and reverence."

And Cassius characteristically adds:

" Your voice shall be as strong as any man's
In the disposing of new dignities."

Brutus promises to make all clear; and Antony "doubts
not his wisdom"; giving manifestation to his confidence
in their rectitude, and to his friendship, by shaking the
" purpled hands" of the conspirators, and addressing them
each kindly by name.   He secures the desired promise:
but upon the departure of the conspirators, his pent up
feelings and his hatred burst forth in a torrent of hot in-
vective,— which, in its energy of execration, reminds us
of the dreadful curses heaped upon the murderer of King
Laius and all those sheltering him, by Œdipus, in Sophocles' Tragedy:

" O, pardon me, thou bleeding piece of earth,
That I am meek and gentle with these *butchers!*
Thou art the ruins of the noblest man

That ever lived in the tide of times.*
Over thy wounds now do I prophesy,—
Which, like dumb mouths, do ope their ruby lips,
To beg the voice and utterance of my tongue,—
A curse shall light upon the limbs of men ;
Domestic fury, and fierce civil strife,
Shall cumber all the parts of Italy :
Blood and destruction shall be so in use,
And dreadful objects so familiar,
That mothers shall but smile when they behold
Their infants quarter'd with the hands of war ;
All pity chok'd with custom of fell deeds :
And Cæsar's spirit, ranging for revenge,
With Ate by his side, come hot from hell,
Shall in these confines, with a monarch's voice,
Cry ' *Havoc!* ' and let slip the dogs of war ;
That this foul deed shall smell above the earth
With carrion men, groaning for burial." †

---

* See Bacon's enconium of Cæsar, in his *Advancement of Learning*, First Book, where he speaks of him as one of the " wonders of time."

† There is an exquisite appropriateness in this reference to Ate. "ATE in *Greek Mythology*, a personification of criminal folly (*Iliad, XIX., 91*). She had misled even Zeus to take a hasty oath, when Heracles was born, for which, seeing his folly, he cast her by the hair out of Olympus, whither she did not again return." *Enc. Brit.* " Justice and Insolence and Ate no longer floated, dream-like, in the back-ground of religious thought ; he [Æschylus] gave them a pedigree, connected them in a terrible series, and established them as ministers of supreme Zeus."—*Studies of the Greek Poets,* by John Addington Symonds.

Craik, in his *The English of Shakespeare,* commenting upon the above line, pertinently asks : " Where did Shakespeare get acquainted with this divinity, whose name does not occur, I believe, even in any Latin author?" Only those of us who have attempted the study of Greek, and after months of application, have utterly failed to master this most difficult of languages, can really appreciate the inherent force of this query.

Bacon was perfectly familiar with the Greek Tragedies, im-

Antony in character, in its quality and the direction of its development, is at the opposite pole from Brutus. Higher, spiritual aspirations are wanting, the edge of scrupulous honor is dull, and considerations of duty press but lightly upon him; while the opinion held of him by others is comparatively a matter of indifference. His is an highly sensuous nature, reveling in the present, strong in its hold upon earth and its joys, and rich in its fruition. And at the core of this nature there is a heart of intense warmth:

> "I am dying, Egypt, dying; only
> I here importune death a while, until
> Of many thousand kisses the poor last
> I lay upon thy lips.—"

His defects, unchecked, like Brutus' at the opposite extreme, become the source and occasion of his ruin; as is afterwards developed in *Antony and Cleopatra*.

And now the heart of this wild player, this "masker and reveler," * is a seething fire; as witness its outburst of

---

bibing their spirit; as is shown, incidentally, in the following remark: "So the poets in Tragedies do make the most passionate lamentations, and those that *fore-run* final despair, to be accusing, questioning, and torturing of a man's self."— *Colors of Good and Evil.*

* Possibly these words were subtly colored with a peculiar significance to the English people, in the Elizabethan age. Spedding writes: "On Tuesday (says Chamberlain, writing on the 18th of February, 1612-3) it came to Gray's Inn and the Inner Temple's turn to come with their masque, whereof Sir Francis Bacon was the chief contriver." And Bacon's mother writes to his brother Antony: "I trust they will not mum nor mask nor sinfully revel at Gray's Inn."

Incidentally, it may be mentioned that Bacon's mother finally became insane. Spedding quotes from Bishop Goodman: "But for Bacon's mother, she was but little better than frantic in her age," adding, "There were times between 1593 and 1597 when

flame. Its repression in the presence of the conspirators, and his pretended friendship over Cæsar's body, reveal his unscrupulousness and his marvelous "nerve": his keen intellect is alert, his faculties excited to their utmost tension, and his heart, the motor power, hot with indignation. He is like a bereaved, infuriated tiger; the incarnation of supple power in destructive activity. He is no theorist, but intensely practical: and to accomplish his purpose, as the means to the end, he is determined to in-

---

almost the same thing might have been said of her." She died in 1610. Spedding says of her:

" Lady Bacon's affections, dispositions, manners, and temper, reveal themselves through her maternal solicitudes, serious and trivial, as clearly as if it were to-day: an affectionate, vehement, fiery, grave, and religious soul, just beginning to fail where such natures commonly fail first, in the power of self-command: in creed a Calvinist, in morals a Puritan. Of the letters which must for many years have been continually passing between her and Francis, only two or three have been preserved. But if we would understand his position, we must not forget that he had a mother of this character and temper living within a few hours' ride of his chambers, anxiously watching over his proceedings, and by advice or authority continually interfering in his affairs." And again: " But Lady Bacon was continually writing: and a great number of her letters (directed to Antony, but addressed generally to both) are preserved among the Tenison *MSS.* at Lambeth. These throw a very full light upon her own character, and upon the relations which subsisted between her and her sons; a relation too important at this period of Francis' life to be lost sight of; for the feelings of such a mother, whether in approbation or disapprobation, could not but enter into his consideration, even where they did not determine his course."

The trend of this maternal anxiety is definitely indicated in a previous remark of Spedding regarding Antony, that he " had lately removed from Gray's Inn to a house in Bishopgate Street, *much to his mother's distress,* who feared the neighborhood of the Bull Inn, where plays and interludes were acted."

fuse his revengeful spirit into the people,—to make them
the instrument of his vengeance.

In his speech, he acts upon them, by acting before them ;
putting to practice the acute suggestion of Volumina to
Coriolanus, about " to speak to the people," to deal largely
in visual manifestations :

> "for in such business
> *Action* is eloquence, and the eyes of the ignorant
> More learned than the ears."

With consummate art, he utterly obliterates the effect of
Brutus' speech : and by his action and his impassioned
words, he enkindles the imagination of the assembled populace, until their hearts also are fired, and they are roused
to a pitch of ungovernable fury.

This " plain blunt man," who has " neither wit, nor
words, nor worth, action, nor utterance, nor the power of
speech to stir men's blood," opens his speech with a "white
lie," following it up, in the same breath, with another,
more dazzling in its glittering generality :

> " Friends, Romans, countrymen, lend me your ears :
> I come to bury Cæsar, *not to praise him.*
> The evil that men do lives after them ;
> The good is oft interred with their bones ;
> So let it be with Cæsar."

He then answers Brutus' charge, by a direct argument
ad hominem ; applying its edge to Brutus himself, with
cutting irony :

> "But Brutus says, he was ambitious ;
> And Brutus is an honorable man.
> He hath brought many captives home to Rome,
> Whose ransoms did the *general coffers* fill :
> Did this in Cæsar seem ambitious?
> When that the poor have cried, Cæsar hath wept :
> Ambition should be made of sterner stuff :
> Yet Brutus says, he was ambitious ;
> And Brutus is an honorable man.

> You all did see that on the Lupercal
> I thrice presented him a kingly crown,
> Which he did thrice refuse.   Was this ambition?
> .   .   .   .   .   .   Bear with me;
> My heart is in the coffin there with Cæsar.
> *And I must pause till it come back to me.*"
> " *Cit.* Mark'd ye his words?   He would not take the crown,
>   Therefore 't is certain he was not ambitious."
> " *2d Cit.* Poor soul! his eyes are red as fire with weeping."

He holds up before them Cæsar's will, hinting at its liberal provisions for their benefit, but withholding its reading:

> " It will *inflame* you, it will make you *mad:*
>   'T is good you know not that you are his heirs;
>   For if you should, O, what would come of it! "

thus whetting their interest to the edge of expectancy, and subtly inciting them to fury.

With Cæsar's robe in hand, he then reënacts the terrible tragedy, with vivid intensity and dramatic power:

> " You all do know this mantle: I remember
>   The first time ever Cæsar put it on;
>   'T was on a summer's evening, in his tent;
>   That day he overcame the Nervii : —
>   *Look!* in this place ran Cassius' dagger through:
>   *See* what a rent the envious Casca made:
>   Through this the well-beloved Brutus stabb'd;
>   And, as he pluck'd his cursed steel away,
>   *Mark* how the blood of Cæsar followed it,
>   As rushing out of doors, to be resolved
>   If Brutus so unkindly knock'd, or no:
>   For Brutus, as you know, was Cæsar's angel:
>   Judge, O you gods, how dearly Cæsar loved him!
>   This was the most unkindest cut of all:
>   For when the noble Cæsar saw him stab,
>   *Ingratitude,* more strong than traitor's arms,
>   Quite vanquished him: then burst his mighty heart:
>   And, in his mantle muffling up his face,
>   Even at the base of Pompey's statua,
>   Which all the while ran blood, great Cæsar fell.

> O, what a fall was there, my countrymen!
> Then I, and you, and all of us fell down,
> Whilst bloody treason flourish'd over us.
> O, now you weep; and, I perceive, you feel
> The dint of pity: these are gracious drops.
> Kind souls, what, weep you, when you but behold
> Our Cæsar's vesture wounded? *Look you here,*
> *Here is himself, marr'd, as you see, with traitors."*

The people are inflamed; and we blame them not. They cry,

> "Revenge! About. — seek! — burn! — fire! — kill! — slay — let not a traitor live!"

Finally, and in climax, he reads them Cæsar's will; reciting his munificent provisions for their welfare with telling power, maddening them beyond control; and they rush forth, an infuriated mob, to wreak vengeance upon the conspirators.

Antony stands back serenely triumphant, his purpose accomplished:

> "Now let it work: mischief, thou art afloat,
> Take thou what course thou wilt: —
> .   .   .   .   . Fortune is merry,
> And in this mood will give us anything:"

Word is brought him, that

> "Brutus and Cassius
> Are rid like madmen through the gates of Rome,"

when, with exultant complacency, he remarks:

> "Belike they had some notice of the people,
> How I had moved them."*

---

* As with Brutus', so with Antony's speech: Bacon has given us sufficient data to enable us to comprehend the nature and source of the power of the one, as well as of the weakness of the other. Indeed, this interpretation of "Action" in eloquence might almost be termed distinctively Baconian; for while our ideas upon the subject have been general and somewhat confused, with him it was a clearly-cut, definite conception.

He gave it remarkable exemplification, in an account of the

action of an "actor," in inciting the people to a like fury, in ancient times:

"And it is not amiss to observe also how small and mean faculties gotten by education, yet when they fall into *great men or great matters*, do work great and important effects; whereof we see a notable example in Tacitus of two stage-players, Percennius and Vibulenus, who by their faculty of playing, put the Pannonian armies into an extreme tumult and *combustion*. For there arising a mutiny amongst them, upon the death of Augustus Cæsar, Blæsus, the lieutenant, had committed some of the mutineers; which were suddenly rescued; whereupon Vibulenus got to be heard speak, which he did in this manner: — 'These poor innocent wretches, appointed to cruel death, you have restored to behold the light. But who shall restore my brother to me, or life unto my brother? that was sent hither in message from the legions of Germany to treat of the common cause, and he hath murdered him this last night by some of his fencers and ruffians, that he hath about him for his executioners upon soldiers. Answer, Blæsus, what is done with his body? The mortalest enemies do not deny burial. When I have performed my last duties to the corpse with kisses, with tears, command me to be slain besides him; so that these my fellows, seeing us put to death for no crime, but only for our good meaning and our true hearts to the legions, may have leave to bury us.' With which speech he put the army into an infinite fury and uproar; whereas truth was, he had no brother, neither was there any such matter, but he played it merely as if he had been upon the stage."—*Advancement of Learning*, Second Book.

And again, in his Essay, *Of Boldness*, he says: "It is a trivial grammar-school text, but worthy a wise man's consideration. Question was asked of Demosthenes, what was the chief part of an orator? He answered, Action: what next?—Action: what next again?—Action. He said it that knew it best, and had by nature himself no advantage in that he commended. A strange thing, that that part of an orator which is but superficial, and rather *the virtue of a player*, should be placed so high above those other noble parts of invention, elocution, and the rest; nay almost alone, as if it were all in all. But the reason is plain. There is in human nature generally more of the fool than of the wise; and therefore, those faculties by which the foolish part of men's minds is taken are most potent."

CHAPTER IX.—Continued.

But though the conspirators have thus escaped with their lives, an inexorable Nemesis still pursues them. Dissensions arise among them; for theirs is a combination of inherently discordant elements, containing within itself the seeds of destruction. They are unequally yoked together, and a quarrel is inevitable. Cassius' unscrupulousness and his corrupt methods of raising money make him odious to the high-minded Brutus; who, nevertheless, is angry because some of this money is not sent to him, in his extremity, to pay his legions:

"For I can raise no money by vile means:
By heaven, I had rather coin my heart,
And drop my blood by drachmas, than to wring
From the hard hands of peasants their *vile trash*
By any indirection."

Cassius, by a supreme effort, conquers peace, and love is restored. But again the victor is vanquished: for Brutus immediately assumes the mastery, and in the blindness that is upon him, orders the fatal movement upon the enemy at Philippi.

Meanwhile, the work of disorganization in Cassius' character is subtly progressing. This Epicurean, whose school "rejected both the necessity of Fate and the fear of the gods," scorning divination, is now changing, becoming superstitious. On the morning of the decisive battle, his mind is filled with gloomy forebodings; oppressed by silent whisperings of coming disaster, forerunners of his impending fate:

19

> "This is my birthday; as this very day
>   Was Cassius born.   Give me thy hand, Messala:
> Be thou my witness that, against my will,
> As Pompey was, am I compelled to set
> Upon one battle all our liberties.
> You know that I hold Epicurus strong,
> And his opinion: now I change my mind,
> And partly credit things that do presage.
> Coming from Sardis, on our former ensign
> Two mighty eagles fell; and there they perch'd,
> Gorging and feeding from our soldiers' hands,
> Who to Philippi here consorted us;
> This morning are they fled away, and gone;
> And in their steads do ravens, crows, and kites,
> Fly o'er our heads, and downward look on us,
> As we were sickly prey; their shadows seem
> A canopy most fatal, under which
> Our army lies, ready to give up the ghost."

Through the influence of Messala, he resolves to be constant: but nevertheless, this rein thus given to the imagination, drawing him towards despair, this under-current of ominous feeling, is sweeping him off his moorings and loosening his hold upon life, even before he is subjected to the final, fatal strain in the hour of battle.

The hand of Nemesis presses heavily upon Brutus also: and its touch is scorching. The smouldering flame within himself, that burst forth in his murderous act, has recoiled upon his household, in a consuming fire. Tidings are brought him that Portia, his devoted wife,—'himself, his part,' by virtue of

> "that great vow
> Which did incorporate and make us one,"—

in her anxiety and her grief, had become *mad*, and that in her madness she had killed herself:

> "with this she fell distract,
> And, her attendants absent, swallow'd fire."

But Brutus bears this blow with heroic resolution. He

is a Stoic, and more than that, his is an inherently noble
nature : and he astonishes the wavering, ignoble Cassius
by his fortitude,—" the virtue of adversity." This Roman
gentleman buries his grief from the sight of his friends ;
sustaining himself solely by his philosophy :

> " With meditating that she must die once,
> I have the patience to endure it now." *

Brutus' resolution is yet again put to test. That very
night, the night before the fateful battle, he encounters a
dreadful portent, personal to himself. We have seen how
merely the sight of the flight of some birds had depressed
Cassius, whose self-conserving powers of resistance had
been palsied, in the disintegration going on within him,—
which, indeed, seems to be one of the final penalties of
guilt, — but the effect of a far more appalling spectacle
upon Brutus was altogether different.

King Richard III., that monster of crime, bold, resolute, and with a heart harder than flint, the night before
his fatal battle, dreamed he saw the ghosts of his murdered victims. He awoke to dire complaints, *to dreadful
questionings and torturing self-accusations*, sharpened to
the edge of " conscience," in its modern conception :

> " Have mercy, Jesu!—Soft; I did but dream.
> O coward conscience, how thou dost afflict me !
> The lights burn blue.— It is now dead midnight.
> Cold fearful drops stand on my trembling flesh.
> What, do I fear? myself? there 's none else by :
> Richard loves Richard; that is, I am I.
> Is there a murderer here? No ;—yes; I am :
> Then fly.—What, from myself? Great reason why?
> Lest I revenge. What? Myself, upon myself?
> Alack, I love myself. Wherefore? for any good
> That I myself have done unto myself?
> O, no : alas, I rather hate myself,
> For hateful deeds committed by myself.
> I am a villain : yet I lie, I am not.

---

* See *ante*, page 150.

Fool, of thyself speak well: — fool, do not flatter.

. . . .

I shall despair.— There is no creature loves me;
And if I die, no soul shall pity me: —
Nay, wherefore should they? since that I myself
Find in myself no pity to myself.
Methought, the souls of all that I had murder'd
Came to my tent: and every one did threat
To-morrow's vengeance on the head of Richard."

But Brutus' imagination, left to itself, in untrammeled
license, in the midnight hour,—

> "in that silent time, when sullen night
> Did hide heav'n's twinkling tapers from his sight,
> And on the earth with blackest looks did lour,"—

conjured up no ghost of the murdered Cæsar. This, in
fact, would have been wholly incompatible with the fixed
idea which possesses him, — of the strict honesty of his
purpose,— as any specialist will tell us. Instead, there
appears before him, as in a phantasma, a horrible apparition of his own evil spirit. It awakens in him no slum-
bering consciousness of guilt, no apprehension of a "to-
morrow's vengeance," and, strange to say, no gloomy forebodings of a coming disaster. It inspires "physical"
terror, but Brutus' soul is undaunted:

"How ill this taper burns! — Ha! who comes here?
I think it is the weakness of mine eyes
That shapes this monstrous apparition.
It comes upon me! — Art thou anything?
Art thou some god, some angel, or some devil,
That mak'st my blood cold, and my hair to stare?
Speak to me what thou art.
Ghost. Thy evil spirit, Brutus.
Bru. Why com'st thou?
Ghost. To tell thee thou shalt see me at Philippi.
Bru. Well: then I shall see thee again?
Ghost. Ay, at Philippi.
Bru. Why, I will see thee at Philippi, then.—
                              [*Ghost vanishes.*

> Now I have taken heart thou vanishest:
> Ill spirit, I would have more talk with thee.—
> Boy! Lucius!—Varro! Claudius! Sirs, awake!"

Strong in the consciousness of his integrity, he thinks of nothing but natural causes for the phenomenon. He ascertains by questioning that the others had neither seen anything nor were aware of having cried out in their sleep, though he notes that Lucius is thus talking; and then, giving no further attention to the matter, he proceeds immediately, and with undiminished vigor, to press forward the movement:

> "Go, and commend me to my brother Cassius;
> Bid him set on his powers betimes before,
> And we will follow."

Later, Cassius, personally interested, puts him to a test of another sort:

> "But since the affairs of men rest still uncertain,
> Let's reason with the worst that may befall.
> If we do lose this battle, then is this
> The very last time we shall speak together:
> What are you then determined to do?"

Brutus, comprehending the sinister significance of this question, again fortifies himself with his philosophy, and answers:

> "Even by the rule of that philosophy
> By which I did blame Cato for the death
> Which he did give himself:—I know not how,
> But I do find it *cowardly and vile*,
> For fear of what might fall, so to prevent
> The time of life:—arming myself with patience,
> To stay the providence of some high powers
> That govern us below."

But Cassius puts upon the question a subtly incisive point:

> "Then if we lose this battle,
> You are contented to be led in triumph
> Through the streets of Rome?"

The question now strikes home, penetrating to the very core of Brutus' sensitive nature. There is somewhere a limit to the strain which this honorable philosophy will endure without collapse, even in the noblest soul. And in this case, the limit, in its anticipation, is passed. Cassius has again applied the torch to Brutus' imagination, and his philosophy is consumed in the flame. The vision that unrolls before him of Brutus, him of noble lineage, upon whom Rome called for redress, and to whom the respect of his fellow men is as the breath of life, presently bound and led in triumph through the streets of Rome, amidst the jeers of the multitude,—the vision of this rape of honor, this infamy, this unutterable shame, is too appalling; and Brutus recoils:

> "No, Cassius, no: think not, thou noble Roman,
> That ever Brutus will go bound to Rome;
> He bears too great a mind."

But Cassius has gained his point. His problem has been solved for himself. For the tables are turned; and this once strong, self-centred man, who had memorably moulded Brutus to his purpose, has at length, in the progress of his deterioration, altogether lost his poise,— become sensitively subject to extraneous influences, both portentous and personal. This is subtly shown in his almost parrot-like repetition of Brutus' farewell speech, at the close of their interview. And now his course is clear. In the event of disaster,—suicide. And with this spectre almost visibly hovering over him, he enters the battle.

Desperation is the immediate antecedent of despair, the iridescent flush of evening, preceding the night. And in Cassius' words of bravado, uttered just before the engagement, we perceive the muffled ring of an undertone of desperation; possibly the antecedent note of an oncoming despair:

"Why, now, blow wind, swell billow, and swim bark!
The storm is up, and *all is on the hazard.*"

For we remember that this was to him a painful chord,—
one of the mournful plaints in the strain of despair he
poured into Messala's ear, as already noted.

And now the battle is on: and its tide, though favor-
ing Brutus, turns at length against Cassius' division. It
becomes hemmed in by Antony's forces: and Pindarus,
Cassius' servant, enters, sounding the alarm:

"Fly further off, my lord, fly further off.
Mark Antony is in your tents, my lord!
Fly therefore, noble Cassius, fly far off."

Cassius finds a safe position upon the side of a hill,
from whence he perceives his burning tents, and also a
body of troops approaching. He mounts Titinius upon
his horse, and sends him in haste to reconnoitre and report
whether the advancing troops be "friends or enemy." In
his anxiety, and because of his weak eyesight, he sends
Pindarus up the hill, to watch Titinius, and to report what
he sees upon the field. And before he hears a word, the
night of black despair closes in upon him, enveloping him
in its gloom:

"This day I breathed first: time is come round,
And where I did begin there shall I end;
My life is run his compass."

His imagination thus pictures before him the fatal end,
and in its vivid realization there is a complete collapse:
he is prepared to surrender all further hold upon life.

In climatic fitness, Pindarus, his servant, in *malice*,
now lies to him; reporting that Titinius is taken prisoner,
and that "they shout for joy"; and the shout is heard in
confirmation,— when in fact, it is the acclaim of Brutus'
advancing forces, welcoming Titinius. Summoning Pindarus, bidding him, "behold no more," and making no
further inquiry, for he is consciously accepting the inev-

itable, Cassius now covers his face and ends his life by falling upon his own sword. It was the sword with which he had pierced Cæsar to his death. In his dying words, he recognizes the profound significance of the fact:

> "Cæsar, thou art *aveng'd*
> Even with the sword that kill'd thee."

His own chalice has at last been pressed to his own lips, with its draught of death.

> "Thus doth He force the swords of wicked men
> To turn their own points on their master's bosoms:
> . . . .
> *Wrong hath but wrong, and blame its due of blame.*" *

Continuing the painful record of crime's painful retribution: Titinius returns, bearing the garland of victory sent by Brutus to Cassius,

> "for Octavius
> Is overthrown by noble Brutus' power,"

and rejoicing in the " comfort " he brings to Cassius, whom he had left " all disconsolate." In his anguish, at the sight of Cassius' corpse, and his ignorance of Pindarus' guile, he exclaims :

> "Mistrust of my success hath done this deed."

> "Why didst thou send me forth, brave Cassius?
> Did I not meet thy friends? and did not they
> Put on my brows this wreath of victory,
> And bid me give 't thee? Didst thou not hear their shouts?
> Alas, thou hast misconstrued everything."

And Messala, Cassius' friend, to whom he had confided his gloomy apprehensions, laboring under the same misconception, in the same partial comprehension of the truth, continues the theme, developing a general principle of profound import :

> "Mistrust of good success hath done this deed.

---

* And in this also, we are but following in Bacon's enlightened footsteps : See *ante*, page 76, note.

O hateful error, melancholy's child!
Why dost thou show to the apt thoughts of men
The things that are not?   O error, soon conceived,
Thou never com'st unto a happy birth,
But kill'st the mother that engender'd thee."

Messala departs, to carry the tidings to Brutus; and we
note with interest the peculiar incisiveness with which
this intelligence is pointed:

" I go to meet
The noble Brutus, *thrusting this report*
Into his ears: I may say *thrusting* it;
For *piercing steel,* and *darts* envenomed,
Shall be as welcome to the ears of Brutus
As tidings of this sight."

Titinius is left behind, plunged into the same gulf of
despair.   Cassius' dismal end, so unnecessary, so inscrutable beneath its surface,—save to his own dying glance,—
is given by Titinius a woful interpretation: it is to him
ominous of the fate of their cause, the setting of its sun,
ushering in the night:

" But Cassius is no more.—O setting sun!
As in thy red rays thou dost sink to-night,
So in his red blood Cassius' day is set;
The sun of Rome is set!   Our day is gone;
Clouds, dews, and dangers come; our deeds are done!" *

---

* Incidentally, Titinius' few words reveal, unmistakably, the
pure and unselfish quality of his patriotism.   Rome was written upon his heart, springing thence spontaneously to his lips,
in this moment of distress preceding his death.   Her welfare
and the existence and intent of their cause were to him identical; and their common fate, their helplessness, and the ensuing
dangers, and not his own personal misfortunes, were the burden of his thoughts.   Evidently he was not one of those whose
minds are self-absorbed, closed to " this universality," and with
little knowledge of the world at large, who, to use Bacon's expressive words, " do refer all things to themselves, and thrust
themselves into the centre of the world, as if all lives should

In the utter abandonment of despair, he kills himself
with the same sword :

> "By your leave, gods : — this is a Roman's part:
> Come, Cassius' sword, and find Titinius' heart."

In the parley preceding the battle, Antony and Octavius had thrust into the conspirators' ears some very
pointed words, of intensive force, breathing of vengeance,
and expressive of a righteous indignation :

> "*Ant.* In your bad strokes, Brutus, you gave good words:
> Witness the hole you made in Cæsar's heart,
> Crying, '*Long live! hail, Cæsar!*'"

> "Villains, you did not so when your vile daggers
> Hack'd one another in the sides of Cæsar:
> You show'd your teeth like apes, and fawn'd like hounds,
> And bow'd like bondmen, kissing Cæsar's feet;
> Whilst damned Casca, like a cur, behind,
> Struck Cæsar on the neck. O you flatterers!"

> "*Oct.* Come, come, the cause : if arguing make us sweat,
> The proof of it will turn to redder drops.
> *Look*,— I draw a sword against conspirators;
> When think you that the sword goes up again? —
> Never, till Cæsar's three-and-thirty wounds
> Be well *avenged;* or till another Cæsar
> Have added slaughter to the sword of traitors;"

declaring further, that he "was not born to die on Brutus'
sword." As might perhaps be expected, these "words,
words" seemingly make but little impression upon the
conspirators, at least upon Brutus. Cassius, indeed, answers with bluster, though he immediately addresses Messala in a strain indicating a sinking heart. But Brutus,
armored in the consciousness of his integrity, replies with
dignity :

> "O, if thou wert the noblest of thy strain,
> Young man, thou couldst not die more honorable."

---

meet in them and their fortunes ; never caring in all tempests
what becomes of the ship of estates, so they may save themselves in the cockboat of their own fortune."

But presently, Brutus encounters a poignant sight, of such penetrating, convicting power, that it pierces even through his darkened understanding. Returning with Messala to look for Cassius' body, he finds by its side, lying face upward, the body of Titinius, self-slain by the self-same sword. Standing there appalled,

"Before this sudden and unlooked-for fate,"

a glimmering of its meaning forces its way into his benighted soul, and what seems to him to be its rightful interpretation; and he exclaims:

"O Julius Cæsar, thou art mighty yet!
Thy spirit walks abroad, and turns our swords
In our own proper entrails." *

---

* The several and varied interpretations given to Cassius' death, by himself, by Titinius and Messala, and by Brutus, are not accidents; for they are too carefully elaborated. They are, in fact, elegant exemplifications (like waters drawn from its fountain, or flowers upon its stem) of Bacon's profound philosophy of human nature in certain of its aspects, to which he gave distinct development in his *Novum Organum*. Its spirit may perhaps be caught from the following brief extract:

"For it is a false assertion that the sense of man is the measure of things. On the contrary, all perceptions as well of the sense as of the mind are *according to the measure of the individual* and not according to the measure of the universe. And the human understanding is like a false mirror, which, receiving rays irregularly, distorts and discolors the nature of things by mingling its own nature with it. . . . For every one (besides the errors common to human nature in general) has a cave or den of his own, which refracts and discolors the light of nature; owing either to *his own proper and peculiar nature;* or to his education and conversation with others; or to the reading of books, and the authority of those whom he esteems and admires; or to the differences of impressions, accordingly as they take place in a mind *preoccupied and predisposed* or in a mind indifferent and settled; or the like. So that the spirit of man (according as it is meted out to different individuals) is in fact variable and full of perturbation, and governed as it were by chance."

But Brutus has by no means awakened to clarity of
vision. He is still walking among the clouds, in the
higher realm of his own ideal world ; or perhaps, to put
it more strongly, he is even yet over and beyond, in the
black cloud of darkness that overshadows the abnormal.

In his early exaltation, it will be remembered, it was
not Cæsar " for the thing he is," the personality to whom
he was bound by ties of affection, in the actuality of things
as they are, but it was Cæsar's embodied potentiality, his
ambitious " spirit," in its ominous possibilities, which occupied his mind, and against which he arrayed himself in
mortal combat ; and Cæsar's physical ' dismemberment '
was to him but the gross, earthly, and repulsive, but nevertheless necessary incident to this higher warfare :

> " We all stand up against the spirit of Cæsar ;
> And in the spirit of man there is no blood ;
> O, that we then could come by Cæsar's spirit,
> And not dismember Cæsar !   But, alas,
> Cæsar must bleed for it."

To this chimera, the offspring of his inflamed imagination, Brutus is destined to remain in thralldom, even unto
the fatal end ; blinded first to the crime, and now to its
consequences, by the attendant delusion that he is all the
while treading in the honorable pathway of heroic self-
sacrifice, and that whatever be the event, he is winning
to himself imperishable glory.   He is in fact still possessed by a fixed idea, that shapes and colors everything to
its own likeness.   And in this awful spectacle, so pregnant with significance, he sees, and only sees, the manifest workings of his old intangible enemy, Cæsar's mighty
" spirit," quenchless even in death, ' walking abroad,' restless in its animosity, and waging, most effectually, a relentless warfare.

But Brutus remains undaunted ; for in his mind, the
justness of his cause is thereby in no respect consciously

impugned. This ray of light is so distorted by the medium through which it enters that it awakens in him no conviction of wrong-doing, nor even its depressing shadow. He, indeed, realizes the tremendous odds against which he contends, as is indicated in his expression, but there is no faltering or wavering of his resolution. Sparing but a moment to pay to the dead his tribute of appreciation and affection, he urges on the conflict with undiminished vigor:

> "Are yet two Romans living such as these?—
> The last of all the Romans, fare thee well!
> It is impossible that ever Rome
> Should breed thy fellow.—Friends, I owe more tears
> To this dead man than you shall see me pay.—
> I shall find time, Cassius, *I shall find time.*—
> Come, therefore, and to Thassos send his body;
> His funerals shall not be in our camp,
> Lest it discomfort us.— Lucilius, come;—
> And come, young Cato: let us to the field.—
> Labeo, and Flavius, set our battles on:—
> 'T is three o'clock; and, Romans, yet ere night
> We shall try fortune in a second fight."

He exhorts his companions, "O yet hold up your heads!" and in concert with young Cato, and to encourage their troops as they charge, he cries:

> "And I am Brutus, Marcus Brutus, I;
> Brutus, my country's friend; know me for Brutus."

But the tide of battle turns against them. Cato is slain, Lucilius taken prisoner, and their forces are utterly routed. Brutus acknowledges himself vanquished; hope is abandoned, and his grief finds vent in manly tears:

> "Now is that noble vessel full of grief,
> That it runs over even at his eyes."

He recalls the apparition with which he had before been visited; now recognizing in it another origin, and a significance of fearfully ominous import:

> " *The ghost of Cæsar* hath appeared to me
> Two several times by night: at Sardis, once;
> And, this last night, here in Philippi fields.
> *I know my hour is come.*"

Accepting his fate, he bids farewell to his friends:

> "Farewell to you — and you; — and you, Volumnius.—
> Strato, *thou hast been all this while asleep;*
> Farewell to thee too, Strato.— Countrymen,
> My heart doth joy that yet, in all my life,
> I found no man but he was true to me.
> *I shall have more glory by this losing day,*
> *More than Octavius and Mark Antony*
> *By this vile conquest shall attain unto.*
> So, fare you well at once; for Brutus' tongue
> Hath almost ended his life's history."

Death is to him welcome; and there is an unutterable longing for the final rest:

> "Night hangs upon mine eyes: my bones would rest,
> That have but labor'd to attain this hour." *

He then runs upon the sword held by Strato, crying:

> "Cæsar, now be still:
> I kill'd not thee with half so good a will."

---

* " Death arrives gracious only to such as sit in darkness, or lie heavy burthened with grief and irons; to the poor Christian, that sits bound in the galley; to despairful widows, pensive prisoners, and deposed kings; to them whose fortune runs back, and whose spirits mutiny; unto such death is a redeemer, and the grave a place for retiredness and rest.

" These wait upon the shore of death, and waft unto him to draw near, wishing above all others to see his star, that they might be led to his place; wooing the remorseless sisters to wind down the watch of their life, and to break them off before the hour. . . .

" The night was even now: but that name is lost; it is not now late but early. Mine eyes begin to discharge their watch, and to compound with this fleshly weakness for a time of perpetual rest; and I shall presently be as happy for a few hours, as I had died the first hour I was born."—*On Death.*

Cæsar is thus finally avenged; a righteous retribution is accomplished; and the play appropriately ends with Mark Antony's touching tribute to Brutus, uttered over his body:

> "This was the noblest Roman of them all:
> All the conspirators, save only he,
> Did that they did in *envy* of great Cæsar;
> He only, in a general honest thought,
> And common good to all, made one of them.
> His life was gentle; and the elements
> So mix'd in him that Nature might stand up,
> And say to all the world, '*This was a man!*'
> *Oct.* According to his virtue let us use him,
> With all respect and rights of burial.
> Within my tent his bones to-night shall lie,
> Most like a soldier, order'd honorably,—
> So, call the field to rest: and let's away,
> To feast the glories of this happy day."

CHAPTER X.

Our labor of love is finished. And possibly the reader
has consciously gained a much clearer insight into the play :
through its study from the standpoint of its author, and in
the strong light continually thrown upon it from his volum-
inous prose. Under this illumination, indeed, the play continually unfolds itself to our comprehension : and, as was
said of his history, its effect is "like that of bringing a
light into a dark room : the objects are there as they were
before, but now you can distinguish them."

"Dramatic poetry," said Bacon, "is a kind of visible
history, giving the images of things as if they were present, whilst history represents them as past." And through
the perfect blending of the historian's and the dramatist's
art, how beautifully is this conception fulfilled in the play
before us !

An important event in ancient times is first definitely
comprehended from the historian's standpoint; with a
clear insight into the character and mould of the principal actors, their motives, and the springs of action; into
its causes and the forces at work, their development and
operation, even to the consummation, and thence, through
its consequences, unto the end. Writing from this standpoint, and with his masterly grasp of the forces "that
work upon the spirits of men," he has given the whole
reproduction in the similitude of life itself; in a perfection of execution, an absolute completeness, an artistic
unity, and a perfectly consistent development, from its inception to its conclusion, that almost surpasses belief —

except in the presence of its accomplishment. In this respect, indeed, and in its revelation of man unto himself, it stands unparalleled in the literature of the world, both ancient and modern,—a veritable masterpiece of the ages.

Sharing in the author's conception, we share also in his delight. Our enhanced pleasure in the more intimate comprehension of the play is even closely akin to the added joy experienced by Helmholtz, when, after a close study and final comprehension of the laws of wave motion in their exquisite harmonies, he again visited the sea; and to which he gave expression in these beautiful words:

"And thus from the distant horizon, where white lines of foam on the steel-blue surface betray the coming trains of wave, down to the sand beneath our feet, where the impression of their arcs remains, there is unfolded before our eyes a sublime image of immeasurable power and unceasing variety, which, as the eye at once recognizes its pervading order and law, enchains and exalts without confusing the mind."

And how clearly has he shown us the true method of approach in the study of the plays! Art and Nature speak in one and the same language—*manifestation*. And therefore, if we would comprehend the work, at least of this Master Artist, we must first learn "the mother tongue." And here also there is no royal road to learning. Accepting him as our master, we must enter the same school in which he studied, and by patient, painstaking labor, learn nature's alphabet, aye her primer; and thus only can we fully understand his language, or adequately comprehend his work. And conversely, the close study of his work teaches us, in turn, how to interpret nature's voice in its expressive accents; opening our minds to its understanding, and initiating that intimate "converse" with her, which he so earnestly enjoined, and which is our exalted privilege.

Nevertheless, in this our present attempt, owing to individual limitations and the ever present " personal equation " of error, the play, in its wealth of significance, is by no means fully comprehended. Thus, even as we were writing the concluding pages, there dawned upon us the glimmering vision of a possibly subtler, more important phase of Brutus' character, as it is unfolded in the play, whose definite perception had previously escaped us, and which seems worthy of further and more careful attention.

In brief: Brutus was manifestly a cultivated Roman, a lover of books and music, and proficient in philosophy. In this expansion of his mind, and under the promptings of a sensitive, sympathetic heart, he seems to have attained to a clear apprehension of the surpassing excellence of duty and self-sacrifice, of honor and of good repute; and such considerations appear to have been ever present before him. But observing the marked contrast between Titinius' spontaneous self-abnegation, manifested in his few brief words, and the predominant tone of Brutus' final utterances, characterized by the utter absence of this quality, and in whose self-absorption there was no word of grief for Rome, or for the loss of their cause, or a thought thereof, we begin to suspect that one of Brutus' most pronounced characteristics was a superb Egotism, which both colored his thoughts and subtly influenced his whole course of action; yea more, that it lay at the very foundation of his ruin; that it was at once the *weakness* that gave Cassius his hold upon him, and in its subtler essence, the *sin* which lay at the core of his error; whose poison festered into his delusion, and whose virulence burst forth in the consequent crime; and that finally, its ascendency, manifested in his headstrong wilfulness and blind self-assertion, ministered directly to the subsequent retribution.

But all this must be left to the enlightened judgment

of the reader : and we beg that he will indeed regard our whole discussion as merely provisional ; as a framework of suggestions, contributory to his own independent and delightful study of the play ; prosecuted with the intent to attain to the innermost thought and conception of its author. Only, we assure him, from our own experience, that however deep he may sound the plummet, he will find, at the end, that there are still unsounded depths beyond, inviting and rewarding further study, — if only he will adopt Bacon's maxim, " that the eye of the mind be never taken off from things themselves, but receive their images truly as they are."

And applying this maxim to our broader study of this truly magnificent creation, do we not clearly *see* and recognize the personality of its author, as it is " revealed in his works " ? Have we not been enabled to " trace his footsteps " throughout its whole compass ? And do we not discern that its " evidences of design " are, in fact, the fulfilment of his own specifications ; that its thoughts are his thoughts, its learning his learning, its conception of human nature strikingly his conception, and its underlying psychology his psychology ? And has not the recognition of his authorship opened to us a mine of untold treasure, affording to these jewels their appropriate setting, and brought with it a flood of light, in whose illumination they glow in a surpassing splendor ? And above all, has it not given us a clearer insight into the kindly, beneficent intent towards mankind which so distinctively characterizes his work, and which is at once its inspiration and its crowning glory ?

But shall this new and enlarged appreciation be merely intellectual and barren ; confined wholly to the gift, and with no accompanying expansion of the soul in a kindly or even merciful thought towards its bountiful giver ?

And what though he chose to veil his personality for a

time : it was doubtless for what were to him good and sufficient reasons :

> "Never believe, though in my nature reign'd
> All frailties that besiege all kinds of blood,
> That it could so preposterously be stain'd,
> To leave for *nothing* all thy sum of good." *

Moreover, whatever the reasons, and however controlling the circumstances, confessedly, he produced the plays under conditions which effectually precluded his enjoyment of the lustrous reputation they might have conferred upon his name. And the very absence of this powerful incentive, taken in connection with their long continued and

---

* In the very beginning, Bacon's regard for the comfort and peace of mind of his pious mother, especially in her precarious condition, would certainly have counted for something: and it would seem, in itself, to have been a sufficient, and indeed a highly creditable reason for withholding his name even from such priceless works. (See *ante*, page 283, note.) And not to mention other pertinent circumstances inviting interesting discussion, it is obvious, from the nature of the case, that binding obligations were likely assumed in the beginning, which placed further check upon him; holding him to honorable silence, —until, as he was serenely confident, the plays themselves enforced the revelation :

> "Because he needs no praise, wilt thou be dumb?
> Excuse not silence so; for it lies in thee
> To make him much outlive a gilded tomb,
> And to be praised of ages yet to be."

The *Sonnets*, from which the above lines are quoted, have generally been regarded as beautiful, but licentious productions, whose theme is illicit love: when in fact, in their rightful interpretation (possibly becoming apparent in a subsequent chapter) they are as pure as is Solomon's Song; the unveiling of the Poet's heart; singing in unmistakable notes of his loving appreciation of the plays, of his grief in his deprivation of their acknowledgment, and of his abiding faith in the ultimate revelation.

prolific composition, but throws into stronger light the higher motives which actuated their production. They were indeed born of an irresistible impulse, whose germinal force was the divinely implanted purpose of service to mankind, and whose allurement was the lofty ambition to thus perpetuate himself in the life of humanity, in a fruition whose maturity could only come long after his departure.

Such greatness, attaining even to grandeur, may seem to some a fanciful picture ; but only to those who are unacquainted with Bacon, and who have perhaps forgotten that these immortal works, so delight-inspiring, are also replete with lessons of the most vital import to each of us. The creation bears the stamp of its design ; and this is the most characteristic imprint of its author.*

---

* Incidentally, it should be mentioned that Bacon had a lofty conception of the legitimate province of the Drama, and of its possible utilization for good, as is clearly shown in the following brief extract from his *De Augmentis*, Second Book :

" Dramatic Poetry, which has the theatre for its world, would be of excellent use, if well directed. For the stage is capable of no small influence, both of discipline and corruption. Now of corruption in this kind we have enough; but the discipline has in our times been plainly neglected. And though in modern states play-acting is esteemed but as a toy, except when it is too satirical and biting; yet among the ancients, it was used as a means of educating men's minds to virtue. Nay, it has been regarded by learned men and great philosophers as a kind of musician's bow by which men's minds may be played upon. And certainly it is most true, and one of the great secrets of nature, that the minds of men are more open to impressions and affections when many are gathered together than when they are alone."

A standard that is as much higher than that of modern playwrights, as are their productions inferior to the plays in moral power, and "as a means of educating men's minds to virtue." For in literature, as in nature, a stream never rises higher than its source.

Goethe said of his work, "*It is bone of my bone and flesh of my flesh*": and the remark is fundamental; applicable to all the great works of genius, which are indeed their authors' progeny, bearing the characteristics of their heredity. Indeed, if we would adequately comprehend the greatness of the plays in the full grandeur of their beneficent intent, and moreover grasp the underlying law of their genesis — in the comprehension of the essential, indispensable germinal element which was their origin and inspiration—we must study intently the mould of their author; laying hold upon the special virile force which dominated his intellectual life, and which found expression in his works,— a force which is the very essence of the greatness indicated, and which rendered him abundantly capable of just such a sacrifice.

We are entering upon a region so lofty, that its paths are unfamiliar. Negligence of the lustre of fame, as a present, personal gratification (so flattering to man's inherent vanity, and so highly esteemed), is indeed difficult to comprehend; but only because of the greater difficulty of comprehending the predominance in motive of the vastly greater good of accomplished service to mankind; which as far transcends it as does the sunlight the lesser lights that illumine the earth.

But such was Bacon's thought, his predominant motive and purpose. It is made clearly manifest in connection with the development of his Inductive Philosophy — unfolded in his *Novum Organum*, "*or True Directions concerning the Interpretation of Nature*"—whose beneficent intent is so obvious and so familiar to all. At an early date, when his mighty project was still a secret confined to himself, to quote from Spedding:

"He believed that he had by accident stumbled upon a Thought, which duly followed out would in the course of generations make man the master of all natural forces.

The 'Interpretation of Nature' was, according to his speculation, the 'Kingdom of Man.' To plant this thought in men's minds under such conditions that it should have the best chance of growing and bearing its proper fruit in due season was the great aspiration of his life. . . . On one of these days, his imagination wandering far into the future, showed him in vision the first instalment ready for publication, and set him upon thinking how he should announce it to the world. The result of this meditation he fortunately confided to a sheet of paper, which being found long after in his cabinet, revealed the secret which it had kept." It is entitled, *Of the Interpretation of Nature,—Proem*, and opens with these pregnant words:

" Believing that I was born for the service of mankind, and regarding the care of the commonwealth as a kind of common property which, like the air and water, belong to everybody, I set myself to consider in what way mankind might be best served, and what service I was myself best fitted by nature to perform."

And in conclusion, he writes:

" For myself, my heart is not set upon any of those things which depend upon external accidents. I am not hunting for fame: I have no desire to found a sect, after the fashion of the heresiarchs; and to look for any private gain from such an undertaking as this, I count both ridiculous and base. Enough for me the consciousness of well-deserving, and those real and effectual results with which Fortune itself cannot interfere."

The unfinished manuscript of this, *Of the Interpretation of Nature*, from whose Proem the foregoing is quoted, was found among Bacon's papers and published after his death. It contains the germ and initial but incomplete development of his proposed Philosophy. And the above utterance is especially significant and helpful to our comprehension of the man, in the light of the astonishing fact (which appears from its title-page, published in facsimile in Vol. III. of Ellis and Spedding's edition of his Works) that Bacon, for reasons known only to himself, originally purposed its publication, not in his own name, but under the pseudonym of "*Valerius Terminus*," "with annotations by *Hermes Stella*," another pseudonym.

Mr. Robert Leslie Ellis, Spedding's co-editor, who wrote its explanatory preface, comments upon this as follows :

" It is impossible to ascertain the motive which determined Bacon to give to the supposed author the name of Valerius Terminus, or to his commentator, of whose annotations we have no remains, that of Hermes Stella. It may be *conjectured* that by the name Terminus he intended to intimate that the new philosophy would put an end to the wandering of mankind in search of truth, that it would be the *terminus ad quem* in which when it was once attained the mind would finally acquiesce. Again the obscurity of the text was to be in some measure removed by the annotations of Stella ; not however wholly, for Bacon in the epitome of the eighteenth chapter commends the manner of publishing knowledge 'whereby it shall not be to the capacity nor taste of all, but as it were single and adapt its reader.' Stella was therefore to throw a kind of starlight on the subject, enough to prevent the student's losing his way, but not much more."

Bacon's motive in thus purposing in the beginning to withhold his name from a work he so highly esteemed, and which might have conferred upon it such lustre and reputation almost at the outset of his career, must remain purely a matter of conjecture. But we may rest assured, from his own utterances, that it was planned in furtherance of his loftier purpose, "to plant this thought in men's minds under such conditions that it should have the best chance of growing and bearing its proper fruit in due season," and that this was with him paramount to any personal considerations.

Afterwards, the conditions changed, and with them his

plans: for when the completed *Novum Organum* was finally published in 1620, his acquired dignity and lofty position as Lord Verulam, High Chancellor of England, gave to the work additional weight and force, and his name in these terms was engraved upon its title-page.*

---

* Upon this point we gain additional light from the following passage, in a letter he wrote in 1591 to his uncle Burghley, seeking his kindly aid towards his advancement:

"Lastly, I confess that I have as vast contemplative ends, as I have moderate civil ends: for I have taken all knowledge to be my province; and if I could purge it of two sorts of rovers, whereof the one with frivolous disputations, confutations, and verbosities, the other with blind experiments and auricular traditions and impostures, hath committed so many spoils, I hope I shall bring in industrious observations, grounded conclusions, and profitable inventions and discoveries; the best state of that province. This, whether it be curiosity, or vain glory, or nature, or (if one take it favorably) *philanthropia*, is so fixed in my mind as it cannot be removed. *And I do easily see, that place of any reasonable countenance doth bring commandment of more wits than a man's own; which is the thing I greatly affect.*"

(See also Professor Adamson's able article on Bacon, in the *Encyclopædia Britannica*, for a concise statement of his striving after lofty ends, "the key to Bacon's life.")

As an aid to our comprehension of its mystery, though not in extenuation (for Bacon said of himself, in just contrition: "I was the justest judge that was in England these fifty years: but it was *the justest censure in parliament* that was these two hundred years."), we venture to add, in this connection, Spedding's charitable interpretation of his downfall:

"So far therefore, his actual course was quite consistent with his first design; and it is even probable that this very constancy was in some degree answerable for the great error and misfortune of his life. That an absorbing interest in one thing should induce negligence of others not less important, is an accident only too natural and familiar; and if he did not allow the *Novum Organum* to interfere with his attention to the causes which came before him in Chancery, it did probably prevent

The dominant spirit which animated his work is manifested repeatedly in further utterances. Thus, in his *De Augmentis*, Seventh Book, he says:

"For myself, most excellent king, I may truly say that

him from attending as carefully as he should and otherwise would have done to the proceedings of his servants and the state of his accounts."

His intimate friend, Sir Tobie Mathew, said of him: "It is not his greatness that I admire, but his virtue: it is not the favors I have received from him (infinite though they be) that have thus enthralled and enchained my heart, but his whole life and character; which are such that, if he were of an inferior condition I could not honor him the less, and if he were my enemy I should not the less love and endeavor to serve him."

And after his fall, Ben Jonson said: "My conceit of his person was never increased toward him by his place or honors: but I have and do reverence him, for the greatness that was only proper to himself, in that he seemed to me, ever by his work, one of the greatest men, and most worthy of admiration, that had been in many ages. In his adversity, I ever prayed that God would give him strength; for greatness he could not want. Neither could I *condole* in a word or syllable for him, as knowing no accident could do harm to virtue, but rather help to make it manifest."

May God grant, that some day, the mystery may be comprehended, in an intelligent, all-embracing charity. And possibly the overruling hand of Providence turned his downfall to good; as was Bacon's faith. In a letter to King James he wrote: "I have now (by God's merciful chastisement and by his special providence) time and leisure to put my talent, or half-talent, or what it is, to such exchanges as may perhaps exceed the interest of an active life."

It should be noted that it was during this period of his retirement that the plays were perpetuated to posterity, through their collection and publication in the folio of 1623; many of them here appearing in print for the first time, and others with material modifications: while they were originally composed (the first of them appearing anonymously) during the period when he was comparatively a briefless barrister.

both in this present work, and in those I intend to publish hereafter, I often advisedly and deliberately throw
aside the dignity of my name and wit (if such thing be)
in my endeavor to advance human interests."

He writes to Dr. Playfer, asking his aid in the translation of the *Advancement of Learning* into Latin:

" If I do not err (for any judgment that a man maketh
of his own doings had need to be spoken with a *Si nun-
quam fellit imago*), I have this opinion, that if I had
sought my own commendation, it had been a much fitter
course for me to have done as gardeners used to do, by
taking their seeds and slips, and rearing them first into
plants, and so uttering them in pots, when they are in
flower, and in their best state. But for as much as my
end was merit of the state of learning to my power, and
not glory; and because my purpose was rather to excite
other men's wits than to magnify my own; I was desirous
to prevent the incertainties of my own life and times, by
uttering rather seeds than plants: nay and furder (as the
proverb is) by sowing with the basket, than with the
hand."

And again, he writes to Bishop Andrews:

" As for my Essays, and some other particulars of that
nature, I count them but as the recreations of my other
studies, and in that sort purpose to continue them; though
I am not ignorant that those kind of writings would, with
less pains and embracement (perhaps) yield more lustre
and reputation to my name than others which I have in
hand. But I account the use that a man should seek of
the publishing of his own writings before his death, to be
but an untimely anticipation of that which is proper to
follow a man, and not to go along with him."

Dr. Rawley, in his Preface to Bacon's *Natural History*,
says:

" I have heard his lordship often say, that if he should
have served the glory of his own name, he had been better
not to have published this Natural History: for it may

seem an undigested heap of particulars, and cannot have
that lustre which books cast into methods have; but that
he resolved to prefer the good of men, and that which
might best secure it, before anything that might have relation to himself."

And especially significant, because of its direct bearing,
is the sentence already quoted from his prayer, found
among his papers after his death:

"I have (though in a despised *weed*) *procured the good
of all men.*" (See *ante*, page 89.)

Moreover, it was strikingly characteristic of Bacon, that
he worked for future ages and for posterity. This is evident in the whole scope and tenor of the great body of his
writings, and also from his utterances in letters, which
fortunately have been preserved. Thus, we find the following, in a letter he wrote to Count Gondomar of Spain,
formerly ambassador in London:

"But for myself, my age, my fortune, yea my Genius,
to which I have hitherto done but scant justice, calls me
now to retire from the stage of civil action and betake myself to letters, and to the instruction of the actors themselves, and the service of Posterity."

He wrote to Father Fulgentio of Venice:

"I wish to make known to your Reverence my intentions with regard to the writings which I meditate and
have in hand; not hoping to perfect them, but desiring
to try; and because I write for posterity; these things
requiring ages for their accomplishment." *

To the Bishop of Ely he wrote:

"Because you were wont to make me believe you took

---

* Truly, there was a foundation for the remarkable expression
in one of the Sonnets:

"Were't aught to me I bore the canopy,
With my extern the outward honoring,
Or laid great bases for eternity,
Which prove more short than waste or ruining?"

liking to my writings, I send you some of this vacation's
fruits ; and thus much more of my mind and purpose. I
hasten not to publish ; *perishing I would prevent.* And
I am forced to respect as well my times as the matter."

And to Sir Tobie Mathew :

" And I must confess my desire to be, that my writings
should not court the present time, or some few places, in
such sort as might make them either less general to persons, or less permanent to future ages."

Such was the mould in which the plays were cast, in
intelligently designed universality and perpetuity. They
are indeed " bone of his bone, and flesh of his flesh," not
only in

> " That every word doth almost tell my name,
> Showing their birth, and where they did proceed,"

but in such marked heredity, that in their every element
they partake of his greatness. They truly require ages
for the maturity of their comprehension. Gervinus, looking backward, said, in 1850, that it had required two centuries to understand them. But succeeding generations find
ever new vistas opening before them. And to-day, after
the lapse of nearly three centuries, we are conscious that
we are only just beginning to comprehend their amazing
depth, their moral power, and the grandeur of their embodied purpose.

And how rich is the legacy in its *Interpretation of Man,*
as he is, in his essential nature, in a veritable " model "
of his constitution, and in absolute fidelity to the realities !
And in this, also, we discern the coursing of the very life-
blood of their creator.

In his *Novum Organum,* he states in a word, his fundamental purpose :

" For I am building in the human understanding a true
model of the world, *such as it is in fact,* not such as a
man's own reason would have it be."

And he thus eloquently advocates his work, in contrast with the methods previously pursued, which for centuries had produced only " a crude liquor like water ":

" Whereas I pledge mankind in a liquor strained from countless grapes, from grapes ripe and fully seasoned, collected in clusters and gathered, and then squeezed in the press, and finally purified and clarified in the vat."

Such is the glorious vintage of the realities; which Bacon inaugurated, and which has since so enriched the life of man; lightening his lot, and gladdening his heart.

And how grandly, almost literally, is the pledge fulfilled in the plays! Poetry that is merely subjective, " evolved from the inner consciousness," or that is ladled from surface pools, is but as " water," compared with this rich, nourishing wine, vitalized with nature's spirit, surcharged with the verities of life, and expressed from grapes that are the objective realities of existence.

In the beginning, we traced the origin of every thought, metaphor, and turn of expression in a lengthy passage from *The Tempest:* afterwards, we entered his Storehouse, and observed in detail the close interweaving of his garnered observations into the innermost texture of the plays: and again, we followed the workings of the same process, upon broader lines, in the whole conception, development, and elaboration of the *Julius Cæsar;* and throughout, and at every turn, we have been brought into intimate, appreciative contact with this continual " expression " of the realities, the most vital element and characteristic of the plays,—their very marrow, substance, and life-blood.

Have we not seen, with our own eyes, grapes that he had collected, laboriously, from every field and province of nature's kingdom; grapes ripe and fully seasoned; and of her infinite variety, from the most commonplace to the least known of her productions ; including the ripest and best fruitage of classic soils, as well as the choicest products of mediæval and modern tillage — and in almost countless numbers ; collected in clusters, in crowding profusion? Have we not also witnessed, how they were squeezed in the press of his powerful intellect, their richest juices expressed, and then purified and clarified in the vast chambers of his capacious mind?

And who can do justice to the quality of the liquor, as it was poured forth so freely to delight the world ? Drawn, every drop, from nature's fount, it partakes of her freshness and vitality. Age has only mellowed it, developing an appreciably richer flavor and a more exquisite bouquet. Its good cheer, both refreshing and inspiring, quickens the intellect, opens the understanding, and broadens the vision : while our enraptured hearts are awakened to larger sympathies, and brought into closer intimacy with humanity. Its exhilaration is expanding, lifting us out of our narrow self-consciousness, into the broad, privileged realm of universal existence, and into touch with its vivifying spirit. It is preëminently an healthful cup, imbued with instruction, and whose essence is the distillation of wisdom. It is the wine of life.

And now that we so much better understand him who thus procured our good, the loving spirit that prompted his labors, his lofty motives, his comprehensive design, and its glorious fulfillment; surely, the hour of our recognition of his work is an appropriate time for the long delayed acknowledgment of his magnificent pledge. The tide at length has turned, and the bread he so freely cast upon the waters is being wafted back towards the shores where time merges into eternity. The divine promise still holds good, unlimited as to time or place. And it may be, that even now, his heart is gladdened, as our mis-

conceptions are swept away, and his dearly beloved mankind is entering into a better comprehension of himself,
his motives, and his accomplishments.

Be that as it may, certainly the draught will be all the
sweeter, if it be mingled with the incense of a grateful
heart. And so, in no extravagance, but in befitting recognition of his inestimable services to mankind, whenever
we partake of the cup he so generously provided, let it be
in grateful acceptance of his eloquent pledge, in the spirit
in which it was given ; and with heart responding to
heart, all over the world, and through all the " ages yet
to be," let us drink it, in glad accord, to the memory of
Francis Bacon, our bountiful, aye twice-bountiful Bene-
factor.

CHAPTER XI.

WE may now confidently widen the range of our inquiry; turning to the consideration of another fundamental quality of the plays, one universally recognized, and especially significant in its expression of the personality of the Poet. To fairly put the question: Had Bacon that wonderful imaginative power, whose display in the Shakespeare has so astonished the world; giving realization to visions, which in their penetration and range are fairly bewildering to our comprehension, in thoughts clothed in the most gorgeous imagery ever fashioned from nature's phenomena?

The poetic faculty is something exceedingly difficult to define, especially in its essential characteristics, as displayed for example in prose writings. One must penetrate beneath the distinctions and peculiarities incident to the widely divergent structural forms of poetry and prose, and fasten upon something underlying all that is fundamental in its character, its vital and vitalizing principle. This we take to be, essentially, *the creative power*. And this is perhaps best comprehended through its limitations. The Divine Creator, through the impartation of himself, brought into existence the universe, whose sustaining power is His energy, and whose development is the evolution of His thought. But man cannot rise to such dignity. He can only deal with materials already in existence. And moreover, created in His image, his creations are also in imagery — whether his instrument be brush, or chisel, or pen, and his vehicle canvas, stone, or words.

21

In common in all these Arts, the first attribute of man's creative power is *vision*, insight into the realm of existence, the discernment of an inner, subtler something which is given manifestation in some department of nature.   In primary terms, it may be some inherent element, quality, attribute, or associative relation, which for convenience we term spiritual, but which is no less real than the material which is the vehicle of its expression. Thus, for illustration, it was through this vision that Corot attained to his magnificent grasp of the supreme quality of joyousness that pervades all nature at the birth of the new day, in its resurrection from the night.

Having thus attained to its clear perception, in part through its isolation in mental conception from the thousand other distracting qualities attendant in nature, man's creative power gives to this quality concrete representation, in the similitude of nature's mode of expression ; but intensified to our comprehension through its subtle accentuation.   For it is reëmbodied in imagery of nature so chosen and combined as to give to this quality "*concentrated manifestation.*"   It is the enshrinement within the outward form of an inner, animating spirit, equally perceptible to our apprehension — the vital element in the organic whole.   The work is thus distinctively a creation, a perpetual source of delight, and in its comprehension, a revelation.   And such is the triumph of art that even things invisible are thus given visible, tangible representation.   Thus, for example, Daniel Chester French, in his masterpiece of modern sculpture, " Death and the Sculptor," has given to the awful mystery of death, in its inscrutable but inexorable sway, physical expression and embodiment, in the enshrouding gloom, the sombre but impassive face, the silently compelling gesture, and in every detail of the figure, — all expressive of things as real as they are manifest.

Coming specifically to words as the medium of expression, the distinctive mode of operation is essentially the same. It is the like work of the same creative power. There is first, vision, penetrating beyond the ordinary sight into the inner life and constitution of things; discerning here or there a subtle, intangible something which nature silently voices, a quality, a vital relation, or it may be a whole congeries of relations. This mighty power lays hold upon it, encompasses it, and compresses it into the condensation of an idea. And so vivid is the conception, that it seemingly comes like an inspiration. There is thence developed an entity, complete in itself, and almost self-existing, once it is born. For there is a birth as well as a conception. The thought is delivered to the world by this wonderful faculty enshrined within a bodily form, concrete and coherent, and fashioned from materials common and familiar to all. It is clothed as in the flesh in a representative imagery, so beautifully adapted, so fitting, and so perfectly analogous in its similitude to the embodied thought, that it seems ordained from the beginning for its investment. The whole is indeed a new creation, instinct with life; for the grosser outer form is quickened by the presence of the subtler spirit within. And their union is so organic, that the thought, in its distinct individuality and its precise shade of meaning, is known to us only under the guise of its material form; while over this it is so dominant that the imagery but reveals to us the beautiful perfection of that which is enshrined within it.

To follow this up by a discussion of the serious prose writings of any of the great dramatic poets of the world, as for example, of Goethe or Schiller, who also wrote upon scientific and philosophical subjects, and to deduce from them, and to delineate in clear outlines the characteristic workings of this unique faculty, as they might be revealed in their mode of thought and style of expression, would be a work of exceeding difficulty. It might perhaps be accomplished, though only by a master critic.

We can hardly realize the fact, but precisely this work has been done on Bacon's prose, and by one of the ablest critics of modern times. And, what is of the utmost significance, it was not done by one seeking specially to find some development of the poetic faculty; but on the contrary, it was the work of one aiming only to grasp and to delineate accurately and comprehensively the essential qualities and distinctive characteristics of Bacon's style and mode of thought. We refer to Taine, whose *History of English Literature* is universally recognized as a masterpiece of literary criticism. A somewhat extended quotation is perhaps admissible; both on account of the interest of the subject, and because of the keen insight displayed by this singularly acute, penetrating, and comprehensive critic. Of Bacon he says:

" In this band of scholars, dreamers, and enquirers, appears the most comprehensive, sensible, originative of the minds of the age, Francis Bacon, a great and luminous intellect, one of the finest of this poetic progeny, who, like his predecessors, was naturally disposed to clothe his ideas in the most splendid dress. In this age, a thought did not seem complete until it had assumed a form and color: but what distinguishes him from the others is, that with him an image only serves to *concentrate* meditation. He reflected long, stamped on his mind all the parts and joints of his subject; and then, instead of dissipating his completed idea in a graduated chain of reasoning, he embodies it in a comparison so expressive, exact, transparent, that behind the figure we perceive all the details of the idea, like a liquor in a fair crystal vase. Judge of his style by a single example:

" ' For as water, whether it be the dew of heaven or the springs of the earth, easily scatters and loses itself in the ground, except it be collected into some receptacle, where it may by union and consort comfort and sustain itself (and for that cause, the industry of man has devised aqueducts, cisterns, and pools, and likewise beautified them with various ornaments of magnificence and state, as well as for use and necessity): so this excellent liquor of knowledge, whether it descend from divine inspiration or spring from human sense, would soon perish and vanish into oblivion, if it were not preserved in books, traditions, conferences, and especially in places appointed for such matters, as Universities, Colleges, and schools, where it may have both a fixed habitation, and means and opportunity of increasing and collecting itself.' 'The greatest error of all the rest, is the mistaking or misplacing of the last or farthest end of knowledge : . . . as if there were sought in knowledge a couch whereupon to rest a searching and restless spirit; or a terrace, for a wandering and variable mind to walk up and down with a fair prospect; or a tower of state, for a proud mind to raise itself upon; or a fort or commanding ground, for strife and contention; or a shop, for profit or sale; and not a rich storehouse, for the glory of the Creator, and the relief of men's estate.'

"This is his mode of thought, by symbols, not by analysis; instead of explaining his idea, he transposes and translates it,—translates it entire, to the smallest details; enclosing all in the majesty of a grand period, or in the brevity of a striking sentence. Thence springs a style of admirable richness, gravity, and vigor, now solemn and symmetrical, now concise and piercing, always elaborate and full of color. There is nothing in English prose superior to his diction. Thence is derived also his manner of conceiving of things. He is not a dialectician, like Hobbs or Descartes, apt in arranging ideas, in educing one from another, in leading his reader from the simple to the complex by an unbroken chain. He is a producer of conceptions and of sentences. The matter being explored he says to us: 'Such it is; touch it not on that side; it must be approached from the other.' Nothing more; no proof, no effort to convince : he affirms, and does nothing more; he has thought in the manner of artists and poets, and he speaks after the manner of prophets and seers. *Cogita et Visa*, this title of one of his books might be the title of all. The most admirable, the *Novum Organum*, is a string of aphorisms,— a collection, as it were, of scientific decrees, as of an oracle who foresees the future and reveals the truth. And to make the resemblance complete, he expresses them by poetical figures, by enigmatic abbreviations, almost in Sibylline verses: *Idola species, Idola tribus, Idola fori, Idola theatri*, every one will recall these strange names, by which he signifies the four kinds of illusions to which man is subject.

" Shakespeare and the Seers do not contain more vigorous or expressive condensations of thought, more resembling inspiration, and in Bacon they are to be found everywhere. In short, his process is that of the creators; it is intuition, not reasoning. When he has laid up his store of facts, the greatest possible, on some vast subject, on some entire province of the mind, on the whole anterior philosophy, on the general condition of the sciences, on the power and limits of human reason, he casts over all this a comprehensive view, as it were a great net, brings up a universal idea, condenses his idea into a maxim, and hands it to us with the words, ' Verify and profit by it.' "

Here is a clear presentation, by a critic of unquestioned ability, of the workings of the creative faculty in a colossal intellect; which, indeed, appears to him, in its various phases, as the very personification of this mighty power.

But another surprise awaits us. When afterwards, Taine comes to consider the characteristics of the author of the Shakespeare, as revealed in his works, his clear insight discerns in him substantially the same peculiarities noted in his description of Bacon's mode of thought and his style of expression. It is perfectly obvious that this was done unconsciously; and it is the more significant, since it could hardly be expected, so great are the differences between prose and poetry, both in style and thought.

After groping around in the dim light afforded by tradition and conjecture regarding William Shakespeare,

Taine turns gladly to the study of the author in his works.
He says:

"Of all this we can but conjecture: if we would see
the man more closely, we must seek him in his works.
Let us then look for the man, and in his style. The style
explains the work; whilst showing the principal features
of the genius, it infers the rest. When we have once
grasped the dominant faculty, we see the whole artist developed like a flower.

"Shakespeare imagines with copiousness and excess;
he spreads metaphors profusely over all he writes; every
instant abstract ideas are changed into images; it is a
series of paintings that is unfolded in his mind. He does
not seek them; they come of themselves; they crowd
within him, covering his arguments; they dim with their
brightness the pure light of logic. He does not labor to
explain or prove; picture on picture, image on image, he
is forever copying the strange and splendid visions which
are engendered one within another, and are heaped up
within him . . . if he speaks thus, it is not from choice,
but of necessity; metaphor is not his whim, but the form
of his thought. . . . Whosoever involuntarily and naturally transforms a dry idea into an image, has his brain on
fire: true metaphors are flaming apparitions, which are
like a picture in a flash of lightning. . . . We pause
stupefied before these convulsive metaphors, which might
have been written by a fevered hand in a night's delirium,
which gather a pageful of ideas and pictures in half a sentence, which scorch the eyes they would enlighten. . . .
In Shakespeare there is no preparation, no adaptation, no
development, no care to make himself understood. Like
a too fiery and powerful horse, he bounds, but cannot run.
He bridges in a couple of words an enormous interval;
is at the two poles in a single instant. The reader vainly
looks for the intermediate track; confounded by these
prodigious leaps, he wonders by what miracle the poet
has entered upon a new idea the very moment when he
quitted the last, seeing perhaps between the two images a

long scale of transitions, which we pace painfully step by step, but which he has spanned in a stride. Shakespeare flies, we creep. . . . All that I have said may be compressed into a few words. Objects were taken into his mind organized and complete; they pass into ours disjointed, decomposed, and fragmentarily. He thought in the lump, we think piecemeal; hence his style and our style—two languages not to be reconciled. We, for our part, writers and reasoners, can note precisely by a word each isolated fraction of an idea, and represent the due order of its parts by the due order of our expressions. We advance gradually; we affiliate, go down to the roots, try and treat our words as numbers, our sentences as equations; we employ but general terms, which every mind can understand, and regular constructions into which every mind can enter; we attain justness and clearness, not life. Shakespeare lets justness and clearness look out for themselves, and attains life. From amidst his complex conception and his colored semi-vision, he grasps a fragment, a quivering fibre, and shows it; it is for you from this fragment, to divine the rest. He, behind the word, has a whole picture, an attitude, a long argument abridged, a mass of swarming ideas; you know them, these abbreviative, condensive words:—" And again: "This creative power is Shakespeare's great gift, and it communicates an extraordinary significance to his words. Every word pronounced by one of his characters enables us to see, besides the idea which it contains and the emotion which prompted it, the aggregate of the qualities and the entire character which produced it—the mood, physical attitude, bearing, look of the man, all instantaneously, with a clearness and force approached by no one. . . . He had the prodigious faculty of seeing in a twinkling of an eye a complete character, body, mind, past and present, in every detail and every depth of his being, with the exact attitude and the expression of the face, which the situation demanded. A word here and there of Hamlet or Othello would need for its explanation three pages of commentaries; each of the half-

understood thoughts, which the commentator may have discovered, has left its trace in the turn of the phrase, in the
nature of the metaphor, in the order of the words ; nowadays, in perusing these traces, we divine the thoughts ;
these innumerable traces have been impressed in a second,
within the compass of a line. In the next line there are
as many, impressed just as quickly, and in the same compass. You can gauge the concentration and the velocity
of the imagination which creates thus."

As we carefully compare, in a broad and comprehensive view, the two pictures here presented and observe
their intimate resemblance, though we well know that the
secret lies in the fact that they are portraitures of one
and the same unique personality, with but slight variations, due solely to differences of attitude, of the medium,
and the surroundings, yet we cannot but express our admiration for Taine, as he also is revealed in his work ;
and we wonder that seeing through a glass darkly, he yet
saw so clearly.

One other pair of pictures must be presented, companion
pieces, though drawn by different artists.

Quoting briefly from the article upon Bacon in the *Encyclopædia Britannica:* Prof. Adamson says, with reference to the Essays : " The style is quaint, original, abound-
ing in allusions and witticisms, and rich, even to gorgeousness, with piled up analogies and metaphors." He continues : " The peculiarities of Bacon's style were noticed
very early by his contemporaries (See Letters and Life
I., 268). Raleigh and Jonson have both recorded their
opinions of it, but no one, it seems to us, has characterized
it more happily than his friend Sir Tobie Mathew : ' A
man so rare in knowledge, of so many several kinds, en-
dued with the facility and felicity of expressing it all in
so elegant, significant, so abundant, and yet so choice and
ravishing a way of words, of metaphors, of allusions, as
perhaps the world hath not seen since it was a world.' "

Compare this with Richard Grant White's graphic portrayal of the distinctive characteristic of the Shakespearean style. This accomplished critic, one of the most appreciative of the Shakespearean scholars, in his *Genius of Shakespeare* says:

"Never did intellectual wealth equal in degree the boundless riches of Shakespeare's fancy. He compelled all art, all that God had revealed, and all that man had discovered, to contribute materials to enrich his style and enforce his thought; so that the entire range of human knowledge must be laid under contribution to illustrate his writings. This inexhaustible mine of fancy, furnishing metaphor, comparison, illustration, impersonation, in ceaseless alternation, often intermingled so that the one cannot be severed from the other, although the combination is clearly seen and leaves a vivid impression on the mind, is the great distinctive intellectual trait of Shakespeare's style."

Recognizing the now familiar lineaments, we can appreciate the acumen displayed by Mr. White, in his epitomized portrayal of Bacon's personality, 'though known under another name.' Seeing not, yet saw he notwithstanding.

These last pictures, though miniature portraits, are well worthy of being placed beside Taine's masterpieces. And as we embrace them all in one comprehensive view, we are amazed at the startling effect. Behold, they are true stereoscopic pictures, notwithstanding the anomalous fact that they are the productions of several artists, working in various styles, and from different standpoints. As we receive their impressions upon the "eye of the mind," note how perfectly they register. There is neither blur, confusion, nor antagonism; nor even a dreamy uncertainty or a hazy obscurity. They fit together completely, blending into one harmonious whole; details in one filling blanks in another, while repetitions only throw the prominent features into bolder relief.

And how lifelike is the portrait thus brought to view! Such were the deep insight and the skill of the artists, and so vivid is the effect produced by the concentration of the fourfold combination, that we are brought, as it were, into the very presence of a great personality. We can almost see the operation of that mighty intellect, in its work of production. Is it true, that " whosoever involuntarily and naturally transforms a dry idea into an image has his brain on fire?" Then witness him at work and gauge, if you can, the white heat of the flame. There is a delusion, to which a large portion of mankind is subject, a whole mass of delusions. To us, they are abstractions, matters of argument and of analytical discussion, part by part, in orderly relation. He comprehends the whole at a glance, sweeping far beyond our reach. He takes in their full meaning and significance: he is at the two poles in a single instant, and he bridges the whole in a couple of words. But he does more than that. In a flash of flame, he creates an impersonation. A creature is born, and into this thing he has injected the whole of one of these delusions. He produces a whole family, and in his *Idola Theatri*, we have the very objects that mankind had all along been unconsciously worshiping.

This great and luminous intellect, one of the finest of the poetic progeny, and the most comprehensive, sensible, and originative mind of the age, takes within his grasp the whole of some vast subject, some entire province of the mind, the general condition of the sciences, the power and limits of human reason, or it may be, a complete character, body, mind, past, and present, in every detail and every depth of his being, with the exact attitude and expression which a given situation demands. From amidst this complex conception, he lays hold upon a fragment and shows it to us, and behind the word, there is a whole picture, an attitude, a long argument abridged, a mass of

swarming ideas. Or casting over all a comprehensive
view, he brings up a universal idea, condenses it into a
maxim, or embodies it in a figure so expressive, exact,
transparent, that behind it we perceive all the details of
the idea, like a liquor in a fair crystal vase. Each of the
half-understood thoughts, which the commentator may
have discovered, has left its trace in the turn of the phrase,
in the nature of the metaphor, in the order of the words:
while every word pronounced by one of his characters
enables us to see, beside the idea which it contains and
the emotion which prompted it, the aggregate of the qualities and the entire character which produced it — the
mood, physical attitude, bearing, look of the man, all instantaneously, with a clearness and force approached by
no one.

He is not a dialectician, like Hobbs or Descartes, apt
in arranging ideas, in educing one from another, in leading his reader from the simple to the complex by an unbroken chain. Objects were taken into his mind organized and complete; they pass into ours disjointed, decomposed, fragmentarily. He thought in the lump, in a
string of aphorisms; we think piecemeal. We, for our
part, writers and reasoners, can note precisely by a word
each isolated fraction of an idea, and represent the due
order of its parts by the due order of our expressions.
We advance gradually, and treat our words as numbers
and our sentences as equations: but his process is that of
the creators; it is intuition, not reasoning. He bridges
in a couple of words an enormous interval; is at the two
poles in a single instant. He is a producer of conceptions
and of sentences: he speaks after the manner of prophets
and seers, or of an oracle who foresees the future and reveals the truth. And to complete the resemblance, his
utterances are expressed in poetical figures, in enigmatic

abbreviations, almost in Sibylline verses. Nor does he dissipate his complete idea in a graduated chain of reasoning: he gathers a pageful of ideas and pictures in half a sentence, which scorch the eyes they would enlighten. The seers do not contain more vigorous or expressive condensations of thought, more resembling inspiration, and in Bacon they are found everywhere.

He does not labor to explain or prove: there is no preparation, no adaptation, no development, no care to make himself understood: there is no proof, no effort to convince; he affirms, and does nothing more.

He thinks after the manner of artists and poets; picture on picture, image on image, he is forever copying the strange and splendid visions which are engendered one within another, and are heaped up within him. His mode of thought is by symbols, not by analysis: he spreads metaphors profusely over all he writes: every instant abstract ideas are changed into images; it is a series of paintings which is unfolded in his mind.

Take, for example, knowledge. We view it in the abstract; to us, it is learning, erudition, perception of the truth. We employ but general terms, which every mind can understand: we attain justness and clearness, not life; we are still dealing with the shadowy, the intangible, the unsubstantial. He lets justness and clearness look out for themselves, and attains life. His poetic eye, glancing from earth to heaven and heaven to earth, in an exquisite frenzy, discerns the twofold origin of this knowledge invisible, its characteristic flux, its hazard of oblivion; and as imagination bodies it forth in befitting form, his pen turns it to shape, and gives to this airy nothing a local habitation and an impersonation. He copies from a strange and splendid vision of the landscape of the universe, that is unrolled before him. He paints for us the picture of an excellent liquor descending from divine inspiration, or springing from human sense, like the dew of heaven or the springs of the earth; easily scattered and lost in the ground, but for union, consort, comfort, and support, collected in receptacles, in aqueducts, cisterns, and pools, beautified with ornaments of magnificence and state. There are heaped up pictures, in series, of men seeking in knowledge a couch, a terrace, for a wandering and variable mind to walk up and down with a fair prospect, a tower of state, a fort, commanding ground, a shop, a rich storehouse, for the glory of the Creator and the relief of man's estate. Truly, metaphor is not his whim, but the form of his thought. And instead of explaining his idea, he transposes and translates it, translates it entire, to the smallest details, enclosing all in the majesty of a grand period, or in the brevity of a striking sentence.

A man so rare in knowledge, of so many several kinds, having at his command all that God had revealed, and all that man had discovered, so that the entire range of human knowledge must be laid under contribution to illustrate his writings, his intellectual wealth is boundless in its riches of imagery. It is an inexhaustible mine of fancy, furnishing him comparison, illustration, impersonation, allusions, witticisms, piled up analogies and metaphors, in exuberant profusion; and he pours forth all in a style rich even to gorgeousness, and in so elegant, significant, so abundant, and yet so choice and ravishing a way of words, as perhaps the world hath not seen since it was a world.

We are lost in wonder and admiration. It is a revelation,—a revelation, indeed, of the splendor, the power, and the inherent greatness of that wonderful personality, Francis Bacon.

Here are unfolded, in accurate portrayal, the distinctive characteristics, the peculiarities, and even the idiosyncrasies of his marvellous intellect, the most phenomenal with which man was ever endowed. And to us, the most striking peculiarity is the manifest presence, throughout, of an integral, inseparable, personal identity; cohering in the perfectly consistent unity underlying and pervading the whole harmony. It is obviously that essential, organic unity which is peculiar to personality, and is found nowhere else. But here, we find everywhere the unmistakable impress of an individuality as definite, distinct, and as recognizable, as is that of Napoleon or of Carlyle. Indeed, the masterful intellects of the world have always been unique; and we call the roll in vain, in our search for another possessing these pronounced characteristics, or of whom any one of these pictures would be a portraiture. Verily, "None but himself could be his parallel."

One, and yet twain; present, and yet absent; owning, and yet dispossessed; exalted, and yet unhonored; seemingly indifferent, and yet fondly appreciative; suffering the bitterness of deprivation, and nevertheless finding solace in the separation; such was the turmoil involved in the enactment of this amazing self-parallelism. And, strange to say, it has been graphically portrayed, over and over again, in picture after picture, in a whole series of powerful pictures, drawn by his master hand. Indeed, it is the one continual theme of the *Sonnets*, their unifying bond, the *motive* and the burden of their song.

The world well knows that the creative artist appreciates, as does no one else, the real worth of his work. The flower of its beauty has unfolded its every petal under the tender touch of his loving hand, and its sweet fragrance is the exhalation of his spirit. It is the blossom of his love, the child of his heart, the embodiment of all that is highest, and holiest, and best within him. And yet his mouth is closed: any adequate expression of appreciation on his part is subtly akin to self-praise, and under ordinary circumstances, is obtrusive and unseemly. As Bacon elegantly puts it, in his Essay, *Of Friendship :* "How many things there are which a man cannot, with any face or comliness, say or do himself? A man can scarce allege his own merits with modesty, much less extol them. . . . But all these things are graceful in a friend's mouth, which are blushing in a man's own."

To give appropriate expression, in unblushing words, to his lofty appreciation of his own work, in perhaps needful contradiction to his apparent neglect, and yet in such a way as to effectually preclude the premature disclosure of his secret, was the truly formidable difficulty which confronted him. But, Sampson-like, by the sheer power of his intellectual might, he slew this lion in his pathway, found honey in its jaws, and put the whole into a riddle, which, as there was really no Delilah in the case, has for ages greatly perplexed both the Phillistines and the Literati ; remaining so utterly inexplicable, that even the scholarly Hallam recorded his heartfelt wish, that the *Sonnets* had never been written.

But none of us, it is to be hoped, will ever join in that wish. For under the shield of their mystic, veiled, allegorical form, sphinx-like, as strangely puzzling in import as is the "Solomon's Song," he has opened to us his heart, portrayed its turmoil, and given expression to his inmost thoughts and feelings, in a series of exquisite verses, which the world will yet cherish as one of its most precious possessions.

Here are a few examples, the pleasure afforded by their detailed solution being left to the reader, who will find some that are even more striking in the complete series. And as we read them, we may almost hear the beatings of his throbbing heart :

"O, how thy worth with manners may I sing,
  When thou art all the better part of me?
What can mine own praise to mine own self bring?
  And what is 't but mine own, when I praise thee?
Even for this let us divided live,
  And our dear love lose name of single one,
That by this separation I may give
  That due to thee, which thou deserv'st alone.
O absence, what a torment wouldst thou prove,
  Were it not thy sour leisure gave sweet leave,
To entertain the time with thoughts of love,
  (Which time and thoughts so sweetly doth deceive,)
    And that thou teachest how to make one twain,
    By praising *him* here, who doth hence remain."

"My tongue-tied Muse in manners holds her still,
  While comments of your praise, richly compiled,
Reserve their character with golden quill,
  And precious phrase by all the Muses filed.
I think good thoughts, while others write good words,
  And, like unlettered clerk, still cry 'Amen'
To every hymn that able spirit affords,
  In polished form of well-refined pen.
Hearing you praised, I say ''T is so, 'tis true,'
  And to the most of praise add something more;
But that is in my thought, whose love to you,
  Though words come hindmost, holds his rank before.
    Then others for the breath of words respect,
    Me for my dumb thoughts, speaking in effect."

"As a decrepit father takes delight
  To see his active child do deeds of youth,
So I, made lame by fortune's dearest spite,
  Take all my comfort of thy worth and truth;
For whether beauty, birth, or wealth, or wit,
  Or any of these all, or all, or more,
Entitled in thy parts do crowned sit,
  I make my love engrafted to this store:
So then I am not lame, poor, nor despised,
  Whilst that this *shadow* doth such substance give,
That I in thy abundance am sufficed,
  And by a part of all thy glory live.
    Look what is best, that best I wish in thee:
    This wish I have; then ten times happy me!"

22

" So are you to my thoughts, as food to life,
  Or as sweet-season'd showers are to the ground;
And for the peace of you I hold such strife
  As 'twixt a miser and his wealth is found:
Now proud as an enjoyer, and anon
  Doubting the filching age will steal his treasure;
Now counting best to be with you alone,
  Then better'd that the world may see my pleasure:
Sometime all full with feasting on your sight,
  And by-and-by clean starved for a look;
Possessing or pursuing no delight,
  Save what is had or must from you be took.
    Thus do I pine and surfeit day by day,
    Or gluttoning on all, or all away."

" Mine eye and heart are at a mortal war,
  How to divide the conquest of thy sight;
Mine eye mine heart thy picture's sight would bar,
  My heart mine eye the freedom of that right.
My heart doth plead that thou in *him* dost lie,
  (A closet never pierced with crystal eyes,)
But the defendant doth that plea deny,
  And says in him thy fair appearance lies.
To 'cide this title is impannelled
  A quest of thoughts, all tenants to the heart;
And by their verdict is determined
  The clear eye's moiety, and the dear heart's part:
    As thus; mine eye's due is thine outward part,
    And my heart's right thine inward love of heart."

" How careful was I, when I took my way,
  Each trifle under truest bars to thrust,
That, to my use, it might unused stay
  From hands of falsehood, in sure wards of trust!
But thou, to whom my jewels trifles are,
  Most worthy comfort, now my greatest grief,
Thou, best of dearest, and mine only care,
  Art left the prey of every vulgar thief.
Thee have I not lock'd up in any chest,
  Save where thou art not, though I feel thou art,
Within the gentle closure of my breast,
  From whence at pleasure thou mayst come and part;
    And even thence thou wilt be stolen, I fear,
    For *truth* proves thievish for a prize so dear."

"Thy glass will show thee how thy beauties wear,
Thy dial how thy precious minutes waste;
The vacant leaves thy mind's imprint will bear,
And of this book this learning mayst thou taste.
The wrinkles which thy glass will truly show,
Of mouthed graves will give thee memory;
Thou by thy dial's shady stealth mayst know
Time's thievish progress to eternity.
Look, what thy memory cannot contain,
Commit to these waste blanks, and thou shalt find
Those children nursed, deliver'd from thy brain,
To take a new acquaintance of thy mind.
  These offices, so oft as thou wilt look,
  Shall profit thee, and much enrich thy *book*."

"How can my Muse want subject to invent,
While thou dost breathe, that pour'st into my verse
Thine own sweet argument, too excellent
For every vulgar paper to rehearse?
O, give myself the thanks, if aught in me
Worthy perusal stand against thy sight;
For who's so dumb that cannot write to thee,
When thou thyself dost give invention light?
Be thou the *tenth Muse*, ten times more in worth
Than those old nine which rhymers invocate;
And he that calls on thee, let him bring forth
Eternal numbers to outlive long date.
  If my slight Muse do please these curious days,
  The pain be mine, but thine shall be the praise."

"Sin of self-love possesseth all mine eye,
And all my soul, and all my every part;
And for this sin there is no remedy,
It is so grounded inward in my heart.
Methinks no face so gracious is as mine,
No shape so true, no truth of such account;
And for myself mine own worth do define,
As I all other in all worths surmount.
But when my glass shows me myself indeed,
Beated and chapp'd with tann'd antiquity,
Mine own self-love quite contrary I read;
Self so self-loving were iniquity.
  'Tis thee (myself) that for myself I praise,
  Painting my age with beauty of thy days."

" O, for my sake do you with fortune chide,
The guilty goddess of my harmful deeds,
That did not better for my life provide,
Than public means, which public manners breeds.
Thence comes it that my name receives a brand,
And almost thence my nature is subdu'd
To what it works in, like the dyer's hand;
Pity me then, and wish I were renew'd;
Whilst, like a willing patient, I will drink
Potions of eysell, 'gainst my strong infection;
No bitterness that I will bitter think,
Nor double penance, to correct correction.
   Pity me, then, dear friend, and I assure ye
   Even that your pity is enough to cure me."

" When thou shalt be dispos'd to set me light,
And place my merit in the eye of scorn,
Upon thy side against myself I'll fight,
And prove thee virtuous, though thou art foresworn.
With mine own weakness being best acquainted,
Upon thy part I can set down a story
Of faults conceal'd, wherein I am attainted;
That thou, in losing me, shall win much glory:
And I by this will be a gainer too;
For bending all my loving thoughts on thee,
The injuries that to myself I do,
Doing thee vantage, double-vantage me.
   Such is my love, to thee I so belong,
   That for thy right myself will bear all wrong."

" Farewell! thou art too dear for my possessing,
And like enough thou know'st thy estimate:
The charter of thy worth gives thee releasing;
My bonds in thee are all determinate.
For how do I hold thee but by thy granting?
And for that riches where is my deserving?
The cause of this fair gift in me is wanting,
And so my patent back again is swerving.
Thyself thou gav'st, thy own worth then not knowing,
Or me, to whom thou gav'st it, else mistaking;
So thy great gift, upon misprision growing,
Comes home again, on better judgment making.
   Thus have I had thee, as a dream doth flatter,
   In sleep a king, but, waking, no such matter."

" That God forbid that made me first your slave,
I should in thought control your times of pleasure,
Or at your hand the account of hours to crave,
Being your vassal, bound to stay your leisure !
O, let me suffer (being at your beck)
The imprison'd absence of your liberty ;
And patience, tame to sufferance, bide each *check*,
Without accusing you of injury.
Be where you list; your charter is so strong,
That you yourself may privilege your time :
Do what you will, to you it doth belong
Yourself to pardon of self-doing crime.
   I am to *wait*, though waiting so be hell ;
   Not blame your pleasure, be it ill or well."

" O truant Muse, what shall be thy amends
For thy neglect of truth in beauty died?
Both truth and beauty on my love depends ;
So dost thou too, and therein dignified.
Make answer, Muse: wilt thou not haply say,
'Truth needs no color with his color fix'd ;
Beauty no pencil, beauty's truth to lay ;
But best is best, if never intermix'd?'
Because he needs no praise, wilt thou be dumb?
Excuse not silence so ; for it lies in thee
To make him much outlive a gilded tomb,
And to be praised of ages yet to be.
   Then do thy office, Muse; I teach thee how
   To make him seem long hence as he shows now."

" Not mine own fears, nor the prophetic soul
Of the wide world dreaming on things to come,
Can yet the lease of my true love control,
Suppos'd as forfeit to a confin'd doom.
The mortal moon hath her eclipse endur'd,
And the sad augurs mock their own presage ;
Incertainties now crown themselves assur'd,
And peace proclaims olives of endless age."

  . . . .
    . . . .

" If Nature, sovereign mistress over wrack,
As thou goest onwards, still will pluck thee back,
She keeps thee to this purpose, that her skill
May time disgrace, and wretched minutes kill.

Yet fear her, O thou minion of her pleasure!
She may detain, but not still keep, her treasure.
Her audit, though delay'd, answer'd must be,
And her quietus is to render thee."

"The mills of the Gods grind slowly." Three centuries have come and gone since the Elizabethan age. They round out a cycle, a unit in the fulness of time. They complete an epoch, one of the numbered periods in the progress of humanity towards its destiny. The dawning of the Twentieth century is to Bacon a resurrection morn. The long eclipse at last is ended, and the full orb has burst upon us, in resplendent glory. His title, supposedly forfeit, is forever confirmed, and his spirit is unloosed from its seemingly confined doom. Nature indeed has time disgraced. But though she long detained, still she could not keep her treasure. Her audit has been answered, her quietus given, and the eternal harmony is restored. Incertainties now have crowned themselves assured,

"And peace proclaims olives of endless age."

His was truly an oracle-like, prophetic soul. As we read his Sibylline verses, obscure, and yet so clear, like the enigma of nature lying all the while an "open secret," we are astonished at his intellectual power. But greater than this power was his faith, his sublime faith in the realities,—in their ultimate triumph. He projected himself into the ages, and amidst their solemnity, we are admitted within the sacred precincts of a human heart, unclosed to our view. We behold, enshrined in the inherent weakness of his nature, a Titanic strength of soul, rising even to grandeur. We begin to comprehend the man: we are at the very core of his personality. He was of antithesis "all compact." It was the origin of his greatness, the source of his infirmity, the genesis of his univer-

sality. His complex being held within it, responsive to
the lightest touch, every chord possible to humanity, while
his very mould brought him into intimate sympathy with
nature, even in her innermost mystery. His plummet
sounded the depths, and his vision pierced the heights.
In his Richard III., he developed the fiend lurking in
man ; and again, he gave emphasis to humanity's subtle
" Intimations of Immortality." His voice, sounding from
the tomb and resounding through the ages, tells us, in
suggestive accents, that he still lives. His soul rose superior to time and place. It is at home in eternity.

The power of realities was Bacon's lifelong theme. It
was his inspiration, his prophetic vision, his message to
man. He embodied it in his Philosophy, and he turned
the tide of human affairs. He gave it representation in
the Shakespeare, and he bestowed upon the world its one
masterpiece in Art and in Literature. And finally, he
afforded a vivid illustration of his theme in his own person, in the enactment of this soul-stirring, living drama,
whose theatre has been the world, and whose hours were
the centuries. And the end is not yet. The twain have
become one, and thereby each has doubled, and the one
has quadrupled his power. We little comprehend the
tremendous force he is yet to exert upon the race : but
the next cycle, like the last, will fully evince his impress.
The realities are still to be the theme, as exhaustless as is
the stream of time. Yea, when time shall be no more, the
eternal realities will still prevail. Immovable, relentless,
inexorable, they are to be feared, and they are to be trusted.
They are the sinews of the Almighty, holding the universe
and all that it contains within the grasp of his Infinite
power. The mills of the gods indeed grind slowly, " but
they grind exceeding fine."

To return for a moment to Taine: To fully appreciate his comprehensive insight into Bacon, we must bear in mind that what he saw, in the first instance, was through the medium of his prose, where his imagination was held under constant check. The fact of this restraint was well understood. Taine adds to the passage already quoted the following, which completes all that he says upon Bacon's style:

" There is nothing more hazardous, more like fantasy, than this mode of thought, when it is not checked by natural and strong good sense. This common sense, which is a kind of natural divination, the stable equilibrium of an intellect always gravitating to the true, like the needle to the north pole, Bacon possesses in the highest degree."

As is befitting, Mr. White discerns also in the Shakespeare the predominant influence of this pronounced personal characteristic, and in the like peculiar antithesis. He says:

" For although of all poets he is most profoundly psychological, as well as most fanciful and most imaginative, yet with him philosophy, fancy, and imagination are penetrated with the spirit of the unwritten law of reason, which we speak of as if it were a faculty, common sense. His philosophy is practical, and his practical views are fused with philosophy and poetry. He is withal the sage and the oracle of this world."

Verily, Buffon was right, " The style is the man himself," a revelation of his personality. Our only wonder now is at the remarkable insight displayed by these accomplished critics, in their clear-visioned discernment of this personality, in its essential characteristics.

No man, indeed, knew better than Bacon the restraints belonging to prose, and no one better observed them. But occasionally, even when dealing with subjects of the most profound thought, he slightly relaxed the rein held so constantly over his exuberant fancy. Thus, he opens the

Third Book of his *Advancement of Learning* in these luxuriant words:

"All history, excellent king, treads the earth, performing the office of a guide rather than of a light: and poetry
is, as it were, the stream of knowledge,—a pleasing thing
full of variations, and affects to be inspired with divine
rapture, to which treasures also pretend. But now it is
time I should awake and raise myself from the earth and
explore the liquid regions of philosophy and the sciences.
Knowledge is like waters; some descend from the heavens,
some spring from the earth."

Again, this gem slips through his fingers:

"—imprinted upon the spirit of man by an inward instinct, according to the law of conscience, which is a
sparkle of the purity of his first estate."

And again, the whole play of life is given a setting, that
embraces the heavens, and in a single sentence:

" But man must know that in this theatre of man's life
it is reserved only for God and the angels to be lookers-on."

And with true poetic instinct, he pertinently asks:

" Who taught the bee to sail through such a vast sea
of air, and to find her way from a field in flowers a great
way off to her hive?"

Note the strange power and the mingled tenderness in
this, from his Essay, *Of Adversity:*

" Prosperity is the blessing of the Old Testament, adversity is the blessing of the New, which carrieth the
greater benediction, and the clearer revelation of God's
favor. Yet even in the Old Testament, if you listen to
David's harp, you shall hear as many hearse-like airs as
carols; and the pencil of the Holy Ghost hath labored
more in describing the affliction of Job than the felicities
of Solomon."

And the sweetness of heaven is wafted unto earth, as
by the breath of inspiration, in another sentence, where a
whole world of thought is compressed into each clause:

" Certainly it is heaven upon earth to have a man's mind move in charity, rest in providence, and turn upon the poles of truth."

In his Preface to the *Great Instauration*, he says:

" Whereas of the sciences which regard nature, the divine philosopher declares that ' it is the glory of God to conceal a thing, but it is the glory of the King to find a thing out.' Even as though the divine nature took pleasure in the innocent and kindly sport of children playing at hide and seek, and vouchsafed, of his kindness and goodness, to admit the human spirit for his playfellow at that game."

We know not at which we most do marvel; at this lofty sweep of the imagination, embracing the two poles, God and man, and bridging the measureless chasm with an airy structure of playful fancy; or at the audacity of the conception, though it be only the daring of the truth-bearer; or at this overwhelming expression of the kindly condescension of the divine nature, in imagery a child could understand. After this, though we may wonder and admire, we need not be surprised at any feat of his imagination. Macaulay says of Bacon:

" He was at once the Mammon and the Surly of his friend Ben. Sir Epicure did not indulge in visions more magnificent and gigantic. Surly did not sift evidence with keener and more sagacious incredulity. Closely connected with this peculiarity of Bacon's temper was a striking peculiarity of his understanding. With great minuteness of observation, he had an amplitude of comprehension, such as has never yet been vouchsafed to any other human being. The small fine mind of Labruyere had not a more delicate tact than the large intellect of Bacon. The Essays contain abundant proofs that no nice feature of character, no peculiarity in the ordering of a house, a garden, or a court-masque, could escape the notice of one whose mind was capable of taking in the whole world of knowledge. His understanding resembled the tent which the fairy Paribanou gave to Prince Ahmed. Fold it; and it seemed a toy for the hand of a lady. Spread it; and the armies of powerful Sultans might repose beneath its shade. In keenness of observation he has been equalled though perhaps never surpassed. But the largeness of his mind·was all his own. The glance with which he surveyed the intellectual universe resembled that which the Archangel, from the golden threshold of heaven, darted down into the new creation."

And again : " Yet we cannot wish that Bacon's wit had been less luxuriant. For, to say nothing of the pleasure it affords, it was in the vast majority of cases employed for the purpose of making obscure truth plain, of making repulsive truth attractive, of fixing in the mind forever truth which might otherwise have left a transient impression.

" The poetical faculty was powerful in Bacon's mind, but not like his wit, so powerful as occasionally to usurp the place of his reason, and to tyrannize over the whole man. No imagination was ever at once so strong, and so thoroughly subjugated. It never stirred but at a signal from good sense. Yet, though disciplined to such obedience, it gave noble proofs of its vigor. In truth, much of Bacon's life was passed in a visionary world, amidst things as strange as any that are described in the Arabian Tales, or in those romances on which the curate and barber of Don Quixote's village performed so cruel an *auto da fè*, amidst buildings more sumptuous than the palace of Aladdin, fountains more wonderful than the golden water of Parizade, conveyances more rapid than the hippogryph of Ruggiero, arms more formidable than the lance of Astolfo, remedies more efficacious than the balsam of Fierabras. Yet in his magnificent day-dreams, there was nothing wild, nothing but what sober reason sanctioned. He knew that all the secrets feigned by poets to have been written in the books of enchanters are worthless, when compared with the mighty secrets which are really written in the book of

nature, and which with time and patience will be read
there.   He knew that all the wonders wrought by all the
talismans in fable were trifles, when compared to the wonders which might reasonably be expected from the philosophy of fruit, and that, if his words sank deep into the
minds of men, they would produce effects such as superstition had never ascribed to the incantations of Merlin
and Michael Scot."

These are truly colossal proportions.   They are orb-
like : they have the girth of the equator, and the antithesis of the poles.   And this luminary is shown to have
been fairly dazzling in its splendor ; but shining upon
mankind in beneficent ministry, affording delight, and
illuminating the pathway.

Nor is the picture overdrawn ; for Schlegel, the eminent
German critic, gives us, in a few words, the like commen-
surate view of this wonderful Personality, unique in all
the ages of the world, and as he saw him through the medium of the Shakespeare.   He says :

" He unites in his soul the utmost elevation and the
utmost depth ; and the most opposite and even apparently
irreconcilable properties subsist in him peaceably together.
The world of spirits and nature have laid all their treasures at his feet: in strength a demi-god, in profundity of
view a prophet, in all-seeing wisdom a guardian spirit of
a higher order, he lowers himself to mortals as if unconscious of his superiority, and is as open and unassuming
as a child."

And the immortal Goethe !   His voice too blends in
this wondrous, majestic harmony, the united pæan of all
nations, and tongues, and succeeding generations ; and
Orpheus-like, he enriches it with the concordant strains
of a sweeter melody.   Though he was looking from afar,
through a veil, the insight of the heart, with which he
was so richly endowed, awakened in him an instant rec-

ognition of the spirit animating this Master Teacher, and he caught thence an inspiration towards a like service.

In his *Conversations with Eckermann*, he says:

" But we cannot talk about Shakespeare; everything is inadequate. I have touched upon the subject in ' *Wilhelm Meister*,' but that is not saying much. He is not a theatrical poet; he never thought of the stage; it was too narrow for his great mind: nay the whole visible world was too narrow. He is even too rich and powerful. . . . This, however, is by no means to be regretted, for what Shakespeare has lost as a theatrical poet, he has gained as a poet in general. Shakespeare is a great psychologist, and we learn from his pieces the secrets of human nature."

Turning to the *Wilhelm Meister*, we find there these impassioned words; descriptive of the profound impression made upon him in his first reading of the Shakespeare:

" Wilhelm had scarcely read one or two of Shakespeare's plays, till their effect on him became so strong that he could go no further. His whole soul was in commotion. He sought an opportunity to speak with Jarno; to whom, on meeting with him, he expressed his boundless gratitude for such delicious entertainment. ' I clearly enough foresaw,' said Jarno, ' that you would not remain insensible to the charms of the most extraordinary and most admirable of all writers.' ' Yes!' exclaimed our friend, ' I cannot recollect that any book, any man, any incident of my life, has produced such important effects upon me, as the precious works, to which by your kindness I have been directed. They seem as if they were performances of some celestial genius, descending among men, to make them, by the mildest instructions, acquainted with themselves. They are no fictions! You would think, while reading them, you stood before the unclosed awful books of fate, while the whirlwind of most impassioned life was howling through the leaves, and tossing them fiercely to and fro. The strength and tenderness, the power and peacefulness of this man have so astonished and transported me, that I long vehemently for the time when I shall have it in my power to read further.'

"' Bravo!' said Jarno, holding out his hand and squeezing our friend's: 'this is as it should be! And the consequences, which I hope for, will likewise surely follow.'

"' I wish,' said Wilhelm, ' I could disclose to you all that is going on within me even now. All the anticipations I have ever had regarding man and his destiny, which have accompanied me from youth upwards, often unobserved by myself, I find developed and fulfilled in Shakespeare's writings. It seems as if he cleared up every one of our enigmas to us, though we cannot say: Here or there is the word of solution. His men appear like natural men, and yet they are not. These, the most mysterious and complex productions of creation, here act before us as if they were watches, whose dial-plates and cases were of crystal : which pointed out, according to their use, the course of the hours and minutes; while, at the same time, you could discern the combination of wheels and springs that turned them. The few glances I have cast over Shakespeare's world incite me, more than anything beside, to quicken my footsteps forward into the actual world, to mingle in the flood of destinies that is suspended over it: and at length, if I shall prosper, to draw a few cups from the great ocean of true nature, and to distribute them from off the stage among the thirsting people of my native land.' "

It is sweet, indeed, thus to visit the company of the Immortals, to listen to their words, to *know* them, as they are self-revealed to our comprehension ; to realize in some measure their greatness, and to be swayed by their deathless spirits. And we may safely render to the summit glories of frail humanity our full tribute of appreciation ; for there, ever before us, towering far above them, up into and through the illimitable heavens, and overshadowing the universe, is the Supreme Love, manifested in the Son of Man, in untarnished glory.

But the great men of the world, they who have benef-
icently ministered to the welfare of the race, advanced
its enlightenment, and contributed to its enrichment, in a
marked degree, are really gifts to humanity, a part of its
priceless heritage. Among these men, Bacon stands foremost. And though the language employed in his delineation may perhaps seem extravagant to those who have not
closely studied the man, yet it was apparently well considered, called forth by the necessities of the case, and
from men who obviously felt that words were scarcely adequate to the portrayal of the man in the magnitude of his
greatness. It comes as the almost involuntary tribute of
the Intellect, the Critical Acumen, and the Genius of the
world to their recognized Master.

United as in one voice, in ever blending harmony, it
reveals to us the man in his true function, as the world's
Great Teacher. This seemingly celestial genius, whose
glance through the intellectual universe resembled that of
the Archangel from the golden threshold of heaven, or of
a guardian spirit of a higher order ; endowed with an amplitude of comprehension such as has never yet been vouchsafed to any other human being ; capable of taking in the
whole world of knowledge, and for whose great mind the
theatrical stage was too narrow, nay the whole visible
world too narrow ; much of whose life was passed in a visionary realm, amidst things as strange as any described
in the Arabian Tales, and yet with nothing in these day-
dreams that was wild, nothing but what sober reason
sanctioned ; indulging in visions more magnificent and
gigantic than those of Sir Epicure, and yet sifting evidence with keen and sagacious incredulity ; gifted with a
largeness of mind all his own, and yet with a keenness
of observation equalled though perhaps never surpassed,
and such that no nice feature of character, no peculiarity
in the ordering of a house, a garden, or a court-masque

could escape; the most opposite and apparently irreconcilable qualities subsisting in him peaceably together;
uniting the utmost elevation and the utmost depth, strength,
and tenderness, power and peacefulness; a psychologist
and a philosopher, but philosophy, fancy, and imagination
penetrated with the spirit of the unwritten law of reason,
his philosophy being practical and his practical views
fused with philosophy and poetry; with the poetical faculty powerful, giving noble proofs of its vigor, but disciplined to obedience to his good sense; no imagination
being ever at once so strong and so thoroughly subjugated;
with nothing in English prose superior to his diction, the
most extraordinary and most admirable of all writers; in
strength called a demi-god, and in profundity of view a
prophet, he spake after the manner of prophets, almost in
Sibylline verses, like an oracle who foresees the future
and reveals the truth, and at times you would think you
stood before the unclosed awful books of fate, while the
whirlwind of most impassioned life was howling through
the leaves, and tossing them fiercely to and fro; but all
the while, as open and unassuming as a child, he was em-
ploying his luxuriant wit, and the pleasure it affords, in
developing and fulfilling our anticipations regarding man
and his destiny, in clearing up the enigmas of life, in
making obscure truths plain, repulsive ones attractive, fixing in the mind forever those otherwise leaving but transient impressions, and in making men by the mildest instructions acquainted with themselves; well knowing, that
when his words should sink deep into the minds of men,
they would produce, in their consequences, effects far surpassing any that are ascribed to the incantations of the
old-time magicians.

Behold the man! And in the man, also, the key to the
Shakespeare; to its beneficient intent, fulfilled in such
glorious accomplishment! It is the befitting accompan-

iment, if, indeed, it be not essentially an integral part of
his *Great Instauration;* entering into his grand, comprehensive scheme, but reserved to himself for exhaustive
development, upon the fundamental lines of the realities.
Man is the subject; man as he is actually found in nature,
good and bad; in his weaknesses, his excesses, his passions, and his crimes; in his rugged strength, in woman's
gentle tenderness, her charming beauty, her constancy,
and her devotion; in his friendship, his magnanimity, his
loyalty, and his love; in all his incongruities and inconsis-
tencies; in every phase of human existence, in almost
every modification, and as developed amidst the complexities of life's experiences. It is a transcript of humanity,
accurate, comprehensive, and well-nigh exhaustive, a vivid
representation to the life of the universal man, in his
essential characteristics, in his myriad forms, aspects, and
experiences; thus both infolding and unfolding "the secrets of human nature." This great philosopher, playing
upon our hearts as with a musician's bow, has made it " a
means of educating men's minds to virtue"; and this is
accomplished so sweetly, and in such perfection, and such
beauty, that it has all the charm of enchantment. His
magic is the only real magic in the world, — the subtle
power of realities, in the intensity of their beauty, and the
might of their verity.

> "Truth needs no color with his color fix'd;
> Beauty no pencil, beauty's truth to lay."

And now, as we read the Shakespeare, we may rise
fully to Goethe's plane of appreciation : we, also, may discern its mighty import, and catch the inspiration of its
beneficent spirit. We may know, to a certainty, that it
was bestowed upon us for our delight, and for our instruction as well. It is, indeed, delicious nutriment, luscious
fruit imbedded in fragrant flowers, a banquet of delectable food provided for our entertainment, "a rich store-

23

house," full of choicest grain, where every kernel contains its living germ of wisdom.

And in our delight over its marvellous beauty, we may know that we are only catching some gleams of Bacon's joy, as he threw off the accustomed restraints, assumed the magic mantle and the enchanter's wand, and gave himself up to a legitimate revel of his imagination. But we cannot know the rapture that filled his soul, ravishing the mental tendrils of all his senses and entrancing his whole being, in the convulsive throes of the creative act. It was the divine rapture, experienced in the impartation of himself.

In the hour of exaltation, when he was all aglow with the flame enkindled by a burning impulse, he gave enshrinement to his clearest visions, in creations that were after the likeness of human souls. They were clothed in imagery fashioned ont of vivid impressions stamped upon his brain : his spirit endowed them with vitality, and his wisdom with its subtle power. And over them all he threw a glittering canopy of wondrous beauty, woven out of beams and gleaming rays that he had drawn from the drapery of the universe.

The travails of their birth were, indeed, thrills of exquisite delight, and their life is everlasting, because they were the joyous outflowings of his immortal soul.

CHAPTER XII.

LET us, for our further satisfaction, delve once more, even into the subsoil of the world's criticism.

Mr. Hamilton W. Mabie, the distinguished critic, in his *Essays in Literary Interpretation* (a little book full of meat, feeding whereon a man grows), in a luminous generalization, places at our command another crucial test of the personality of the Poet. He says:

"Every dramatist of the first order has had a fundamental thought about life which, expressed in his own way, has been in some essential things different from the thought of all his fellows; and that thought has contained the very essence of his personality. The great writers speak not from report, but from personal knowledge. They differ from the lesser writers, not only in quality of workmanship, but still more in the fact that they are witnesses of the truth which they express. They have seen and felt, therefore they speak. And that which thus sees and feels and knows is the man's whole nature, not observation only, nor thought only, nor feeling only. All the faculties, the aptitudes, the sensibilities, the experiences which make us what we are, are involved in this process. So that which lies deepest in a man, his thought of the movement of things in which he finds himself, expresses completely and most profoundly his personality."

We have already been unconsciously applying this test, in our discussion of the play of *Julius Cæsar*, which indeed strikingly illustrates the truth of the proposition,— for else were it meaningless.* But to further prolong this

---

* For a more specific example, see the peculiar view enter-

exposition, showing in detail the continual unfolding within the plays, in the like perfect harmony, of Bacon's "fundamental thought about life" and of "the movement of things in which he finds himself," would far exceed our limits. Nor is it here necessary. For yet another surprise awaits us. Strange to say, the work, in its essentials, has already been performed, years ago, and by a critic of unquestioned ability, who has condensed what might fill a volume into a compact summary which covers the ground.

For this, as is fitting, we are indebted to Germany, the land of diligent, profound, and accurate scholarship. Gervinus, to whom we refer, stands perhaps foremost among the Shakespearean critics of the world. Dr. Furnivall, the eminent English Shakespearean scholar, in his Introduction to the English translation of his *Shakespeare Commentaries*, says of him:

"What strikes me most in Gervinus is his breadth of culture, his rightness and calmness of judgment, his fairness in looking at both sides of a question, his noble earnest purpose, his resolve to get at the deepest meaning of his author, and his reverence and love for Shakespeare. No one can read his book without seeing evidence of a range of reading rare indeed among Englishmen."

"In his last section, 'Shakespeare,' Gervinus sets before us his view of the poet and his works as a whole, and rightly claims for him the highest honor as the greatest dramatic artist, the rarest judge of men and human affairs, *the noblest moral teacher*, that Literature has yet known."

And again: "The profound and generous *Commentaries* of Gervinus—an honor to a German to have written, a pleasure to an Englishman to read—is still the only book known to me that comes near the true treatment and the

---

tained of Hope, the direct outgrowth also of "a fundamental thought about life." (See *ante*, page 142, note.)

dignity of its subject, or can be put into the hands of the student who wants to know the mind of Shakespeare."

Fortunately, Gervinus was an equally profound student of Bacon in his prose writings ; citing them repeatedly throughout his *Commentaries*, in elucidation of the meaning of the plays. And in his last section, above referred to, he institutes, in a careful summary, a direct comparison between Bacon, *in propria persona*, and him who was known to him only as " Shakespeare,"—in their course of thought, their attitude towards life, and their views of its movements, as they are revealed in their works.

This exposition is the more significant, since it was written at the close of the last half century, and by an earnest, devoted critic, who felt impelled to note the likeness, but who was utterly unconscious that he was all the while dealing with the same personality. But such was the depth of his insight, his intellectual grasp, and his intimate knowledge of the subject, that, unlike Plutarch, with his parallels of different men, there is here unfolded no shading of contrast, indicating a difference in individuality.

The importance of the subject, and its able treatment, fully warrant an extended quotation ; and especially as, at the end, it leaves no occasion for detailed comment. He says :

" For just as Shakespeare was an interpreter of the secrets of history and of human nature, Bacon was an interpreter of lifeless nature. Just as Shakespeare went from instance to instance in his judgment of moral actions, and never founded a law on a single experience, so did Bacon in natural science avoid leaping from one experience of the senses to general principles ; he spoke of this with blame as anticipating nature ; and Shakespeare, in the same way, would have called the conventionalities in the poetry of the Southern races an anticipation of human nature. In the scholastic science of the middle ages,

as in the chivalric poetry of the romantic period, approbation and not truth was sought for; and with one accord
Shakespeare's poetry and Bacon's science were equally
opposed to this. As Shakespeare balanced the one-sided
errors of the imagination by reason, reality, and nature,
so Bacon led philosophy away from the one-sided errors
of reason to experience; both, with one stroke, renovated
the two branches of science and poetry by this renewed
bond with nature; both, disregarding all by-ways, staked
everything upon this 'victory in the race between art and
nature.'

"Just as Bacon with his new philosophy is linked with
the natural science of Greece and Rome, and then with
the latter period of philosophy in western Europe, so
Shakespeare's drama stands in relation to the comedies of
Plautus and to the stage of his own day; between the two
there lay a vast wilderness of time, as unfruitful for the
drama as for philosophy. But while they thus led back
to nature, Bacon was yet as little of an empiric, in the
common sense, as Shakespeare was a poet of nature.
Bacon prophesied that if hereafter his commendation of
experience should prevail, great danger to science would
arise from the other extreme, and Shakespeare even in his
own day could perceive the same with respect to his poetry; Bacon, therefore, insisted on the closest union between experience and reason, just as Shakespeare effected
that between reality and imagination. While they thus
bid adieu to the formalities of ancient art and science,
Shakespeare to conceits and taffeta-phrases, Bacon to logic
and syllogisms, yet at times it occurred that the one fell
back into the subtleties of the old school, and the other
into the constrained wit of the Italian style.

" Bacon felt himself quite an original in that which was
his peculiar merit, and so was Shakespeare: the one in
the method of science he had laid down, and in his suggestions for its execution, the other in the poetical works
he had executed, and in the suggestions of their new law.
Bacon, looking back to the waymarks he had left for

others, said with pride, that his words required a century
for their demonstration and several for the execution;
and so too it has demanded two centuries to understand
Shakespeare; but very little has been executed in his
sense. And at the same time, we have mentioned what
deep modesty was interwoven in both with their self-reliance, so that the words which Bacon liked to quote hold
good for the two works:—'The kingdom of God cometh
not with observation.'

"Both reached this height from the one starting point,
that Shakespeare despised the million, and Bacon feared
with Phocion the applause of the multitude. Both are
alike in the rare impartiality with which they avoided
everything one-sided; in Bacon we find, indeed, youthful
exercises in which he endeavored in severe contrasts to
contemplate a series of things from two points of view.
Both, therefore, have an equal hatred of sects and parties; Bacon of sophists and dogmatic philosophers, Shakespeare of Puritans and zealots. Both, therefore, are
equally free from prejudices, and from astrological superstition in dreams and omens. Bacon says of the alchem-
ists and magicians in natural science, that they stand in
similar relation to true knowledge as the deeds of Amadis
to those of Cæsar, and so does Shakespeare's true poetry
stand in relation to the fantastic romance of Amadis.

"Just as Bacon banished religion from science, so did
Shakespeare from art; and when the former complained
that the teachers of religion were against natural philosophy, they were equally against the stage. From Bacon's
example, it seems clear that Shakespeare left religious
matters unnoticed on the same grounds as himself, and
took the path of morality in worldly things; in both this
has been equally misconstrued, and Le Maistre has proved
Bacon's lack of Christianity, as Birch has done that of
Shakespeare.

"Shakespeare would, perhaps, have looked down just
as contemptuously on the ancients and their arts as did
Bacon on their philosophy and natural science, and both

on the same grounds; they boasted of the greater age of
the world, of more enlarged knowledge of heaven, earth,
and mankind. Neither stooped before authorities, and an
injustice similar to that which Bacon committed against
Aristotle, Shakespeare *perhaps* has done to Homer.*

" In both, a similar combination of different mental powers was at work; and as Shakespeare was often involuntarily philosophical in his profoundness, Bacon was not seldom surprised into the imagination of the poet. Just as
Bacon, although he declared knowledge in itself to be much
more valuable than the use of invention, insisted throughout generally and dispassionately upon the practical use of
philosophy, so Shakespeare's poetry, independent as was
his sense of art, aimed throughout at bearing upon the
moral life. Bacon himself was of the same opinion; he
was not far from declaring history to be the best teacher
of politics, and poetry the best instructor in morals.

" Both were alike deeply moved by the picture of a ruling Nemesis, whom they saw, grand and powerful, strid-
ing through history and life, dragging the mightiest and
the most prosperous as a sacrifice to her altar, as the victims of their own inward nature and destiny. In Bacon's
works we find a multitude of moral sayings and maxims
of experience, from which the most striking mottoes might
be drawn for every Shakespearean play, aye, for every
one of his principal characters (we have already brought
forward not a few proofs of this), testifying to a remarkable harmony in their mutual comprehension of human
nature.

" Both, in their systems of morality rendering homage to

* We note the following, from Bacon's *Advancement of Learning*, Second Book: "Surely of those poets which are now extant, even Homer himself (notwithstanding he was made a kind
of Scripture by the later schools of the Grecians), yet I should
without any difficulty pronounce that his fables had no such in-
wardness in his own meaning; but what they might have upon
a more original tradition, is not easy to affirm; for he was not
the inventor of many of them."

Aristotle, whose ethics Shakespeare, from a passage in
Troilus,* may have read, arrived at the same end as he
did — that virtue lies in a just medium between two ex-
tremes.   Shakespeare would have also agreed with him
in this, that Bacon declared excess to be ' the fault of
youth, as defect is of age '; he accounted ' defect the worst,
because excess contains some sparks of magnanimity, and,
like a bird, claims kindred of the heavens, while defect,
only like a base worm, crawls upon the earth.'   *In these
maxims lie at once, as it were, the whole theory of Shakespeare's dramatic forms and of his moral philosophy.*"

---

* The passage referred to is especially interesting, not only in
its disclosure of the same views regarding the liability of youth
to the disturbance of their judgment through the very warmth
of their nature, but also, as showing the committing of the same
negligent *mistake* regarding the tenor of Aristotle's doctrine :

> " Paris, and Troilus, you have both said well ;
> And on the cause and *question now in hand*[1]
> Have glozed,[2]— but superficially ; not much
> Unlike young men, whom Aristotle thought
> *Unfit* to hear *moral* philosophy :
> The reasons you allege do more conduce
> To the *hot passion of distemper'd* blood,
> Than to make up a free determination
> 'Twixt right and wrong ; for pleasure and revenge
> Have ears more deaf than adders to the voice
> Of any true decision."[3]
> —*Troilus and Cress., II., 2.*

In his *De Augmentis*, Seventh Book, Bacon says : " Is not
the opinion of Aristotle very wise and worthy to be regarded,
' that young men are *no fit* auditors of *moral* philosophy,' because the *boiling heat of their affections* is not yet settled, nor
tempered with time and experience ? "

In a note to this passage, Spedding says : " Arist. Eth. ad
Nicom., i. 3. Aristotle, however, speaks not of moral but of *political* philosophy."

So that their identity is manifested even in their errors.

[1] See *ante*, page 70.   [2] See *ante*, page 45.   [3] See *ante*, page 61.
See, also, page 135, note.

This concludes Gervinus' really wonderful summary; which, over and beyond its clear delineation of these unmistakable manifestations of a single, unique mentality, in its distinctive characteristics and its homogeneous phases, has, somehow, brought us into intimate acquaintance with the man himself, personally, and into almost conscious contact with his living, vitalizing spirit; which animated his whole work, in its perfectly consistent development, its comprehensive harmony, and its underlying unity, and which was "the very essence of his personality."

Returning again for a moment to Taine : It may not be amiss, in this connection, to note a now manifest error into which this distinguished critic fell in his discussion of the Shakespeare, and, if possible, to explain its occurrence. He finds, indeed, in the plays, and especially in the *Sonnets*, the organic manifestation and expression of the Poet's personal *immorality*.   He says :

" He had many loves of this kind, amongst others one for a sort of Marion Delorme [a famed French courtesan], a miserable, deluding, despotic passion, of which he felt the burden and the shame, but from which, nevertheless, he could not and would not free himself.   Nothing can be sadder than his confessions, or mark better the madness of love, and the sentiment of human weakness :

'When my love swears that she is made of truth,
　I do believe her, though I know she lies.'—*Sonnet 138*.
So spoke Alceste of Célimène ; but what a soiled Célimène is the creature before whom Shakespeare kneels, with as much of scorn as of desire !

'— those lips of thine,
That have profaned their scarlet ornaments,
And seal'd false bonds of love as oft as mine,
Robb'd others' beds' revenues of their rents.
Be it lawful I love thee, as thou lov'st those
Whom thine eyes woo as mine importune thee.'
—*Sonnet 142*.

This is plain-speaking and deep shamelessness of soul, such as we find only in the *stews ;* and these are the intoxications, the excesses, the delirium into which the most refined artists fall, when they resign their own noble hand to these soft, voluptuous, and clinging ones. They are higher than princes, and they descend to the lowest depths of sensual passion."

And again : " Falstaff has the passions of an animal ; and the imagination of a man of wit. There is no character which better exemplifies the fire and *immorality* of Shakespeare.* Falstaff is a great supporter of disreputable places, swearer, gamester, idler, wine-bibber, as low as he well can be. . . . This big, pot-bellied fellow, a coward, a cynic, a brawler, a drunkard, a lewd rascal, a pot-house poet, is one of Shakespeare's favorites. The reason is, that his morals are those of pure nature, and Shakespeare's mind is congenial with his own."

The explanation is not far to seek. Taine had the happy faculty of penetrating, at once, to what he conceived to be the heart of a subject, and working thence from within outward. And what is the heart of a book but the personality of its author ? A worthy book, indeed, is a stream of thought, flowing from a fountain-head, and partaking of its properties : or as Milton eloquently puts it, in his prose :

" For books are not absolutely dead things, but do contain a potency of life in them, to be as active as that soul

---

* It is now evident that the Poet no more exemplifies himself in Falstaff, than in Richard III., or Iago, or Edmund. In all these he simply "holds the mirror up to nature," reflecting objects "as they are ": and it is in this, that he most truly reveals his personality.

If at all, it is perhaps in Prospero, in *The Tempest* (that exquisitely symbolical creation, whose depth of meaning it is reserved for other ages to fathom) that the Poet gives expression to his own individuality.

was whose progeny they are ; nay, they do preserve as in
a vial the purest efficacy and extraction of that living intellect that bred them. . . . Many a man lives a burden
to the earth ; but a good book is the precious life-blood
of a master-spirit, embalmed and treasured up on purpose
to a life beyond life."

Consequently, Taine went at once to the fountain-head,
to determine the quality of the flowing waters. And in
this, as is often the case, he became the victim of his own
underlying, inexorable logic. His major premise, perfectly sound, was that a book, in its essence, is a manifestation of the personality of its author. His minor premise was, that this was the work of *William Shakespeare*.
His conclusion, after a careful study of the man, and to
one of Taine's calibre, was inevitable.

For this is what he finds and reports regarding William
Shakespeare:

" His father, a glover and wool-stapler, in very easy circumstances, having married a sort of county heiress, had
become high-bailiff and chief alderman in his little town ;
but when Shakespeare was nearly fourteen, he was on the
verge of ruin, mortgaging his wife's property, obliged to
resign his municipal offices, and to remove his son from
school to assist him in his business. The young fellow
applied himself to it as well as he could, not without some
scrapes and frolics : if we are to believe tradition, he was
one of the thirsty souls of the place, with a mind to support the reputation of his little town in its drinking powers.
Once, they say, having been beaten at Bideford in one of
these ale-bouts, he returned staggering from the fight, or
rather could not return, and passed the night with his
comrades under an appletree by the roadside. . . . At
all events, he was not a pattern of propriety, and his passions were as precocious as they were impudent. While
not yet nineteen years old, he married the daughter of a
substantial yeoman, about eight years older than himself
—and not too soon, as she was about to become a mother.

Other of his outbreaks were no more fortunate. It seems that he was fond of poaching, after the manner of the time, being 'much given to all unluckinesse in stealing venison and rabbits,' says the Rev. Richard Davies; 'particularly from Sir Thomas Lucy, who had him oft whipt and sometimes imprisoned, and at last made him fly the country.' . . . He went to London, and took to the stage: took the lowest part, was a 'servant' in the theatre, that is, an apprentice, or perhaps a supernumerary. They even said that he had begun still lower, and that to earn his bread he had held gentlemen's horses at the door of the theatre. At all events, he tasted misery and felt, not in imagination, but in fact, the sharp thorn of care, humiliation, disgust, forced labor, public discredit, the power of the people. He was a comedian, one of 'His Majesty's poor players'—a sad trade, degraded in all ages by the contrasts and the falsehoods which it allows; still more degraded then by the brutalities of the crowd, who not seldom would stone the actors, and by the severities of the magistrates, who would sometime condemn them to lose their ears. . . . But the worst of this under-valued position is, that it eats into the soul. In the company of actors we become actors: it is vain to wish to keep clean, if you live in a dirty place; it cannot be. No matter if a man braces himself; necessity drives him into a corner and sullies him. The machinery of the decorations, the tawdriness and medley of the costumes, the smell of the tallow and the candles, in contrast with the parade of refinement and loftiness, all the cheats and sordidness of the representation, the bitter alternative of hissing or applause, the keeping of the highest and lowest company, the habit of sporting with human passions, easily unhinge the soul, drive it down the slope of excess, tempt it to loose manners, green-room adventures, the loves of strolling actresses.

" Shakespeare escaped them no more than Molière, and grieved for it, like Molière:

'O, for my sake do you with Fortune chide,
The guilty goddess of my harmful deeds,
That did not better for my life provide,
Than public means which public manners breeds.'

—*Sonnet 111.*

"They used to relate in London, how his comrade Burbadge, who played Richard III., having a rendezvous with the wife of a citizen, Shakespeare went before, was well received, and was pleasantly occupied, when Burbadge arrived, to whom he sent the message, that William the Conqueror came before Richard III. We may take this as an example of the tricks and somewhat coarse intrigues which are planned, and follow in quick succession, on this stage. Outside the theatre, he lived with fashionable young nobles, Pembroke, Montgomery, Southampton, and others, whose hot and licentious youth gratified his imagination and senses by the example of Italian pleasures and elegancies. . . . Under a sway so imperious and sustained, what sentiment could maintain its ground? That of family? He was married and had children,—a family which he went to see ' once a year'; and it was probably on a return from one of these journeys that he used the words above quoted. Conscience? 'Love is too young to know what conscience is.' . . . Neither glory, nor work, nor invention satisfy these vehement souls : love alone can gratify them, because, with their senses and heart, it contents also their brain ; and all the powers of man, imagination like the rest, find in it their concentration and employment. 'Love is my sin,' he said, as did Musset and Heine ; and in the *Sonnets* we find traces of yet other passions, equally abandoned; one in particular, seemingly for a great lady. . . .

"Such as I have described him, however, he found his resting-place. Early, at least what regards outward appearances, he settled down to an orderly, sensible, almost humdrum existence ; engaged in business, provident of the future. He remained on the stage for at least seventeen years, though taking secondary parts ; he set his

wits at the same time to the touching up of plays with so
much activity, that Greene called him 'an upstart crow
beautified with our feathers; . . . an absolute *Johannes
factotum*, in his owne conceyt, the onely shake-scene in a
countrey.' At the age of thirty-three he had amassed
money enough to buy at Stratford a house with two barns
and two gardens, and he went on steadier and steadier in
the same course. A man attains only to easy circumstances by his own labor; if he gains wealth, it is by making others labor for him. This is why, to the trades of
actor and author, Shakespeare added those of manager
and director of a theatre. He acquired a share in the
Blackfriars and Globe theatres, farmed tithes, bought
large pieces of land, more houses, gave a dowry to his
daughter Susanna, and finally retired to his native town
on his property, in his own house, like a good landlord,
an honest citizen, who manages his fortune fitly, and takes
his share of municipal work. He had an income of two
or three hundred pounds, which would be equivalent to
about eight or twelve hundred at the present time, and
according to tradition, lived cheerfully and on good terms
with his neighbors; at all events, it does not seem that
he thought much about his literary glory, for he did not
even take the trouble to collect and publish his works.
One of his daughters married a physician, the other a
wine merchant; the last did not even know how to sign
her name. He lent money, and cut a good figure in this
little world. Strange close; one which at first sight re-
sembles more that of a shopkeeper than of a poet."

Richard Grant White, in his *Life and Genius of
Shakespeare*, though with a loving hand, applies the knife
with even greater severity. He says:

" But for this loss there is recompense in the authen-
ticity of a court record, by which we know that in August,
1608, Shakespeare sued John Addenbroke of Stratford,
got a judgment for £6, and £1 4*s.* costs, and that Addenbroke being returned *non est inventus*, Shakespeare sued

his bail, Thomas Hornby, the proceedings lasting until June, 1609. Four years before, Shakespeare had sued one Philip Rogers in the Stratford Court of Record for £1 15s. 10d. He had sold Rogers malt to the value of £1 19s. 10d., and had lent him 2s., of which the debtor had paid but 6s. And so Shakespeare brought suit for what is called in trade the balance of the account, which represented about $9 of our money. These stories grate upon our feelings with a discord as much harsher than that which disturbs us when we hear of Addison suing poor Steele for £100, as Shakespeare lives in our hearts the lovelier as well as the greater man than Addison. But Addison's case was aggravated by the fact that the debtor was his life-long friend and fellow-laborer. Debts are to be paid, and rogues who can pay and will not pay must be made to pay; but the pursuit of an impoverished man, for the sake of imprisoning him and depriving him both of the power of paying his debt and supporting himself and his family, is an incident in Shakespeare's life which it requires the utmost allowance and consideration for the practice of the time and country to enable us to contemplate with equanimity,— satisfaction is impossible.

"The biographer of Shakespeare must record these facts, because the literary antiquaries have unearthed and brought them forward as 'new particulars of the life of Shakespeare.' We hunger, and we receive these husks; we open our mouths for food, and we break our teeth against these stones."

As was inevitable, we have come at length to the intersection, where the two pathways squarely cross each other. It is incumbent upon us to choose the path in which we will hereafter tread,—between Francis Bacon and William Shakespeare, — which, in view of all the data, we will accept as the actual author of the plays.

If we choose William Shakespeare, we shall have this advantage, that the Shakespeare who is the idol of our affections, whom we love and revere, will continue to be, as in the past, an *ideal* character, almost exclusively the creation of our own imagination. Every mental quality and power of the intellect, knowledge of "all that God had revealed, and all that man had discovered," familiarity with court life in its amenities and nice gradations, the delicacy of refined cultivation, the exquisite harmony of soul, attuned to the finer issues, broad, comprehensive views of life and its movements, and of the moral relations of the individual, every excellence and beauty of soul, and all the "loveliness" that we find reflected in the plays will inevitably be interwoven and incorporated in this ideal that is enshrined in our hearts. And the finer our own natures, and the more delicate our sensibilities, the sweeter, the richer, and the lovelier will be our creation.

Only, we shall from time to time be rudely shocked by the "discord," our "equanimity" disturbed, and our satisfaction turned into disgust, as was the case with Richard Grant White, when we are involuntarily brought into contact with the cold, hard facts of the *reality;* unearthed by the pestiferous antiquarians, those iconoclasts who have so repeatedly been destructive to our illusions. And at such moments, we shall be haunted by the lurking suspicion that some future psychologist, master of his theme, will use us to exemplify his proposition, that such is the inherent weakness of human nature, that the most enlightened people, at the close of the Nineteenth century, could cling with devotion to a long-cherished illusion; even after their eyes had been opened to its inconsistency, and to its glaring absurdities. And in the end, we shall find that there is no rest for our souls.

But, on the other hand, if through our continual recognition of his unmistakable personality in its essential phases; of his sweet, kindly spirit, with its grandly beneficent intent; of his wonderful imaginative power, tempered with the utmost good sense; of his rich mentality,

24

in its thousand-fold manifestations; exemplified in underlying principles, in broad outlines, and in the minutest
details; comprising every department of thought, the accumulated knowledge of the ages, the widest range of observation, and the most sage reflections and "maxims of
experience," underlying 'the whole theory of the plays'
dramatic forms'; in a universality unparalleled; including
an equally unparalleled "comprehension of human nature," and a distinctive moral philosophy, 'from which
the most striking mottoes might be drawn for every play,
aye, for every one of the principal characters'; and all
blending in that unity and perfect consistency which is
solely the attribute of individuality, we are led to intelligently accept Francis Bacon as the actual author of the
plays, we descend at once from the clouds to the solid
earth, and are ushered into the legitimate domain of the
realities; where harmony dwells, where study meets with
an ample, continuous, and enduring reward, and wherein
we experience continually the gratification and the joy of
conscious growth.

We find, back of the creation, its greater creator; of
whom it is "bone of his bone, and flesh of his flesh." A
rich mine is opened to our possession, almost exhaustless
in its treasure. And every vein that we work, in every
direction, not only affords us striking confirmation, but
yields to us additional resources; contributing materially
to our better comprehension of the plays, of the sources
of their power, of the laws underlying their development,
and of the methods of the Master.

And above all, when our minds shall have once been
disabused of the idea of the semi-miraculous origin of the
plays; when we shall discern, in their every element and
development, the orderly relation of cause and effect, and
shall realize that they are actually the production of the
normal human intellect in its highest development, the

glittering fetters that have hitherto insensibly enchained the race will be broken asunder. In the newly awakened consciousness of their inherent powers, the youth of succeeding generations, appreciating the conditions involved, will be inspired to like effort, in a devotion that will pay the price: and if we mistake not, we shall then be blessed with another Golden Age in Literature, of even greater lustre, more widely extended, more productive, and more enduring, than any the world has ever known:

> "There shall be sung another golden age,
>   The rise of empire and of arts,
> The good and great uprising epic rage,
>   The wisest heads and noblest hearts.
>
>   .   .   .   .
>
> "Westward the course of empire takes its way;
>   The first four acts already past,
> The fifth shall close the drama with the day;
>   Time's noblest offspring is the last."

With the abundant data now before us, and where so much is involved, it is due to ourselves, that we come to a conclusion; for indecision, as was shown in Cicero, is destructive to both the mental and the moral fibre. Moreover, as with Taine, the conclusion at which we arrive will unavoidably color our whole conception and understanding of the plays; of their morality, of the quality of their inspiration, and of the sordidness or the grandeur of their embodied purpose.

Personally, as was said in the Prologue, we have long been convinced "beyond a reasonable doubt": we are now consciously resting upon a certainty; and there is contentment, aye joy in the harmony.

CHAPTER XIII.

IF we would adequately comprehend Bacon's potent influence upon the destinies of the race, we must cast a glance through the long vista of the preceding ages, and, if possible, take the bearings of the great currents of the world's thought.

Looking thus backward, our eye is at once arrested by a bright light, whose steady glow effectually pales the few dim, phosphorescent lights that flicker behind it. Our attention is thus fastened upon ancient Greece, the centre and source of this illumination.

The Greeks were, indeed, a race of intellectual giants; developing a power and a mastery of their materials which not only raised them to the summit of ancient civilization, but wrought their enduring impress upon the human race; subtly moulding its thought, its science, its art, and its philosophy; strongly influencing even our minds to-day.

Somehow, possibly through Homer's all-pervasive influence, they drew close to nature; catching from her inspiration, and entering into sympathy with her diverse moods; her joyousness, and her infinite tragedy; her intense activity, and her impassive repose, eternal as Mount Olympus. Feeding in its infancy upon Homer, and for generations continually assimilating his poetry—the simplest, the most faithful objective reflection of nature and humanity—the nation grew and developed upon these lines, until, in the time of Pericles, it attained to its Golden Age, of surpassing lustre. It was the age of Anaxagoras

and Democritus, of Thucydides, Herodotus, and Xenophon, of Pericles and Lysias, of Simonides and Pindar,
of Æschylus, Sophocles, Euripides, and Aristophanes, of
Myron, Polyclites, and Phidias.

It is an accepted truism, that the spirit of an age is
reflected in its art. And Charles Waldstein, in his masterly *Essays on the Art of Pheidias*, has opened for us
this window; enabling us to look through it into the very
soul of the Greek nation in that age.* He says:

"In the third place, having examined the causes, we
have to indicate several manifestations of the 'simply'
observing and plastic spirit of the Greeks, which we notice as the most striking characteristic in all the spheres
of their life and thought.†

---

* Mr. Charles Dudley Warner, in Harper's Magazine for
Dec., 1893, says: "We all recall three noteworthy essays in
criticism: Lessing's *Laocoon;* Charles Walstein's *The Art of
Pheidias;* and Matthew Arnold's *The Function of Criticism at
the Present Time.* These all relate to the higher criticism —
the application of principles to details — but they are examples
of it."

† Our author explains that he uses the word "plastic" in a
special, peculiar sense, in conformity with the German usage:
"Plastic art," he says, "corresponds rather to things in themselves; painting (and this is still more the case with poetry) corresponds rather to the relation between things. The plastic mind
is simply observing; the pictorial and poetic minds are less intuitive, more reflective and associative.

"Hence the plastic mind, in the active sense of the term,
comes to mean the mind which acts through the senses alone,
by pure and simple sensuous observation; while the pictorial or
the poetic tendency is less intuitive, more reflective and associative. The word 'plastic' in this active sense has been so long
in use in Germany to express this definite idea, that though less
widely used in England, it becomes a necessity to adopt it in
dealing with the present subject.

"The ancient Greeks were thus 'simply' observing and plastic in mind; while we of modern times are, so to say, verbal
rather than plastic. The Greeks thought by means of the in-

"Their very language is immediately based upon *observation of nature*. The Greek drew his words from the direct source of nature, while the Roman introduces some abstraction, some mental association. . . . The words πρόβατου and εἰλίποδες βοῦς evidence their minute observation of outer nature, denoting that the sheep in walking places one foot before the other, while cattle drag one foot after the other. It is most interesting to read through Homer or any one of the great poets with this question in view, and to see how perfectly simple and sensuous are the attributes and compound words used by them. The more we study their language the more strongly will this characteristic impress itself upon us.

" In their building, too, and engineering, the first step with the Greeks is the clinging to nature and the adaptation to the natural environment. The Romans, however, construct almost irrespective of the environing nature, appearing almost to repel the suggestions made to their senses by the material at hand. . . .

" The religion of the Greeks has ever been recognized as intimately connected with their feeling for form and its manifestation in their sculpture. As Greek art was strongly influenced by their mythology, so their works of art again reacted upon and modified their religious feeling. Yet both in their mythology and in their religious art, *they clung to nature and avoided abstraction.* While the gods

ner representations of the things themselves, while we think by the representations of words ; be it in recalling their sound or their written symbols. We have lost the power of simple observation and our interest in the things themselves, that is, things independent of their relation to other things or to us. The Greek carried his humanity into inanimate nature, endowed it with a self-centered life of its own ; we draw nature into the sphere of humanity and regard it in the light of use or conscious pleasure."

It is in this sense of the word that he observes that, " The distinctive characterististic of the descriptions of Homer is that they are essentially plastic."

of the Greeks arose out of nature, and did not transcend it, even when they developed into personality, the specifically Roman gods, such as Saturnus, Ops, Terminus, arose from preconceived notions of human needs. . . . [After discussing the Oriental gods, he continues]. . . . Therefore it is, that these Oriental types must remain the same and there can be no development, or else the known difference between man and gods would not remain fixed; while the Greek gods may develop in their type and in their representation, because influenced and essentially modified by impressions from nature. The Oriental is the upshot of reflection and abstraction, the Greek of ' simple ' observation, *which directs the course of the imagination.*

" It has further been universally acknowledged that Greek poetry is essentially plastic in character. Its imagery, beginning with the Homeric attributes, appeals above all things to the eye. The persons and things described stand before our eyes in their visible form before they appeal to our sympathy with their spiritual qualities; nay, in Homer, who manifests his appreciation of form and his study of nature in his detailed descriptions of the anatomy of the body in his wounded or falling heroes, spiritual qualities, such as majesty, power, kindliness, effeminacy, vileness, are merely conveyed by the description of their physical correlatives. And we must not ignore this element in the representation of the Greek dramas. . . .

" I have devoted all this space to suggesting in some way the plastic character of the Greek mind, because it is *the fundamental characteristic* of Greek culture. If we are ignorant of this quality, it is in vain for us to strive at appreciating Greek antiquity, and at conceiving justly the position of classical archæology. We may now say with Welcker: ' That the plastic spirit which distinguishes the Greeks, gives to their mythology and poetry the highest worth and penetrates their whole culture, stands forth in greater clearness and richness in the art which takes its name from it than in all others. Therefore the plastic arts are a school of the science of antiquity in general, and a necessary and important constituent element of the studies of antiquity.'"

And again: "The palæstra was the real school for the Greek artist: here he spent his time and studied the human form; but not only in individuals. Constantly from his earliest youth, day by day, he had before his eye numbers of well-built youths in all attitudes and all actions, and these series of individual forms impressed themselves upon his mind, until they became an intrinsic part of his visual memory and imagination, forming, as it were, an *alphabet*, with which he could create at will things of great and new meaning. Just as letters, words, and grammar have become to us elements and units of thought, which lie ready to be composed, without effort, as far as they are concerned, into phrases, sentences, periods, books, poems, and orations, with great and new meaning and perfect form, so the existing human bodies and their changes in various attitudes and actions became such elements to the visual and imaginative mind of the ancient Greek artists. They did not require conscious attention, but became the parts of a great and new composition, with a meaning and spirit as a whole, lofty and high, yet ever intelligible, *because composed of these elements familiar to man from the daily suggestion of nature.*"

We have here placed within our grasp "the fundamental characteristic of Greek culture," its source, its method of development, and the secret of its power. In a word, it was the close observation of nature, in the intimacy of constant, familiar "converse," the acquirement of the "alphabet" of her elements, and their subsequent elaboration into new works of profound significance, through the legitimate, normal union of the imagination and realities,—based upon an observation "which directs the course of the imagination." In the light of its glorious results, it stands forth as a great "object lesson" to ourselves, teaching us, by its exemplification, the inestimable importance of the fundamental precept, "that the eye of the mind be never taken off from things themselves, but receive their images truly as they are,"—not only in science, but in the higher departments of thought, in poetry, in literature, and in art itself.

And now there came into activity an antagonistic force, in the person of one of the greatest intellects the world has ever known. This was the philosopher, Plato, "the father of Idealism in philosophy, in politics, in literature."

Gifted with natural endowments of the highest order, he developed a power of concentration in abstract contemplation that has perhaps never been equalled. And to this, he added the acquirement of all that the Greek "plastic" culture could afford in its best estate: so that he was enabled to clothe his ideas in such perfectly fitting material forms, and in such beautiful guise, that his prose, in the original, has almost the power and the charm of poetry.

Thus equipped, however, he taught, with singular power, a philosophy aggressively hostile to the plastic spirit which had produced his culture; weakening man's hold upon material existence, in this bond with nature; sundering its ties, through his emancipation into the joys of a more glorious liberty; diverting his mind from the close, objective study of the realities about him, and concentrating it upon the inward, subjective contemplation of "higher" ideals, evolved from within, paramount in value, and which were alone worthy of the soul's regard.

He gave this Idealism distinct utterance in his *Phaedo*, perhaps the most powerful of his works; modestly putting all into the mouth of Socrates, his deceased master. The following extracts, whose length seems justified by their importance, will give the reader a clear insight into the spirit, and the inherent tendencies of Plato's doctrine:

"And were we not saying long ago that the soul, when

using the body as an instrument of perception, that is to
say, when using the sense of sight or hearing or some
other sense (for the meaning of perceiving through the
body is perceiving through the senses)—were we not saying that the soul too is then dragged by the body into the
region of the changeable, and wanders and is confused;
the world spins round her, and she is like a drunkard,
when she touches change?

" Very true.

" But when returning into herself she reflects, then she
passes into the other world, the region of purity, and eternity, and immortality, and unchangeableness, which are
her kindred, and with them she ever lives, when she is by
herself and is not let or hindered; then she ceases from
her erring ways, and being in communion with the un-
unchanging is unchanging. And this state of the soul is
called wisdom?

" That is well and truly said, Socrates, he replied.

" The Lovers of knowledge are conscious that the soul
was simply fastened and glued to the body — until philosophy received her, she could only view real existence
through the bars of a prism, not in and through herself;
she was wallowing in the mire of every sort of ignorance,
and by reason of lust had become the principal accom-
plice in her own captivity. This was her original state;
and then, as I was saying, and as the lovers of knowledge
are well aware, philosophy, seeing how terrible was her
confinement, of which she was to herself the cause, received and gently comforted her and sought to release
her, pointing out that the eye and the ear and the other
senses are full of deception, and persuading her to retire
from them, and abstain from all but the necessary use of
them, and be gathered up and collected into herself, bidding her trust in herself and her own pure apprehension
of pure existence, and to mistrust whatever comes to her
through other channels and is subject to variation; for
such things are visible and tangible, but what she sees in
her own nature is intelligible and invisible."

" Is there or is there not an absolute justice?

" Assuredly there is.

" And an absolute beauty and absolute good?

" Of course.

" But did you ever behold any of them with your eyes?

" Certainly not.

" Or did you ever reach them with any other bodily sense? — and I speak not of these alone, but of absolute greatness, and health, and strength, and of the essence or true nature of everything. Has the reality of them ever been perceived by you through the bodily organs? or rather, is not the nearest approach to the knowledge of their several natures made by him who so orders his intellectual vision as to have the most exact conception of the essence of such thing which he considers?

" Certainly.

" And he attains to the purest knowledge of them who goes to each with the mind alone, not introducing or intruding in the act of thought sight or any other sense together with reason, but with the very light of the mind in her own clearness searches into the very truth of each; he who has got rid, so far as he can, of eyes and ears and, so to speak, of the whole body, these being in his opinion distracting elements which when they infect the soul hinder her from acquiring truth and knowledge—who, if not he, is likely to attain to the knowledge of true being? "

" When I was young, Cebes, I had a prodigious desire to know that department of philosophy which is called the investigation of nature; to know the causes of things, and why a thing is and is created or destroyed, appeared to me a lofty profession; and I was always agitating myself with the consideration of questions such as these: — Is the growth of animals the growth of some decay which the hot and cold principle contracts, as some have said? Is the blood the element with which we think, or the air, or the fire? or perhaps nothing of the kind — but the brain may be the originating power of the perceptions of

hearing and sight and smell, and memory and opinion
may come from them, and science may be based on memory and opinion when they have attained fixity. And then
I went on to examine the corruption of them, and then to
the things of heaven and earth, and at last I concluded
myself to be utterly and absolutely incapable of these
inquiries, as I will satisfactorily prove to you. . . . I
thought that as I had failed in the contemplation of true
existence, I ought to be careful that I did not lose the
eye of my soul; as people may injure their bodily eye by
observing and gazing on the sun during an eclipse, unless they take the precaution of looking at the image reflected in the water, or in some similar medium. So in
my own case, I was afraid that my soul might be blinded
altogether, if I looked at things with my eyes or tried to
apprehend them by the help of the senses. And I thought
that I had better have recourse to the world of mind, and
seek there the truth of existence. I dare say the simile
is not perfect—for I am very far from admitting that he
who contemplates existences through the medium of
thought, sees them only 'through a glass darkly,' any
more than he who considers them in action and operation.
However this was the method which I adopted: I first
assumed some principle which I judged to be the strong-
est, and then I affirmed as true what seemed to agree with
this, whether relating to the cause or to anything else:
and that which disagreed, I regarded as untrue."

The subtly seductive charm of this philosophy, or what
has been called its "intoxicating power," seems due, first,
to its insidious appeal to man's Egotism and his pride of
intellect: "Ye shall be as gods,"—and of your own might
partake of their nectar! And, as Bacon afterwards developed, this is but a refined form of idolatry — one of the
Idola of mankind.

And second, its power is intensified by the delusive sat-
isfactions it continually affords to the highest aspirations
of the soul. The beauty of goodness, absolute justice,

beauty and good, the perfection of wisdom and of virtue, are indeed lofty themes, whose profound contemplation awakens visions of heavenly bliss, and exalts the soul. But an ideal, nevertheless, in its essence, is an *abstraction*, —and abstractions, to just the extent in which they are insufficient representations of the reality, are inadequate, delusive, and inefficient.

This is exemplified even in the Mathematics, the home and very throne of abstractions. We would be the last to underrate the power of mathematical analysis; especially in view of the remarkable achievements of Clerk Maxwell, in its application to electricity,—working out the same conclusions at which Faraday had previously arrived by experiment, and also others which have since been verified. Nevertheless, and because of the inadequate correspondence of its abstractions to the reality, this analysis utterly breaks down before the simplest problem of the form of matter in its solidity.

Take the simple solid, the right, rectangular parallelopiped, and given the sum of all its lines, its aggregate surface, and its solid contents, determine its three dimensions. Or to put it in the usual form: let the sum of its three dimensions be a, the sum of their products, taken two and two, be b, and their direct product be c; find the value of these dimensions. As every high-school graduate knows, this involves the solution of an equation of the third degree, $x^3 - ax^2 + bx = c$, reducible to the form $x^3 - 3px = 2q$, where p and q are known values. This is resolved in the final formula,

$$x = \sqrt[3]{q + \sqrt{q^2 - p^3}} + \sqrt[3]{q - \sqrt{q^2 - p^3}}$$

which fulfils the requisite condition, that the value of the unknown quantity be expressed in terms of the known values. But as in this case, the roots are all *real*, the formula is a delusion, involving the *imaginary* quantity, $\sqrt{-1}$; and we have to throw away our analysis, and resort, in each instance, to long, tedious methods of arithmetical approximation.

This analysis is based upon fundamental abstractions. " A point is that which has neither length, breadth, nor thickness." " A line is that which has length, but neither breadth nor thickness." " A surface is that which has length and breadth, but no thickness." These are all imaginations: there are no such things in reality. But turning to our parallelopiped, we find that a point, in its actual, *mathematical* relations to this solid, is a *corner* where three of its surfaces intersect; and which partakes of the relations of each of those surfaces. There are eight of them: and as each has thus three aspects, there is a total of twenty-four aspects or relations under which the point exists upon this solid. In like manner, we find that the line is an *edge*, where two of its adjacent surfaces intersect; partaking of the relations of each of them. There are four of these lines, of equal length, in each of the three dimensions; and as each of them has its double aspect, there are again twenty-four aspects or relations in which the line subsists upon the solid. We find, also, that a surface, in its relations to the solid, is one of its *sides*, which are combined in three pairs of equals that are *opposite* each other, the opposite sides obliterating the surface when two blocks are superimposed,—as also the line is obliterated in the same way—thus disclosing the subsisting relations of "positive" and "negative," co-equal in their mutuality, and uniting in obliteration; the line, however, being thus capable of obliteration upon *each* of its two sides or aspects. (As each of the six sides of the solid may be viewed from any one of its four corners, in its relations thereto and to the other intersecting sides, it may be that here, also, there are twenty-four aspects or relations under which a surface may be regarded upon this solid.)

However meagre the foregoing " observations," it would seem clear, that there exists in the form of matter, in its solidity, a body of relations which find very inadequate expression in our present analysis. It may be possible, that this analysis might be so expanded, by the introduction of additional signs and symbols, that the final formula for the value of x would even infold the expression of each of the twelve lines of the solid, four of them, of the same length, in each dimension.

The method of approach would seem to lie in this direction : that laying aside, for the time, our conceptions based upon the present abstractions, with their ever unfolding and continually discouraging limitations, (the first of the formidable difficulties to be surmounted), and possibly availing ourselves of an expansion of Descartes' relations of " position," we go back to first principles, and study our blocks attentively, aye *inductively*, to discover the relations of their form in their actuality, and, if possible, to embody an expression of these relations in our analysis, —and thus, and thus only, may we ever hope to resolve this simplest, but fundamental problem of the form of matter in its actual solidity.

Again, and for further exemplification, let us turn to religion and ethics, where the noblest souls fondly cherish the highest ideals.

Remembering that the life of a people is reflected in its art, and studying the religious paintings of Italy in the time of Raphael, Andrea del Sarto, Sassoferrato and Carlo Dolci, we find there continually reflected a lofty, most beautiful ideal of the summit of religion in man. It is contemplative adoration, often rising even to the height of rapturous ecstacy. One has only to look into the faces of some of Carlo Dolci's sainted women, to see the satisfaction afforded to the soul by this blissful contemplation.

But this beautiful ideal was a wholly inadequate representation of the reality : it scarcely expressed a fraction of a tithe of true religion, in its rightful relations,—and witness the meagreness of the whole religious life of the people.

On the other hand, Professor Hoffman, in his masterpiece of religious painting of the Nineteenth century, "Christ in the Temple," has given expression, perhaps unconsciously, to the new spirit beginning to animate the religious life of our time, in its youth-like awakening into the dawning recognition of religion in its reality ; as an *activity*, flowing from within outward, in beneficent self-impartation to others. This is reflected in the picture, in the whole attitude and mien of Christ, in his manifest activity of mind and soul, in its outward movement, streaming forth through his eyes, informing his face, and expressed even in the poise of his fingers ; and with his whole energy concentrated upon his auditors.

In Jesus Christ, we have ever before us the living embodiment of pure, true religion, in its reality ; embracing all its relations both to God and humanity. As yet, we know but little of this reality, in its heights, and depths, and breadth ; simply because we have not closely studied him objectively, or inductively if you please, but instead, have allowed ideals, of our own forming, to cloud our minds and obscure our vision. But there, and there only, and through this objective study, will be found, not only the content of our own individual happiness and destiny, but the ultimate solution of the mighty ethical problems that are enforcing themselves upon society, and which must be solved.

Christ also unfolded the new law of wisdom : " He that doeth my will shall know the doctrine." Not idealization, but realization is the pathway to the highest wisdom: and Plato's Idealism is but the delusive shadow of the substance embodied in Christ.

Nor must we forget, what is too often overlooked, the actual weakness of humanity, and our pressing need for divine aid; which, in reality, has been provided, in the gift of the Holy Spirit, which, when the avenue is once opened by the sincere desire and the attitude of faith, illumines, aids, and comforts the soul, — working eventually the normal union of Divinity and humanity in our being, the ultimate destiny of the race. "That they all may be one: as thou, Father, art in me, and I in thee, that they also may be one in us."

In the presence of such realities, pride of intellect is extinguished in humility of soul: and ideals, of man's creation, pale and shrivel into nothingness. In life, in a word, an ideal, in so far as it is satisfying, in so far as it is reverenced in itself, in so far as it diverts the mind from the continued study of the reality, is *vicious*.

Having thus caught a glimpse, not only into the spirit and tendency of Plato's doctrine, and its essential hostility to the plastic spirit animating the Greek culture, but also into its sweetly seductive power, and its tenacious hold upon man, we need not wonder at the marked and long-continued decadence that immediately ensued. With Aristotle, Plato's disciple, and his delusive blending of the Platonic spirit and the plastic tendency in the power of logic, this growing bond with nature was finally and effectually broken, and the light which had been the source of this illumination was extinguished.*

---

* Other powerful forces, social, political, and material, doubtless contributed to this end: but obviously, within the limitations of a single chapter, we can merely touch upon outlines, and these only of the intellectual forces. Throughout, what we have not said, but which ought to be said, would indeed fill volumes: and we trust that the reader will regard our work merely as a thread of suggestion, perhaps, in this respect, helpful in his own independent and profitable study of the theme.

25

What followed Plato is thus pointedly outlined by Professor Jowett, in the last edition (1892) of his admirable *Translation of Plato's Dialogues*, from which the foregoing extracts were quoted :

" The dreary waste which follows, beginning with the Alexandrian writers and even before them in the platitudes of Isocrates and his school, spreads over much more than a thousand years. And from this decline the Greek language and literature, unlike the Latin, which has come to life in new forms and been developed into the great European languages, never recovered. This monotony of literature, without merit, without genius, and without character, is a *phenomenon* which deserves more attention than it has hitherto received ; it is a phenomenon unique in the history of the world. How could there have been so much cultivation, so much diligence in writing, and so little mind or real creative power ? Why did a thousand years invent nothing better than Sibylline books, Orphic poems, Byzantine imitations of classical histories, Christian reproductions of Greek plays, novels like the silly and obscene romances of Longus and Heliodorus, innumerable forged epistles, a great many epigrams, biographies of the meanest and most meagre description, a sham philosophy which was the bastard progeny of the union between Hellas and the East ? Only in Plutarch, in Lucian, in Longinus, in the Roman emperors Marcus Aurelius and Julian, in some of the Christian fathers, are there any traces of good sense or originality, or any power of arousing the interest of later ages. And when new books ceased to be written, why did hosts of grammarians and interpreters flock in, who never attain to any sound notion either of grammar or interpretation ? Why did the physical sciences never arrive at any true knowledge or make any real progress ? Why did poetry droop and languish ? Why did history degenerate into fable ? Why did words lose their power of expression ? Why were ages of external greatness and magnificence attended by all the signs of decay in the human mind which are possible ?

"To these questions many answers may be given, which if not the true causes are at least recorded among the symptoms of decline." *

But though he discusses a variety of matters, they are, as he frankly states, rather the "symptoms" than the causes: and singularly enough, possibly because he was so imbued with the Platonic spirit, he fails to even touch upon the root of the difficulty.

---

* The mind, like the body, subsists upon nutriment, neither can it evolve this nutriment from within itself. And, obviously, when its hold upon the exterior sources of supply is weakened, its growth will be stunted, and "decay" will follow. Or as Goethe puts it:

"Just so with the poet;—he deserves not the name while he only speaks out of his few subjective feelings; but as soon as he can appropriate to himself and express the world, he is a poet. Then he is inexhaustible, and can be always new, while a subjective nature has soon talked out his little internal material, and is at last ruined by mannerism. . . . I will now tell you something which you will often find in your experience. All eras in a state of decline and dissolution are subjective; on the other hand, all progressive eras have an objective tendency. Our present time is retrograde, for it is subjective: we see this not merely in poetry, but also in painting, and much besides. Every healthy effort, on the contrary, is directed from the inward to the outward world, as you will see in all great eras, which have been really in a state of progression, and all of an objective nature."

Again, referring to himself: "I have never observed nature with a view to poetical production; but because my early drawing of landscapes and my later *studies in natural science* led me to a constant, close observation of natural objects, I have gradually learned nature by heart, even to the minutest details, so that, when I need anything as a poet, it is at my command; and I cannot easily sin against truth."

And again, in criticism of a certain poem: "I also think the poem a very weak production. It bears no traces of external observation; it is wholly mental, *and that is not in the right way*."—*Conversations with Eckermann.*

But three centuries ago, there was one mind that thoroughly grasped the situation. Francis Bacon, in the very midst of this waste and in its darkness, discerned, first, and perhaps foremost, that it *was* a waste ; second, its cause ; and third, the remedy. All this, which appears in detail in his works, is concisely indicated in the opening sentence of his *Great Instauration:*

" *FRANCIS OF VERULAN reasoned thus with himself, and judged it to be for the interest of the present and future generations that they should be made acquainted with his thoughts :*

" Being convinced that the human intellect makes its own difficulties, not using the true helps which are at man's disposal soberly and judiciously ; whence follows manifold ignorance of things, and by reason of that ignorance mischiefs innumerable ; he thought all trial should be made, whether that commerce between the mind of man and the nature of things, which is more precious than anything on earth, or at least than anything that is of the earth, might by any means be restored to its perfect and original condition, or if that may not be, yet reduced to a better condition than that in which it now is."

This great Thought, of the inestimable preciousness to man of this bond with nature in an intercourse of rightful intimacy, of the innumerable mischiefs wrought through his abnormal divorcement, and of the countless blessings that would follow its restoration, was the inspiring theme of his work, whose purpose was to effect this restoration. And later, in a glow of enthusiasm, awakened by the grandeur of the thought, he sings the new song of this reunion, in these eloquent words :

" The explanation of which things, and of the true relation between the nature of things and the nature of the mind, is as the strewing and decoration of the bridal chamber of the Mind and the Universe, the Divine Goodness

assisting ; out of which marriage let us hope (and be this
the prayer of the bridal song) there may spring helps to
man, and a line and race of inventions that may in some
degree subdue and overcome the necessities and miseries
of humanity."

Possessed of this thought when he was but a youth, he
then devoted himself, single-handed and alone, "not even
communicating my thoughts to a single individual," to its
development and implantation in the mind and heart of
mankind ; confident that he would thereby turn the tide
which for two thousand years had borne the race through
a barren waste, and set it irrevocably towards regions
fruitful in blessings.

He therefore besought man to look into nature, through
his senses, and in an humble spirit :

" Wherein if I have made any progress, the way has
been opened to me by no other means than the true and
legitimate humiliation of the human spirit. For all those
who before me have applied themselves to the invention
of arts have but cast a glance or two upon facts and examples and experience, and straightway proceeded, as if
invention were nothing more than an exercise of thought,
to invoke their own spirits to give them oracles. I, on the
contrary, dwelling purely and constantly among the facts
of nature, withdraw my intellect from them no further
than may suffice to let the images and rays of natural objects meet in a point, as they do in the sense of vision ;
whence it follows that the strength and excellency of the
wit has but little to do in the matter."

And again : " The access also to this work hath been
by that port or passage, which the divine Majesty (who
is unchangeable in his ways) doth infallibly continue and
observe ; that is, the felicity wherewith he hath blessed
an humility of mind, such as rather laboreth to spell and
so by degrees to read in the volume of his creatures, than
to solicit and urge and, as it were, to invocate a man's own
spirit to divine and give oracles unto him. For as in the

inquiry of divine truth, the pride of man hath ever inclined to leave the oracles of God's word and to vanish in
the mixture of their own inventions; so in the self-same
manner, in the inquisition of nature they have ever left the
oracles of God's works, and adored the deceiving and deformed imagery which the unequal mirrors of their own
minds have represented unto them. Nay, it is a point fit
and necessary in the front and beginning of this work,
without hesitation or reservation to be professed, that it
is no less true in this human kingdom of knowledge than
in God's kingdom of heaven, that no man shall enter into
it, *except he become first as a little child.*"

"Again, it will be thought, no doubt, that the goal and
mark of knowledge which I myself set up (the very point
which I object to in others) is not the true or the best;
for that *contemplation of truth* is a thing worthier and
loftier than all utility and magnitude of works; and that
this long and anxious dwelling with experience and matter and the fluctuations of individual things, drags down
the mind to earth, or rather sinks it to a very Tartarus
of turmoil and confusion; removing and withdrawing it
from the serene tranquility of abstract wisdom, a condition far more heavenly. Now to this I readily assent;
and indeed this which they point at as so much to be preferred, is the very thing of all others which I am about.
For I am building in the human understanding a true
model of the world, such as it is in fact, not such as a
man's own reason would have it to be; a thing which cannot be done without a very diligent dissection and anatomy of the world. But I say that those foolish and apish
images of worlds, which the fancies of men have created
in philosophical systems, must be utterly scattered to the
winds. Be it known then how vast a difference there is
(as I said above) between the Idols of the human mind
and the Ideas of the divine. The former are nothing more
than arbitrary *abstractions;* the latter are the creator's
own stamp upon creation, impressed and defined in matter by true and exquisite lines. Truth therefore and util-

ity are here the very same things: and works themselves
are of greater value as *pledges of truth* than as contributing to the comforts of life." *

And again : " For we copy the sin of our first parents
while we suffer for it. They wished to be like God, but
their posterity wish to be even greater. For we create
worlds, we direct and domineer over nature, we will have
it that all things *are* as in our folly we think they should
be, not as seems fittest to the Divine wisdom, or as they
are found to be in fact; and I know not whether we more
distort the facts of nature or our own wits; but we clearly
impress the stamp of our own image on the creatures and
works of God, instead of carefully examining and recognizing in them the stamp of the Creator himself. Wherefore our dominion over creatures is a second time forfeited,
not undeservedly; and whereas after the fall of man some
power of resistance of creatures was still left to him—the
power of subduing and managing them by true and solid
arts—yet this too, through our insolence, and because we
desire to be like God, and to follow the dictates of our
own reason, we in great part lose. If, therefore, there be
any humility towards the Creator, any reverence for or
disposition to magnify His works, any charity for man and
anxiety to relieve his sorrows and necessities, any love of

---

* " But it is manifest that Plato in his opinion of Ideas, as
one that had a wit of elevation situate as upon a cliff, did descry
that forms were the true object of knowledge; but lost the real
fruit of his opinion; by considering of forms as abstracted from
matter, and not confined and determined by matter; and so
turning his opinion upon Theology, wherewith all his natural
philosophy is infected."

" Again, the age in which natural philosophy was seen to
flourish most among the Greeks, was but a brief particle of
time; for in early ages the seven Wise Men, as they were called,
(all except Thales) applied themselves to morals and politics;
and in later times, when Socrates had drawn down philosophy
from heaven to earth, moral philosophy became more fashionable than ever, and *diverted* the minds of men from the philosophy of nature."

truth in nature, any hatred of darkness, any desire for the
purification of the understanding, we must entreat men
again and again to discard, or at least set apart for a while,
these volatile and preposterous philosophies, which have
preferred theses to hypotheses, led experience captive, and
triumphed over the works of God: and to approach with
humility and veneration to unroll the volume of Creation,
to linger and meditate therein, and with minds washed
clean from opinions, to study it in purity and integrity.
For this is that sound and language which went forth into
all lands, and did not incur the confusion of Babel; this
should men study to be perfect in, and becoming again as
little children, condescend to take the alphabet of it into
their hands, and spare no pains to search and unravel the
interpretation thereof, but pursue it strenuously and persevere even unto death."

Behold the sharp contrast and the essential antagonism
between the Platonic and the Baconian spirit, — and by
their fruits ye shall know them!

Bacon, also, with comprehensive wisdom, warned mankind against the errors to which the senses are liable, and
also against the subtle infirmities to which the mind itself
is subject; providing for these defects safeguards and
efficient remedies. He exposed the weakness of Logic,
in that it " is not nearly subtle enough to deal with nature ":

" The syllogism consists of propositions; propositions
of words; and words are the tokens and signs of notions.
Now if the very notions of the mind (which are the soul
of words and the basis of the whole structure) be improp-
erly and over-hastily abstracted from facts, vague, not
sufficiently definite, faulty in short in many ways, the
whole edifice tumbles. I therefore reject the syllogism;
and that not only as regards principles (for to principles
the logicians themselves do not apply it) but also as regards middle propositions; which, though obtainable no
doubt by the syllogism, are, when so obtained, barren of

works, remote from practice, and altogether unavailable
for the active department of the sciences."

And for Logic he substituted his " *Interpretation of
Nature*" by orderly Induction; unfolding at length both
its spirit and its method in his *Novum Organum*, to which
the reader is referred. Regarding its purpose:

" For I consider induction to be that form of demonstration which upholds the sense, and closes with nature,
and comes to the very brink of operation, if it does not
actually deal with it. . . . Now my plan is to proceed
regularly and gradually from one axiom to another, so that
the most general are not reached till the last: but then,
when you do come to them, you find them to be not empty
notions, but well defined, and such as nature would really
recognize as her first principles, and such as lie at the
heart and marrow of things. . . . For the induction of
which the logicians speak, which proceeds by simple enu-
meration, is a puerile thing; concludes at hazard; is
always liable to be upset by a contradictory instance;
takes into account only what is known and ordinary; and
leads to no result. Now what the sciences stand in need
of is a form of induction which shall analyse experience
and take it to pieces, and by a due process of exclusion
and rejection lead to an inevitable conclusion. And if
that ordinary mode of judgment practised by the logicians
was so laborious, and found exercise for such great wits,
how much more labor must we prepare to bestow upon
this other, which is extracted not merely out of the depths
of the mind, but out of the very bowels of nature. . . .
And lastly, the information of the sense itself I sift and
examine in many ways. For certain it is that the senses
deceive; but then, at the same time, they supply the means
of discovering their own errors; only the errors are here,
the means of discovery are to seek. . . .

" To meet these difficulties, I have sought on all sides
diligently and faithfully to provide helps for the sense —
substitutes to supply its failures, rectifications to correct

its errors ; and this I endeavor to accomplish not so much by instruments as by *experiments.* For the subtlety of experiments is far greater than that of the sense itself, even when assisted by exquisite instruments ; such experiments, I mean, as are skilfully and artificially devised for the express purpose of determining the point in question. To the immediate and proper perception of the sense therefore I do not give much weight ; but I contrive that the office of the sense shall be only to judge of the experiment, and that the experiment itself shall judge of the thing. And, thus I conceive that I perform the office of a true priest of the sense (from which all knowledge in nature must be sought, unless men mean to go mad) and a not unskilful interpreter of its oracles ; and that while others only profess to uphold and cultivate the sense, I do so in fact. Such then are the provisions I make for finding the genuine light of nature and kindling and bringing it to bear."

And finally, he put this Induction to a crucial test, in the discovery of the then unknown nature of Heat. A discovery so true, so far in advance of his age, that it has given rise to one of the profound misconceptions regarding Bacon, which this generation has *inherited.*

Some of us doubtless remember studying in our youth Professor Comstock's *Natural Philosophy,* where we were taught, that " Heat is an imponderable substance called *caloric.*" And while the scientific world was under the sway of such a philosophy, Bacon's conclusion could only be regarded as visionary and preposterous. Whewell, in his *Philosophy of the Inductive Sciences,* says :

" But we cannot be surprised, that in attempting to exemplify the method which he recommended, he should have failed. For the method could be exemplified only by some important discovery in physical science ; and great discoveries, even with the most perfect methods, do not come at command. . . . Accordingly, Bacon's *Inqui-*

sition into the nature of Heat, which is given in the Second Book of the *Novum Organum* as an example of the mode of interrogating nature, cannot be looked upon otherwise than as a complete failure."

Devey and Spedding, editors of Bacon's works, take the same view. And as late as 1886, Richard A. Proctor, the eminent astronomer, accepting the traditional opinion, in a letter published in the *Arena* of Nov., 1893, speaks of Bacon as " failing egregriously in his attempt on the sole detail to which he applied his own method."

But was it an egregious failure ? Turning to his *Novum Organum*, we find that Bacon, at the end of his orderly Induction, arrives at this conclusion :

" From a survey of the instances, all and each, the nature of which heat is a particular case appears to be Motion. . . . When I say of Motion that it is the genus of which heat is a species, I would be understood to mean, not that heat generates motion or that motion generates heat (though both are true in certain cases), but that Heat itself, *its essence and quiddity*, is Motion and nothing else. . . .

" Heat is an expansive motion, whereby a body strives to dilate and stretch itself to a larger sphere or dimension than it had previously occupied . . . that heat is a motion of expansion, not uniformly of the whole body together, but in the smaller parts of it ; and at the same time checked, repelled, and beaten back, so that the body acquires a motion alternative, perpetually quivering, striving and struggling, and irritated by repercussion, whence springs the fury of fire and heat. . . .

" Now from this our First Vintage it follows that the Form or true definition of heat (heat, that is, in relation to the universe, not simply in its relation to man) is, in few words, as follows : *Heat is a motion, expansive, restrained, and acting in its strife upon the smaller particles of bodies.*" (Bacon's italics.)

Professor George F. Barker, of the University of Pennsylvania, in his able work on *Physics*, recently published, states the present view of the nature of heat in these words :

"*Heat the Energy of Molecular Motion.* — Is heat-energy in the kinetic or in the potential form ? Davy said in 1812 : 'The immediate cause of the phenomenon of heat, then, is motion, and the laws of its communication are precisely the same as the laws of the communication of motion.' This in modern language is equivalent to the statement that heat is kinetic energy ; not evidently of the mass, since the hot body may be at rest ; but of the molecules. We know that one of the ways in which a hot body cools is by transferring its energy to another and a colder body not in contact with it ; and we shall study later the mechanism of this radiating process. One thing about it is certain, however, and that is that it consists in a motion of the intervening medium. The hot body communicates motion to the medium, and the cold body receives motion from this medium. We conclude, therefore, that the surface of a hot body must be in motion ; and because radiation may take place as well from the interior of a body as from its exterior, we also conclude that the body must be in motion throughout its entire mass. This view of the case is in entire accord with the kinetic theory of matter already discussed, which supposes the molecules of matter to be actively in motion. The motion to which heat-energy is due ' must therefore be a motion of parts too small to be observed separately ; the motions of different parts at the same instant must be in different directions ; and the motion of any one part must, at least in solid bodies, be such that however fast it moves it never reaches a sensible distance from the point from which it started ' (Maxwell)."

As we carefully compare the foregoing statements, we can hardly realize that the one is a conclusion put forth three centuries ago, when there were comparatively no science or scientific instruments, and wrought out from the necessarily crude observations of the unaided senses ;

and that the other is the expression of the latest conclusion of science, the product of a century of special research, conducted with the most delicate instruments, and by the brightest men of the time.

Indeed, Bacon's achievement is so extraordinary, that we are tempted to do an injustice to his Induction, and to ascribe his success to his insight "into the heart and marrow of things," in this intimacy with nature which to him was so precious, in the comprehension of her voice.

And this inclination is encouraged by some of his observations, which exhibit a perception almost intuitive in its penetration. Thus regarding gravity: While he sometimes spoke of the motion of things towards the centre of the earth, "which was the opinion of the ancients," in its serious consideration, he says:

"Inquire what is the line and direction of the motion of gravity; how far it follows the centre or mass of the earth, how far the centre of the body itself, that is the *strife* and pressure of its parts. For these centres, though convenient for demonstration, are of no effect in nature." And again: "For as for what is said of motion to the earth's centre, it would indeed be a potent kind of Nothing that should *draw* such great things to it; nor is body acted upon, except by body."

And again, he says: "For whoever shall set aside the imaginary divorce between superlunary and sublunary things, and shall well observe the most universal appetites and passions of matter (which are powerful in both globes and make themselves felt through the universal frame of things), will obtain clear information of heavenly things from those that are seen amongst us." And again: "For these supposed divorces between ethereal and sublunary things seem to me but figments, superstitions mixed with rashness; seeing it is most certain that very many effects, as of expansion, contraction, impression, cession, collection into masses, *attraction*, repulsion, assimilation, union, and the like, have place not only here with us, but also in the heights of heaven and the depths of the earth."

A general proposition which has since become one of the fundamental recognitions of modern science, not only regarding gravity, but as to all the other properties of matter.*

---

* "And yet this is not more certain than that the bodies of both globes have common inclinations, passions, and motions. We should therefore follow *the unity of nature*, and rather distinguish than sever such things and not make a breach in the contemplation of them. . . . And these things I have spoken not out of zeal to introduce *a new opinion*, but because I foresee, not without experience, but instructed by example, that these fabulous divorces and distinctions of things and regions, beyond what truth admits of, will be a great obstacle to true philosophy and the contemplation of nature."

We may profitably compare the foregoing with the following concise statement of our present advancement, by Professor John Fiske:

"In these latter days, since the law of gravitation has been extended to the sidereal heavens, and spectrum analysis has begun to deal with nebulæ, there is abundant proof that properties of matter and processes with which we are familiar on this earth are to be found in some of the remotest bodies which the telescope can reach, and it is thus forcibly impressed upon us that all are parts of one stupendous whole."

It is true, there are many crudities found in Bacon's works: but they arose out of the old scholastic philosophy from which he emerged. And obviously, the just and fair judgment of his work is to formed by regarding it from the standpoint of what preceded him, though under the illumination afforded by our present knowledge. Thus, he has been criticised for his use of "Forms"; when, in fact, he took the old, empty, scholastic formula, "of the Forms of things," and infused life into it by his definition:

"And even in the case of simple natures I would not be understood to speak of abstract forms and ideas, either not defined in matter at all, or ill defined. For when I speak of forms I

Again, one of the most vital and fruitful conceptions of modern science is that matter is not a dead, inert thing, but is itself the seat of energy, in intense activity. But this was with Bacon a fundamental perception, strongly urged. In his *Principles and Origins*, he says:

" Now an abstract principle is not a being; and again, a mortal being is not a principle; so that a necessity plainly inevitable drives men's thoughts (if they would be consistent) to the *atom;* which is a true being, having matter, form, dimension, place, *resistance*, appetite, *motion*, and emanations; which likewise, amid the destruction of all natural bodies, remains unshaken and eternal." Again: " Notwithstanding in the body of the atom are the elements of all bodies, and in the motion and virtue of the atom are the beginnings of all motions and virtues." He accordingly criticises Telesius for coupling with the idea of the constant quantity of matter that it is inert and passive: " Now in these assertions there is a great mental error,—an error truly wonderful, were it not that consent and common and inveterate opinion take away the wonder. For there is scarce any error comparable to that of taking this virtue implanted in matter (by which it saves itself from destruction, insomuch that not the smallest portion of matter can either be overpowered by the whole mass of the world, or destroyed by the force and power of all agents together, or in any way so annihilated and reduced to order, but that it both occupies some space, and *maintains a resistance with impenetrable dimensions*, and itself attempts something in its turn, and never deserts itself) not to be an *active* virtue; whereas, on the contrary, it is of all virtues far the most powerful, and

---

mean nothing more than those laws and determinations of absolute actuality, which govern and constitute any simple nature, as heat, light, weight, in every kind of matter and subject that is susceptible of them. Thus the Form of Heat or the Form of Light is the same thing as the Law of Heat or the Law of Light."—*Novum Organum.*

plainly insuperable, and as it were mere fate and necessity."

Moreover, there is here an acceptance of the principle
of the Conservation of Matter, and its statement in terms
that touch to the quick its occasion. And elsewhere, he
says: "The sum of matter in the universe is always the
same ; and there is no operation either from nothing or
to nothing."

Professor Barker, in his *Physics*, following the recognized authorities, (for who has cared to study at first hand
Bacon's works?—while all seem unaware of their wonderfully quickening power), states the present view of scientific men as follows :

"The close of the last century was made memorable in
science by the discovery of the illustrious Lavoisier that
matter is indestructible by human agency; and that consequently the amount of matter in the universe is constant."
And as to its importance: "As the result of modern investigation, it is believed that matter is absolutely unalterable
in quantity by any agency at the command of man. This
great principle, which has been called the law of the Conservation of Matter, lies at the basis of chemistry and
demands absolute equality in mass on the two sides of all
chemical equations." *

---

* "*V. That the Quantity of Matter is fixed, and that Change
takes place without Loss.* — That all things are changed, and
that nothing really perishes, and that the sum of matter remains
exactly the same, is sufficiently certain. And as it needed the
omnipotence of God to create something out of nothing, so it
requires the same omnipotence to reduce something to nothing.
. . . From these positions therefore I have now thought good
to draw three precepts or counsels for use, in order that men
may deal with nature more skilfully, and by that means more
successfully. Of these the first is, that men should frequently
call upon nature to render her account ; that is, when they perceive that a body which was before manifest to the sense has
escaped and disappeared, *they should not admit or liquidate*

And in the same connection, Bacon gives clear state-ment to a principle of profound interest to-day:

"For the summary law of being and nature, which pen-etrates and runs through the vicissitudes of things (the same which is described in the phrase, 'the work which God worketh from the beginning to the end'), that is, the *force* [in the Latin, *vis*, which would now be translated "energy"] implanted by God in these first particles, from the multiplication whereof all the variety of things pro-ceeds and is made up, is a thing which the thoughts of man may offer at but can hardly take in. . . . But in the meantime I make this assumption; that the ancients set down the first matter (such as may be the beginning of things), as having form and qualities, not as abstract, potential, and unshapen. And certainly that despoiled and passive matter seems altogether a fiction of the human mind. . . . But almost all the ancients, as Epedocles, Anaxagoras, Anaximenes, Heraclitus, and Democritus, though in other respects they differed about the first mat-ter, agreed in this, that they set down matter as *active*, as having some form, as dispensing that form, and as *having the principle of motion in itself*. Nor can anyone think otherwise, unless he plainly deserts experience. Therefore all these submitted their minds to the nature of things. Whereas Plato made over the world to thoughts; and Aristotle made over thoughts to words; men's studies even then tending to dispute and discourse, and forsak-ing the stricter inquiry of truth. Hence such opinions are rather to be condemned in the whole, than confuted separately in the parts; for they are the opinions of those who wish to talk much, and know little. And this abstract matter is the matter of disputation, not of the universe. But one who philosophises rightly and in order, should dissect nature and not abstract her (but they who will

---

the account before it has been shown them where the body has gone to, and into what it has been received."—*Thoughts on the Nature of Things.*

not dissect are obliged to abstract); and must by all means
consider the first matter as united to the first form, and
likewise to the first principle of motion, as it is found.
For *the abstraction of motion* also has begotten an infinite number of fancies about souls, lives, and the like; as
if these were not satisfied by matter and form, but de-
pended on principles of their own.   But these three are
by no means to be separated, only distinguished; *and
matter (whatever it is) must be held to be so adorned,
furnished, and formed, that all virtue, essence, action,
and natural motion, may be the consequence and emana-
tion thereof.*"

Truly a mighty evolution — wherein all physical phenomena, in their almost infinite variety and complexity,
are but developments of the simple, primal forces inherent
in matter! *

We have seen (see *ante*, page 101) how Bacon's extraordinary, but normal, intellectual development had its
" birth " in his youthful conviction of the inestimable
importance of the renewal of this bond with nature and
his devotion to its accomplishment.   It brought him into
such intimate sympathy with nature that his powers grew
and developed in a vitality and vigor, and with a sound-

---

* "Now those motions are to be chiefly inquired, which are
simple, primitive, and fundamental, whereof the rest are composed.   For it is most certain that by how much the more simple motions are discovered, by so much will the power of man
be increased and made independent of materials special and
prepared, and strengthened for the production of new works.
Surely as the words or terms of all languages, in an immense
variety, are composed of a few simple letters, so all the actions
and powers of things are formed by a few natures and original
elements of simple motions.   And it were shame that men
should have examined so carefully the tinklings of their own
voice, and yet should be so ignorant of *the voice of nature;* and
as in the early ages (before letters were invented), should discern only compound sounds and words, not distinguishing the
elements and letters."—*Thoughts on the Nature of Things.*

ness of sense, only possible to one drawing nourishment continually from her inexhaustible fount, — as was likewise the case with the ancient Greeks ; and which seems, indeed, to be nature's divinely appointed reward for this absolute ' submission of the mind unto things.'

The same force brought him into a like sympathetic comprehension of humanity, a part of the Creator's universal kingdom. His mastery of the human heart, its motives, its passions, its affections, and its springs of action, was so complete that we ever recognize, instinctively, the verity of his utterances. He not only came into touch with the great heart of humanity, but he deeply felt the power and mystery of its common bond, in the unity of its origin, its nature, and its destiny. This is shown, incidentally, in a remark in his *Natural History:*

"The delight which men have in popularity, fame, honor, submission, and subjection of other men's minds, wills, or affections, (although these things may be desired for other ends) seemeth to be a thing in itself, without contemplation of consequence, grateful and agreeable to the nature of man. This thing (surely) is not without some signification, *as if all spirits and souls of men came forth out of one divine limbus;* else why should men be so much affected with that which others think or say?"

And again, in his *Novum Organum:* "The Idols of the Tribe have their foundation in human nature itself, and *in the tribe or race of men.* . . . Such then are the idols which I call *Idols of the Tribe;* and which take their rise either from the homogeneity of the substance of the human spirit, or from its preoccupation, or from its narrowness, or from its restless motion, or from an infusion of the affections, or from the incompetency of the senses, or from the mode of impression."

This profound realization of the common bond of humanity, wherein we all partake of the same nature, and are one in origin and destiny, was undoubtedly one of the sources of Bacon's universality, in his interpretation of mankind. Indeed, the creative artist (whether in literature, or working upon canvas or stone) must bathe in these deep waters, losing his own petty self-consciousness in the broader, deeper consciousness of the race, if he would adequately " voice" nature and humanity in their characteristic universality, informing even the particularity he unfolds,— the lofty, but rightful standard by which he must measure his work.

We have also seen how the " plastic " spirit penetrated all the higher activities of the Greeks, animating their literature and their art,—the underlying source of their surpassing excellence. And Bacon also carried this renovating bond with nature, with its vivifying spirit, into literature.

He thus dignified immeasurably the work of the Historian ; elevating him to the side of the poet, as a revealer and interpreter of mankind. (See *ante*, page 123.) And he reinaugurated in practice what is just beginning to be recognized as the rightful function of the historian—" making history a living expression of the character of man,— a continuous revelation of the laws and forces of life." (Mabie.)

He wrote the first *live* history of modern times, though he was dealing with an uneventful period ; " nearer to the merits of Thucydides than any English history that I know," says Spedding ; tracing effects to their causes, and developing the action out of the workings of the motives and passions of the human heart, as they were brought into play by the circumstances; so that we are enabled to " learn the secrets of human nature " even from his history,— another " object lesson " of profound import to future historians, who, in writing the records of his life, would reveal man unto himself, through the developments of his past experience.

And in the Shakespeare, he thus dignified Poetry itself ; making it the highest, the most beautiful and complete objective expression and revelation of nature and humanity,—the authentic reflection and interpretation of universal life. Recognizing the inner source of this power, we discern that, in reality, he *exalts* the poet, in making him 'perform the office of a true priest of the sense, and an interpreter of its oracles.' Gervinus, with comprehensive vision, recognizes this fundamental characteristic of the Poet, and gives it expression in these significant words :

"Shakespeare was a sensualist [in the German sense of "plastic "] of a thoroughly intuitive nature. He was perhaps even more than Goethe, 'devoted to the holy spirit of the senses,' and averse to one-sided *abstractions* and philosophic speculations. Nature and humanity were his book of revelation, and experience the source of his wisdom. His sense must have been the soundest that ever man possessed ; his eye a smooth mirror, his ear an echo, which repeated all sounds and images with the utmost fidelity." *

* See, in exemplification, Perdita's exquisite handling of the Flowers, *ante*, page 147.

In this connection, a further remark of Charles Waldstein is very significant, especially in its bearing upon the lines of our future cultivation, — for " observation " is as fundamental and as vital to art (including poetry) as to science :

"We are bad observers. For several years I have made a point of inquiring into the power or rather feebleness of observation of people I meet, and it was strange to notice the effect when their attention was directed to this side of their nature. Unlike the M. Jourdain who was not aware of a power which he really possessed, they are astonished to find that they are hardly possessed of a faculty, with which they were always in the habit of crediting themselves. With a view to testing the above. I asked one who was present while I was writing these lines the color of his mother's eyes. He informed me that she was dead. ' But do n't you remember it ?' After some attempts he found he could not. But later on he started up with, ' they

And Richard Grant White says: "One of them, himself
a poet, Pope, passed in happy phrase one of the most
penetrative judgments that has ever been uttered upon
him, when he said: 'The poetry of Shakespeare is inspiration indeed. He is not so much an imitator as an instrument of Nature; and it is not so just to say that he speaks
for her, as that she speaks through him.'"

This absolute fidelity to "the voice of nature," heard
and focussed through the senses, is the foundation principle of the "new law" of poetry to which Gervinus refers:
though, unfortunately, he is compelled to remark, that while
it has taken two centuries to understand the Poet, "but
very little has ever been executed in his sense." The
secret of this lamentable paucity, however, is enwrapped
in the irrepressible conflict still waging between the Plat-
tonic and the Baconian spirit.

Plato and Bacon! these two powerful intellects stand
forth in lofty grandeur, as the self-consecrated apostles of
two mighty, antagonistic forces, contending for supremacy over the world's thought and activities. In the domain
of physical science, the issue has already been happily
determined. But elsewhere, plainly, the conflict is still
on: though even now its final glorious outcome can be
clearly foreseen.

We have heard from Goethe's own lips (see *ante*, page
349) how in early youth he caught from Bacon, through
the medium of his Shakespeare, the flame of the inspiration which thereafter animated his whole life's work,—and
we all know the result. This influence was received through
the instinctive comprehension of Bacon's work in its essential principles, and through the touch of his vivifying spirit.

And if we rightly estimate the forces and the conditions
were blue.' 'How comes it that you know now and did not
know before?' I asked. 'Because I remembered that two years
ago we spoke about it.' He had no image in his eye, but he
remembered the words."

involved, as this intimate comprehension of his work becomes more general, the validity and the universality of his principles more widely acknowledged, and as the quickening power of his spirit is more deeply felt, and its inspiration more generally diffused, Bacon's influence, in its growing predominance over the Platonic spirit, is destined ultimately to effect a revolution, as pronounced, as felicitous, and as complete and enduring, in poetry, in literature, in art, and in all man's higher activities, as it has wrought in the past in physical science. For it concerns " not only the contemplative happiness, but the whole fortunes, and affairs, and powers, and works of men."

CHAPTER XIII.—Continued.

AND yet, as the reader has doubtless remarked, there is much in the Shakespeare that transcends the reality. And here again, we recognize the thoroughly consistent personality of its author: for, as has been well said, "It is the characteristic of genius to comprehend all contradictories in itself." In his many-sided, broad "whole-mindedness," Bacon clearly distinguished the difference between art and science; recognizing that art occupies a distinct realm, having laws and principles of its own, and with well defined lines of demarkation separating it from the domain of science. These distinctions are based upon the fundamental fact that a work of art is essentially a *creation* of man, bearing the impress of his formative hand. Thus, in contradistinction to science, one of its controlling principles, contributing materially to its power —because it is responsive to a deep craving of the human spirit—is *intensification*. (The word is used in the broadest sense; for the Greeks in their art gave intensity even to *repose*.)*

---

* This intensification is aptly illustrated in Greek art, in its representation of the human form in a substantial perfection unknown in real life: "The Greek sculptor could readily form in his constructive imagination an individual figure, which, *true to nature in all its parts*, was still the bearer of these characteristics of typical life. Especially among the athletes of the Palæstra his eye received impressions of numberless individual forms, which became as it were his materials, with which, without an effort, he could construct new and great forms, individual works of art unmatched in real life."—*Essays on the Art of Pheidias.*

This essential principle, exemplified upon almost every page of the Shakespeare, was fundamental with Bacon, who gave it clear exposition in his *Advancement of Learning*, Second Book:

"Poetry is a part of learning in measure of words for the most part restrained, but in all other parts extremely licensed, and doth truly refer to the Imagination; which, being not tied to the laws of matter, may at pleasure join that which nature hath severed, and sever that which nature hath joined, and so make unlawful matches and divorces of things: *Pictoribus atque poetis*, etc. (Painters and poets have always been allowed to take what liberties they would.) It is taken in two senses, in respect of words or matter. In the first sense it is but a character of style, and belongeth to arts of speech, and is not pertinent for the present.* In the latter it is (as hath

---

* Later, in the Sixth Book of his *De Augmentis*, he touches upon versification, concluding in these masterful words:

"Precepts should be added as to the kinds of verse which best suit each matter or subject. The ancients used hexameter for histories and eulogies; elegiac for complaints; iambic for invectives; lyric for odes and hymns. Nor have modern poets been wanting in this wisdom, as far as their own languages are concerned. The fault has been, that some of them, out of too much zeal for antiquity, have tried to train the modern languages into the ancient measures (hexameter, elegiac, sapphic, etc.): measures incompatible with the structure of the languages themselves, and no less offensive to the ear. *In these things the judgment of the sense is to be preferred to the precepts of art,* — as the poet says,

Coenæ fercula nostræ
Mallem convivis quam placuisse cocis.

["The dinner is for eating, and my wish is
That guests and not that cooks should like the dishes."]

And it is not art, but abuse of art, when instead of perfecting nature, it perverts her."

This original, but preëminently sound artistic principle, is the distinctive law of the Shakespearean versification; universally

been said) one of the principal portions of learning, and
is nothing else but Feigned History, which may be styled
as well in prose as in verse.

"The use of this Feigned History hath been to give some
shadow of satisfaction to the mind of man in those points
wherein the nature of things doth deny it; the world
being in proportion inferior to the soul; by reason whereof
there is agreeable to the spirit of man a more ample greatness, a more exact goodness, and a more absolute variety,
than can be found in the nature of things. Therefore,
because the acts or events of true history have not that
magnitude which satisfieth the mind of man, poetry feigneth acts and events greater and more heroical; because
true history propoundeth successes and issues of actions
not so agreeable to the merits of virtue and vice, therefore poetry feigns them more just in retribution, and
more according to revealed providence; because true his-

----

recognized as such by the critics. Thus, Richard Grant White
says:

"Shakespeare's freedom in the use of words was but a part of
that *conscious irresponsibility to critical rule* which had such an
important influence upon the development of his whole dramatic
style." And Gervinus says: "But Shakespeare soon stepped
forth from this constraint, in a manner scarcely indicated by
Marlowe; *he intertwined the sense more clearly through the
verses according to the degree of passion expressed;* and yield-
ing to this inward impulse, he removed the monotonousness of
the older blank verse by constantly interrupting its regular course,
by abbreviation into verses of one, two, or three feet, by repeated
cesures and pauses, by concluding these cesures with amphi-
brachs, by exchanging the iambic metre with the trochaic, by
alternately contracting or extending many-syllabled words, and
by combining words and syllables, capable of different scanning.
Especially schooled by Spenser's melodious versification, he thus
blended its manner with Marlowe's power, and with exquisite
tact of sound and feeling, he broke up the stiff severity of the
old verse into a freedom which was foreign to his predecessors,
and yet in this freedom he retained a moderation which, on the
other hand, is partly lost by his successors."

tory representeth actions and events more ordinary and less interchanged, therefore poetry endueth them with more rareness, and more unexpected and alternative variations. So it appeareth that poetry serveth and conferreth to magnanimity, morality, and to delectation." *

Gervinus has unfolded so clearly the exemplification of this principle in the Shakespeare, that its brief quotation gives us a clearer understanding of the matter than would a lengthy discussion. He says:

" From the chronicles of history Shakespeare conveyed into his poetry the idea and image of a just ruling Nemesis, so familiar in his age ; Bacon, who only at times saw this Nemesis prominently distinguished in history, demanded straightway of poetry that she should in this take the place of history, that in her kingdom the images of things should conform themselves to the will of the mind, and not, as in reality, that the mind should accommodate itself to the things. And no demand is more just than this. . . . Bacon was struck by the wonderful instances in experience in which God's justice is even here made manifest; whoever has the opportunity of looking at once into the inner and outer life of men will indeed not unfrequently detect the track of this Nemesis : this exceptional appearance in the actual world is the rule in Shakespeare's poetical one. It is not the stars which with him determine the fate of men, but their works ; justice lies throughout just at the point where it is most fruitful for the poetic representation ; that the cause of the descending fate is prepared by the man himself, that the end lies in the beginning, that the cup mixed by himself is placed at the lips of the evil-doer, and that even here retribution happens for that which is here done." †

---

* There is here developed by this master " Realist," the essential, fundamental principle of " Romanticism "; whose contending schools likewise find their perfect blending and complete reconciliation in his work in the plays.

† Gervinus continues: " Shakespeare has certainly taken the

But Bacon further amplifies his conception of the license permissible in poetry. In his *Description of the Intellectual Globe*, he says:

"History is referred to the memory; poetry to the Imagination; philosophy to the Reason. And by poetry here I mean nothing else but feigned history. History is properly concerned with individuals; the impressions whereof are the first and most ancient guests of the human mind, and are as the primary material of knowledge. With these individuals and this material the human mind perpetually exercises itself, and sometimes sports. For as all knowledge is the exercise and work of the mind, so poetry may be regarded as its *sport*. In philosophy, the mind is bound to things; in poetry, it is released from that bond, and wanders forth, and feigns what it pleases. That this is so any one may see, who seeks ever so simply and without subtlety into the origins of intellectual impressions. For the images of individuals are received by the sense and fixed in the memory. They pass into the memory whole, just as they present themselves. Then the mind recalls and reviews them, and (which is its proper office) compounds and divides the parts of which they consist. For the several individuals have something in common one with another, and again something different and manifold. Now this composition and division is either according to the pleasure of the mind, or according to the

---

liberty on some few occasions of practising an injustice, though only in the case of subordinate characters, which may tend to the exercise of a justice all the more severe on the principal characters. He has besides permitted Banquo, Duncan, Hastings, and Cordelia to perish, only for the sake of the error of imprudence. Yet from Shakespeare's moral system, tending as it does to an active use of life, that lesson would result which Bacon enforced with so much emphasis, that men must expand their thoughts and look circumspectly around them, if they would truly advance their happiness; that, as it says in Troilus,

'omission to do what is necessary,
Seals a commission to a blank of danger.'"

nature of things, as it exists in fact. If it be according
to the pleasure of the mind, and these parts are arbitra-
rily transposed into the likeness of some individual, it is
the work of imagination; which, not being bound by any
law and necessity of nature or matter, may join things
which are never found together in nature, and separate
things which in nature are never found apart; being nevertheless confined therein *to these primary parts of individuals.* For of things which have been in no part objects of the sense, there can be no imagination, not even
a dream."

Here we have a firm grasp, and the distinct enunciation of an underlying principle of art, in its development
of human "sport," to which Herbert Spencer has since
given such able exposition, and which finds its supreme
exemplifications in *The Midsummer Night's Dream* and
The Tempest.

The critics have often commented on the extraordinary
verisimilitude of the most fanciful creations in the plays,
—"creatures that act just as such creatures ought to act."
Of this, Ariel, in *The Tempest,* (whose name partakes of
the symbolism of the play), is a striking example.

Prospero continually addresses Ariel as a "spirit":
"My brave spirit;" "Why, that's my spirit!" "Dost
thou think so, spirit?" "Spirit, fine spirit!" etc. In his
De Augmentis, Fourth Book, Bacon says:

"Let us now proceed to the doctrine which concerns
the Human Soul, from the treasures whereof all other
doctrines are derived. The parts thereof are two; the
one treats of the rational soul, which is divine; the other
of the irrational, which is common with brutes. . . . the
one springing from the breath of God, the other from the
womb of the elements. . . . Now this soul (as it exists
in man) is only the *instrument* of the rational soul, and
has its origin like that of the brutes in the dust of the
earth." In his *History of Life and Death,* after discuss-

ing what he terms the "spirits" in inanimate things, he continues: "The other difference between the spirits is, that the vital spirit has in it a degree of inflammation, and is like a breath compounded of flame and air. . . . But the inflammation of the vital spirits is gentler by many degrees than the softest flame, whether of spirits of wine or other; and besides it is largely mixed with an *aerial* substance, so as to be a mysterious combination of a flammeous and aerial nature." "Likewise the spirit gets from air its easy and delicate impressions and receptions, but from flame its noble and powerful motions and activity. In like manner, also, the duration of the spirit is a compound thing, not so momentary as flame, nor yet so permanent as air."

Ariel is a perfect embodiment of this conception. Prospero addresses him:

"Hast thou, which art but air, a touch, a feeling
Of their afflictions?"

And again, Ariel says:

"All hail, great master! grave sir, Hail! I come
To answer thy best pleasure; be 't to fly,
To swim, to dive into the fire, to ride
On the curl'd clouds; to thy strong bidding task
Ariel, and all his quality.
Prospero. Hast thou, spirit,
Perform'd to point the tempest that I bade thee?
Ariel. To every article.
I boarded the king's ship; now on the beak,
Now in the waist, the deck, in every cabin
I flamed amazement: sometimes *I'd divide
And burn in many places;* on the topmast,
The yards and bowsprit, *would I flame distinctly,
Then meet and join.*" *

---

* And even here, the "alphabet" of nature's elements is utilized: "The ball of fire, called Castor by the ancients, that appears at sea, prognosticates a severe storm (seeing it is Castor the dead brother), *which will be much more severe if the ball does not adhere to the mast, but rolls or dances about.* But if there

Professor Richard G. Moulton, in his lecture on *The Tempest as a Drama of Enchantment*, discerningly remarks, " We see in him [Ariel] just the qualities of air and fire. He is invisible, but, like the lightnings, can take shape as he acts. Like air and fire, he can penetrate everywhere, treading the ooze of the salt deep, running upon the sharp winds of the north, doing business in the veins of the earth when it is baked with frost. His natural speech is music, or waves of the air. His ideas are the ideas associated with the atmosphere — liberty and omnipresence : to be ' free as mountain winds,' to fly on the bat's back merrily, couch in the cowslip's bell, live under the blossom that hangs from the bow." †

And through our additional comprehension of Bacon's distinctive, underlying conception of the reality, peculiar to himself, we are, in fact, placed in command of the innermost secret of the evolution of this unembodied " spirit," and of the wonderful verisimilitude, and perfectly consistent action, of what is perhaps the most original of all the fanciful creations ever produced in this " sport " of the human mind.

Returning to our main theme : Though the Greeks gave to the productions of their art, in a striking degree, an interior unity in an all-pervading harmony (the essential characteristic of a truly organic structure), thus evincing their progress into a deep sympathy with nature in its inner constitution and its animating spirit, yet in their

---

are two of them (that is if Pollux the living brother be present), and that too when the storm has increased it is reckoned a good sign. But if there are three of them (that is, if Helen, the general scourge, arrive), the storm will become more fearful. The fact seems to be, that one by itself seems to indicate that the tempestuous matter is crude; two, that it is prepared and ripened; *three or more*, that so great a quantity is collected as can hardly be dispersed."—*History of the Winds.*

† *Shakespeare as a Dramatic Artist*, by Richard G. Moulton.

treatment of form (which is the domain of sculpture) their supreme excellence lay in their development of that which appeals more directly to the "physical" eye, and thence to the emotions naturally aroused by this sight,— as witness the perfection of their human figures, and their comparatively expressionless faces ; as compared with the best products of modern sculpture, in its search after a larger expression compatible with the enduring marble. And the same characteristic is discernible in their Tragedies, where, whenever nature is touched upon (and in Æschylus, its sympathetic reflection is simply marvellous), it is presented in its purely external aspects, and with the like comparative, though much less pronounced inexpression of its subtler meanings. In a word, the power of the Greeks, and the excellence of their art, were in large measure the outgrowth and natural development of their customary close observation of things, coupled with their resulting exquisite sensitiveness to the *immediate* impressions of the senses, and their general and strongly moving impulse towards expression.

But Bacon, in addition, or indeed more intelligently and to a much greater extent, opened "the eye of the mind," not, as did Plato, in the direction of its inner recesses, but outwardly, through the senses, into the recesses of nature, — into "the heart and marrow of things." He thus, in effect, opened up to man's possession what was to him a "new world," lying all the while at his feet unrecognized and unappreciated ; exhaustless in its resources, and fathomless in its profundity — the new world of God's universe. The province of art is its objective revelation and interpretation ; the revelation of its inner life and spirit, and the interpretation of its thought. And in his Shakespeare, Bacon inaugurated the new art of this new world, — a living art, whose growth and expansion will be limited only by the growth of the race and the expanse of the universe. It is the artistic development and expression, in appropriately beautiful forms, of all that this opened eye of the mind discerns in nature and humanity.

We have repeatedly caught glimpses of Bacon's penetrative vision into the innermost recesses of nature, and of his artistic embodiment of its results in the plays,—in their very constitution, in their "coloring," and in their detailed elaboration. (See especially *ante*, page 258, note, and context.) And for a single brief example of still another, and perhaps more incidental phase : Sleep has its purely physical aspects, and also its inner, subtler significations ; which latter are beautifully unfolded in *Macbeth, Act II.:*

> " *Macbeth.* The innocent sleep:
> Sleep, that knits up the ravell'd sleeve of care,
> The death of each day's life, sore labor's bath,
> Balm of hurt minds, great nature's second course,
> Chief nourisher in life's feast."

> " *Macd.* Confusion now hath made his masterpiece!
> Most *sacriligious* murder hath broke ope
> The Lord's annointed temple, and stole thence
> The life o' the building. . . .
> Banquo, and Donalbain! Malcolm! Awake!
> Shake off this downy sleep, death's counterfeit,
> And look on death itself!—up, up, and see
> The great doom's image! Malcolm! Banquo!
> *As from your graves* rise up, and walk like sprites,
> To countenance this horror! Ring the bell."

And again, we have seen in the *Julius Cæsar*, the like artistic expression and revelation of man himself, in the inner recesses of his constitution, and as he is affected by the subtle forces that act upon him both from within and without,—the embodiment in the domain of art of the results achieved through this close, penetrative study of humanity, "such as it is in fact," in its actual reality.

Through the marvellous progress of science, under the dominating influence of the Baconian spirit, our acquaint-

27

ance with nature has since become much more intimate, with a vastly enlarged comprehension of her beautiful workings, of her manifold subtleties, her exquisite harmonies, her inexhaustible variety, and of the continually unfolding similitudes, that are the outward, salient manifestations of her inner, constitutional unity. And when Art shall awaken from its semi-lethargy, throw off the deadening Platonic influence, with its resultant inattention to nature, and becoming alike dominated by the Baconian spirit, shall turn itself, devotedly, to the direct utilization within its own domain of these magnificent results, then, indeed, will the world enter upon its long foretold Golden Age, that will endure, with ever brightening lustre, till the end of time. For science and art are sisters, both drawing their sustenance from nature's bosom : both were for centuries untimely weaned, and in consequence, they were both nearly starved ; and alike, in each case, a return to the original fount is the indipensable condition of their healthy growth.

The glorious opportunities afforded to art, especially in literature, through the continual advancement of science, are eloquently set forth by Professor Thomas C. Chamberlain, of the University of Chicago, in an address delivered at one of its first Convocations, upon *The Mission of the Scientific Spirit* (published in the Chicago *Standard* of April 6, 1893). He first states the essential characteristic of this truly Baconian spirit:

"It has for its supreme attribute a controlling love of determinate truth ; not truth in a vague mystical sense, but rigid, solid knowledge. It is a search for facts, and the immediate and necessary inductions from facts. It is a pervading desire for actualities, stripped of imperfections and quasi-truths ; stripped of mists and fogs and veils of obscurity, and set forth in their pure, naked simplicity. It is a zeal for uncolored realities. . . . When demonstrative realities are brought forth they are embraced to the exclusion of all else. They displace all preconceptions, all deductions from general postulates, all favorite theories. The dearest doctrines, the most fascinating hypotheses, the most cherished creations of the imagination or of the reason, are cast aside, that the new light may freely enter and illuminate the mind. Previous intellectual affections are crushed, without hesitation and without remorse. Demonstrative facts are placed before reasonings, and before ideals, even though the reasonings and the ideals seem, from previous bias, to be more beautiful, to be more lofty, yea, even though they should seem for the time, until the clearer vision come, to be truer."

In his summary, but comprehensive survey of the workings of this spirit in the various departments of man's activity, he comes at length to literature. And here, he traces first its destructive influence upon much of the artistic literature of the past:

"The growth of present knowledge, the love of pure truth it enkindles, and the truer views of the constitution of things it brings, cannot be without their profound effects upon literary tastes and literary productions. . . . In the mythical realms in which the literature of the free imagination has found much of its favorite material, this advance has been destructive, and the ruin it has wrought may cause a tinge of regret, until the higher gifts it brings are realized. . . . Dante's *Inferno* is a literary phenomenon that will never recur. . . . Milton's cosmos, equally with his chaos, is only a picture of the past. And this simply because it was not true. The heavens are not as they were imagined. The beauty of thought does not make it true. The loveliness of thought does not make it immortal. Only the true is enduring. We still love these literary products of days and conditions that are gone. They rightly teach us, as all past life-productions teach the appreciative soul. Rightly viewed, their value is even heightened by the very fact that their day is gone, to return no more. The bone that lies in the gutter is matter for the scavenger. The bone that is imbedded in the Cambrian shales is beyond price. And so it is with the literature that marks the evolution of the thoughts and feelings of the age. As products of the past their value is beyond estimate. As factors of present and future creations they have lost their potency."

He then continues: "But though, thus within the earth, and on the earth, and in the heavens, science has been a destroyer of literary fields, by the same act, a new heavens and a new earth were created. New fields, and new functions for literature were brought forth. When the new heavens, pictured by a true imagination, in lieu of a wild fantasy, shall become as vivid in realization to the scientific generation that is coming as the old heavens were to the generations of the past, they will be as rich in literary possibilities as those that are gone; nay more, they will be richer, by as much as the truth of a creation of the Infinite is richer than the fantasy of the human mind. Just now, we stand between the wreck of the past and the growth of the future. Our thoughts and sentiments are not yet cleared of the *débris* of past concepts, nor have they yet taken up, in their fulness and beauty, the actualities and possibilities of the present and the future. The significance of the face of the earth we do not read as we will come to read it. The depths of the new heavens we do not fathom as we will come to fathom them. The refined light thrown on other fields does not yet inspire us as it will come to inspire us. Our souls do not throb at the touch of the soul of the new universe. When the higher, and the deeper truths that lie in all these spheres shall have permeated our common thought, and awakened responsive sentiments, they will form the ground of a literature more rich, and more enduring than any they have displaced."

Such are the materials awaiting the moulding of the imagination into artistic forms which will afford to mankind their vivid realization. For this is the function of art. The soul of the true artist throbs at their touch : and he gives them such manifestation, that it awakens in our souls an answering throb; thus bringing us into communion with "the soul of the new universe."

Science, Art, and Religion, are the blessed trinity of man's higher activities. Religion, the highest, has its seat "in the very citadel of the mind and understanding"; and its province is the immediate fulfilment of the highest aspiration of the soul. Within its domain, we are brought to an understanding of God, the Father, through his direct revelation in Jesus Christ; and to his realization, through the ministration of the Holy Spirit.

But God is also revealed in his works; which, in a profound sense, are his outward, physical manifestation. But here, in divine wisdom, man is happily thrown wholly upon the exercise of his own powers, unaided by a direct revelation. And accordingly, the intellectual comprehension of the universe, and of God as he is revealed therein, is the especial office and function of Science; whose specific subject matter, in its last analysis, is *power*, the power of God, as it is manifested in its manifold workings in the universe; and whose effect is to be the immeasurable increase of the power of man, through his divinely ordained subjection of the forces of nature to his service.

But the intellectual comprehension of these matters, in the cold, clear, "dry light" of reason, is one thing; and their vivid *realization*, in the heart and soul of mankind, is another and a greater thing. And this latter is the true function and province of Art, in its beneficent ministry to man.

Realization is effected through the legitimate workings of the imagination. This is true even in religion. As Bacon aptly observes: "Not that divine illumination resides in the imagination; its seat being rather in the very citadel of

the mind and understanding; but that the divine grace
uses the motions of the imagination as an instrument of
illumination; just as it uses the motions of the will as an
instrument of virtue."

The true, divinely appointed artist discerns, beyond his
fellows, the inner animating spirit, that enlivens the manifestations he observes. He discerns, not merely their
unfolding power, but the inherent *beauty* of that power.
And in his deeper insight into *what* is manifested, he is
thrilled to the core. His imagination is fired at the sight,
and in the illumination, he attains to its vivid realization.
It becomes thenceforward a part of himself, and of the
environment in which he consciously dwells.

Coming thus into contact with "the soul of the universe," he has caught thence the divine impulse towards
expression. He would give also to his fellows, if possible,
and to mankind forever, the like vision, appreciation, and
vivid realization of this "good." He cannot deal in abstractions; for he must work through the imagination,
quickening it into activity. He therefore, according to
his power, gives to his particular vision incarnation in concrete form; giving to what he has seen *concentrated manifestation*, in an intensity that compels its recognition.
His work is the act of the whole man, mind, heart, and
soul, and with all his powers in their highest activity. It
is suffused with emotion, or rather with that which has
produced his emotion. Its sight consequently enkindles
our imagination, and awakens in our hearts like emotions:
and thus through his work, we indeed enter into the realization of his vision.

Thus for a new familiar example: Many of us are blind
to the fact, or perhaps have not yet awakened to its realization, that God's retributive justice runs through the
thread of man's life. Bacon, however, with clear vision,
discerned its presence and operation; though in the daz-

zling play of the shuttle, it can be detected only here and there, in the barest glimpses. And in the plays, in the fulfilment of the end of art, he intensifies its manifestation. He "writes it and reports it to view in such capital letters that (as the Prophet sayeth) 'He that runneth by may read.'" We behold continually, that "the cup mixed by himself is placed at the lips of the evil-doer," and that, as in Cassius' case,

"Thus doth he force the swords of wicked men
To turn their own points on their masters' bosoms."

The sight is so impressive, that we awaken to the consciousness that this justice is indeed a reality, and to a vivid realization that it is actually a working element in life; though its operations are often obscured from view, through the intermingling of other elements in life's complexities. Our eyes are opened to its closer observation, and its recognition becomes a deterring force, tending to restrain us from evil courses. But it is not "abstract justice" thus engaging our contemplation: instead, we are entering into the comprehension and the realization of *the justice of God*.

And in like manner, the true artist, viewing nature closely, catches evanescent glimpses, here and there, of the exquisite beauty and the harmony that are actually present in her manifestations; though to the duller vision they are too often obscured from view, in the bewildering whirl of her incessant activities. Possessed by this vision of loveliness, he gives it incarnation, in a concentrated manifestation. Beholding it, we also attain to his vision, and we awake to the perception of a beauty existing in nature which was before by us unrecognized and unknown; and our hearts, also, are thrilled in its presence. And we shall yet learn, that it is not "abstract beauty" thus engaging our contemplation, but that, through this instrumentality, we are indeed brought into realizing contact with the beauty and the harmony inherent in the Soul of the universe. It is, in effect, a disclosure of *the beauty of God, and of His harmony*, as they are reflected in his works.

Again, God is love: and self-impartation is love's instinctive impulse, its characteristic mode of action. And in reality, the Love of God is thus displayed in the universe. But the scientist of to-day, using the dry light of reason, and discerning everywhere the presence and operation of *power*, manifested, for example, in the phenomena of light, heat, and electricity, has exalted it into a veritable "entity," which he calls "energy," the primal force in the universe. But this fails to satisfy the human heart, with its instinctive aspiration after God, and for the realization of his actual and active presence. And the world to-day is awaiting, with deep longing, the advent of the artist poet, or poets, of truly creative power, who shall sing, "in mighty verse," the new song of this new universe; unfolding to our vision its spiritual and material realms in their essential, organic unity; wherein this "energy," in its Protean phases, is itself a *phenomenon*, the physical expression and manifestation of the Supreme Love, in the self-impartation of His sustaining power to the universe and all that it contains, and in the evolution of His thought, in its ever unfolding harmony; thus awakening in our souls a keener perception, and a more profound, and more vivid realization of His power, His wisdom, and His lovliness, as He is revealed in his works.

It is not without its deep significance, that art, in its early rudiments, and in all the ages, has ever been intimately associated with religion. Because the heathen worshipped false gods, we do not discard worship: but instead, in the fulfilment of an instinctive impulse turned in the right direction, we worship God in sincerity and truth. And likewise, the Christian, of all men in the world, should foster art, encourage its development, and strive for its elevation to its rightful plane; for it is clearly evident, that in the ages to come, it will be through the blessed ministrations of Art, that mankind will ultimately attain to the burning consciousness, and the living realization of the unutterable *glory* of God, as it shines forth in his universe.

Man's thirst for beauty, with his deep satisfaction in its fulfilment, is a divinely implanted instinct; feeble, flickering at first, but "growing upon what it feeds," with a continual attunement to finer harmonies. Bacon, mindful of the revelation of man's creation and fall, said, in felicitous phrase, that conscience " is a sparkle of the purity of his first estate." And likewise, and with equal validity, it may be said that this love of beauty is the lingering glow of the glory of that first estate, whose refulgence filled the heavens, in ineffable harmony, and "when the morning stars sang together for joy." So that what Plato taught and poets have sung of man's reminiscence of a previous existence is true, not of the individual, but of the race, that

'trailing clouds of glory, did we come
From God, who is our home.'

But this feeble, flickering reflection can only be brightened from its original source. We must learn the harmony inherent in those stars, if we would again listen to their song. The new heavens and the new earth are indeed radiant with the light of God's glory, and resonant with His harmony: and our ever growing thirst for beauty, with our instinctive delight in its enjoyment, will only find its abundant fulfilment and satisfaction in the unutterable joy experienced in their conscious realization.

Such is the divinely appointed mission and the lofty goal of this new art of the new universe, which Bacon inaugurated; and whose immediate and serious purpose, even in the midst of the delightful exercise of its recreative "sport," is the interpretative revelation of the *realities* of this universe in their intrinsic beauty and harmony, and in such power as to effect their vivid realization; and whose possibilities "will be richer, by as much as the truth of the creation of the Infinite is richer than the fantasy of the human mind."

It is profoundly significant that, of all man's creations, only the artistic is enduring in its hold upon his affections. Only things of beauty are "a joy forever." Indeed, the glory of the Greek nation, yea its perpetuity, not only in history, but in the life and being of the race, and thus what we call its immortality, was largely the outcome and product of its magnificent development of art, in its various forms. And when our age shall awaken to its immeasurably greater opportunities, through its growing possession of this new and truly inexhaustible universe, and shall generally recognize and appreciate the surpassing *worth* of art and its enduring quality, and shall, accordingly, turn its superabundant energies directly and with like devotion to its development; then, indeed, and over and beyond what is wrought through our triumphs in science, will we most effectually and endurably impress ourselves upon and within the future life of the race, and most preciously contribute to its enrichment. We shall then pay our debt to the past, by our greater benefactions to the future: and, in the ensuing progress, it will yet be seen and appreciated that this Greek art, in its beautiful perfection but limited scope, was but the opening vestibule into the greater, more glorious, and the truly consecrated Temple of Art, which in its ever expanding proportions is destined ultimately to fill the earth: and the light of this temple is to be the glory of God.

Nor can this art, which in its blessed ministry to man might properly be termed the lovely handmaid of religion, ever usurp her place and function. Bacon's words of wisdom are both pertinent and of commanding force. In his *De Augmentis*, Ninth Book, he says:

"Wherefore we conclude that Sacred Theology ought to be derived from the word and oracles of God, and not from the light of nature, or the dictates of reason. For it is written, 'The heavens declare the glory of God,' but it is nowhere written, 'The heavens declare the will of God'; but of that it is said, 'To the law and to the testimony; if men do not according to this word, etc.' And this holds not only in those great mysteries which concern the Deity, the Creation, and the Redemption; but it pertains likewise to a more perfect interpretation of the moral law, 'Love your enemies'; 'do good to them that hate you,' and so on; 'that ye may be the children of your father who is in heaven, that sendeth rain upon the just and the unjust.' To which words this applause may well be applied, 'that they do not sound human'; since it is a voice beyond the light of nature. . . . So then religion, whether considered with regard to morals or mysteries, depends on revelation from God."

It is very noticeable that the few great creative artists of modern times, those whom we are wont to count upon our fingers, were profoundly reverent. This is especially true of Michael Angelo, of Dante, and of Milton; and the great Goethe has opened to us the recesses of his heart, in these expressive words:

"*Credo Deum!* That is a fine, a worthy thing to say; but to recognize God where and as he reveals himself, is the only true bliss on earth." "Man must be capable of elevating himself to the highest Reason, to come into contact with the Divinity, which manifests itself in the elemental phenomena, which dwells behind them, and from which they proceed." "But this is the divine energy everywhere diffused, and divine love everywhere active."

"In Faust himself there is an activity which becomes

constantly higher and purer to the end, and from above, there is eternal love coming to his aid. This harmonizes perfectly with our religious views, according to which we cannot obtain heavenly bliss through our own strength alone, but with the assistance of divine grace."

And Bacon, the greatest of them all, bowed in unfeigned reverence before the Father; regarding the universe as His handiwork, and earnestly striving to afford to man "a revelation and true vision of the traces and moulds of the Creator in his creatures."

This reverent spirit not only brings the soul into intimate sympathy with the great Heart pulsating through all existence, but somehow it opens the door to the incoming of the *divine* impulse, which lies at the core of all great creative production. The divine origin of this impulse, and its workings within himself, are shadowed forth by Bacon, in these few, fervent words: "— ever earnestly desiring, *with such a passion as we believe God alone inspires*, that this which has been hitherto unattempted may not now be attempted in vain." In a word, it is not the instinct of self-glorification, but the unselfish devotion of the soul, devotion to the Father, and to His children, the burning impulse of service to mankind, of self-impartation to others, which is the germ, the source, the fountain of all great creative work; for it is the nearest approach to the likeness of the inspiration of the Divine Artist

Goethe, profoundly impressed by the fact, gave it expression in his criticism of a German poet, "who had lately gained a great name," but who has since been almost forgotten: "We cannot deny that he has many brilliant qualities, but he is wanting in — *love*. He loves his readers and his fellow poets as little as he loves himself, and thus we may apply to him the maxim of the apostle, ' *Though I speak with the tongues of men and angels, and have not love, I am become as sounding brass and a tinkling cymbal.'* I have lately read the poems of Platen, and cannot deny his great talent. But, as I said, he is deficient in *love*, and thus he will never produce the effect which he ought."

The first attribute of the creative artist is vision, in the clarity afforded by " purity of illumination "; the second is the power of manifestation, in giving incarnation to his visions ; and the third is love, the divine impulse. And here again, the greatest of these is love ; for love is the inspiration and the sustaining power, both the flame and the oil in the lamp.

All of which, in a word, is but a glimpse of the profound truths exemplified in Bacon's authorship of the plays.

AN AFTER-WORD.

OF INTEREST TO LAWYERS.

FRANCIS BACON was an accomplished lawyer, bred in the profession, himself the son of a lawyer.* In the beginning, and for eight years a briefless barrister, he rose successively through the various gradations to the highest eminence in his profession, becoming, in 1618, Lord Chancellor of Great Britain. His pleas, many of which have been preserved, and his legal writings fully attest his

---

* "And since I am upon the point whom I will hear, your Lordships will give me leave to tell you a fancy. It falls out, that there be three of us the King's servants in great place, that are lawyers by descent, Mr. Attorney, son of a judge, Mr. Solicitor, likewise son of a judge, and myself, a chancellor's son. Now, because the law roots so well in my time, I will water it at the root thus far, as besides these great ones, I will hear any Judge's son before a Sergeant, and any Sergeant's son before a Reader, if there be not many of them."—*Speech on taking his seat in Chancery.* *Works,* Vol. 13, page 192.

("They were trained together in their childhood; and there *rooted* betwixt them such an affection which cannot choose but branch now. Since their more mature dignities and royal necessities made separation of their society, their encounters, though not personal, have been royally attorneyed, with interchange of gifts, letters, loving embassies."—*A Winter's Tale, I., 1.*

"I have spoke this, to know if your affiance
Were deeply rooted."—*Cymbeline, I., 6.*

"But I, having a good *affiance* in your Grace's judgment, will tell you my reason why I thus think, and so leave it."—*Works,* Vol. 14, page 450.)

mastery of the law. They show that its principles, its technique, and its recondite phraseology were thoroughly at his command. The law, indeed, was his livelihood, his lifelong profession, in youth at the bar, and in old age upon the bench : and dwelling thus continually in the atmosphere of the court, it might reasonably be expected that some of its air would be wafted into the plays ; in metaphor, illustration, and in unmistakable notes and chords.

Such is the fact, and, in the words of Lord Campbell, there is there abundantly displayed ' a familiar, profound and accurate knowledge of juridical principles and practice.'

This is a phenomenon of exceeding interest, especially as such " profound and accurate " professional knowledge could not have been acquired by intuition, but only by the closest study. Moreover, it illustrates how, in the hands of the master, the driest technical details were inwrought into the texture of an imaginative work, and thus made to contribute their quota to its amplitude of expression, and, therefore, to its artistic power.

And here, once more, original research is unnecessary ; for this work has already been performed, and its results are ready to our hand. In 1859, in reply to an inquiry of Mr. Peter Collier, Lord John Campbell, one of Bacon's successors as Lord Chancellor of Great Britain, published an essay upon " *Shakespeare's Legal Acquirements*," in which he collated, with pertinent annotations, passages from the plays, which, in his judgment, evidenced the possession by the Poet of a thorough knowledge of the law. Coming from such an eminent legal authority, absolutely impartial, — for obviously the question of Bacon's authorship of the plays was unknown to him,— his words have far greater weight than anything which might now be said.

The following are quotations from his book (with added annotations from Bacon's *Works*):

"In writing the second scene of Act IV. *The Merry Wives of Windsor*, Shakespeare's head was so full of the recondite terms of the law, that he makes a lady thus pour them out, in a confidential *tête-à-tête* conversation with another lady, while discoursing of the revenge they two should take upon an old gentleman for having made an unsuccessful attempt upon their virtue:

Mrs. Page. I'll have the cudgel hallowed and hung o'er the altar: It hath done meritorious service.

Mrs. Ford. What think you? May we, with the *warrant* of womanhood, and the *witness* of a good conscience, pursue him with any further revenge?

Mrs. Page. The spirit of wantonness is, sure, scared out of him: if the devil have him not *in fee simple, with fine and recovery,* he will never, I think, in the way of *waste,* attempt us again.

"This merry Wife of Windsor is supposed to know that the highest estate which the devil could hold in any of his victims was *a fee simple,* strengthened by *fine and recovery.*"

"The following is part of the dialogue between Antipholus of Syracuse and his man Dromio, in *The Comedy of Errors*, Act II., Sc. 2:

Dro. S. There's no time for a man to *recover* his hair, that grows bald by nature.

Ant. S. May he not do it by *fine and recovery?*

Dro. S. Yes, to pay a *fine* for a periwig, and *recover* the lost hair of another man.

"These jests cannot be supposed to arise from anything in the laws or customs of Syracuse; but they show the author to be very familiar with some of the most abstruse proceedings in English jurisprudence."

"So in *All's Well that Ends Well*, Act IV., Sc. 3, Parolles, the bragging cowardly soldier, is made to talk like a conveyancer in Lincoln's Inn:

He will sell the *fee simple* of his salvation . . . and *cut the entail from all remainders.*" *

" Hamlet's own speech, on taking in his hand what he supposed might be the skull of a lawyer, abounds with lawyer-like thoughts and words :

Where be his quiddits now,† his quillets,‡ his tenures, and

---

* " The last and greatest estate of land is *fee simple*, and beyond this there is none. All the former, for years, lives. or *entails*, have further beyond them the estate of *fee simple;* but fee simple itself is the greatest, last, and utmost degree of estates in land. Therefore he that maketh a lease for life to one, or a gift in tail, may appoint a *remainder* to another for life or in tail after that estate, or to a third in fee simple; but after a fee simple he can limit no other estate. And if a man do not dispose of the fee simple by way of remainder when he maketh the gift in tail, or for lives, then the fee simple resteth in him as a reversion. . . . This slight was first invented when entails fell out to be so inconvenient, as is before declared, so that men made no conscience *to cut them off* if they could find law for it. And now, by use, these recoveries are become common assurances against entails and against the remainders and reversions, and are the greatest security purchasers have for their money ; for a *fine* will bar the heir in tail, and not the remainder, nor reversion, but a common *recovery* will bar them all."— *Works*, Vol. 7, page 492.

† " And the Queen's Counsel did again enforce that point, setting forth that it was no mystery or *quiddity* of the common law, but it was a conclusion infallible of reason and experience." — *Works*, Vol. 9, page 286.

‡ " Which perpetuities, if they should stand, would bring in all the former inconveniences of entails, that were cut off by the former mentioned statutes; and far greater: for, by the perpetuity, if he that is in possession start away never so little, in making a lease, or selling a little *quillet*, forgetting after two or three descents, as often they do, how they are tied : the next heir must enter."— *Works*. Vol. 7, page 491. " The states of Italy, they be like little quillets of freehold lying intermixed in the midst of a great honor or lordship."—*Discourse in Praise of the Queen, Works*, Vol. 8, page 136.

28

his tricks?* Why does he suffer this rude knave to knock him about the sconce with a dirty shovel, and will not tell him of his action of battery? Humph! This fellow might be in 's time a great buyer of land, with his statutes, his recognizances, his fines, his double vouchers, his recoveries : is this the fine of his fines, and the recovery of his recoveries, to have his fine pate full of fine dirt? will his vouchers vouch him no more of his purchases, and double ones too, than the length and breadth of a pair of indentures?†

" These terms of art are all used seemingly with a full knowledge of their import; and it would puzzle some practising barristers with whom I am acquainted to go over the whole *seriatim*, and to define each of them satisfactorily."

" So fond was he of law terms that in *King Henry the Fourth*, Part I., when Henry IV. is made to lecture the Prince of Wales on his irregularities, and to liken him to

---

* " He will never do his tricks clean."—*Promus.*, *Works*, Vol. 7, page 205.

" Which it pleased you to say were no tricks or novelties, but true passages of business."—*Works*, Vol. 11, page 311.

† The reason why the heirs in tail, remainders, and reversions are thus barred is, because in strict law the recompense adjudged against the crier, that was *vouched*, is to go in succession of estate as the land lost should have done. . . . Upon feoffments, fines, and recoveries, the estate of the land doth settle as the use and intent of the parties is declared, by word or writing, before the act was done; as, for example, if they make a writing that one of them shall levy a fine, or make a feoffment, or suffer a recovery to the other, but the use and intent is, that one should hold it for his life, and after his death, a stranger should have it in tail, and then a third in fee simple : in this case the land settleth in estate according to the use and intent declared."
—*Works*, Vol. 7, page 494. The attempted pun upon the word " fine " reminds us of the following : " It makes me remember what I heard one say of a judge that sat in Chancery, that he would make 80 orders in a morning out of the way, and it was *out of the way* indeed, for it was nothing to the end of the business."—*Works*, Vol. 13, page 190.

Richard II., who, by such improper conduct, lost the
crown, he uses the forced and harsh figure that Richard—

Enfeoffed himself to popularity (Act III., Sc. 2) *

---

* "So if I make a feoffment in fee upon condition that the
feoffee shall enfeoff over, and the feoffee be disseised, and a
descent cast, and then the feoffee bind himself in a *statute*,
which statute is discharged before the recovery of the land:
this is no breach of the condition, because the land was never
liable to the statute; and the possibility that it should be liable
upon the recovery the law doth not respect."— *Works*, Vol. 7,
page 328.

> "Enfeoff'd himself to popularity:
> That being daily swallow'd by men's eyes,
> They surfeited with honey, and began
> To loathe the taste of sweetness, whereof a little
> More than a little is much too much:
>
> . . . .
>
> Being with his presence glutted, gorged and full."

And again:

> "For as a surfeit of the sweetest things
> The deepest loathing to the stomach brings."
> —*Midsummer Night's Dream, II., 2.*

"Some food we may use long, and much without *glutting;*
as bread, flesh that is not fat or rank, etc. Some other (though
pleasant) glutteth sooner; as sweet meats, fat meats, etc. The
cause is for that appetite consisteth in the emptiness of *the
mouth of the stomach;* or possessing it with somewhat that is
astringent, and therefore cold and dry. But things that are
sweet and *fat* are more filling, and do swim and hang more
about the mouth of the stomach, and go not down so speedily;
and again turn sooner to *choler*, which is hot, and ever abateth
the appetite. We see also another cause of satiety is an over
custom, and of appetite is novelty; and therefore meats, if the
same be continually taken, induce *loathing*."—*Natural History*, § 300.

"One word more, I beseech you. If you be not too much
cloyed with fat meat, our humble author will continue the story."
—*II., Henry, Epilogue.*

> "Thus do I pine and surfeit day by day,
> Or gluttoning on all or all away."—*Sonnet LXXV.*

"I copy Malone's note of explanation on this line :—
'Gave himself up absolutely to popularity. A feoffment
was the ancient mode of conveyance, by which all lands
in England were granted in fee simple for several ages,
till the conveyance of lease and release was invented by
Serjeant Moor about the year 1630. Every deed of feoffment was accompanied with livery of seisin, that is, with
the delivery of corporal possession of the land or tenement
granted in fee.' "

"To 'sue out livery' is another law term used in the
play (Act IV., Sc. 3)—a proceeding to be taken by a ward
of the crown, on coming of age, to obtain possession of
his lands, which the king had held as guardian in chivalry
during his minority. Hotspur, in giving a description of
Henry the Fourth's beggarly and suppliant condition
when he landed at Ravenspurg, till assisted by the Percys,
says :

> And when he was not six-and-twenty strong,
> Sick in the world's regard, wretched and low,
> A poor unminded outlaw, sneaking home,
> My father gave him welcome to the shore:

"*Kath.* I pr'ythee go, and get me some repast;
I care not what, so it be wholesome food.
Gru. What say you to a neat's foot?
Kath. 'Tis passing good; I pr'ythee let me have it.
Gru. I fear, it is too *choleric* a meat:
How say you to a fat tripe, finely broiled?
Kath. I like it well; good Grumio, fetch it me.
Gru. I cannot tell; I fear, 'tis *choleric*."
— *Taming of the Shrew, IV., 3*

"Nor *custom stale* her *infinite* variety."
— *Antony and Cleopatra, II.. 3.*

"But now thy uncle is removing hence;
As princes do their courts, when they are *cloy'd*
With long continuance in a settled place."
— *I., Henry VI., II.. 5.*

"My banquet is *to close our stomachs up*,
After our great good cheer."
— *Taming of the Shrew, V., 2.*

And when he heard him swear, and vow to God,
He came but to be Duke of Lancaster,
To *sue his livery*, and beg his peace,
With tears of innocency and terms of zeal,
My father in kind heart and pity mov'd,
Swore him assistance." *

" In *All's Well that Ends Well*, we meet with proof
that Shakespeare had an accurate knowledge of the law
of England respecting the incidents of military tenure, or
tenure in chivalry, by which the greater part of the land
in this kingdom was held till the reign of Charles II.
The incidents of that tenure here dwelt upon are ' *wardship of minors* ' and ' the right of the guardian to dispose
of the minor in *marriage* at his pleasure.' The scene lies
in France, and, strictly speaking, the law of that country
ought to prevail in settling such questions : but Dr. John-
son, in his notes on *All's Well that Ends Well*, justly
intimates his opinion that it is of no great use to inquire
whether the law upon these subjects was the same in
France as in England, ' for Shakespeare gives to all nations the manners of England.'

" According to the plot on which this play is constructed,
the French King labored under a malady which his physicians had declared incurable ; and Helena, the daughter
of a deceased physician of great eminence, knew of a cure
for it. She was in love with Bertram, Count of Rousil-
lon, still a minor, who held large possessions as tenant *in*

---

* " The fourth institution was, that for recognition of the
king's bounty by every heir succeeding his ancestor in these
knight-service lands, the king should have *primer seisin* of the
land, which is one year's value of the land ; and until this be
paid, the king is to be in possession of the land, and then to
deliver it to the heir, which continueth in use until this day, and
is the very cause and business of *suing livery*, and is as well
where the heir hath been in ward as otherwise."--- *Works*, Vol. 7,
page 482. " Nay, the king's wards, after they had accomplished their full age, could not be suffered to have livery of
their lands, without paying excessive fines, far exceeding all
reasonable rates."— *History of Henry VII*.

capite under the crown, and was in ward to the King. Helena undertook the cure, making this condition:

> *Hel.* Then shalt thou give me with thy kingly hand
> What husband in thy power I will command,

" Adding however:

> Exempted be from me the arrogance
> To choose from forth the royal blood of France. . .
> But such a one, thy vassal, whom I know
> Is free for me to ask, thee *to bestow.*—*Act II.*, *Sc. 1.*

" She effects the cure, and the King showing her all the noble unmarried youths whom he then held as wards, says to her:

> Fair maid, send forth thine eye: this youthful parcel
> Of noble bachelors stand at my bestowing. . . .
> . . . . thy frank selection make:
> Thou hast power to choose, and they none to forsake.

" Helena, after excusing herself to several others, comes to Bertram, and, covered with blushes, declares her election:

> *Hel.* I dare not say I take you; but I give
> Me and my service, ever while I live,
> Into your guiding power.—This is the man.
> *King.* Why then young Bertram, take her: she's thy wife.

" Bertram at first strenuously refuses, saying:

> In such a business give me leave to use
> The help of mine own eyes.

" But the King, after much discussion, thus addresses him:

> It is in us to plant thine honor where
> We please to have it grow.   Check thy contempt:
> Obey our will, which travails in thy good. . . .
> . . . . Take her by the hand,
> And tell her she is thine. . . .
> *Bert.* I take her hand.—*Act II.*, *Sc. 3.**

---

* " The grief was, That every man's eldest son or heir (the dearest thing he hath in the world) was, by Prerogative warranted by the laws of the land, to be in ward to the King for his body and lands; than which they conceived (to a free na-

"The ceremony of marriage was immediately performed, and no penalty or forfeiture was incurred. But

---

tion) nothing to be more grievous. But they esteemed it only a grief, no wrong: sithence it had been patiently endured by our ancestors, and by ourselves."—*Report of Conference concerning Wardship. Works*, Vol. 10, page 179.

("Which I held my duty, speedily to acquaint you withal; *sithence*, in the loss that may happen, it concerns you something to know it."—*All's Well, I., 3.*)

"First therefore his Majesty hath had this princely consideration with himself, that as he is *pater patriæ*, so he is by the ancient law of this kingdom *pater pupillorum*, where there is any tenure by knight's service of himself; which extendeth almost to all the great families noble and generous of this kingdom: and therefore being a representative father, his purpose is to imitate and approach as near as may be to the duties and offices of a natural father, in the good education, well *bestowing in marriage*, and preservation of the houses, woods, lands, and estates of his wards."—*Works*, Vol. 11, page 285.

Curiously enough, it appears from Bacon's *History of Henry VII.* that he was aware that this was also the law in France:

"So as the marriage halted upon both feet, and was not clear on either side. But for the contract with King Charles [of France], the exception lay plain and fair; for that Maximilian's daughter was under years of consent, and so not bound by law, but a power of disagreement left to either part. But for the contract made by Maximilian with the lady herself, they were harder driven: having nothing to allege but that it was done without the consent of her sovereign lord, King Charles, whose ward and client she was, and he to her in place of a father: and therefore it was void and of no force for want of such consent. King Charles thereupon sent embassadors to King Henry VII. ' to treat a peace and league with the king; accoupling it with an article in the nature of a request, that the French king might with the king's good will, *according unto his right of seigniory and tutelage* dispose of the marriage of the young duchess of Britain as he should think good; offering by a judicial proceeding to make void the marriage of Maximilian by proxy.' "—*History of Henry VII.*

And even the laws and legal customs of mediæval Venice

the law not extending to a compulsion upon the ward to live with the wife thus forced upon him, Bertram escapes from the church door, and abandoning his wife, makes off for the wars in Italy, where he unconsciously embraced the deserted Helena.

"For the cure of the King by the physician's daughter, and her being deserted by her husband, Shakespeare is indebted to Boccaccio; but the wardship of Bertram and the obligation of the ward to take the wife provided for him by his guardian, Shakespeare drew from his own knowledge of the common law of England, which, though now obsolete, was in full force in the reign of Elizabeth, and was to be found in Littleton."

"In the speeches of Jack Cade and his coadjutors in *King Henry VI.*, Part II., we find a familiarity with the law and its proceedings which strongly indicates that the author must have had some professional practice or education as a lawyer.

"The indictment on which Lord Say was arraigned, in Act IV., Scene 7, seems drawn by no inexperienced hand:

Thou hast most traitorously corrupted the youth of the realm in erecting a grammar-school: and whereas, before, our forefathers had no other books but the score and the tally, thou hast caused printing to be used; and *contrary to the king, his crown*

were better understood than many modern critics have supposed. The following is from a recent speech by Colonel Robert G. Ingersoll:

"Shakespeare has been criticised on account of the trial scene in *The Merchant of Venice*. The critics pointed out that nothing could be more absurd than a young fellow coming along and taking the place of the judge and proceeding to try a case. All these objections to Portia, however, have been found to have no foundation. At that time it was the custom for students of the great law school at Padua to assist legal judges. Many of these judges knew nothing of the law and when in doubt or trouble, they sent to Padua asking that some one learned in the law might be sent. And it was in accordance with this custom that Portia presided at the trial."

and dignity, thou hast built a paper-mill. It will be proved to thy face that thou hast men about thee that usually talk of a noun and a verb, and *such abominable words as no Christian ear can endure to hear.* ('*Inter Christianos non nominand.*' —Camp.) Thou hast appointed justices of peace, to call poor men before them about matters they were not able to answer. Moreover thou hast put them in prison; and *because they could not read*, thou hast hanged them, when indeed only for that cause they have been most worthy to live.

"How acquired I know not, but it is quite certain that the drawer of this indictment must have had some acquaintance with 'The Crown Circuit Companion,' and must have had a full and accurate knowledge of that rather obscure and intricate subject—'Felony and Benefit of Clergy.' " *

---

* "But because some prisoners that can read have their books, and be burned in the hand and so delivered, it is necessary to show the reason thereof. This having their books is called their clergy, which in ancient time began thus: For the scarcity of men that could read, and the multitude requisite in the clergy of the realm to be disposed into religious houses, priests, deacons, and clerks of parishes, there was a prerogative allowed to the clergy that if any man that could read as a clerk were to be condemned to death, the bishop of the diocese might, if he would, claim him as a clerk; and he was then to see him tried in the face of the court, whether he could read or not. The book was prepared and brought by the bishop, and the judge was to turn to some place as he should think meet; and if the prisoner could read, then the bishop was to have him delivered unto him to dispose in some place to the clergy, as he should think meet: but if either the bishop would not demand him, or that the prisoner could not read, then was he to be put to death." — *Works*, Vol. 7, page 473.

Touching the "grammar-school" the following is pertinent:

One Thomas Sutton, dying, left a large estate which he bequeathed by will to various charities, among others, to the foundation of a grammar-school. Bacon, retained by the heir, brought suit to break the will: prior to which he wrote a letter of advice to the King upon the matter, in which he argued as follows:

"Concerning the advancement of Learning, I do subscribe

"Cade's proclamation which follows, deals with still

to the opinion of one of the wisest and greatest men of your
kingdom : That for grammar-schools there are already too many,
and therefore no providence to add where there is excess. For
the great number of schools which are in your Highness' realm,
doth cause a want, and doth cause likewise an overflow, both
of them inconvenient, and one of them dangerous. For by
means thereof they find want in the country and towns, both of
servants for husbandry and apprentices for trade; and on the
other side, there being more scholars bred than the state can
prefer and employ, and the active part of that life not bearing
a proportion to the preparation, it must needs fall out that many
persons will be bred unfit for other vocations, and unprofitable
for that in which they are brought up; which fills the realm
full of indigent, idle and wanton people, which are but *materia
rerum novarum.*"

He urges, instead, that the salaries of the teachers in the universities be increased : " Therefore I could wish that in both
the universities, the lecturers as well of the three professions,
Divinity, Law, and Physic, as of the three heads of science,
Philosophy, Arts of Speech, and Mathematics, were raised in
their pensions unto 100 *l.* per annum apiece. Which, though it
be not so great as they are in some other places, where the greatness of the reward doth whistle for the ablest men out of all
foreign parts to supply the chair, yet it may be a portion to content a worthy and able man, if he be likewise contemplative in
nature, as those spirits are that are fittest for lectures.[1] Thus
may learning in your kingdom be advanced to a further height."
—*Works*, Vol. 11, page 252.

[1] " Our Court shall be a little Academe,
      Still and contemplative in living art."—*L. L. L., I., 1.*

In reply to a possible criticism, it should be observed that
Lord Bacon, living in the Sixteenth century, is to be judged by
the standards of that time ; while it has been reserved for America to demonstrate the incomparable value of the " common
school," as well as the fundamental principles underlying the
dignity, the worth, and the advancement of *the people.* Bacon
undoubtedly expressed to the king his honest sentiments; and
therein lies another harmony :

Richard Grant White, in his *Genius of Shakespeare,* says :

more recondite heads of jurisprudence. Announcing his policy when he should mount the throne, he says:

The proudest peer in the realm shall not wear a head upon his shoulders unless he pay me tribute: there shall not a maid be married but she shall pay me her maidenhead ere they have it. Men shall hold of me *in capite;** and we charge and com-

---

"It has been objected to the assertion of the amplitude of Shakespeare's mind, and to the generosity of his character, that *he always represents the laborer and the artisan in a degraded position, and often makes his ignorance and his uncouthness the butt of ridicule.*"

To this charge Mr. White aptly replies: " Three hundred years ago the husbandman and the mechanic were degraded in the world's eyes; and Shakespeare, the healthiness of whose understanding is as remarkable as any trait of his genius, knew that the world's appreciation is generally right of men in mass, and that these hard-handed men had all the consideration that was their due, though not all the rights or advantages. It is always so. Individual men may fail to receive a just appreciation; but as surely as water finds its level, classes of men always rise to the standing that they can maintain. It is because the working-man, whether his labor be rude or skilled, has raised himself, has in fact become another man, that the world now awards him a consideration which he did not receive in the days of Queen Elizabeth."

George Wilkes, in his *Shakespeare from an American Point of View*, is less generous, verging even upon injustice. Regarding the Poet, he says:

" Nay, worse than this, worse than his servility to royalty and rank, we never find him speaking of the poor with respect, or alluding to the working classes without detestation or contempt. We can understand these tendencies as existing in Lord Bacon, born as he was to privilege, and holding office from a queen; but they seem utterly at variance with the natural instincts of a man who had sprung from the body of the people, and who, through the very pursuits of his father, and likewise from his own beginning, may be regarded as one of the working classes himself."

* " This case concerneth one of the greatest and fairest flowers of the crown, which is the King's tenures, and that in their

mand that their wives be *as free as heart can wish, or tongue can tell.*

" He thus declares a great forthcoming change in the tenure of land and in the liability to taxation : he is to have a poll-tax like that which had raised the rebellion ; but, instead of coming down to the daughters of blacksmiths who had reached the age of fifteen, it was to be confined to the nobility. Then he is to legislate on the *merchcta mulierum.* According to Blackstone and other high authorities this never had been known in England ; although till the reign of Malcolm III., it certainly appears to have been established in Scotland ; * but Cade inti-

creation, which is more than their preservation: for if the rules and maxims of law in the first raising of tenures *in capite* be weakened, this nips the flower in the bud, and may do more hurt by a resolution in law, than the losses which the King's tenures do daily receive by oblivion or suppression, or the neglect of officers, or the iniquity of jurors, or other like blasts, whereby they are continually shaken. And therefore it behooveth us of the King's counsel to have a special care of this case as much as in us is to give satisfaction to the court. Therefore, before I come to argue these two points particularly, I will speak something of the favor of law towards tenures *in capite,* as that which will give a force and edge to all that I shall speak afterwards. . . . But now further, amongst the tenures by knight-service, that of the King *in capite* is the most high and worthy ; and the reason is double ; partly because it is held of the King's crown and person, and partly because the law createth such a privity between the line of the Crown and the inheritors of such tenancies, as there cannot be an alienation without the King's license ; the penalty of which alienation was by the common law the forfeiture of the estate itself, and by the statute of E. III. is reduced to fine and seisure. And although this also have been unworthily termed by the vulgar *captivity* and thralldom ; yet that which they count bondage the law counteth honor."—*Argument in Lowe's Case of Tenures, Works,* Vol. 7, page 547.

* " For although *I have read and read with delight the Scottish statutes,* and some other collection of their laws; with delight I say, partly to see their brevity and propriety of speech, and

mates his determination to adopt it,—with this alteration, that instead of conferring the privilege on every lord of a manor, to be exercised within the manor, he is to assume it exclusively for himself all over the realm, as belonging to his prerogative royal.

"He proceeds to announce his intention to abolish tenure in *free soccage*, and that all men should hold of him *in capite*, concluding with a licentious jest, that although his subjects should no longer hold in free soccage, their wives should be 'as free as heart can wish, or tongue can tell.' Strange to say, this phrase, or one almost identically the same, ' as free as tongue can speak or heart can think,' is feudal, and was known to the ancient law of England. In the tenth year of King Henry VII., that very distinguished judge, Lord Hussey, who was Chief Justice of England during four reigns, in a considered judgment delivered the opinion of the whole Court of King's Bench as to the construction to be put upon the words, ' as free as tongue can speak or heart can think.' See *Year Book, Hil. Term, 10 Hen. VII.*, fol. 13, pl. 6."

"In *As You Like It*, Act I., Sc. 2, Shakespeare makes the lively Rosalind, who, although well versed in poesy and books of chivalry, had probably never seen a bond or a law-paper of any sort in her life, quite familiar with the commencement of all deeds poll, which in Latin was, *Noverint universi per presentes*, in English, ' Be it known to all men by these presents':

Le Beau. There comes an old man and his three sons,—
Cel. I could match this beginning with an old tale.

---

partly to see them come so near to our laws; yet I am unwilling to put my sickle in another's harvest, but leave it to the lawyers of the Scottish nation: the rather, because I imagine with myself that if a Scottish lawyer should undertake, reading of the English statutes, or other our books of law, to set down positively in articles what the law of England were, he might oftentimes err: and the like errors, I make account, I might incur in theirs."—*A Preparation for the Union of Laws, Works,* Vol. 7, page 732.

Le Beau. Three proper young men, of excellent growth and presence.

Ros. With bills on their necks,—'*Be it known unto all men by these presents,—* *

"This is the technical phraseology referred to by Thomas Nash in his 'Epistle to the Gentlemen Students of the two Universities,' in the year 1589, when he is supposed to have denounced the author of *Hamlet,* as one of those who had 'left the trade of *Noverint, whereto they were born,* for handfulls of tragical speeches,'— that is an attorney's clerk become a poet, and penning a stanza when he should engross.

"*As You Like It* was not brought out until shortly before the year 1600, so that Nash's *Noverint* could not have been suggested by it. Possibly Shakespeare now introduced the 'Be it known unto all men,' etc., in order to show his contempt for Nash's sarcasm." †

---

* Bacon embodies this humor in one of his Apothegms. Indeed, we do not appreciate the point of the joke in the play, until we have read the Apothegm:

"Jack Roberts was desired by his tailor, when the reckoning grew somewhat high, to have a bill of his hand. Roberts said: *I am content, but you must let no man know it.* When the tailor brought him the bill, he tore it, as in choler, and said to him: *You use me not well; you promised me nobody should know it, and here you have put in, Be it known unto all men by these presents.*"— *Works,* Vol. 7, page 129.

† Regarding Lord Campbell's remarks, the inquiry at once arises,— Did Nash have an inkling of the truth?

When, however, he comes to the direct consideration of the hypothetical question of fact regarding William Shakespeare, put by Mr. Collier, in attempted explanation of the "familiar, profound, and accurate" knowledge of the law displayed in the plays, to wit: "Whether Shakespeare was a clerk in an attorney's office at Stratford, before he joined the players in London?" Lord Campbell, in withholding his assent, forcibly observes:

" You must likewise remember that you require us implicitly

" In Act III., Sc. 1, a deep technical knowledge of law is displayed, howsoever it may have been acquired.

" The usurping Duke, Frederick, wishing all the real property of Oliver to be seized, awards a writ of *extent* against him, in the language which would be used by the Lord Chief Baron of the Court Exchequer:

Duke Fred. Make an *extent upon his house and lands —* *

an *extendi facias* applying to house and lands, as a *fieri facias* would apply to goods and chattels, or a *capias ad satisfaciendum* to the person."

" In the first scene of Act IV., Shakespeare gives us the true legal meaning of the word 'attorney,' viz., *representative* or *deputy.* (Celui qui vient à tour d' autrui ; Qui alterius vices subit ; Legatus ; Vakeel.)

Ros. Well, in her person, I say — I will not have you.

Orl. Then, in my own person, I die.

Ros. No, faith, *die by attorney.* The poor world is almost six thousand years old, and in all this time there was not any man died in his own person, *videlicet*, in a love cause."

---

to believe a fact, which, were it true, positive and irrefragable evidence in Shakespeare's own handwriting might have been forthcoming to establish it. Not having been actually inrolled as an attorney, neither the records of the local court at Stratford, nor of the superior courts at Westminster, would present his name, as being concerned in any suits as an attorney ; but it might have been reasonably expected that there would have been deeds or wills witnessed by him still extant ; — and after a very diligent search, none such can be discovered. Nor can this consideration be disregarded, that between Nash's Epistle in the end of the 16th century, and Chalmers' suggestion more than two hundred years after, there is no hint by his foes or his friends of Shakespeare having consumed pens, paper, ink, and pounce in an attorney's office at Stratford."

* " To the fifteenth article of the charge, *videlicet*, William Compton being to have an *extent* for a debt of one thousand and two hundred pounds, the Lord Chancellor stayed it, and wrote his letter, upon which part of the debt was paid presently, and part at a future day."— *Works*, Vol. 14, page 257. See also page 366.

" Near the end of the same scene Shakespeare again evinces his love for legal phraseology and imagery by converting Time into an aged Judge of Assize, sitting on the Crown side:

Ros. Well Time is the old *Justice* that examines all such offenders, and let Time try.

" As in *Troilus and Cressida* (Act IV., Sc. 5) Shakespeare makes Time an *Arbitrator:*

> And that old common *Arbitrator*, Time,
> Will one day end it." *

---

* This was a favorite thought with Bacon, to which he gave manifold expression:

"Every man knows that Time is the controller of laws."— *Works*, Vol. 10, page 19. "For the law (as has been said before) cannot be framed to meet all cases; but is adapted to such as generally occur. But Time, as was said of old, is the wisest of things, and the author and inventor every day of new cases."— *Works*, Vol. 14, page 96. "Neither are they of authority to judge this question against all *the precedents of Time.*"—*Id.*, page 477.

"And if any one take this general acquiescence and consent for an argument of weight, as being *the judgment of Time,* let me tell him that the reasoning on which he relies is most fallacious and weak . . . so neither the births nor the miscarriages of Time are *entered in our records.*"— *Works*, Vol. 4, page 15. "Time hath *tried* it, and we find it to be the best."— *Works*, Vol. 14, page 174. "Sixthly, if it be said the number of fees is much increased because causes are increased, that is a benefit which Time gives and Time takes away."— *Works*, Vol. 10, page 285. "Let me so give every man his due, as I give Time his due, which is to discover Truth."— *Works*, Vol. 8, page 125.

> (" Time's glory is to calm contending kings,
> To unmask falsehood, and bring truth to light."
> —*The Rape of Lucrece.*)

" — and the inseparable property of Time, which is ever more and more to disclose truth. . . . For the *appeal* is (lawful though it may be, it should not be needful) from the first cogitations of men to their second, and from the nearer times to the times further off."— *Advancement of Learning*, Second Book. *Works*, Vol. 3, page 477.

" *The Merchant of Venice*, in the last scene of the last act, contains another palpable allusion to English legal procedure. In the Court of Queen's Bench, when a complaint is made against a person for a contempt, the practice is that before sentence is finally pronounced, he is sent into the Crown Office, and being there '*charged upon interrogatories*,' he is made to swear that he will '*answer all things faithfully*.' Accordingly, in the moonlight scene in the garden at Belmont, after a partial explanation

---

And *per contra*: — " But on the other side, who knoweth not that Time is truly compared to a stream, that carrieth down fresh and pure waters into that salt sea of corruption which environeth all human actions? And therefore if man shall not by his industry, virtue, and policy, as it were with the oar row against the stream and inclination of Time, all institutions and ordinances, be they never so pure, will corrupt and degenerate." — *Works*, Vol. 10, page 105.

We find flowing, as from an inexhaustible fountain, yet other variations of the theme:

"I, that please some, *try* all; both joy and terror
Of good and bad; that make and unfold error,—
Now take upon me, in the name of Time,
To use my wings. Impute it not a crime
To me, or my swift passage, that I slide
O'er sixteen years, and leave the growth untried
Of that wide gap; since *it is in my power*
To o'erthrow law, and in one self-born hour
To plant and o'erwhelm custom. Let me pass
The same I am, ere ancient'st order was,
Or what is now received. I witness to
The times that brought them in: so shall I do
To the *freshest* things now reigning, and *make stale*
The glistering of this present, as my tale
Now seems to it."
— *Time as Chorus in A Winter's Tale, IV.*

"We see which way the stream of Time doth run."
— *II., Henry IV., IV., 1.*

See also the characterization of Time in *Troilus and Cressida*, Act III., Sc. 3.

29

between Cassanio, Gratiano, Portia, and Nerissa, about their rings, some further inquiry being deemed necessary, Portia says :

> Let us go in,
> And *charge us there upon inter'gatories*,
> And *we will answer all things faithfully*.

" Gratiano assents, observing :

> Let it be so : the first inter'gatory
> That my Nerissa shall be sworn on is,
> Whether till the next night she had rather stay,
> Or go to bed now, being two hours to day." *

" In *Othello*, Act I., Sc. 3, in the trial of Othello before the Senate, as if he had been indicted on Stat. 33 Hen. VII. c. 8, for practising ' conjuration, witchcraft, enchantment, and sorcery, to provoke to unlawful love,' Brabantio, the prosecutor, says :

> She is abused, stol'n from me, and corrupted
> By spells and medicines bought of mountebanks;
> For Nature so proposterously to err.   .   .   .
> *Sans witchcraft* could not.

" The presiding judge at first seems alarmingly to favor the prosecutor, saying :

> *Duke.* Who'er he be that in this foul proceeding
> Hath thus beguil'd your daughter of herself,
> And you of her, the bloody book of law
> You shall yourself read, in the bitter letter,
> After your own sense.

" The Moor, although acting as his own counsel, makes

---

* " In other words, I mean (according to the practice in civil causes) in this great Plea or Suit granted by the divine favour and providence (whereby the human race seeks to recover its right over nature), to examine Nature herself and the arts upon interrogatories."—*Parasceve, Works*, Vol. 4, page 263.

The following is another example of Bacon's apt employment of legal terms in his non-professional writings : " For since they have debarred Christ's wife of a great part of her dowry, it were reason they made her a competent jointure."—*On the Pacification and Unification of the Church, Works*, Vol. 10, page 125.

a noble and skilful defense, directly meeting the statutable misdemeanor with which he is charged,— and referring pointedly to the very words of the indictment and the Act of Parliament:

> I will a round unvarnish'd tale deliver
> Of my whole course of love; *what drugs, what charms,*
> *What conjuration, and what mighty magic*
> (For such proceedings I am charged withal)
> I won his daughter with.

"Having fully opened his case, showing that he had used no forbidden arts, and having explained the course which he had lawfully pursued, he says in conclusion:

> This only is the *witchcraft* I have used:
> Here comes the lady — let her witness it.

"He then examines the witness, and is honorably acquitted." *

"Act III., Sc. 3, shows that Shakespeare was well acquainted with all courts, low as well as high; — where Iago asks:

> Who has a breast so pure,
> But some uncleanly apprehensions
> *Keep leets and law-days,* and *in session sit*
> With meditations lawful?"

"In *The Taming of the Shrew,* in the *Induction,* Shakespeare betrays an intimate knowledge of the matters which may be presented as offences before the *Court Leet,* the lowest court of criminal judicature in England. He puts this speech into the mouth of a servant who is trying to persuade Sly that he is a great lord, and that he had

---

* "For *witchcraft,* by the former law it was not death, except it were actual and gross invocation of evil spirits, or making covenant with them, or taking away life by witchcraft. But now by an act in his Majesty's times, *charms and sorceries in certain cases of procuring of unlawful love* or bodily hurt, and some others, are made felony the second offence; the first being imprisonment and pilory."—*Charge on Opening the Court, Works,* Vol. 11, page 268.

been in a dream for fifteen years, during which time he
thought he was a frequenter of ale-houses:

> For though you lay here in this goodly chamber,
> Yet would you say, ye were beaten out of door,
> And rail upon the hostess of the house,
> And say you would *present her at the leet*,
> Because she brought stone jugs, and no sealed quarts."

"Now, in the reigns of Elizabeth and James I., there
was a very wholesome law, that, for the protection of the
public against 'false measures,' ale should be sold only in
sealed vessels of the standard capacity; and the violation
of the law was to be presented at the 'Court Leet' or
'View of Frankpledge,' held in every hundred, manor, or
lordship, before the steward of the leet." *

"In *Much Ado About Nothing*, if the different parts
of Dogberry's charge are strictly examined, it will be found

---

* "There have been by use and statute law, besides survey-
ing pledges of freemen, and giving the oath of allegiance, and
making constables, many additions of power and authority given
to the stewarts of *Leets and Law-days*, to be put in use in their
courts. As for example, they may punish innkeepers, victual-
lers, bakers, brewers, butchers, poulterers, fishmongers, and
tradesmen of all sorts *selling at underweight or measure*, or at
excessive prices."— *Works*, Vol. 7, page 467.

In 1601, during the reign of Queen Elizabeth, "Mr. Bacon
stood up to prefer a new bill" in Parliament. In his speech,
he said:

"This, Mr. Speaker, is no bill of state nor of novelty, like a
stately gallery for pleasure, but neither to dine in nor sleep
in; but this bill is a bill of repose, of quiet, of profit, of true
and just dealing; the title whereof is an 'Act for the Better
Suppressing of Abuses in Weights and Measures.' . . . I'll
tell you, Mr. Speaker, I'll speak out of mine own experience
that I have learned and observed, having had causes of this
nature referred to my report, that this fault of using false
weights and measures is grown so intolerable and common that,
if you would build churches, you shall not need for battlements
and bells other things than false weights of lead and brass."—
Works, Vol. 10, page 18.

that the author of it had a very respectable acquaintance with crown law. The problem was to save the constables from all trouble, without any regard to the public safety :

Dogb. If you meet a thief you may suspect him, by virtue of your office, to be no true man ; and for such kind of men, the less you meddle or make with them, why, the more is for your honesty.

2d Watch. If we know him to be a thief, shall we not lay hands on him?

Dogb. Truly, by your office you may ;* but, I think, they that touch pitch will be defiled. The most peaceable way for you, if you do take a thief, is to let him show himself what he is, and steal out of your company.

" Now there can be no doubt that Lord Coke himself could not more accurately have defined the power of a peace-officer."

" We find in several of the 'Histories' Shakespeare's fondness for law terms ; and it is still remarkable, that whenever he indulges this propensity, he uniformly lays down good law.

" Thus, in the controversy, in the opening scene of *King John*, between Robert and Philip Faulconbridge, as to which of them was to be considered the true heir of the deceased Sir Robert, the King, in giving judgment, lays down the law of legitimacy most perspicuously and soundly,— thus addressing Robert, the plaintiff :

Sirrah, your brother is legitimate :
Your father's wife did after wedlock bear him ;
And if she did play false, the fraud was hers,
Which fault lies on the hazards of all husbands

---

* " For, first, if any man will lay murder or felony to another's charge, or do suspect him of murder or felony, he may declare it to the constable, and the constable ought, upon such declaration or complaint, to carry him before a justice of peace ; and *if by common voice or fame any man be suspected*, the constable ought to arrest him, and bring him before a justice of peace, though there be no other accusation or declaration."— *Works*, Vol. 7, page 752.

That marry wives. Tell me, how if my brother,
Who, as you say, took pains to get this son,
Had of your father claim'd this son for his?
In sooth, good friend, your father might have kept
This calf, bred from his cow, from all the world:
In sooth, he might: then, if he were my brother's,
My brother might not claim him, nor your father,
Being none of his, refuse him. This concludes —
My mother's son did get your father's heir;
Your father's heir must have your father's land.

"This is the true doctrine, '*Pater est quem nuptiæ
demonstrat.*' It was likewise properly ruled that the
father's will, in favor of his son Robert, had no power to
dispossess the right heir." *

"In *King Lear*, Act II., Sc. 1, there is a remarkable
example of Shakespeare's use of technical legal phraseology. Edmund, the wicked illegitimate son of the Earl
of Gloster, having succeeded in deluding his father into
the belief that Edgar, the legitimate son, had attempted
to commit parricide, and had been prevented from accomplishing the crime by Edmund's tender solicitude for the
Earl's safety, the Earl is thus made to express a determination that he would disinherit Edgar (who was supposed
to have fled from justice), and that he would leave all his
possessions to Edmund:

Glo.   Strong and fasten'd villain!
. . . .

---

* "This only yet remains: if the father has any patrimony
and the son be disobedient, he may disinherit him; if he will
not deserve his blessing he shall not have his living. But this
device of perpetuities has taken this power from the father likewise; and has tied and made subject (as the proverb is) the
parents to their cradle, and so notwithstanding he has the curse
of his father, yet he shall have the land of his grandfather.
And what is more, if the son marry himself to a woman dif-
famed, so that she bring bastard slips and false progeny into
the family, yet the issue of this woman shall inherit the land,
for that the first perpetuator will have it so, who is dead a long
time before."— *Works*, Vol. 7, page 634.

All ports I 'll bar ; the villain shall not 'scape.

. . . .

      Besides, his picture
I will send **far** and near, that all the kingdom
May have due note of him ; and of my land,
Loyal and natural boy, I 'll work the means
To make thee capable.

" In forensic discussions respecting legitimacy, the question is put, whether the individual whose *status* is to be determined is ' capable,' *i. e.,* capable of inheriting ; but it is only a lawyer who would express the idea of legitimizing a natural son by simply saying :

     I 'll work the means
  To make him capable." *

" In *Antony and Cleopatra*, Act I., Sc. 4, Lepidus, in trying to palliate the bad qualities and misdeeds of Antony, uses the language of a conveyancer's chambers in Lincoln's Inn :

  His faults, in him, seem as the spots of heaven,
  More fiery by night's blackness ; *hereditary*
  Rather than *purchas'd.*

" That is to say, they are taken by *descent*, not by *purchase.*

" So in the Second Part of *Henry IV.*, Act IV., Sc. 4, the King, who had *usurped* the crown, says to the Prince of Wales :

  For what in me was *purchas'd*

---

* " It is also to be noted, that persons attainted of felony or treason have no *capacity* to take, obtain, or purchase, save only to the use of the King, until they be pardoned."—*Works*, Vol. 7, page 487.

" For Richard the Third had a resolution, out of his hatred to both his brethren, King Edward and the Duke of Clarence, and their lines, having had his hand in both their bloods, to *disable* their issues upon false and incompetent pretexts — the one of attainder, the other of *illegitimation.*"—*History of Henry VII.*

Falls upon thee in a more fairer sort.

i. e., I took by *purchase*, you will take by *descent*."

"Laymen (viz., all except lawyers) understand by 'purchase' buying for a sum of money, called the price : but lawyers consider that 'purchase' is opposed to *descent*, — that all things come to the owner either by *descent* or by *purchase*, and that whatever does not come through operation of law by *descent* is *purchased*, although it may be the free gift of a donor. Thus, if land be devised by will to A. in fee, he takes by *purchase*, or to B. for life, remainder to A. and his heirs, B. being a stranger to A., A. takes by purchase ; but upon the death of A., his eldest son would take by *descent*."*

"In *The Winter's Tale*, Act I., Sc. 2, there is an allu-

---

* And therefore we see what an endless work the King of Spain hath had to recover the Low Countries, although it were to him *patrimony and not purchase.*"— *Of the True Greatness of the Kingdom of Britain, Works,* Vol. 7, page 51.

"Wherein I may not omit to give *obiter* that answer which law and truth provide, namely, that when any king obtaineth by war a country whereunto he hath right *by birth*, that he is ever in upon his ancient right, and not upon his *purchase* by conquest."— *Case of the Post-nati of Scotland, Works,* Vol. 7, page 673.

"Which you hope likewise will be the *hereditary* issue of this late *purchase* of the Palatinate."— *Works,* Vol. 14, page 463.

"The ancient councils and synods (as is noted by the ecclesiastical story) when they deprived any bishop, never recorded the offence, but *buried it in perpetual silence.* Only Cham *purchased* his curse with revealing his father's disgrace."— *On the Controversies of the Church, Works,* Vol. 8, page 82.

"Bethink you father ; for the difference
Is, *purchase of a heavy curse* from Rome,
Or the light loss of England for a friend."
　　　　　　　—*King John, III.,* 1.

"Then, as my gift, and thine own acquisition
Worthily *purchased*, take my daughter."
　　　　　　　—*Tempest, IV.,* 1.

sion to a piece of English law procedure, which, although it might have been enforced till very recently, could hardly be known to any except lawyers, or those who had themselves actually been in prison on a criminal charge, — that whether guilty or innocent, the prisoner was liable to pay a fee on his liberation. Hermione, trying to persuade Polixenes, King of Bohemia, to prolong his stay at the court of Leontes in Sicily, says to him:

> You put me off with limber vows; but I,
> Though you would seek t' unsphere the stars with oaths,
> Should yet say, 'Sir, no going' . . . .
> Force me to keep you *as a prisoner*,
> Not like a guest; *so you shall pay your fees*
> *When you depart*, and save your thanks.

"I remember when the Clerk of Assize and the Clerk of the Peace were entitled to exact their fee from all acquitted prisoners, and were supposed in strictness to have a *lien* on their persons for it. I believe there is now no tribunal in England where the practice remains, excepting the two Houses of Parliament; but the Lord Chancellor and the Speaker of the House of Commons still say to prisoners about to be liberated from the custody of the Black Rod or the Sergeant-at-Arms, 'You are discharged, *paying your fees*.'"[*]

"In Act III., Sc. 2, it is likewise remarkable that Cleomenes and Dion, the messengers who brought back the response from the oracle of Delphi, to be given in evidence, are sworn to the genuineness of the document they produce almost in the very words now used by the Lord Chancellor when an officer presents at the bar of the House of Lords the copy of a record of a court of justice:

---

[*] *K. Hen.* Master lieutenant, now that God and friends
Have shaken Edward from the regal seat,
And turn'd my captive state to liberty,
My fear to hope, my sorrows unto joys,
At our *enlargement* what are thy due fees?
—*III., Henry VI., IV., 6.*

> You here shall swear . . . .
> That you, Cleomenes and Dion, have
> Been both at Delphos; and from thence have brought
> The seal'd-up oracle, by the hand delivered
> Of great Apollo's priest; and that, since then,
> You have not dar'd to break the holy seal,
> Nor read the secrets in 't."

"In *Hamlet*, Act I., Sc. 1, Marcellus inquires what was the cause of the warlike preparations in Denmark:

> And why such daily cast of brazen cannon,
> And foreign mart for implements of war?
> *Why such impress of shipwrights, whose sore task*
> *Does not divide the Sunday from the week?*

"Such confidence has there been in Shakespeare's accuracy, that this passage has been quoted, both by text writers and by judges on the bench, as an *authority* upon the legality of the press-gang, and upon the debated question whether *shipwrights*, as well as *common seamen*, are liable to be pressed into the service of the royal navy. (See Barrington on the Ancient Statutes, p. 300.)"

Lord Campbell cites many other examples, both from the Plays and the Poems,* showing also conclusively (in

---

* The experienced chancery lawyer will discern in the 87th Sonnet the embodiment of a profound principle of equity. Moreover, light is thrown upon the text by the following unique, but scholarly legal definition:

"And herein I note the wisdom of the law of England, which termeth the highest contempts and excesses of authority *Misprisions;* which (if you take the sound and derivation of the words) is but *mistaken*"; (The italics are Bacon's).—*Works*, Vol. 14, page 134.

> "Thyself thou gav'st, thy own worth then not knowing,
> Or me, to whom thou gav'st it, else *mistaking;*
> So thy great gift upon *misprision* growing,
> Comes home again, on better judgment making.
>   Thus have I had thee, as a dream doth flatter,
>   In sleep a king, but, waking, no such matter."

("Have not many, which take themselves to be inward coun-

a discussion too extended for quotation) that the "crowners
quest law," set forth in the Grave-digger's scene in *Hamlet*, "the mine which produces the richest legal ore," is a
direct travesty upon the celebrated case of *Hales vs. Petit*,
tried in the reign of Philip and Mary, and reported in
Plowden ; making it clear that the Poet "intended to
ridicule the counsel who argued and the judges who decided it."

He then continues :

"Having concluded my examination of Shakespeare's
juridical phrases and forensic allusions,—on the retrospect
I am amazed, not only by their number, but by the accuracy
and propriety with which they are uniformly introduced.
There is nothing so dangerous as for one not of the craft
to tamper with our free-masonry. (Let a non-professional
man, however acute, presume to talk law, or to draw illus-
trations from legal science in discussing other subjects, and
he will very speedily fall into some laughable absurdity.)
In the House of Commons I have heard a country member,
who meant to intimate that he entirely concurred with the
last preceding speaker, say, 'I join issue with the honorable gentleman who has just sat down;' the legal sense of
which is, 'I flatly contradict all his facts and deny his infer-
ences.' *Junius*, who was fond of dabbling in law, and
who was supposed by some to be a lawyer (although Sir
Philip Francis, then a clerk in the War Office, is now ascer-
tained, beyond all doubt, to have been the man), in his
address to the English nation, speaking of the House of
Commons, and wishing to say that the beneficial interest

sellors with Nature, proved but idle believers, that told us tales
which were *no such matter ?* "—*Works*, Vol. 8, page 383.)

And again :

"What hast thou done? thou hast *mistaken* quite,
And laid the love-juice on some true-love's sight,
Of thy *misprision*, must perforce ensue
Some true-love turn'd, and not a false turn'd true."
—*Midsummer Night's Dream*, III., 2.

in the state belongs to the people, and not to their repre-
sentatives, says, 'They are only *trustees :* the *fee* is in us.'
Now every attorney's clerk knows that when land is held
in trust, the *fee* (or legal estate) is in the trustee, and that
the beneficiary has only an equitable interest. While Novel-
ists and Dramatists are constantly making mistakes as to
the law of marriage, of wills, and of inheritance,—*to Shakespeare's law, lavishly as he propounds it, there can neither
be demurrer, nor bill of exceptions, nor writ of error.*"

And thus, travel in what direction we may, all roads lead
to Rome : and everywhere, we may trace the footsteps of
the Master.

The tenure of all our knowledge is "scientific faith,"
or in another word, *recognition*, the goal of induction.
This recognition is attained through insight, and insight
through close observation,—through this entrance gate of
homely horn. Moreover, every fact is environed in voice-
ful harmonies, the subtly entrancing concord of its relations to all other facts ; and it is through their delightful
comprehension that we enter into its possession. This is
essentially the scientific method ; applicable in every department of knowledge. And always and everywhere,
"The capital precept for the whole undertaking is this, that
the eye of the mind be never taken off from things themselves, but receive their images truly as they are."

And again we hear, as in a refrain, the exquisite harmony in the Poet's words :

> " Why write I still all one, ever the same,
>   And keep invention in a noted weed,
>   *That every word doth almost tell my name,*
>   *Showing their birth, and where they did proceed?*"

We cannot conclude without a brief word of tribute to
DELIA BACON. Alone, and first in all the world, she discerned Bacon's authorship of the plays. Realizing profoundly the value of her discovery, this noble woman freely
devoted her life to its development. Crossing the Atlantic
to prosecute her researches in London, she was compelled
by her poverty to live there in a garret, and almost literally upon bread and water. Through the effect of her
privations, while thus absorbed in her work, her mind
at length became clouded, and her life went out in darkness,—a sacrifice to her devotion. But through her untiring efforts, her discovery had been published : and since
then, all who have dealt with the theme have but labored
in the exploration and development of the rich mine she
first discovered and disclosed to the world ;—and to her be
the wreath of immortality.